BBC Bitesize

Bitesize
Pearson Edexcel
GCSE (9-1)

COMBINED SCIENCE

REVISION GUIDE

Foundation

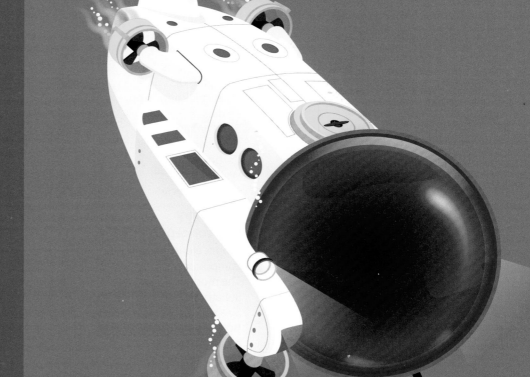

Series Consultant:
Harry Smith

Authors:
Sam Holyman
Aidan Gill
Mike Smith

Contents

GCSE Science

☑ Tick off each topic as you go.

 Each bite-sized chunk has a **timer** to indicate how long it will take. Use them to plan your revision sessions.

 Scan the **QR codes** to visit the BBC Bitesize website. It will link straight through to revision resources on that subject. You can also access these by visiting www.pearsonschools.co.uk/BBCBitesizeLinks.

How to use this book

Use the features in this book to focus your revision, track your progress through the topics and practise your exam skills.

 Features to help you revise

Scan the **QR codes** to visit the BBC Bitesize website. It will link straight through to more revision resources on that subject.

Questions that test **maths skills** are explained in callouts and in the *Exam skills* section at the back of the book.

Topics that are related to **working scientifically** are explained in callouts throughout the book.

Each bite-sized chunk has a **timer** to indicate how long it will take. Use them to plan your revision sessions.

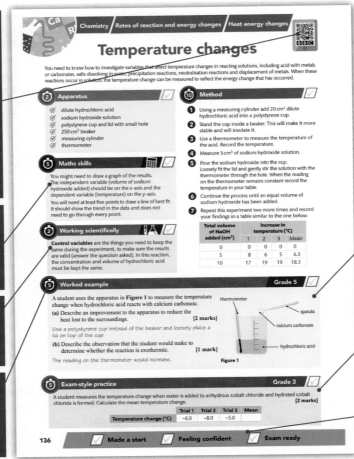

Completed **worked examples** demonstrate how to approach exam-style questions.

Test yourself with **exam-style practice** at the end of each page and check your answers at the back of the book.

Tick boxes allow you to track the sections you've revised. Revisit each page to embed your knowledge.

 Exam focus features

The *About your exam* section at the start of the book gives you all the key information about your exams, as well as showing you how to identify the different questions.

You will also find green *Exam skills* pages and purple *Practical* pages. These work through an extended exam-style question and provide further opportunities to practise your skills.

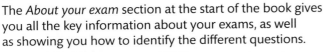

 ActiveBook and app

This Revision Guide comes with a **free online edition**. Follow the instructions from inside the front cover to access your ActiveBook.

You can also download the **free BBC Bitesize app** to access revision flashcards and quizzes.

If you do not have a QR code scanner, you can access all the links in this book from your ActiveBook or visit **www.pearsonschools.co.uk/BBCBitesizeLinks**.

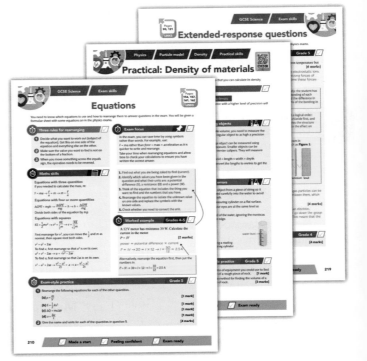

Your Science GCSE

This page will tell you everything you need to know about the structure of your upcoming Pearson Edexcel GCSE (9–1) in Combined Science (Foundation Tier) exams.

About the exam papers

You will have to take **six** papers as part of your Pearson Edexcel GCSE (9–1) in Combined Science (Foundation Tier) qualification: **two biology**, **two chemistry** and **two physics**. The papers will test your knowledge and understanding of different topic areas and your ability to work scientifically.

Paper 1 Biology 1 1 hour 10 minutes 60 marks in total	**Paper 2** Biology 2 1 hour 10 minutes 60 marks in total	**Paper 3** Chemistry 1 1 hour 10 minutes 60 marks in total	**Paper 4** Chemistry 2 1 hour 10 minutes 60 marks in total	**Paper 5** Physics 1 1 hour 10 minutes 60 marks in total	**Paper 6** Physics 2 1 hour 10 minutes 60 marks in total

Exam topics

Topics include: key concepts of physics; energy – forces doing work; forces and their effects; electricity and circuits; magnetism and the motor effect; electromagnetic induction; particle model; forces and matter

Topics include: key concepts of physics; motion and forces; conservation of energy; waves; light and the electromagnetic spectrum; radioactivity

Topics include: key concepts in chemistry; groups in the periodic table; rates of reaction and energy changes; fuels and Earth science

Paper 6 Physics 2 16.7%

Paper 5 Physics 1 16.7%

Paper 4 Chemistry 2 16.7%

Paper 1 Biology 1 16.7%

Paper 2 Biology 2 16.7%

Paper 3 Chemistry 1 16.7%

Topics include: key concepts in biology; cells and control; genetics; natural selection and genetic modification; health, disease and the development of medicines

Topics include: key concepts in biology; plant structures and their functions; animal coordination, control and homeostasis; exchange and transport in animals; ecosystems and material cycles

Topics include: key concepts in chemistry; states of matter and mixtures; chemical changes; extracting metals and equilibria

Maths skills

You will be required to demonstrate the following mathematical skills in your GCSE Science exams:

- rearranging equations
- interpreting data from graphs and tables, including finding a gradient
- converting units
- using standard form
- using ratios, fractions and percentages
- calculating mean, mode and median
- using geometry (volumes, areas, angles, working out sides of triangles).

Working scientifically

There are 21 required practical activities you will carry out during your GCSE Science course.

Practical activities are an opportunity for you to apply your knowledge and understanding, while developing relevant practical skills and techniques.

You need to know how to:

- plan and carry out an investigation
- use apparatus correctly and safely
- take accurate measurements and record data appropriately
- analyse your findings
- evaluate your investigation.

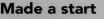 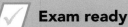

Multiple-choice questions

Multiple-choice questions give you several options to choose from. You must indicate the correct answer by marking your choice clearly.

 Types of multiple-choice question

- ☑ tick box
- ☑ linking boxes
- ☑ sentence completion

 Exam focus

Bold words usually give important instructions. Read them carefully.

e.g. Give **one** way in which a second allele for eye colour might be different.

 Exam explainer

Clearly mark the answer you think is correct with a tick in the box. If you change your mind, draw a line through the incorrect answer and tick the correct answer.

A cricket ball is hit by a bat. The bat and ball exert a force on each other. Which of the following statements about the two forces is true? **[1 mark]**

- ☐ **A** The force on the bat and the force on the ball are in the same direction
- ☐ **B** The bat has a larger mass so it exerts a larger force on the ball
- ☑ **C** The two forces are equal
- ☐ **D** The two forces give the bat and ball equal accelerations

If you are unsure of the answer, use what you know to rule out the incorrect options.

Use a pencil to draw lines, so you can change your answer easily, if necessary.

Draw **one** line from each diagram to the name of the cell. **[3 marks]**

| **Diagram** | **Name of cell** |

red blood cell

sperm cell

root hair cell

Read the question carefully. Here, you are instructed to only use words from the box provided. You would not be awarded marks for using similar words.

The pH scale is a measure of the acidity or alkalinity of a solution.

Use words from the box to complete the sentences. **[3 marks]**

| neutral | acidic | alkaline |

A solution with a pH value of 5 is _____.

A solution with a pH value of 7 is _____.

A solution with a pH value of 13 is _____.

☑ **Made a start**   ☑ **Feeling confident**   **Exam ready**

Short-answer questions

Short-answer questions come in a variety of forms and are the most common type of questions.

 5 **Exam explainer**

Underline key information, such as numbers and units. Make sure you include the correct units in your answer.

A power station has an efficiency of 0.45. Its energy comes from burning coal, which it uses at a rate of 300 MW.

(a) Calculate the useful output of electrical power. **[2 marks]**

(b) Describe the advantages and disadvantages of this type of power station compared to a wind turbine. **[3 marks]**

It is important to show your working when answering a calculation question. If done correctly, you will get method marks even if the final answer is wrong.

For a sketch question, you only need to draw approximately. You should only use a ruler if it helps you to make your answer clear.

Sketch a reaction profile for an endothermic reaction. **[3 marks]**

A student investigated the rate of reaction between calcium carbonate and hydrochloric acid.

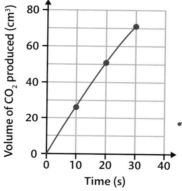

You will need to be able to interpret information from a graph, photo, table or image in any of your exam papers.

Figure 1 The student's results for one concentration of hydrochloric acid.

The table shows the student's results when the concentration was two times greater than the results shown in **Figure 1**.

Time (s)	Volume of CO_2 (cm³)
0	0
10	41
20	62
30	71

(a) Plot the results shown in the table on the grid in **Figure 1**. Draw a line of best fit. **[3 marks]**

(b) Give **one** conclusion about how the rate of reaction changed when the concentration of hydrochloric acid was changed. **[1 mark]**

Extended-response questions

You will find one extended open response question towards the end of each examination paper. They are shown by an asterisk * and are worth 6 marks each.

② Command words

- ✓ **explain** – give reasons for why or how something happens, including calculations if necessary
- ✓ **describe** – give an account of something
- ✓ **plan** – invent or work out a method based on ideas and experiments you already know
- ✓ **discuss** – explore all aspects of something, such as its benefits and drawbacks
- ✓ **comment on** – bring together information or data so that you can make a judgement

② Structure your answers

1. Make a **point** – for example: *Embryo screening is an expensive procedure.*
2. **Develop** your point – for example: *This means that the procedure is available only to people who can afford it.*
3. **Link** your point back to the question – for example: *This is a socio-economic issue because the procedure is not accessible to everyone.*

⑤ Exam explainer

For this type of question, you should provide specific examples for each of the issues mentioned, interpreting them in an objective way, and finishing with a reasoned conclusion.

> * Evaluate the use of embryo screening for cystic fibrosis. In your answer discuss the economic, social and ethical issues. **[6 marks]**

These questions are more open-ended than others, and they are marked using a system based on three levels. At each level, the examiner is looking for evidence that you know and understand your science, and can use this clearly and logically. For each level, your answer typically:

Level 1 attempts to use relevant scientific knowledge and understanding, but at a basic level with unclear or unsupported reasoning.

Level 2 is mostly supported by scientific knowledge and understanding with some logical connections, and supported by some clear reasoning.

Level 3 is well supported throughout using scientific knowledge and understanding with clear, logical and correct connections and reasoning.

In this question you will need to consider the ways in which these two metals are extracted.

If you are told what to include, make sure you cover it. Here you would need to describe factors such as the reactivity series and the cost of each method.

> * Different metals require different methods to extract them from their ores.
>
> Discuss the methods chosen to extract iron and aluminium.
>
> In your answer, you should describe the factors involved in choosing suitable methods of extraction. **[6 marks]**

Read carefully any information at the start of the question. This sentence tells you that the question will be about types of radiation that can remove electrons from atoms and molecules.

> * The electromagnetic spectrum includes ionising radiation such as high-frequency ultraviolet light, X-rays and gamma rays.
>
> Discuss the uses of these types of radiation, the dangers they pose, and the precautions needed to reduce the risk of harm from them. **[6 marks]**

You will need to include three aspects of each of the three types of radiation. Remember that there will be similarities that you can describe together, and differences that you can highlight.

✓ **Made a start** ✓ **Feeling confident** ✓ **Exam ready**

Levels of organisation

You need to understand the principles of organisation within living organisms.

(10) Organisation

Cells are the building blocks of all living things (**organisms**). Simple organisms, such as bacteria, consist of just one single cell and are described as **unicellular**. **Multicellular** organisms have various levels of organisation within them, from the individual cell to the entire organism.

Cells contain **organelles**, also known as sub-cellular structures, which perform specific functions within the cell. Individual cells can perform specific functions (page 4). Groups of specialised cells which all have a similar structure and function are called **tissues**. Groups of tissues that perform specific jobs are known as **organs**. Groups of organs form **organ systems**.

Cells are very small. You need a microscope to be able to examine them. Go to pages 5 and 6 for more about microscopy.

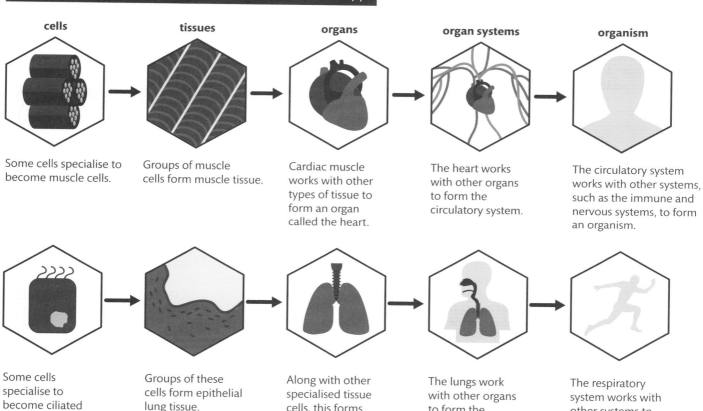

cells	tissues	organs	organ systems	organism
Some cells specialise to become muscle cells.	Groups of muscle cells form muscle tissue.	Cardiac muscle works with other types of tissue to form an organ called the heart.	The heart works with other organs to form the circulatory system.	The circulatory system works with other systems, such as the immune and nervous systems, to form an organism.
Some cells specialise to become ciliated epithelial cells.	Groups of these cells form epithelial lung tissue.	Along with other specialised tissue cells, this forms an organ called the lungs.	The lungs work with other organs to form the respiratory system.	The respiratory system works with other systems to form an organism.

Figure 1 The levels of organisation within the circulatory and respiratory systems

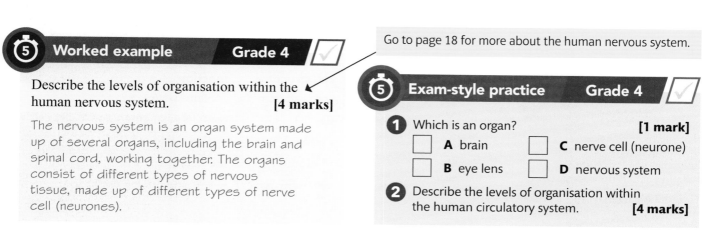

Go to page 18 for more about the human nervous system.

(5) Worked example — Grade 4

Describe the levels of organisation within the human nervous system. **[4 marks]**

The nervous system is an organ system made up of several organs, including the brain and spinal cord, working together. The organs consist of different types of nervous tissue, made up of different types of nerve cell (neurones).

(5) Exam-style practice — Grade 4

1 Which is an organ? **[1 mark]**

☐ **A** brain ☐ **C** nerve cell (neurone)

☐ **B** eye lens ☐ **D** nervous system

2 Describe the levels of organisation within the human circulatory system. **[4 marks]**

Eukaryotic and prokaryotic cells

You need to know the structures and functions of eukaryotic and prokaryotic cells, as well as the differences between them.

⏱ 10 Eukaryotes and prokaryotes

Cells can be classified as either **eukaryotic cells** (eukaryotes) or **prokaryotic cells** (prokaryotes). Animals and plants consist of eukaryotic cells. Bacteria consist of prokaryotic cells. Eukaryotic cells are larger and more complex than prokaryotic cells. Eukaryotic cells contain membrane-bound **organelles** (sub-cellular structures) which are not found in prokaryotic cells. Animal cells contain the organelles nuclei and mitochondria; plant cells contain these, as well as chloroplasts.

> There is more about the different structures of plant and animal cells on page 3.

Ribosomes are tiny structures where proteins are made.

Cytoplasm is a jelly-like substance where chemical reactions take place.

The **cell membrane** controls the movement of substances into and out of the cell.

The **nucleus** is a large membrane-bound structure which contains DNA. DNA controls the growth and development of every living thing.

Mitochondria release energy for cell processes. The energy is a product of respiration.

Figure 1 An animal cell – an example of a eukaryotic cell

A single loop of DNA, called **chromosomal DNA**, not contained within a nucleus.

cytoplasm

cell membrane

A **cell wall** protects the cell.

ribosome

Plasmids are small rings of DNA, which contain additional genes that are not present in chromosomal DNA.

Flagella enable the cell to move.

Figure 2 A bacterial cell – a prokaryotic cell

⏱ 2 Working scientifically

Most cells are microscopic. You need to understand the scale and size of cells and use the correct prefixes.

The following are compared to one metre.

centimetre (cm) = one hundredth or 10^{-2} m

millimetre (mm) = one thousandth or 10^{-3} m

micrometre (μm) = one millionth or 10^{-6} m

nanometre (nm) = one billionth or 10^{-9} m

picometre (pm) = one trillionth or 10^{-12} m

> Prokaryotic means 'before nucleus'. Prokaryotic cells do not have a nucleus. They contain a single DNA loop (chromosomal DNA) and small rings of DNA called plasmids.

⏱ 5 Worked example   Grade 2

Complete the table to show in which type of cell each cell structure is found.   **[6 marks]**

Cell structure	Prokaryotic cell	Eukaryotic cell
cell membrane	✓	✓
cytoplasm	✓	✓
mitochondria		✓
nucleus		✓
plasmid	✓	
ribosome	✓	✓

⏱ 5 Exam-style practice   Grade 2

Draw **one** straight line from each cell structure to its function.   **[4 marks]**

cell structure	function
cell membrane	contains DNA
flagella	controls what enters and leaves cell
nucleus	enable cell to move
ribosome	protects cell
cell wall	where proteins are made

 Made a start 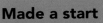 Feeling confident   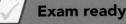 Exam ready

Biology	Key concepts	Cells

Animal and plant cells

You need to be able to describe the structures of animal and plant cells, and the differences between them.

⑩ Animal and plant cell structures

Although both animal and plant cells are eukaryotic, there are important structural differences between them. Plants stay in the same place and produce their own food. Animals move around in search of an external supply of food. These differences are the main reasons why animal and plant cell structures differ.

Algal cells have a similar structure to plant cells. They also have a cellulose cell wall that strengthens the cell.

Go to page 2 to revise the functions of cell components.

Cell components	Plant cell	Animal cell
nucleus	✓	✓
cytoplasm	✓	✓
cell membrane	✓	✓
cell wall	✓	✗
mitochondria	✓	✓
ribosomes	✓	✓
chloroplasts	✓	✗
permanent vacuole	✓	✗

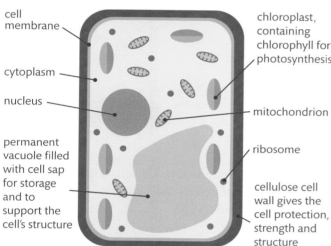

Figure 1 A plant cell

cell membrane

cytoplasm

nucleus

permanent vacuole filled with cell sap for storage and to support the cell's structure

chloroplast, containing chlorophyll for photosynthesis

mitochondrion

ribosome

cellulose cell wall gives the cell protection, strength and structure

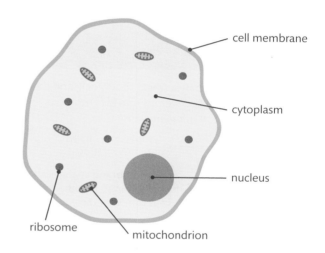

Figure 2 An animal cell

cell membrane

cytoplasm

nucleus

ribosome

mitochondrion

⑤ Worked example — Grade 4

(a) Give **three** structures that plant cells have which animal cells do not have. **[3 marks]**

Cell wall, permanent vacuole and chloroplasts.

(b) State the function of each of these three structures. **[3 marks]**

The cell wall supports the cell and gives it its shape; the permanent vacuole contains cell sap to support the cell; chloroplasts carry out photosynthesis.

② Exam-style practice — Grade 2

Look at **Figure 1**, the diagram of a plant cell. Complete the table by writing numbers 1–5 in the boxes to show the cell structures in order of size. Start with 1 for the smallest. **[2 marks]**

Cell structure	Order of size
chloroplast	
mitochondrion	
nucleus	
permanent vacuole	
ribosome	

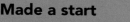 **Made a start**   **Feeling confident**   **Exam ready**

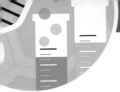

Specialised animal cells

Multicellular organisms are large organisms, like animals, made up of more than one type of cell. You need to know about the structural adaptations of specialised cells that enable them to perform specific functions. Go to page 47 to read about specialised plant cells.

(5) Specialised animal cells

You need to know how the following animal cells are specialised to carry out a particular function.

Sperm cells swim and fertilise egg cells.

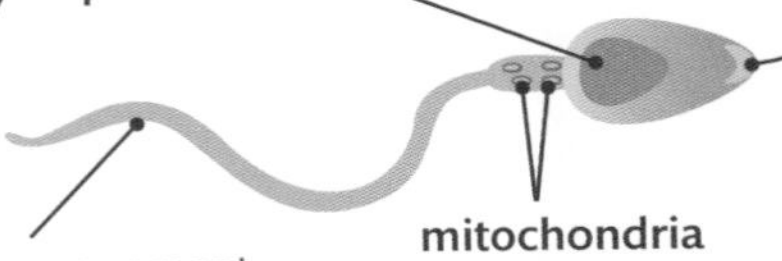
haploid nucleus
acrosome contains enzymes that digest outer layers of an egg cell
tail for movement
mitochondria provide energy for tail movement (swimming)

Figure 1 A sperm cell

A haploid nucleus contains half the normal number of chromosomes found in body cells.
See page 19 for more about haploid cells.

Each **egg cell** is fertilised by a single sperm cell, and then divides several times as it develops into an embryo.

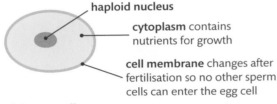

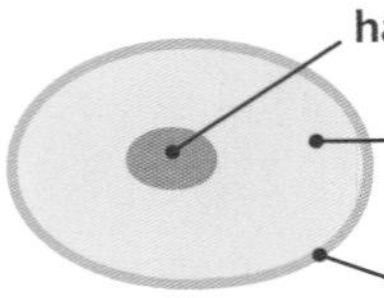
haploid nucleus
cytoplasm contains nutrients for growth
cell membrane changes after fertilisation so no other sperm cells can enter the egg cell

Figure 2 An egg cell

Ciliated epithelial cells, such as those in the trachea, move substances in a particular direction.

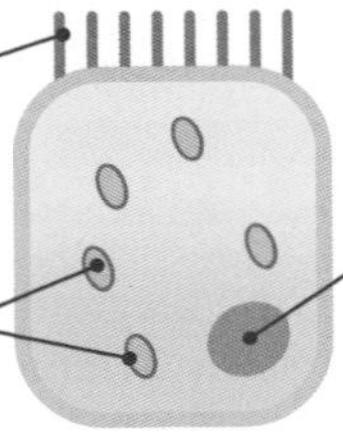
cilia sweep mucus carrying dirt and bacteria away from the lungs
mitochondria
nucleus

Figure 3 A ciliated epithelial cell

Red blood cells and white blood cells are other types of specialised cell.

(5) Worked example — Grade 5

1 **Figure 4** shows a nerve cell (neurone). Describe **two** ways nerve cells are adapted for their function. **[2 marks]**

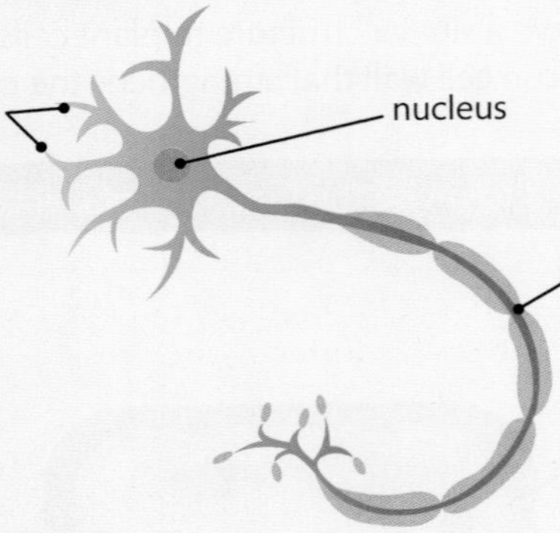
dendrites
nucleus
axon

Figure 4

Nerve cells have long axons so they are able to transmit nerve impulses between distant parts of the body. They also have branched endings called dendrites that connect with other nerve cells.

2 **Figure 5** shows a muscle cell. Suggest a reason why muscle cells contain many mitochondria. **[1 mark]**

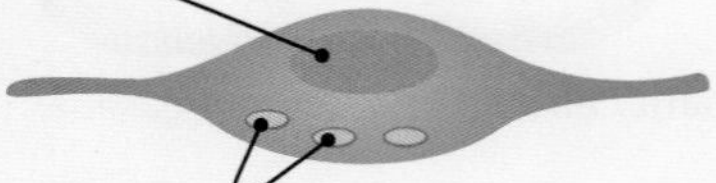
nucleus
mitochondria

Figure 5

Mitochondria are where respiration happens, they release the energy needed for muscles to contract.

See page 57 for more about the functions and adaptations of red blood cells and white blood cells.

(10) Exam-style practice — Grade 5

Describe **two** ways that each of the following are specialised to perform their functions:

(a) egg cells **[2 marks]**

(b) sperm cells **[2 marks]**

(c) ciliated epithelial cells. **[2 marks]**

Microscopy

You need to know how microscopes have developed, allowing scientists to examine increasingly smaller cellular structures.

⑤ Types of microscope

Microscopes are used to study cells. Over time, different kinds of microscope have been developed. The earliest light microscope that could be used to observe simple cell structures was invented about 350 years ago. This was gradually improved upon and refined to give the compound light microscopes that we use today. Very small cell structures can be studied with electron microscopes which were first developed in the 1930s.

Tiny cell organelles can be observed with an electron microscope. Ribosomes can be seen with an electron microscope but they are too small to be seen with a light microscope. The nucleus and mitochondria can be seen with a light microscope. The nucleus is larger so can be seen more clearly.

⑩ Magnification and resolution

Magnification is the measure of how many times bigger the image is than the object.

If a microscope has an eyepiece lens of ×10 and an objective lens of ×50, the image looks 10 × 50 times bigger, that is, 500 times bigger.

Light microscopes use light to see an image. They can only magnify clearly up to about ×1200, due to problems with resolution.

Resolution is the measure of how well a microscope can distinguish between two very close objects.

Above ×1200, light microscopes cannot distinguish between two close objects. This is due to the wavelength of light.

Electron microscopes use electrons rather than light. Electrons have a much shorter wavelength than light. This means they can resolve two very close objects at a much higher magnification, some even reaching up to ×1 000 000.

⑤ Worked example — Grade 5

Figure 1 shows a scale drawing of a cell.

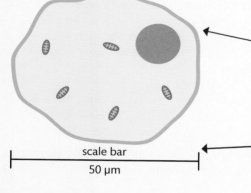

scale bar
50 μm

Figure 1

Calculate the magnification of the image in **Figure 1** using the equation: **[3 marks]**

$$\text{magnification} = \frac{\text{size of image}}{\text{size of real object}}$$

size of image = 5 cm

5 cm = 50 000 μm

size of real object = 50 μm ◄─ from scale bar

$$\text{magnification} = \frac{\text{size of image}}{\text{size of real object}} = \frac{50\,000}{50}$$

= ×1000

Maths skills

You need to know how to work out magnification using the equation:

$$\text{magnification} = \frac{\text{size of image}}{\text{size of real object}}$$

Use a ruler to measure the size of the image.

② Maths skills

Sometimes you may see numbers written in standard form. Standard form is an efficient way of writing very big or very small numbers. For example:

35 000 000 can be written as:

3.5 × 10 × 10 × 10 × 10 × 10 × 10 × 10

or 3.5×10^7 in standard form.

Both figures need to be in the same units.

⑩ Exam-style practice — Grade 5

1 A cell has a width of 0.1 mm. A scale drawing of the same cell has a width of 20 cm. Calculate the magnification of the drawing using the equation: $\text{magnification} = \dfrac{\text{size of image}}{\text{size of real object}}$. **[2 marks]**

2 A microscope has an eyepiece lens of ×15 and an objective lens of ×50. Calculate the total magnification. **[2 marks]**

☑ **Made a start**   ☑ **Feeling confident**   ☑ **Exam ready**

Practical: Using microscopes

You need to know how to set up and use a microscope to look at cells. You also need to be able to draw and label cell images from a microscope.

5 Using a microscope

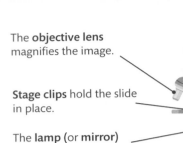

The **eyepiece lens** magnifies the image.

The **objective lens** magnifies the image.

The **coarse focus knob** is used first, to bring the image into focus.

Stage clips hold the slide in place.

The **fine focus knob** is then used to bring the image into sharp focus.

The **lamp** (or **mirror**) illuminates the specimen.

Figure 1 A light microscope

10 Worked example   Grade 5

1 Explain how you would prepare a slide of onion epidermal tissue. You may use a diagram to help you answer. **[3 marks]**

Peel off a one-cell-thick layer of cells and place it on a glass slide. Add one drop of stain, such as iodine solution, to the tissue. Use a mounted needle to lower the cover slip slowly and carefully to avoid trapping any air bubbles.

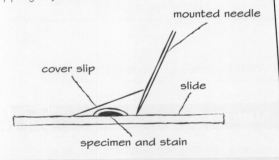

mounted needle

cover slip

slide

specimen and stain

Tissue samples are stained to add contrast because most cells are colourless. Samples should be one cell thick so that cells can be seen clearly.

- You should only draw the things that you can see.
- Do not use shading.
- Keep the labels simple and clearly identified.

2 Explain how you would view the slide under a microscope. **[4 marks]**

Place the prepared slide under the stage clips of the microscope. Use the coarse focus knob to lower the low power objective lens to just above the slide. Look through the eyepiece lens and raise the lens until the image is nearly in focus. Use the fine focus knob to get a clear sharp image. To see parts of the specimen in more detail, move the slide so the parts you are interested in are in the middle of your field of view. Then use a higher power objective lens, and focus as before.

3 **Figure 2** shows an onion cell. Draw and label a diagram of the onion cell. **[2 marks]**

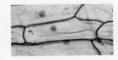

Figure 2

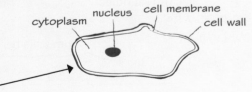

cytoplasm   nucleus   cell membrane   cell wall

5 Exam-style practice   Grade 5

1 Explain why tissue samples must be very thin to be viewed with a microscope. **[2 marks]**

2 Explain why scientists often stain tissue samples before viewing them with a microscope. **[1 mark]**

Made a start   Feeling confident   Exam ready

Enzyme action

You need to know how enzymes work and the factors that affect their activity.

⑩ Enzymes

Enzymes are biological **catalysts**. This means they speed up reactions without themselves being changed. Most chemical reactions that occur in living organisms involve enzymes, because otherwise processes such as respiration or photosynthesis would happen far too slowly for organisms to survive.

The enzymes you will be most familiar with are those involved in digestion. See pages 8 and 9.

Enzyme molecules are **specific**, with each enzyme having a 3D shape that corresponds to the shape of the molecule (**substrate**) it works with. The part of the enzyme that binds to the substrate molecule is the **active site**.

High temperatures or extremes of pH affect an enzyme's molecular structure, irreversibly changing the shape of the active site. This means that the active site will not fit the substrate and the enzyme will no longer work. It has become **denatured**.

⑤ Lock and key model

1 Substrate collides with active site of enzyme and becomes attached.

2 Enzyme catalyses breakdown of substrate.

enzyme — active site — substrate —

Enzyme molecule is unchanged and can be reused.

3 Products released from active site.

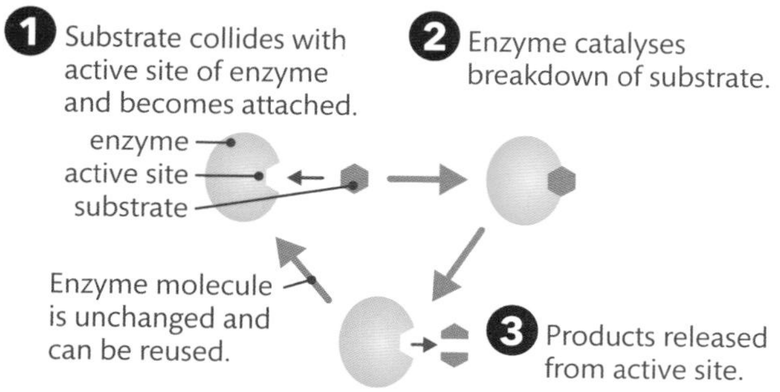

Figure 1 The lock and key model helps explain how enzymes work. Each type of enzyme has a differently shaped active site so can only work with a specific complementary shape of molecule.

As substrate concentration increases, the rate of reaction increases due to more frequent collisions between enzyme and substrate molecules. Eventually the rate of reaction levels off as each enzyme active site is fully occupied.

⑤ Worked example — Grade 4

A student wants to speed up the rate of an enzyme-catalysed reaction by heating the reactants. Explain why this might **not** work. **[2 marks]**

If the temperature is increased above the optimum temperature, the enzyme will become denatured and the reaction will slow down or stop.

⑩ Factors affecting enzymes

The rate of an enzyme-catalysed reaction is affected by temperature, pH and substrate concentration.

Temperature

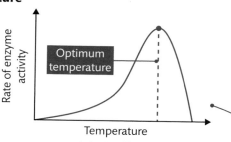

Figure 2 How enzyme activity is affected by temperature

As temperature increases, particles move and collide more quickly increasing the rate of reaction up to a maximum (its **optimum temperature**). Above this temperature, the enzyme molecules become denatured, reducing the rate of reaction.

pH

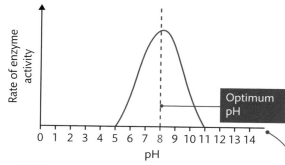

Figure 3 How enzyme activity is affected by pH

Each enzyme has its own **optimum pH**. Above or below this, the enzyme becomes denatured so the rate of reaction decreases.

Substrate concentration

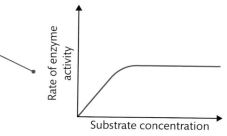

Figure 4 How enzyme activity is affected by substrate concentration

⑤ Exam-style practice — Grade 4

Explain why each enzyme only works with a specific substrate. **[2 marks]**

Practical: Enzymes

You need to know how to investigate the effect of pH on the rate of reaction of an enzyme. Most enzymes will only work efficiently within a narrow pH range.

2 Apparatus

- three beakers containing the same amount of water
- three test tubes containing starch solution
- three test tubes containing amylase solution in a buffer solution
- water bath
- spotting tile
- iodine solution
- thermometer
- pipettes
- glass rod
- stopwatch

Working scientifically

You must control temperature during this investigation, as it affects the behaviour of enzymes.

Working scientifically

Interpreting these results is tricky. Iodine solution turns from yellow to black in the presence of starch.
When the spots of iodine on the tile no longer turn black or brown, but remain yellow, all the starch has been broken down into maltose by the amylase.

You need to make a sensible judgement of when all the starch has been broken down.

10 Method

1. Add one drop of iodine solution to each well in the spotting tile.
2. Make up three beakers of water, each containing a test tube of starch solution and a test tube of amylase solution in a buffer solution. (Buffer solutions maintain constant pHs.) Each buffer solution should be at a different pH, for example: pH 7, pH 8 and pH 9.
3. Using a water bath, heat the three beakers to 25 °C.
4. Pour each test tube of amylase solution into a separate test tube of starch and stir.
5. Starting at 0 seconds, take a drop from each test tube every 30 seconds and add each drop to a separate well on the dropping tile using a pipette.

2 Maths skills

You need to know how to calculate the rate of a reaction. The rate of a reaction is inversely proportional to the time taken for it to complete.

$$\text{rate} \propto \frac{1}{\text{time}}$$

10 Worked example — Grade 5

1. **Figure 1** shows the results of the breakdown of starch by the enzyme amylase. At what pH is starch broken down the quickest? Justify your answer. **[2 marks]**

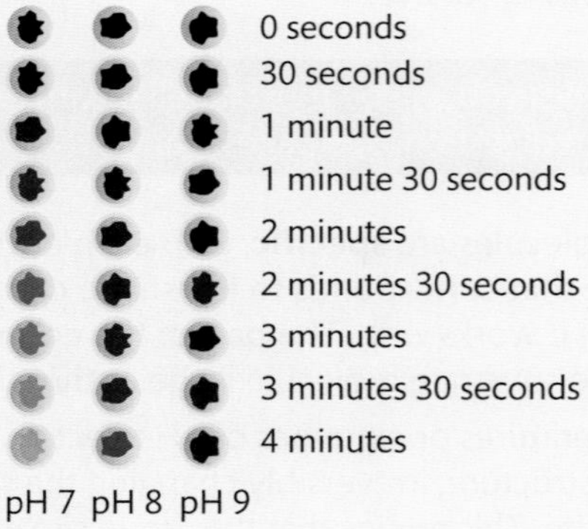

0 seconds
30 seconds
1 minute
1 minute 30 seconds
2 minutes
2 minutes 30 seconds
3 minutes
3 minutes 30 seconds
4 minutes
pH 7 pH 8 pH 9

Figure 1

pH 7 – at pH 7 the drops go from black to yellow the quickest, showing that the starch breaks down the quickest at pH 7.

2. It can be difficult to decide exactly when the iodine stops changing colour. Describe **one** method that would help this. **[2 marks]**

Have some unchanged yellow iodine in another well, and use this as a comparison each time.

3. A student investigated the time taken for amylase to break down starch at different pH values. Calculate the rate of reaction for each pH value. Use the equation:

$$\text{rate of reaction} = \frac{1}{\text{time of reaction}}.$$

Give your answers to two significant figures. **[3 marks]**

pH	Time taken for starch to disappear (s)	Rate of reaction (per second)
4	480	0.0021
6	120	0.0083
8	270	0.0037

5 Exam-style practice — Grade 5

1. During this experiment temperature must be controlled. State **one** other variable that must also be controlled. **[1 mark]**
2. Describe **one** way the experiment could be improved. **[1 mark]**

Digestion and enzymes

You will have already studied the digestive system in Key Stage 3 Science. For the GCSE exam, you need to know how the digestive enzymes, carbohydrase, protease and lipase, act.

 Digestion and enzymes

Digestion is the process of enzymes breaking down large insoluble food molecules into small soluble molecules that can be absorbed into the bloodstream. Enzymes catalyse and speed up chemical reactions. They work best at specific temperatures and pH levels.

Protease enzymes

- Proteases, such as pepsin, break down proteins into amino acids in the stomach and small intestine.
- They are produced in the stomach, small intestine and pancreas.
- Protease enzymes in the stomach need acidic conditions to work.

Carbohydrase enzymes

- Carbohydrases, such as amylase and maltase, break down carbohydrates into simple sugars.
- Amylase is produced in the salivary glands, small intestine and pancreas. Maltase is produced in the small intestine. Amylase and maltase work together to break down starch into glucose, starting in the mouth and finishing in the small intestine.

Lipase enzymes

- Lipases break down lipids (fats and oils) into fatty acids and glycerol in the small intestine.
- They are produced in the pancreas and the small intestine.
- They need alkaline conditions.

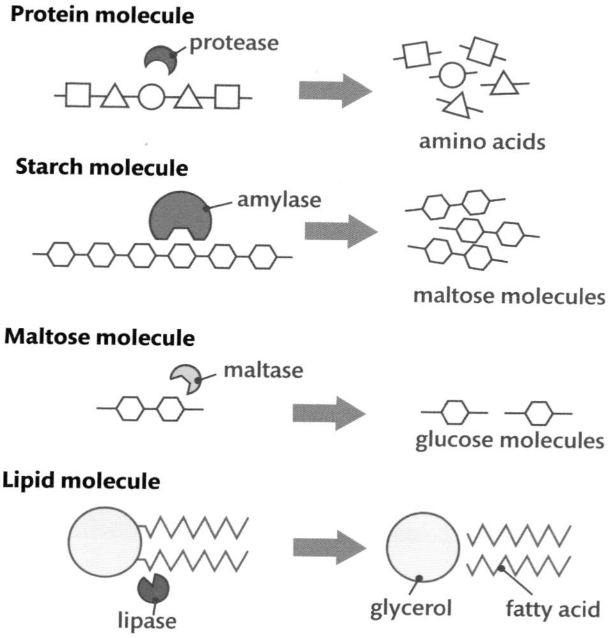

The products of digestion are used by the body in many ways, for example, some of the glucose produced is used for respiration and the release of energy. Other products of digestion are used to build up new proteins, carbohydrates and lipids in the body. These processes are also controlled by enzymes.

Protein molecule
protease → amino acids

Starch molecule
amylase → maltose molecules

Maltose molecule
maltase → glucose molecules

Lipid molecule
lipase → glycerol   fatty acid

Figure 1 Enzymes in digestion

 Worked example — Grade 5

Figure 2 shows the effect of pH on two different protease enzymes, **A** and **B**, found in the human digestive system.

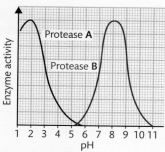

Figure 2

(a) Give the optimum pH for protease **A** and for protease **B**. **[2 marks]**

The optimum pH of protease **A** is pH 2 and the optimum pH of protease **B** is pH 8.

(b) The pH in the stomach is normally in the range of 1.5 to 3.5. Explain whether the two protease enzymes could be active in the stomach. **[2 marks]**

Protease **A** would be active because its optimum pH is in the pH range found in the stomach. Protease **B** would not be active in the stomach because it is completely denatured at the pH range found there.

 Exam-style practice — Grade 4

Explain why food has to be digested in order to be used by the body. **[2 marks]**

 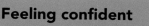

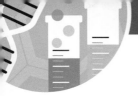

Diffusion

You need to know how some substances move in and out of cells by diffusion and how multicellular organisms have adaptations to enable the effective exchange of substances.

5 Rate of diffusion

Diffusion is the **net** (overall) **movement** of particles of gas or in solution, down a **concentration gradient**, from an area of higher concentration to an area of lower concentration. Diffusion is an important process that occurs in both plants and animals. Useful substances such as oxygen and glucose diffuse into cells. Waste products diffuse out of cells. For example, carbon dioxide is a waste product of respiration, given out during gas exchange in fish gills, leaf cells and the lungs. Urea is a waste product made by the liver, which diffuses into the blood plasma and is then excreted by the kidney.

Certain factors affect the rate of diffusion:

- **difference in concentrations** – the greater the concentration gradient, the greater the rate of diffusion
- **temperature** – the higher the temperature, the higher the rate of diffusion because molecules have more kinetic energy so move faster
- **surface area** – the greater the surface area, the greater the rate of diffusion.

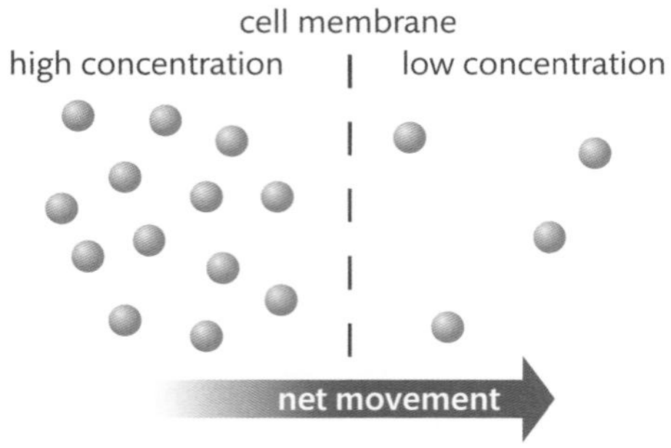

Figure 1 Diffusion occurs due to the random movement of particles. Particles move into and out of cells by diffusion until they are evenly distributed.

The surface area : volume ratio is even more important. Go to page 55 to read more about this.

5 Exchange surfaces

Substances diffuse into and out of small unicellular organisms by passing through their cell surface membrane. Multicellular organisms have evolved to have specialised exchange surfaces and organ systems that maximise diffusion by having:

- a large surface area
- a thin membrane for a short diffusion path
- a good transport system to maintain maximum concentration gradients.

In animals, an efficient blood supply and continuous ventilation maintain the concentration gradient required for efficient gaseous exchange of oxygen and carbon dioxide.

Examples of specialised exchange surfaces include:

- alveoli (air sacs) in the lungs, which provide a large surface area and short diffusion distance for gaseous exchange
- root hair cells in plants, which have a large surface area for absorbing water and mineral ions from the soil.

Find out more about adaptations on pages 56 (lungs) and 47 (plant roots).

5 Worked example — Grade 4

Figure 2 shows three cells, **A**, **B** and **C**, which contain different concentrations of oxygen. The darker the shading, the higher the oxygen concentration. Draw arrows on the diagram to show how oxygen will diffuse between the cells. Explain your answer. **[2 marks]**

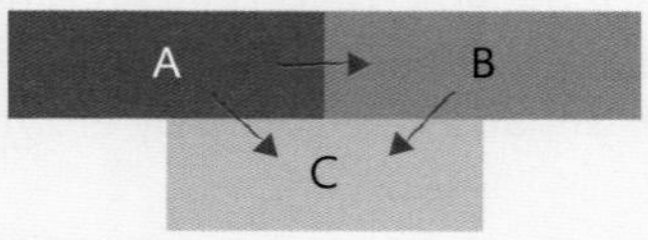

Figure 2

Oxygen will diffuse from areas of higher concentration to areas of lower concentration.

2 Exam-style practice — Grade 2

Use words from the box to complete the following sentence. **[2 marks]**

acid	equal	higher	lower

Diffusion is the net movement of particles from an area of ____________ concentration to an area of ____________ concentration.

Osmosis

You need to understand the process of osmosis and be able to interpret labelled diagrams that model the diffusion of water molecules.

(10) Diffusion of water molecules

Osmosis is a special type of diffusion in which water diffuses across a **partially permeable membrane**. The water travels from a **more dilute solution** (high concentration of water molecules) to a **more concentrated solution** (low concentration of water molecules). The solute molecules (e.g. salt or sugar) are too large to pass through the partially permeable membrane. The water molecules are smaller, so they are able to pass through the pores in the membrane.

> When answering exam questions about osmosis it can be easier to refer to the concentrations of water rather than the concentrations of the solute. Water always moves from a high concentration of water (i.e. a dilute solution) to a low concentration of water (i.e. a more concentrated solution).

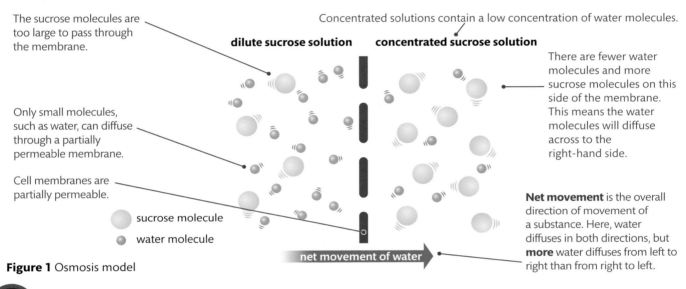

The sucrose molecules are too large to pass through the membrane.

Only small molecules, such as water, can diffuse through a partially permeable membrane.

Cell membranes are partially permeable.

○ sucrose molecule
• water molecule

Concentrated solutions contain a low concentration of water molecules.

dilute sucrose solution **concentrated sucrose solution**

There are fewer water molecules and more sucrose molecules on this side of the membrane. This means the water molecules will diffuse across to the right-hand side.

Net movement is the overall direction of movement of a substance. Here, water diffuses in both directions, but **more** water diffuses from left to right than from right to left.

net movement of water

Figure 1 Osmosis model

(5) Worked example Grades 3–4

1 During osmosis, water molecules move through the partially permeable membrane, but the solute molecules, such as sucrose, do not. Explain why only the water molecules move through the membrane. **[2 marks]**

Water molecules are small enough to pass through the membrane pores but the solute molecules are not.

2 **Figure 2** shows three cells, **A**, **B** and **C**, which contain different concentrations of sucrose. The darker the shading, the higher the sucrose concentration. Draw three arrows on **Figure 2** to show how water will move by osmosis between the cells.

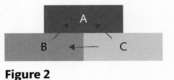

Figure 2

> Remember, the higher the concentration of sucrose, the lower the concentration of water.

[2 marks]

(5) Exam-style practice 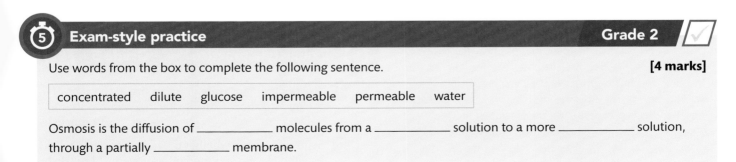 Grade 2

Use words from the box to complete the following sentence. **[4 marks]**

concentrated	dilute	glucose	impermeable	permeable	water

Osmosis is the diffusion of _____ molecules from a _____ solution to a more _____ solution, through a partially _____ membrane.

 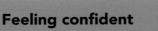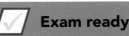

Practical: Osmosis

You need to know how to investigate the effect of different concentrations of sugar solution on osmosis in potatoes.

Worked example — Grade 5

A student placed equal-sized raw potato chips in different concentrations of sugar solution for two hours. The table shows the change in mass of each of the potato chips.

Sugar solution concentration (g dm^{-3})	Initial mass of chip (g)	Final mass of chip (g)	Percentage change in mass (%)
0	2.50	2.95	+18
50	2.50	2.45	−2
100	2.50	2.20	
150	2.50	2.05	−18
200	2.50	1.98	−21

The student's results are shown in **Figure 1**.

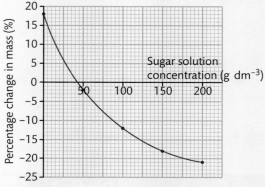

Figure 1

(a) One of the results is missing from the table.
Calculate the missing result. **[2 marks]**

$$100 \times \frac{(2.20 - 2.50)}{2.50} = -12\%$$

(b) Explain **one** way the student could improve the method. **[2 marks]**

The student could do the investigation several more times under the same conditions to see whether the results are repeatable.

(c) Describe and explain the pattern of results shown in **Figure 1**. **[2 marks]**

At about 43 g dm^{-3} sugar solution concentration there is no gain or loss of mass, showing there is no net osmosis because the cells have the same water concentration as the sugar solution. As the solution becomes more dilute, the potato chips increase in mass as they take in more water by osmosis. As the solution becomes more concentrated, the chips decrease in mass as they lose water by osmosis.

Apparatus

- ☑ five equal-sized raw potato chips
- ☑ five different concentrations of sugar solution:
  - 0 g dm^{-3}
  - 50 g dm^{-3}
  - 100 g dm^{-3}
  - 150 g dm^{-3}
  - 200 g dm^{-3}
- ☑ ruler
- ☑ balance

Maths skills

You can calculate percentage change in mass by subtracting the initial mass from the final mass, then dividing by the initial mass and multiplying by 100.

$$\text{percentage change} = \frac{\text{change in mass} \times 100}{\text{initial mass}}$$

Method

1. Using the balance, measure the masses of five equal-sized raw potato chips.
2. Place each potato chip in a different concentration of sugar solution.
3. Leave the chips for the same amount of time, a minimum of two hours.
4. Remove each of the chips, pat them dry and measure their masses.
5. Record the data in a table of results and calculate the percentage changes in mass.
6. Plot a line graph of the results.

Working scientifically

You should be able to produce a suitable hypothesis based on your understanding of osmosis. For example, a student's hypothesis for this investigation could be:

The greater the concentration of sugar solution, the greater the increase in mass.

Exam-style practice — Grade 5

1. The potato chips were equal in size at the start of the investigation. Explain why this was important. **[2 marks]**

2. State and explain whether the hypothesis in the box above was supported or disproved. **[2 marks]**

 Made a start **Feeling confident** **Exam ready**

Active transport

You need to understand how substances are transported by active transport and be able to describe how it differs from osmosis and diffusion.

⏱ 10 Active transport

Active transport is the movement of a substance from an area of low concentration to an area of higher concentration against the **concentration gradient**. This is in the *opposite* direction to how substances would move by diffusion. For this reason, active transport requires energy, which comes from respiration.

One example of active transport is the uptake of mineral ions by plant roots. Plants absorb mineral ions needed for healthy growth from the soil. But the concentration in the soil is very low, so the ions would not enter the roots by diffusion – active transport is needed.

> 'Active' means that it uses energy.

In humans, active transport allows glucose to be absorbed through the wall of the small intestine as food passes along the digestive system. The glucose is absorbed into the blood. The concentration of glucose is usually higher in the blood than in the small intestine so the glucose will not enter the blood by diffusion. The glucose is then taken in the blood to cells and used for respiration.

Active transport involves special proteins in the membranes of cells. These proteins are called **carrier molecules**. **Figure 1** shows how carrier molecules move glucose across membranes from the small intestine into the blood.

> Go to page 47 for more about specialised root hair cells.

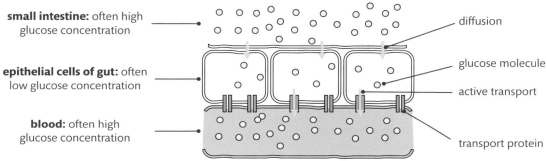

small intestine: often high glucose concentration

epithelial cells of gut: often low glucose concentration

blood: often high glucose concentration

diffusion

glucose molecule

active transport

transport protein

Figure 1 Cell membrane lining small intestine showing active transport in the small intestine

⏱ 5 Worked example — Grade 5

Figure 2 shows a plant growing in a solution of mineral ions. Oxygen is bubbled through the solution.

(a) Give the conclusion that you can make from the graph in **Figure 2**. **[1 mark]**

There is an increase in mineral uptake when extra oxygen is added to the solution.

(b) Suggest an explanation for your answer to part **(a)**. **[3 marks]**

Mineral ions are absorbed by active transport. Extra oxygen allows more respiration to occur, providing more energy for active transport.

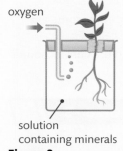

oxygen

solution containing minerals

Figure 2

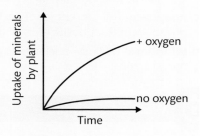

Uptake of minerals by plant

+ oxygen

no oxygen

Time

⏱ 5 Exam-style practice — Grade 4

1 Describe **two** ways active transport is different from diffusion. **[2 marks]**

2 Give **two** examples of active transport in living organisms. **[2 marks]**

Mitosis and the cell cycle

Multicellular organisms grow and develop using a type of cell division called mitosis. You need to know how this occurs.

⏱ (5) Chromosomes: key facts

- ✓ Chromosomes are found in the nucleus of nearly all types of cell.
- ✓ There are two copies of each chromosome in nearly all body cells. In humans, there are 23 pairs of chromosomes giving a total of 46 chromosomes in each cell (but not in the sex cells – see page 24).
- ✓ Chromosomes consist of long strands of DNA coiled up.
- ✓ The full number of chromosomes, found in nearly all body cells, is called the **diploid** number. For humans the diploid number is 46.
- ✓ Each chromosome carries many **genes**. Genes are sections of DNA which control our characteristics.

⏱ (10) The cell cycle

The life-cycle of a cell is called the **cell cycle** and it is made up of different stages.

1 Interphase

The cell grows and the number of sub-cellular structures such as ribosomes and mitochondria increases. The DNA replicates (copies) itself in preparation for cell division. The chromosomes are not yet visible because the DNA is uncoiled.

2 Mitosis

There are four stages of mitosis (**prophase**, **metaphase**, **anaphase** and **telophase**) during which the genetic material is split up so each new cell will have a full diploid set of chromosomes.

a **prophase**: The chromosomes become visible as the DNA coils up tightly.

b **metaphase**: The chromosomes lie in the centre of the cell. Each chromosome is made of two copies.

c **anaphase**: The two copies of each chromosome are pulled apart to opposite ends of the cell.

d **telophase**: Two new nuclei form and the chromosomes uncoil again.

3 Cytokinesis

The cell itself divides into two daughter cells – this is called **cytokinesis** – and the cells begin interphase again. The new daughter cells have identical sets of chromosomes to each other and to the original parent cell – they are all genetically identical and have the full diploid number of chromosomes.

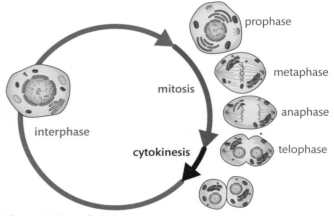

Figure 1 The cell cycle

⏱ (5) Worked example — Grade 3

Draw **one** straight line from each stage of mitosis to its description. **[3 marks]**

stage — description

anaphase — chromosomes become visible

metaphase — chromosomes lie in centre of cell

prophase — chromosomes uncoil and two new nuclei form

telophase — two copies of each chromosome are pulled apart

⏱ (5) Exam-style practice — Grades 4–5

1 Describe **two** things that happen in a cell during interphase to prepare the cell for dividing. **[2 marks]**

2 Describe what happens during cytokinesis. **[1 mark]**

 Made a start **Feeling confident** **Exam ready**

Importance of mitosis

You need to know the importance of mitosis for growth, repair and asexual reproduction. Sometimes cells can divide uncontrollably. This is called cancer.

② The importance of mitosis

Mitosis is the process of cell division involved in body growth, in repair (the replacement of damaged cells) and asexual reproduction. The new daughter cells produced by mitosis are genetically identical to each other and to the parent cell. They are all diploid cells.

⑤ Asexual reproduction

Asexual reproduction only involves one parent. There is no joining of male and female gametes. (A **gamete** is a sex cell such as an egg or sperm which contains genetic information.)

This means that there is no mixing of genetic information, so when the cells divide, all the offspring are genetically identical to the parent and to each other.

The only type of cell division involved in asexual reproduction is mitosis. These offspring are called **clones**. Organisms which can produce asexually include bacteria, fungi and many plants, such as potatoes and daffodils.

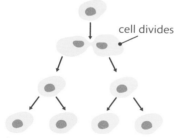

cell divides

Figure 1 Asexual reproduction involves only cell division by mitosis

⑤ Worked example   Grades 3–4

1 **(a)** Describe how cell division in cancer cells is different from that in other cells. **[2 marks]**

The cells divide uncontrollably which means they do not stop dividing.

(b) Give **three** lifestyle risk factors that can increase the likelihood of cancer. **[3 marks]**

Smoking, too much sunbathing, drinking too much alcohol.

2 Which process in humans does not involve mitosis? **[1 mark]**

- [ ] **A** growth
- [ ] **B** repair
- [ ] **C** cancer
- [✓] **D** egg and sperm production

⑤ Cancer

Cancer is caused by changes to genes in the DNA inside cells that lead to uncontrolled cell division and tissue growth. A change in the DNA of a cell is called a **mutation** (page 25).

Risk factors

Some people inherit versions of genes, or alleles, that are more likely to mutate (change) than other alleles. This means these people are born with certain genetic risk factors which make them more likely to develop cancer later in life.

Go to page 22 for more about alleles.

Lifestyle risk factors linked to cancer include sunbathing, smoking, heavy drinking of alcohol, being obese, exposure to some types of radiation and working with carcinogenic (cancer-causing) materials such as asbestos.

Nuclei is the plural of nucleus.

⑤ Sexual reproduction

Sexual reproduction involves the joining of male (sperm) and female (ova or egg) gametes. Gametes in reproductive organs are produced by a type of cell division called meiosis (see page 19).

During fertilisation, the nuclei of the male and female gametes fuse together to make a fertilised egg cell called a **zygote**. The zygote divides many times by mitosis (page 14), eventually forming an embryo. The mixing of genetic information from the male and the female parent provides variation.

Go to page 25 for more about variation.

Also, being obese, too little exercise, exposure to radiation or other cancer-causing substances, such as asbestos.

⑤ Exam-style practice   Grade 1

Draw **one** straight line from each term to its definition. **[2 marks]**

term	definition
asexual reproduction	getting larger
growth	producing offspring from one parent only
repair	replacement of damaged cells

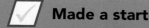 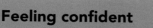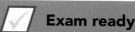

Cell differentiation and growth

You need to understand the importance of cell **differentiation** in plants and animals. You also need to understand how percentile charts can be used to monitor human growth.

 10 Cell differentiation

As an organism develops, its cells differentiate. This means they form different types of specialised cell. Cells need to differentiate so they can carry out different functions. For example:

- muscle cells contract to cause movement
- nerve cells transmit electrical impulses to communicate with other parts of the organism
- plant root hair cells have a large surface area to absorb water and mineral ions from the soil.

Differentiation in animal cells

Most types of animal cell are formed by differentiation at an early stage in life. In adult animals, cell division is restricted mainly to repair and replacement, such as making new blood cells, hair and fingernail growth, and healing skin cuts and broken bones.

Differentiation in plant cells

Many types of plant cell retain the ability to differentiate throughout the life of the plant. Cells can differentiate to grow new leaves, flowers, branches, xylem and phloem. This is why plants can regrow branches that are cut off during pruning. Cells in meristems (page 17) in plants can divide, elongate (get longer) and then differentiate into any type of plant cell, throughout the life of the plant.

5 Monitoring growth

The weight and height of babies and children are regularly measured to make sure they are growing properly and are healthy. Percentile charts show the normal range of variation. **Figure 1** shows a **percentile chart** for boys' heights. For example, if a child is on the 75th percentile line at a particular age, then they are the same height or taller than 75% of boys of the same age.

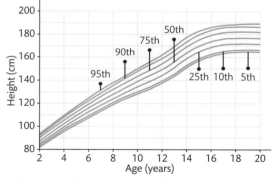

Figure 1 A percentile growth chart for height in boys

5 Exam-style practice — Grade 2

Draw **one** straight line from each term to its definition. **[2 marks]**

term	definition
cell differentiation	when cells become bigger
cell division	when cells become specialised
cell elongation	when cells split into two

5 Worked example — Grades 3–5

Look at **Figure 1**.

(a) Describe the general trend shown in **Figure 1**. **[2 marks]**

To begin with, as age increases, height increases, but after the age of about 17 or 18 years, height stays the same.

(b) At age 10 years, what is the height of the 95th percentile? **[1 mark]**

150 cm

(c) At age 12 years, the height of the 10th percentile is 140 cm. Which of the following statements is true? **[1 mark]**

☐ **A** At age 12 years, 10% of boys are 140 cm tall.

☐ **B** At age 12 years, 10% of boys are 140 cm or taller.

☑ **C** At age 12 years, 10% of boys are 140 cm or shorter.

Stem cells

Stem cells are undifferentiated cells. They can develop into different types of body cell. You need to know where stem cells can be found and how they can be used.

10 Stem cell applications

Stem cells may one day be used to cure diseases by replacing faulty cells. They could cure diseases such as diabetes, paralysis, hearing and vision loss, and Parkinson's disease. If the stem cells are used to treat the donor, then there is no danger of the cells being rejected.

Embryonic stem cells

Stem cells from human embryos can be cloned and made to differentiate into most types of human cell when instructed. They have the potential to cure many genetic conditions by replacing damaged cells. However, embryos cannot choose to donate and they are destroyed in the process. Unwanted embryos from fertility clinics are often used that would otherwise be destroyed.

Adult stem cells

Adult human stem cells can be taken from bone marrow. They can form many, but not all, types of cell, as they are used naturally in the body for the repair and replacement of some tissues. Adult stem cells are useful in the treatment of people suffering from blood disorders as they can form new blood cells.

An advantage is that donation of adult stem cells is a choice and no life is destroyed, but it can be a painful procedure.

Meristem tissue in plants

In animals, growth can occur anywhere in the body. However, plants only grow in certain areas called **meristems**. Meristems consist of stem cells that can differentiate into any type of plant cell throughout the life of the plant. Growth occurs in meristems as they are the only points on the plant with actively dividing cells. Meristems are found, for example, at the tips of shoots and roots. They can be used to quickly and cheaply produce cloned plants (by taking cuttings) and are useful for growing rare species of plants to protect them from extinction. They can be used to grow lots of identical crops exhibiting desired traits such as disease resistance.

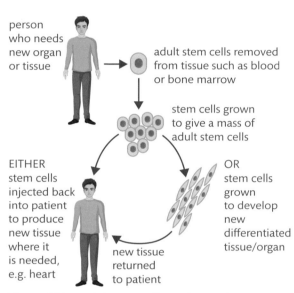

Figure 1 How adult stem cells can be used

1 Working scientifically

Stem cell research is controversial. Some people have ethical and religious objections to the process if human embryos are destroyed in the process, but others believe the advantage of using stem cells to cure diseases or injured people outweighs the rights of an embryo.

5 Worked example   Grade 4

Explain why stem cells might be used to treat many different health conditions.   **[2 marks]**

Stem cells can differentiate into many different types of cell, so might be used to replace many different types of cell, tissue or organ.

1 Exam focus

You do not need to know details about stem cell techniques for the exam, but you are expected to be able to evaluate the risks and benefits.
You also need to know about some of the social and ethical issues in science.

5 Exam-style practice   Grade 4

Give **two** benefits of using adult stem cells from an ill patient to treat the same patient.   **[2 marks]**

The human nervous system

The nervous system senses changes in the environment (called stimuli) and controls the body's responses. This is called **coordination**. You need to be able to explain how the human nervous system is involved in coordination.

5 Coordination

Stimuli are detected by **sensory receptors**, for example, when light stimulates receptors in the retina in the eye. Then, **electrical impulses** are sent to the **central nervous system (CNS)**, which consists of the brain and spinal cord. The CNS coordinates suitable responses to stimuli by sending impulses to **effectors** (muscles or glands). This pathway is known as a **reflex arc**:

stimulus ➔ receptor ➔ coordinator ➔ effector ➔ response

10 Types of neurone

Neurones are cells in the nervous system.
Sensory neurones carry information from sensory receptors to the CNS. **Motor neurones** carry instructions from the CNS to effectors. **Relay neurones** are found in the CNS. Sensory and motor neurones are covered in an insulating **myelin sheath** which insulates the axon to enable the axon to transmit impulses quickly.

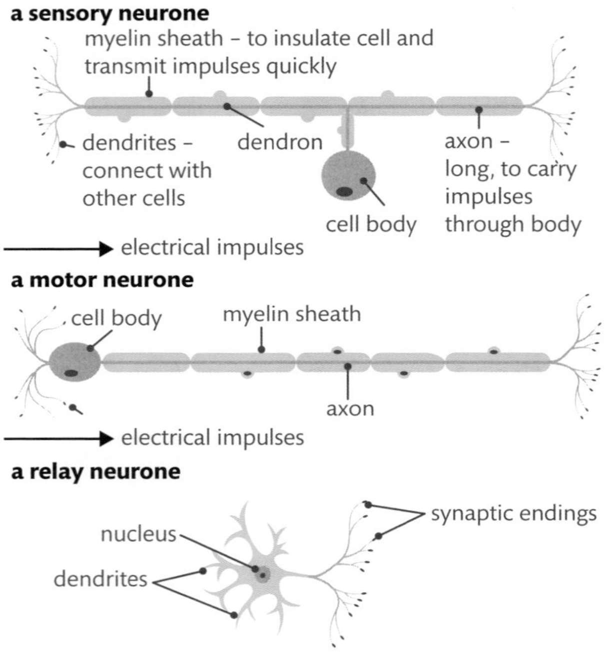

Figure 1 Neurones

5 Worked example Grade 3

Explain why many neurones have a long axon and many dendrites. **[2 marks]**

The axon is long to carry impulses from one part of the body to another. There are many dendrites so one neurone can connect to many others.

Synapses are gaps between neurones. When electrical impulses arrive at a synapse they cause the release of chemical messengers called **neurotransmitters** which diffuse across the gap and trigger an electrical impulse along the next neurone.

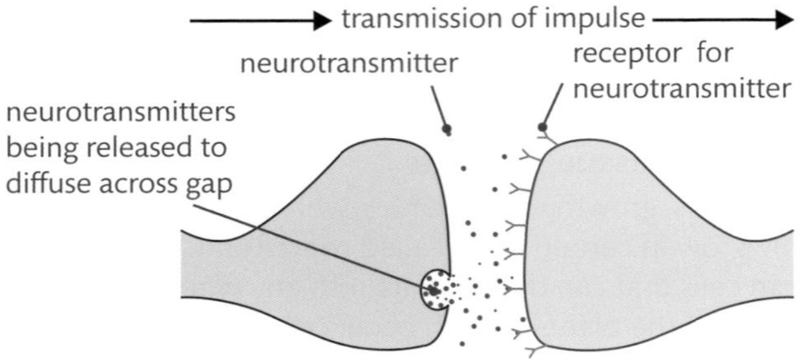

Figure 2 A synapse

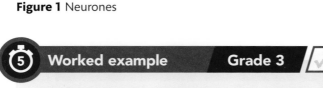

5 Reflex arcs

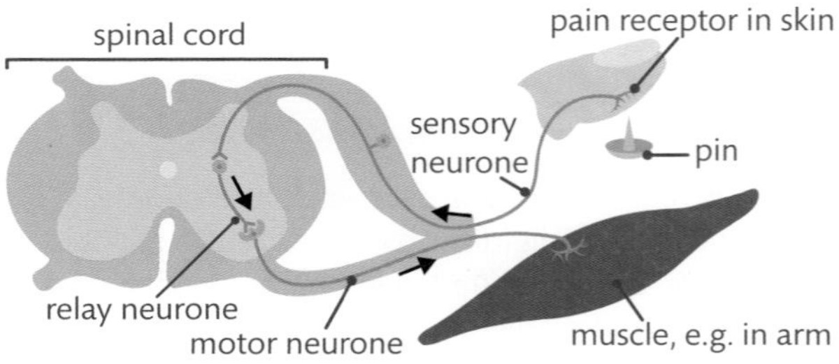

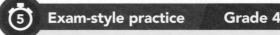

Figure 3 An example of a reflex arc

Reflex arcs are automatic and do not involve the conscious part of the brain. This is important to speed up reaction times.

Not all impulses go via the brain: some impulses just go to the spinal cord and straight back out to an effector. Sensory and motor neurones are connected by **relay neurones**.

receptor ➔ sensory neurone ➔ relay neurone ➔ motor neurone ➔ effector

5 Exam-style practice Grade 4

A student puts his hand against a hot oven. He pulls his hand away in an automatic reflex action. Draw and label the reflex arc. **[5 marks]**

Meiosis

Meiosis is the type of cell division that produces the cells called gametes, which are needed for sexual reproduction. You need to know how this occurs.

(10) The stages of meiosis

Meiosis in humans and other animals results in sperm and egg cells. These are known as sex cells or **gametes**.

Although similar to mitosis (see page 14), meiosis is a two-stage cell division process, resulting in the production of four cells, each containing a single set of chromosomes.

The gametes produced by meiosis are genetically different from each other and from both parent cells.

During fertilisation, one male gamete and one female gamete join up to form a cell with the typical full number (diploid) of chromosomes in a body cell (in humans, 46 chromosomes arranged in 23 pairs). This cell is called a **zygote**.

The zygote will then divide by mitosis forming a ball of cells called the **embryo**. As the embryo develops, cells differentiate.

The final stage of division during meiosis will always produce genetically different cells containing half the number of chromosomes (haploid number) as the parent cell (which has the full or diploid number).

(2) Key terms

- **gametes** – sex cells: sperm and egg cells
- **diploid** – a cell containing two sets of chromosomes
- **haploid** – a cell containing a single set of unpaired chromosomes

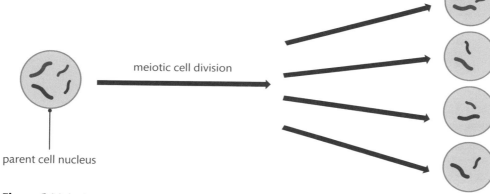

each gamete produced is genetically different

meiotic cell division

parent cell nucleus

Figure 1 Meiosis

(5) Worked example — Grades 3–4

(a) Explain why gametes (sex cells) are described as haploid. **[1 mark]**

They contain half the number of chromosomes of normal body cells.

(b) Explain why it is important that gametes are haploid. **[2 marks]**

So that when they combine in fertilisation the normal number of chromosomes is restored.

(1) Exam focus

In your exam, be very careful with your spellings of 'mitosis' or 'meiosis', so it is clear which one you are writing about. If it is not clear, you may lose marks.

(5) Exam-style practice — Grade 2

Use words from the box to complete the sentences. **[4 marks]**

different	four	gametes	half	identical
meiosis	mitosis	twice	two	zygotes

Sex cells or gametes are produced by a type of cell division called _____.

From each original parent cell _____ daughter cells are produced.

Each daughter cell has _____ the number of chromosomes compared with the parent cell.

The daughter cells are genetically _____ to each other and the parent cell.

The structure of DNA

You need to know about the substance that makes up the genetic material: DNA, or deoxyribonucleic acid.

(10) DNA

DNA (deoxyribonucleic acid) is the genetic material – the substance that genes are made of. Understanding its structure has allowed advances such as genetic engineering (page 30) and 'DNA fingerprinting'.

DNA consists of two strands made of sugars and phosphates. The strands are coiled to form a spiral called a **double helix**. The strands are linked by pairs of bases held together by weak intermolecular bonds called **hydrogen bonds**. There are four different bases: A, T, C and G. They always form the same pairs: A-T and C-G. These are known as **complementary base pairs**. Each gene has a different sequence of base pairs along its length.

DNA is a **polymer**, meaning that it is a very long molecule made up of repeating sub-units (see page 91). Each sub-unit is made of a sugar molecule attached to a phosphate group and a base, and is known as a **nucleotide**.

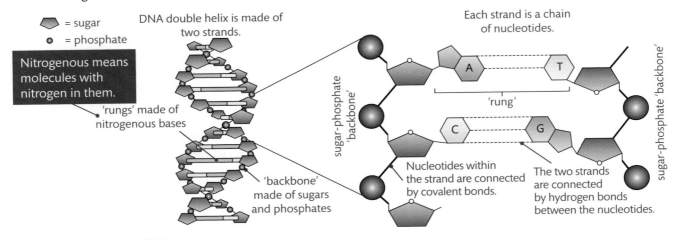

Figure 1 The structure of DNA

(5) Worked example   Grade 5

1 State why DNA is described as a 'polymer'. **[1 mark]**

Each strand is a repeating series of nucleotides.

2 Everyone has a unique 'DNA fingerprint'. What makes one person's DNA different from someone else's. **[2 marks]**

DNA contains a sequence of base pairs.
Each person has a slightly different sequence.

(2) Working scientifically

The structure of DNA was worked out in 1953 by James Watson and Francis Crick, using research from other scientists like Rosalind Franklin to help them. In 1962, together with Maurice Wilkins, Watson and Crick were awarded a Nobel prize, recognising the importance of their discovery. Unfortunately, Rosalind Franklin did not receive the Nobel prize because she died in 1958 and the prize is only awarded to living people.

(10) Extracting DNA

DNA can be extracted from fruit and vegetables. The process works well with kiwi fruit, bananas and strawberries.

Method

1 Remove any tough skin and mush up the fruit.

2 Add a prepared mixture made of water, salt and detergent to the mushed fruit and leave for about 20 minutes.

3 Filter the mixture to remove pips and pulp, collecting the liquid in a test tube.

4 Carefully pour some cold ethanol or methylated spirits down the side of the test tube so it collects on top of the fruit extract. The ethanol needs to have been kept in a freezer so that it is very cold.

5 After about 10 minutes, white 'stringy' material will appear at the interface with the ethanol. This is DNA.

(10) Exam-style practice   Grade 3

Explain why DNA is described as a 'double helix'. **[2 marks]**

DNA and the genome

The whole genetic material of an organism is called its genome. You need to know about how genes work and the importance of the Human Genome Project.

 Genes and the genome

The whole genetic material of an organism is called its **genome**.

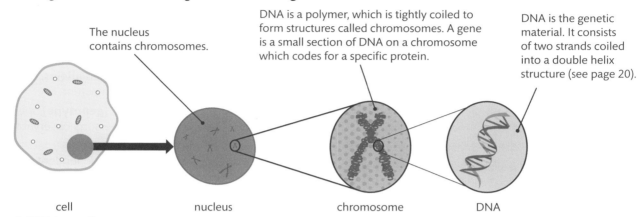

The nucleus contains chromosomes.

DNA is a polymer, which is tightly coiled to form structures called chromosomes. A gene is a small section of DNA on a chromosome which codes for a specific protein.

DNA is the genetic material. It consists of two strands coiled into a double helix structure (see page 20).

cell   nucleus   chromosome   DNA

Figure 1 DNA in a cell

 Worked example   Grades 4–5

1 Explain the difference between a gene and a person's genome. **[2 marks]**

A gene is a section of DNA that codes for a particular protein. The genome is all the DNA or genes of a person.

2 Give **two** reasons why it could be useful to find out if a person is carrying a gene for a genetic disorder, even if they are showing no symptoms or signs of illness. **[2 marks]**

They can be prepared if symptoms develop in future. They can decide whether to have children who might inherit the genetic disorder.

3 The Human Genome Project took 13 years to complete. This was shorter than had originally been planned. Suggest **two** reasons why it was completed sooner than originally planned. **[2 marks]**

Many different scientists worked together on the project. Technology was developed that speeded up the process.

You could also have said that humans had fewer genes than scientists originally thought.

 **Working scientifically**

Completed by 2003, the purpose of the **Human Genome Project** was to map and identify all the genes in the human genome. It was an international project involving scientists from 20 organisations, in six different countries.

Information about DNA can be very useful for forensic science, and for the understanding and treatment of inherited genetic disorders. The project helps scientists to:

- diagnose diseases before symptoms develop
- identify the genetic changes that are responsible for an already diagnosed disease
- help doctors to determine the best treatment
- identify genetic mutations that may increase the risk of developing a disease
- identify gene changes that could be inherited
- screen babies for treatable conditions.

Exam-style practice   Grades 3–5

1 What does a gene code for? **[1 mark]**

☐ **A** carbohydrate   ☐ **C** lipid

☐ **B** DNA   ☐ **D** protein

2 Arrange the following in order of size, starting with the smallest. **[2 marks]**

| cell | chromosome | gene | nucleus |

3 Suggest how knowledge of DNA could help forensic scientists investigate a crime scene at which blood has been found. **[2 marks]**

Genetic inheritance

Many of our characteristics are controlled by the genes we inherit. You need to know how alleles, the different forms of each gene, cause variation between individuals.

(5) Key terms

- ✓ **gene** – a short section of DNA which codes for a protein
- ✓ **allele** – different version of a gene
- ✓ **dominant** – only one dominant allele is needed for a characteristic to be seen in the phenotype (expressed)
- ✓ **recessive** – two recessive alleles are needed for a characteristic to be seen in the phenotype (expressed)
- ✓ **homozygous** – both alleles for a gene are identical
- ✓ **heterozygous** – the alleles for a gene are different
- ✓ **genotype** – the alleles of a gene present in an individual
- ✓ **phenotype** – the physical characteristics, determined by the alleles

(5) Genes

Some characteristics are controlled by a single **gene**, such as red–green colour blindness in humans, and fur colour in mice.

Most characteristics are controlled by multiple genes interacting. For example, multiple genes affect eye colour and skin colour.

The different forms of a gene are called **alleles**; one allele for each gene is inherited from each parent.

The combination of alleles present (**genotype**) operates at a molecular level to develop a person's observable characteristics (**phenotype**).

The appearance of a characteristic is dependent on both the type of alleles present and whether they are **dominant** or **recessive**.

(10) Worked example   Grades 3–5

In mice, the allele for grey fur, **G**, is dominant to the allele for white fur, **g**.

(a) Give the phenotype of a mouse with the genotype **gg**.   **[1 mark]**

White fur.

(b) Give **one** of the possible genotypes of a mouse with grey fur.   **[1 mark]**

GG. ◄

(c) If the allele **G** is dominant, give the term that describes the allele **g**.   **[1 mark]**

Recessive.

(d) Complete the Punnett square to show the result of a cross between two mice with grey fur. Include both the genotypes and the phenotypes of the offspring.
State the chance of the offspring having white fur.   **[3 marks]**

		mother	
		G	g
father	G	GG grey	Gg grey
	g	Gg grey	gg white

There is a 25% chance of the offspring having white fur.

(2) Working scientifically

You need to know how to draw genetic cross diagrams, such as **Punnett squares**, to predict the probability of the results of a single gene cross.
The results of genetic crosses are usually represented as either a ratio or a percentage.

Another type of genetic diagram is shown on page 24.

The other possible genotype is Gg.

Dominant alleles are represented by capital letters, and recessive alleles are shown by lower case letters. In an exam, if you have a choice of the letters you use for alleles, choose letters where the upper and lower cases are easily told apart, for example, A and a. Do **not** choose letters such as O and o, which can look very similar when handwritten.

(5) Exam-style practice   Grades 2–3

Use words from the box to complete the sentence.
[2 marks]

alleles	chromosomes	genes
genotypic	phenotypic	

Some characteristics are controlled by single genes with several _____, but most _____ features are controlled by several genes, which can make it very difficult to predict the characteristics of offspring.

Genetic diagrams

You need to know how genetic diagrams, such as Punnett squares and family pedigrees, show how some characteristics, including genetic disorders, are inherited.

Family pedigree diagrams

Family pedigree diagrams are family trees showing how inherited disorders are passed down through different generations. The example in **Figure 1** shows the inheritance of polydactyly.

Polydactyly is a disorder where the person has extra fingers or toes. It is caused by a dominant allele.

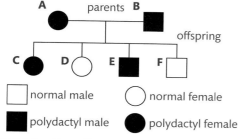

Figure 1 This family pedigree diagram shows the inheritance of polydactyly within a family

Worked example | Grades 3–5

Look at **Figure 1**. Polydactyly is caused by a dominant allele.

(a) Give the sex for both **C** and **F**. For each person, also state whether or not they have polydactyly. **[2 marks]**

C is a female with polydactyly. F is a male who does not have polydactyly.

(b) Explain why both **A** and **B** have polydactyly, but have had some children who do **not** have polydactyly. **[2 marks]**

Polydactyly is caused by a dominant allele, so A and B must both be heterozygous and also carry a recessive allele. The children without polydactyly must have inherited two recessive alleles, one from each parent.

Exam focus
When writing out heterozygous genotypes, it is usual to put the capital letter first: e.g. write Bb rather than bB.

Exam focus

In the exam, you could be asked to:

- complete a Punnett square diagram
- extract and interpret information from genetic cross and family pedigree diagrams.

Maths skills

When explaining the results of genetic diagrams, you may be asked to give your answers as:

- percentages (%)
- probabilities
- ratios.

A chance of 100% is the same as a probability of 1.0, and a chance of 50% is the same as a probability of 0.5.

Always give ratios in the lowest form. For example, if the ratio is 2:2, then write this as 1:1.

Exam focus

If a question asks you to draw a 'genetic diagram', then it is up to you which type you draw. There are other types of genetic diagram, however, a Punnett square is usually the easiest to draw.

Exam-style practice | Grades 3–5

The allele for brown eyes **B** is dominant to the allele for blue eyes **b**. Use this information to answer the following questions.

(a) Complete the Punnett square to show the possible offspring of a couple where one parent has blue eyes and the other parent has brown eyes but is heterozygous for eye colour.

Include both the genotypes and the phenotypes of the offspring.

State the probability of one of the children having blue eyes. **[3 marks]**

	blue eyes	
	b	b
B		
b		

heterozygous brown eyes

(b) Explain whether two parents with blue eyes can have a child with brown eyes. **[2 marks]**

 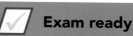

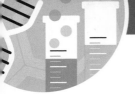

Sex determination

You need to know how sex is determined by chromosomes.

5 Sex chromosomes

Human body cells each contain 23 pairs of chromosomes, 22 of which control characteristics that do not depend on whether you are male or female.

The 23rd pair carries the genes that determine whether a person is male or female.

The female sex chromosomes are XX. The male sex chromosomes are XY.

Sex cells (gametes) only contain 23 chromosomes, one of each pair. Female sex cells (gametes) therefore only contain one X chromosome. The male sex cells (gametes) can either contain one X or one Y, depending on how the chromosomes are separated during meiosis. Therefore an X chromosome is always inherited from the egg but there is a 50% chance of inheriting either an X or a Y chromosome from the sperm, which determines the sex of the offspring.

5 Genetic diagrams

On pages 22 and 23 you saw one type of genetic diagram called a Punnett square. In the **Worked example** you can see a different type of genetic diagram. In the example, the diagram is being used to determine the sex of offspring.

1. To construct this type of genetic diagram, the phenotype of each parent must be written on the top line.
2. The next stage is to write the genotype for each parent, underneath their phenotype.
3. The next line shows the genotypes of all the gametes which can be passed on to the offspring. These are usually drawn in circles.
4. The final stage in the genetic cross diagram is to show all of the combinations of gametes which could occur which give the different genotypes possible.

You are expected to know the genotype for a male and a female.

- In males, the two sex chromosomes are different. They are XY.
- In females, the two sex chromosomes are the same. They are XX.

5 Worked example — Grade 5

There is a 1 : 1 chance of a child being a boy or a girl. Complete the genetic diagram to explain this. **[4 marks]**

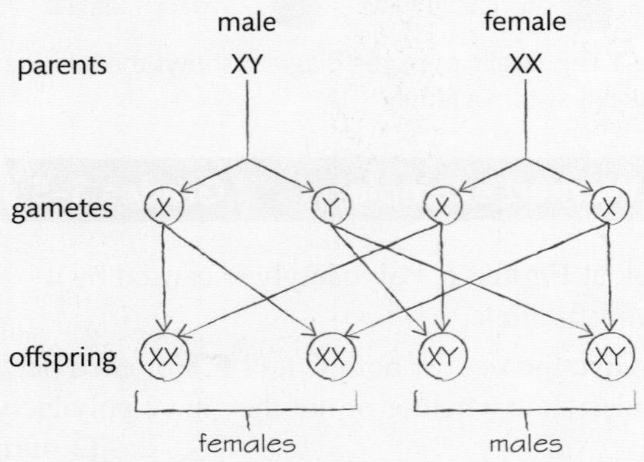

The diagram shows that there is a 2 : 2 chance of female : male offspring, which is simplified to a 1 : 1 chance.

You could also show your answer as a Punnett square diagram:

		Male	
		X	Y
Female	X	XX	XY
	X	XX	XY

1 Working scientifically

Although it is possible to identify the sex of an unborn baby, it is illegal to choose the sex of a baby unless you have a serious genetic condition which could put a child at risk if inherited, such as haemophilia or muscular dystrophy. (The alleles for these conditions are carried on the sex chromosomes.)

5 Exam-style practice — Grades 1–2

1 **(a)** What sex chromosomes are in a human egg cell? **[1 mark]**

☐ **A** X ☐ **B** Y ☐ **C** X or Y ☐ **D** X and Y

(b) What sex chromosomes are in a human sperm cell? **[1 mark]**

☐ **A** X ☐ **B** Y ☐ **C** X or Y ☐ **D** X and Y

2 Give the probability of a baby being a girl. **[1 mark]**

Variation and mutation

You need to know how both variation and mutation occur in a species.

10 Causes of variation

The differences between different individuals' phenotypes are called **variation**.

Variation occurs due to differences in:

- inherited alleles
- the environment – this includes anything that happens to an individual during their lifetime
- the interaction between genes and the environment.

Some characteristics caused by genes include blood group and eye colour.

Some characteristics caused by the environment include language spoken and the presence of scars. Characteristics caused by the environment are sometimes called **acquired characteristics**.

Most examples of variation are influenced by both environmental and genetic factors. For example, a person may have the genetic potential to be tall, but an unhealthy diet can cause poor growth.

There is usually a lot of genetic variation within a population of a species.

Genetic variation in individuals is caused by sexual reproduction (see pages 15 and 19) and by genetic changes called **mutations**. Most mutations will have no effect on the phenotype; some mutations have a small effect on the phenotype; rarely, a single mutation will significantly affect the phenotype. Mutations occur continuously. If the new phenotype is suited to an environmental change it can lead to a new species – this is evolution (see page 26).

Mutations can have positive or negative effects:
- 👍 improve chances of survival
- 👍 increase genetic diversity
- 👎 can lead to diseases, such as cancer (pages 15 and 41)
- 👎 can lead to genetic disorders (page 23).

5 Mutations: key facts

- ☑ A mutation is a change in genetic material (DNA).
- ☑ Mutations occur naturally and continuously, usually when DNA is being copied before cell division takes place.
- ☑ The effect of a mutation on an individual's characteristics may be neutral, harmful or beneficial.
- ☑ Mutations cause variation within a species, which can be vital to ensure the survival of the species.
- ☑ Some mutations are caused by substances such as tar from cigarettes.
- ☑ Radiation, including gamma rays, X-rays and UV rays, can also cause genetic mutations.

5 Worked example — Grades 2–4

1 Complete the table to show whether each example of variation is caused by genetic factors, environmental factors, or both. **[3 marks]**

Example	Genetic	Environmental	Both
blood group	✓		
body mass			✓
eye colour	✓		
hair length		✓	
height			✓
scars		✓	

2 Identical twins have the same DNA but sometimes can grow up to look quite different. Give **two** reasons why they might look different. **[2 marks]**

Live in different climates. Eat different foods. ◀

5 Exam-style practice — Grades 4–5

1 What is the best definition of a mutation? **[1 mark]**

- [ ] **A** change caused by growth
- [ ] **B** change caused by radiation
- [ ] **C** change in someone's DNA
- [ ] **D** change in the environment

2 Which of the following does **not** always cause variation between individuals? **[1 mark]**

- [ ] **A** ageing
- [ ] **B** environmental factors
- [ ] **C** mutation
- [ ] **D** sexual reproduction

Other possible answers include: different lifestyles, whether or not they smoke, different levels of activity.

Evolution by natural selection

You need to know how the theory of evolution by natural selection explains the development of species over time.

Natural selection

The theory of **evolution** by natural selection states that all species of living things have evolved, over more than three billion years, from simpler life forms, through a process called natural selection. **Natural selection** is the theory that organisms which are best suited to their environment are more likely to survive and reproduce. Therefore, their offspring are more likely to inherit genes that give rise to phenotypes (see pages 22 and 25) most suited to the environment, causing changes to the population over time.

The stages in natural selection are:

1 **Variation**: there are differences within a population – e.g. some giraffes are taller than others.

2 **Survival of the best adapted (sometimes called 'survival of the fittest')**: individuals with the best suited characteristics are more likely to survive – e.g. taller giraffes can reach more food in trees.

3 **Inheritance**: individuals with the best characteristics are more likely to breed and pass on their genes (alleles) to their offspring – e.g. taller giraffes are more likely to breed and have offspring who are tall.

4 **Change in species**: over many generations, genes (alleles) for the successful characteristics spread through the species – e.g. the average height of the giraffe population increases.

Figure 1 Taller giraffes have an advantage because they can reach leaves to eat that others cannot

New species can form when the genes of groups within a species become so different that their phenotype changes and they can no longer interbreed with other groups to form fertile offspring. This is known as **speciation**.

You do not need to learn how particular species have evolved, and in the exam you will be given the information you need to answer the question.

You could also be asked to suggest a reason why a feature has evolved. For example, the whale's fin developed so that the whale could swim efficiently.

Working scientifically

Charles Darwin developed the theory of natural selection after observing many examples of variation, for example, between different species of tortoise or of birds while voyaging around South America and the Galapagos Islands. Another scientist, Alfred Russel Wallace, also developed similar ideas.

As more evidence surrounding genetic inheritance (page 22) was discovered and more of the fossil record was found, the theory of evolution by natural selection became widely accepted. There is further evidence for evolution in the process by which bacteria become resistant to certain antibiotics over time (page 39), and in how some pests, such as rats or mosquitoes, become resistant to particular poisons or insecticides.

The theory of evolution by natural selection was not widely accepted at first because:

- the theory challenged the idea that God made all the animals and plants that live on Earth
- there was insufficient evidence at the time the theory was first published to convince all scientists
- how genes are inherited was not known until about 100 years after the theory was published.

Worked example — Grade 4

Stage 1   Stage 2
Stage 3   Stage 4

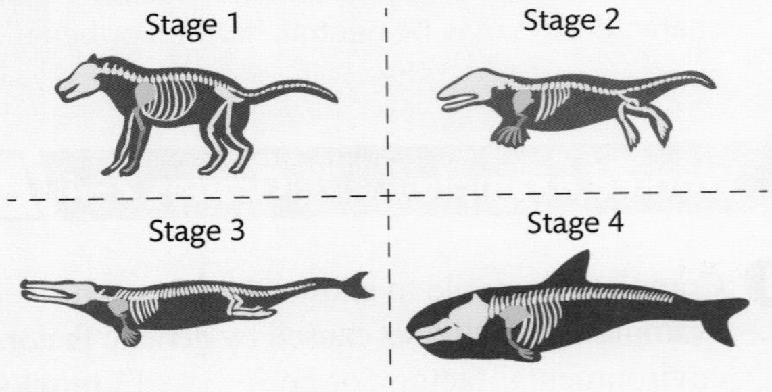

Figure 2

Figure 2 shows how the whale is thought to have evolved from its land-dwelling ancestors.

Give **two** ways in which the whale has evolved since Stage 1. **[2 marks]**

The early ancestor had four limbs, and the whale alive today doesn't.

The whale has a fin on its back unlike its ancestors.

Exam-style practice — Grades 3–5

1 Name the theory that Charles Darwin and Alfred Russel Wallace developed. **[1 mark]**

2 Cheetahs live in Africa and hunt antelope and other prey. Cheetahs are the fastest land animal in the world. Describe the stages of natural selection by which cheetahs evolved from slower-moving ancestors. **[4 marks]**

Made a start   Feeling confident   Exam ready

Evidence for human evolution

Fossils are the preserved remains of organisms that lived millions of years ago. You need to know that fossils can show us how life, including humans, has evolved on Earth. Stone tools provide further evidence of human evolution.

 ## Evidence for human evolution

Evidence for how humans have evolved includes fossils and stone tools.

Fossils

- Ardi (*Ardipithecus ramidus*) is a fossil of a female human-like animal from 4.4 million years ago. She could probably walk upright but had much longer arms than a human, which would help with moving through trees.

- Lucy (*Australopithecus afarensis*) is another human-like fossil from 3.2 million years ago. She also could walk upright but her feet were more similar to modern humans than Ardi's.

- Turkana Boy (*Homo erectus*) is a fossil discovered by a team of archaeologists led by Richard Leakey. He is about 1.6 million years old and is more similar to modern humans than Ardi or Lucy, for example, in having a much larger brain size.

Stone tools

The oldest known fossil remains of modern humans, *Homo sapiens*, are about 0.3 million years old. However, stone tools have been found that are 3.3 million years old and so were almost certainly made by early humans living at that time. Scientists have worked out the age of the tools from the surroundings and environment where they were found.

 ## Working scientifically

Richard Leakey's parents, Louis and Mary Leakey, made many important discoveries of early human fossils in Kenya, showing that humans first evolved in Africa. His wife and daughter also work in the field of paleoanthropology.

 ## Worked example **Grade 5**

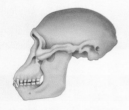 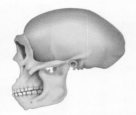 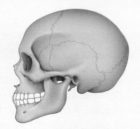

Australopithecus afarensis 'Lucy' – 3.2 million years ago	*Homo erectus* 'Turkana Boy' – 1.6 million years ago	*Homo sapiens* modern humans – from about 0.3 million years ago

Figure 1

Describe **two** ways, shown by the fossil skulls in **Figure 1**, that humans have changed as they evolved.

[2 marks]

Their brains became larger and their faces became more flattened.

 ## Exam-style practice **Grades 3–5**

Figure 2 shows how stone tools changed over time.

(a) Describe **one** way the tools changed over time. **[1 mark]**

(b) Explain what your answer to part **(a)** suggests about the way that the early humans changed over this period. **[2 marks]**

Time

Figure 2

Classification

Classification is the process used to arrange living organisms into groups based on their similar structures and characteristics. You need to know how species are classified and how the process of classification has changed over time.

(10) The five kingdoms

In the 18th century, Carl Linnaeus introduced a system for classifying living organisms and giving them scientific names. Linnaeus divided all living things into large groups called **kingdoms** according to the organisms' features. Then he divided the kingdoms into smaller and smaller groups, as shown in **Figure 1**.

You need to know about five kingdoms:

1. Animals – eukaryotic organisms that move around to get their food

> As the classification groups get smaller, the organisms have more characteristics in common.

2. Plants – eukaryotic organisms that photosynthesise to make their own food

3. Fungi – eukaryotic organisms that secrete enzymes into their surroundings to digest their food and then absorb the products

4. Protists – mostly single-celled eukaryotic organisms

> Page 2 has more information about eukaryotic and prokaryotic cells.

5. Prokaryotes – bacteria.

Kingdom	animal
Phylum	chordate
Class	mammal
Order	primate
Family	hominid
Genus	*Pongo*
Species	*albelii*

Figure 1 Classification of a Sumatran orangutan

Naming species

It is important for a species to have a unique scientific name as it allows scientists to identify and refer to individual species quickly and accurately. Organisms are named after the genus and species that they belong to. This double name is called the **binomial system** of naming. The scientific name for the Sumatran orangutan is *Pongo albelii*.

Figure 2 A Sumatran orangutan

(5) The three domains

Over time, scientists' understanding of biochemistry and cell structure has changed as scientific equipment and techniques have developed. Advances, such as more powerful microscopes and DNA analysis and sequencing, have led to several new classification systems.

In 1977, Carl Woese proposed, on the basis of genetic analysis, that all living organisms can be divided into three **domains**:

- **archaea** – primitive bacteria, many of which live in extreme environments
- **bacteria** – true bacteria
- **eukaryota** (or eukaryotes) – protists, fungi, plants and animals.

The archaea and bacteria have prokaryotic cells, which, unlike eukaryotic cells, do not contain nuclei and many other organelles. (See pages 2 and 3 for more about these different types of cell.) The differences between the archaea and bacteria are in their chemical make-up and cannot be seen with a microscope.

> This mnemonic can help you remember the classification hierarchy:
> **K**ing **P**hilip **c**ame **o**ver **f**rom **g**reat **S**pain

(5) Worked example — Grade 5

For a long time, the domains archaea and bacteria were classified together in the same kingdom.

(a) Name the kingdom that corresponds with the archaea and bacteria. **[1 mark]**

Prokaryotes

(b) Explain why it took until 1977 to separate the archaea and bacteria into two different groups. **[2 marks]**

The differences between them can only be shown by genetic analysis, which was not available before then.

(5) Exam-style practice — Grade 3

1 Before scientists used the binomial system for naming species, they used different local names. Suggest **one** reason why using the binomial system was an improvement. **[1 mark]**

2 Give **one** reason why we now have more information to classify organisms. **[1 mark]**

Made a start — Feeling confident — Exam ready

Selective breeding

You need to know about selective breeding and the positive and negative impacts it can have.

 Selective breeding

Selective breeding is like natural selection (page 26), except it is humans who choose the desired characteristics to produce the best offspring. Selective breeding is also called **artificial selection**. It involves selecting individuals with the desired characteristic from a population showing variation in that characteristic. These individuals are then bred together and the offspring with the desired characteristic are then also selected and used for breeding. This continues over many generations, until all the offspring show the desired characteristic. Selective breeding can sometimes lead to inbreeding, where problems are caused by inherited defects or being prone to certain diseases.

Impacts of selective breeding

Positive	Negative
plants 👍 improved crop yield 👍 improved disease resistance 👍 large or unusual flowers **animals** 👍 improved quality of meat 👍 increased milk production 👍 increased meat production 👍 sociable domesticated animals 👍 large eggs	👎 A new disease could put the whole species at risk as the lack of genetic diversity makes them all equally vulnerable. 👎 The reduction in the stock of different alleles in the population could restrict the ability to produce new varieties in the future. 👎 Inbreeding can lead to inherited defects or susceptibility to disease.

wild cabbage plant (*Brassica oleracea*)

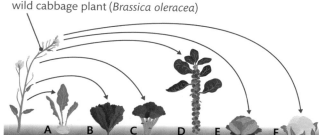

Crop	Modified trait
A kohlrabi	stem
B kale	leaves
C broccoli	flower buds and stem
D Brussels sprouts	lateral leaf buds
E cabbage	terminal leaf bud
F cauliflower	flower buds

Figure 1 Wild cabbage has been selectively bred to produce a variety of modern crops

Worked example

Grades 2–4

1 The table shows some of the stages used to breed cattle to produce an increased milk yield. Complete the table by writing the numbers 1–4 in the boxes to show the correct order of the stages. **[2 marks]**

Stage	Order
Breed the bull and cows together.	2
Choose cows that have a high milk yield and a bull that is the offspring of a female with a high milk yield.	1
Continue this over many generations until all cows have a high milk yield.	4
Select the highest milk-yielding offspring that are produced and breed them.	3

2 A farmer wants to improve their apples using selective breeding. Give **two** characteristics the farmer might select for. **[2 marks]**

Large size, sweet taste. ◄── Other possible answers include: attractive colour, long shelf life, early ripening.

Exam-style practice

Grades 2–4

1 A farmer wants to improve their herd of sheep using selective breeding. Give **two** characteristics the farmer might select for. **[2 marks]**

2 Give **two** problems caused by selective breeding. **[2 marks]**

 Made a start   **Feeling confident**   **Exam ready**

Genetic engineering

You need to know how genetic engineering is used to change the genome of an organism.

⑤ Genetic engineering

Genetic engineering (also known as **genetic modification** or **GM**) is a process used to alter the genetic material (genome) of an organism, by inserting a gene from another organism (usually another species) to give a desired characteristic. For example, bacterial cells can be genetically modified to produce substances that are useful to humans, such as insulin for the treatment of diabetes. Scientists are working on cures for genetic disorders based on genetic engineering. However, some people believe it is unethical to genetically modify living things, and are concerned about the possible effects on other organisms.

GM crops are crops that have had genes inserted into them to alter their characteristics. For example, some GM plant crops have been genetically engineered to produce higher-quality plants with increased yield, for example, by being disease-, herbicide- and insect-resistant. Crops can also be engineered to grow containing additional nutrients, such as golden rice, which provides high levels of vitamin A. This is useful for countries where vitamin deficiencies are common.

Figure 1 White rice

Figure 2 Genetically modified Golden rice

⑤ Working scientifically

Although many people have concerns about potential risks of genetic engineering, some examples have been very successful for many years. One of the earliest examples involves treating diabetes. People with diabetes are not able to make enough of the hormone insulin. In the past, they had to be injected with insulin extracted from other animals.

Today, human insulin is used, but it is obtained from genetically-engineered bacteria. A functioning human insulin gene was inserted into bacteria, and every time the bacteria reproduced, the gene was reproduced too. Soon, there were many millions of bacteria all producing human insulin. This insulin has been treating patients very successfully since 1982.

⑤ Worked example — Grade 5

1 Give **three** reasons why some people are against the growth of GM crops. **[3 marks]**

GM crops might cross-pollinate with wild plants.

We do not know if there are potential health risks for humans.

They may pass on features such as herbicide resistance to wild plants or weeds.

2 Give **one** advantage to growing herbicide-resistant crops. **[1 mark]**

Farmers can spray the crops with herbicide as the crops will not be harmed (only the weeds).

⑤ Exam-style practice — Grade 5

1 The characteristics of living things can be changed by both selective breeding and genetic engineering. Explain **one** advantage of genetic engineering compared with selective breeding. **[2 marks]**

2 Give **two** concerns associated with GM crops that are herbicide resistant. **[2 marks]**

✓ **Made a start**   ✓ **Feeling confident**   ✓ **Exam ready**

Health issues

According to the World Health Organization (WHO), health is the complete state of physical, mental and social well-being, including being free from disease. You need to know about the things that can affect health.

 Types of disease

Some diseases are communicable and some are not.

Communicable diseases are diseases that can be spread from one person to another. They are often called **infectious diseases**. They are caused by **pathogens** – microorganisms which cause disease.

> Examples include flu, measles and food poisoning. Go to page 32 for more about communicable diseases and their causes.

Non-communicable diseases are diseases that cannot be passed on from one person to another.

They are usually caused by lifestyle factors, such as diet, stress, drinking alcohol or smoking, and/or failures within the body's own systems, such as auto-immune diseases or old age.

Disease interaction

Some diseases are more complex and may be caused by multiple factors. Different types of disease may interact.

- Defects in the immune system mean a person is more likely to suffer from infectious diseases.
- Viruses living inside cells can sometimes be the cause of cancer.
- The immune system, which is designed to destroy invading pathogens, can sometimes be the cause of allergies and asthma.
- Severe illnesses can lead to depression and other mental illnesses.

> Go to pages 41, 42 and 43 for more about non-communicable diseases and their causes. Examples include cardiovascular disease, cancer and diabetes.

 Worked example Grade 4

The table shows the number of cases of Ebola and the number of deaths caused in four different countries during a recent outbreak.

Country	Number of cases of Ebola	Number of deaths caused by Ebola	Case fatality rate
Guinea	2871	1876	0.65
Liberia	8478	3605	0.43
Mali	8	6	0.75
Sierra Leone	10340	3145	

The case fatality rate is calculated using the equation

$$\text{case fatality rate} = \frac{\text{number of deaths}}{\text{number of cases}}$$

(a) Calculate the case fatality rate for Sierra Leone. **[2 marks]**

$\frac{3145}{10340} = 0.30$ (2 decimal places)

(b) One newspaper reported that three-quarters of all the people who catch Ebola die. Does the data support this conclusion? Explain your answer. **[2 marks]**

In countries with a substantial number of cases the death rate is much lower than three-quarters, so this conclusion is not supported.

 Exam focus

In the exam, you could be expected to interpret data from a table, graph or chart. Before answering any questions, make sure you know the data and its units, and if there are any trends.

 Exam-style practice Grade 5

1 Explain the differences between communicable and non-communicable diseases. **[2 marks]**

2 Explain what is meant by a pathogen. **[2 marks]**

 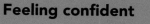

Communicable diseases

Communicable diseases are diseases that can be spread from one person to another. They are sometimes called infectious diseases. You need to know how infections spread.

Pathogens

Pathogens are microorganisms such as **bacteria** and **viruses** that cause infectious diseases.

Once inside the body they reproduce rapidly. Viruses enter cells, and force them to make more copies of the virus. This causes the cells to die and other cells are then invaded by the viruses.

Bacteria produce poisonous waste products called toxins. These toxins damage tissue and can make you feel ill.

Four types of pathogen

1 viruses
2 bacteria
3 fungi
4 protists

For more about diseases caused by the different types of pathogen go to pages 33 (viral diseases), 34 (bacterial diseases), 35 (fungal diseases) and 36 (protist diseases).

Spread of communicable diseases

Communicable diseases can be spread by:

1 **direct contact**, which involves touching or coming into contact with the diseased person

2 **indirect contact**, which involves touching objects that have been contaminated with the disease-causing organism, breathing in airborne disease-causing organisms, or eating or drinking contaminated food or water.

Go to page 37 to revise human defence systems.

The spread of communicable diseases can be reduced or prevented by:

- reducing contact with the microorganism which causes the disease
- using physical barriers such as surgical masks
- using hygiene measures such as washing hands
- using the immune system to destroy the pathogen
- using drugs such as antibiotics to destroy bacteria
- immunisation (vaccination).

Worked example — Grade 5

Some bacteria can divide once every 20 minutes.
The table shows the number of bacteria produced from a single bacterium after 180 minutes.

(a) The number of bacteria for 120 minutes is missing from the table. Calculate the missing number. **[1 mark]**

64 (double 32)

(b) Calculate the number of bacteria a single bacterium could produce in 4 hours. **[1 mark]**

4096 (doubling every 20 minutes means there are 1024 after 200 minutes, 2048 after 220 minutes, and 4096 after 240 minutes)

(c) Use information from the table to suggest a reason why infectious diseases should be treated as early as possible. **[1 mark]**

There will be fewer bacteria present so it will be easier to treat.

You could also say that treating early will mean that less harm will come to the patient.

Time (minutes)	Number of bacteria
20	2
40	4
60	8
80	16
100	32
120	
140	128
160	256
180	512

Exam-style practice — Grades 4–5

1 Give the meaning of 'infectious disease'. **[1 mark]**

2 Airborne diseases spread much faster than diseases which are spread through contact. Suggest an explanation for this. **[2 marks]**

Made a start   Feeling confident   Exam ready

Viral diseases

A virus is an infective agent that is too small to be seen using a light microscope. You need to know about the characteristics of viruses and some examples of them.

5 Viruses

Viruses are much smaller than bacteria.
They are so small that for many years scientists did not know that they existed.
They consist of small fragments of genes enclosed by protein.
They invade other cells and the genes in the virus take over the cell.
The genes instruct the host cell to make more copies of the virus.
This kills the cell and thousands more viruses are released into the body to invade other cells.

Viruses are classed as pathogens, although, as they cannot reproduce without a host cell, they are not usually regarded as being alive.

10 Viral diseases

Measles

Measles is a viral disease which affects humans. It is spread by breathing in airborne droplets from sneezes and coughs.

Symptoms include a fever, sore eyes and a red skin rash. Most people recover from the disease but serious complications can sometimes arise, and it can be fatal. These complications include swelling of the brain, called encephalitis, and ear and eye infections. One in 20 children who get measles may also get pneumonia. This is why most young children in the United Kingdom are vaccinated against measles.

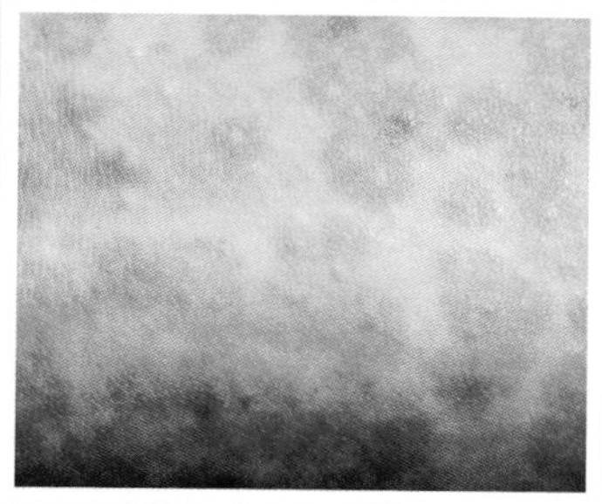

Figure 1 Measles is usually accompanied by a fever and a red skin rash

Human Immunodeficiency Virus (HIV)

HIV causes flu-like symptoms. The virus attacks the human immune system by destroying white blood cells, which is why the body cannot destroy the virus.

In the final stage of HIV infection, when the immune system is badly damaged, it can no longer protect the body from other pathogens or cancers. This is called Acquired Immune Deficiency Syndrome (AIDS). The infected person will develop other diseases. It is these diseases that can kill a person with HIV.

People infected with HIV can take antiviral drugs to prevent the virus from damaging their immune system by stopping it from replicating.

HIV is spread by sexual contact or other exchanges of bodily fluids, such as blood when drug users share needles.

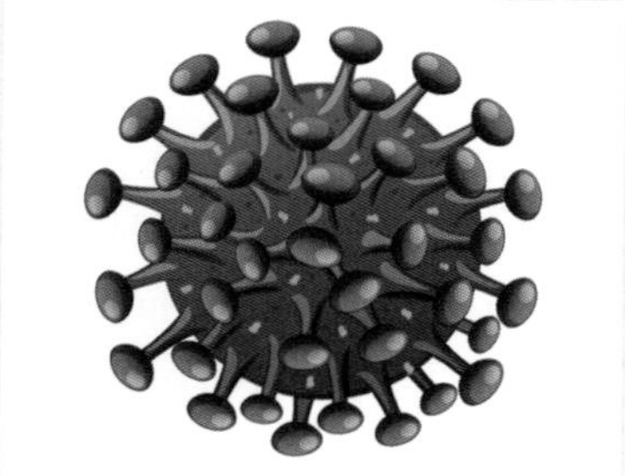

Figure 2 A highly magnified view of the HIV virus

Diseases spread by sexual contact are known as sexually transmitted infections (STIs). The spread of STIs can be reduced in several ways, for example, by avoiding sexual contact, or by using condoms.

Go to page 34 for another example of an STI.

2 Worked example — Grade 4

Describe how HIV is spread. **[2 marks]**

HIV is passed from one person to another through bodily fluids, for example, during sex, in blood, or through unsterilised needles.

5 Exam-style practice — Grades 3–5

1. Give **three** characteristics of viruses. **[3 marks]**
2. Give **two** ways to prevent the spread of HIV. **[2 marks]**

Bacterial diseases

You need to know about the different kinds of bacteria. Most are harmless, some are very useful and some can cause diseases in humans.

 Bacteria

Bacteria are microscopic, single-celled prokaryotic organisms. Once they have entered the body, they can reproduce rapidly.

Some produce toxins that kill tissues and make us feel unwell.

Unlike viruses, bacteria can be treated with antibiotics. However, many strains of bacteria have become resistant to antibiotics. Scientists are trying to find new antibiotics that will be effective against disease-causing bacteria.

> See page 39 for more about antibiotic-resistant bacteria.

 Bacterial diseases

Cholera

Cholera is caused by a bacterium spread through unclean water, for example, water contaminated by sewage.

Symptoms include severe watery diarrhoea, vomiting and cramps. It can be treated with antibiotics and rehydration.

The spread of cholera can be prevented by good water sanitation.

Tuberculosis

Tuberculosis (TB) is caused by a bacterium spread through the air when people with TB cough or sneeze.

Tuberculosis mainly damages the lungs, and can cause blood to be coughed up. Other symptoms include fever and weight loss.

The disease can be treated with antibiotics. Although TB is very common in some parts of the world, in the UK most children are vaccinated against it.

Chlamydia

Chlamydia is a bacterium that is spread through sexual contact.

Some infected people show no symptoms but it can cause painful discharges in both sexes and can lead to infertility in women. If diagnosed at an early stage, it can be treated successfully with antibiotics.

Like other STIs (see page 33), its spread can be prevented by avoiding sexual contact, by using condoms and by regular screening.

 Worked example Grades 4–5

In 1854, before the cause of cholera was known, there was an outbreak in London. A doctor, John Snow, realised that affected people got their water from a pump in Broad Street. Dr Snow thought that the disease was being spread by drinking water from this pump and persuaded the local council to remove the pump handle so it could not be used.

Figure 1 shows the number of deaths due to cholera during the 1854 outbreak.

(a) Give **one** piece of evidence that **supports** Dr Snow's theory that cholera was being spread by drinking water from the Broad Street pump. **[1 mark]**

The number of deaths fell after the handle was removed.

(b) Give **one** piece of evidence that goes **against** Dr Snow's theory that cholera was being spread by drinking water from the Broad Street pump. **[1 mark]**

The number of deaths was already falling before the handle was removed.

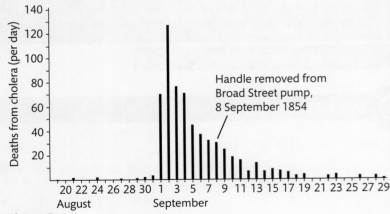

Handle removed from Broad Street pump, 8 September 1854

Figure 1

 Exam-style practice Grades 3–5

1 State what many bacteria produce that can cause the symptoms of a disease. **[1 mark]**

2 Give **two** ways to prevent the spread of *Chlamydia*. **[2 marks]**

Fungal diseases

You need to know about fungal diseases and how they can affect other living things.

5 Fungus

A **fungus** is a living eukaryotic organism, but it is neither a plant nor an animal. Fungi include moulds, yeast, mushrooms and toadstools.

Unlike plants, they do not contain chlorophyll so cannot make their own food. Instead, they secrete enzymes onto organic matter, and then absorb the digested organic products. Fungi can live on dead organisms or invade living ones.

How are fungal diseases spread?

Fungi reproduce by producing microscopic spores, which can each grow into a new fungus. The spores of different types of fungi are spread in different ways, for example, in droplets of rainwater or blown by the wind.

5 Chalara ash dieback

Chalara ash dieback is a fungal disease affecting ash trees. Ash trees are important because they provide habitats for many other species, as well as being widely used for timber. The disease causes death of the growing shoots of the tree, loss of leaves, and lesions (openings) in the bark. It can be fatal, but death can also be caused by the weakened trees being attacked by other fungi or pests.

The fungus causing chalara ash dieback is spread through the air by wind. Its spread can be prevented by cutting down infected plants, and collecting up, burning, burying or composting infected leaves.

Scientists have discovered that some ash trees are naturally resistant to the disease, and that this resistance has a genetic cause.

Figure 1 Chalara ash dieback

5 Worked example — Grade 5

1 How is the chalara ash dieback fungus spread? **[1 mark]**

- [ ] **A** by insects
- [x] **B** through air
- [ ] **C** through soil
- [ ] **D** through water

2 Scientists have discovered that some ash trees are genetically resistant to chalara ash dieback. Explain how this knowledge can be used to combat the spread of chalara ash dieback. **[2 marks]**

Collect cuttings or seedlings from the resistant trees. Plant these to replace infected or dead trees.

2 Exam focus

One way to check that your answers to multiple-choice questions are correct is by using a process of elimination to rule out the other options.

Remember that multiple-choice questions can be more difficult than you might at first think because the other options may seem like plausible answers at first glance.

5 Exam-style practice — Grades 3–5

1 Explain why people are so concerned about chalara ash dieback. **[2 marks]**

2 Describe what should be done with trees infected by chalara ash dieback. **[2 marks]**

Protist diseases

Protists (see page 28) are a group of organisms that are usually unicellular (made of just one cell) and have a nucleus. You need to know how protist diseases like malaria are spread.

 Malaria

Malaria is spread from person to person by mosquitoes which carry the protist that causes the disease. Animals like mosquitoes that spread disease-causing pathogens are called **vectors**. Malaria causes damage to blood and the liver and, if left untreated, can be fatal.

The spread of malaria can be controlled by using mosquito nets and insect repellents to avoid being bitten. Mosquitoes can also be controlled by killing them with insecticides. They can be prevented from breeding by draining the stagnant water, for example, in ditches, where they lay their eggs.

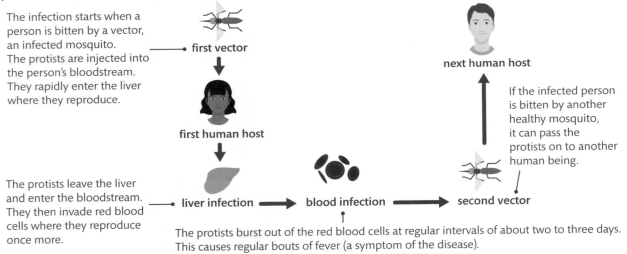

The infection starts when a person is bitten by a vector, an infected mosquito. The protists are injected into the person's bloodstream. They rapidly enter the liver where they reproduce.

first vector

first human host

If the infected person is bitten by another healthy mosquito, it can pass the protists on to another human being.

next human host

The protists leave the liver and enter the bloodstream. They then invade red blood cells where they reproduce once more.

liver infection → blood infection → second vector

The protists burst out of the red blood cells at regular intervals of about two to three days. This causes regular bouts of fever (a symptom of the disease).

Figure 1 The life-cycle of the malarial protist

 Worked example   **Grade 5**

Figure 2 is a photomicrograph showing malarial protists invading human blood.

(a) Label **Figure 2** to show a malarial protist and a red blood cell. **[2 marks]**

> **Figure 2** shows what a red blood cell looks like. There is more about red blood cells on page 57.

(b) Explain what is meant by 'protist'. **[2 marks]**

An organism made of a single cell with a nucleus that is not a fungus, animal or plant.

(c) The malarial protist is transferred from one person to another. Explain how. **[2 marks]**

An infected person is bitten by a mosquito, which then bites another person, infecting them with the protist.

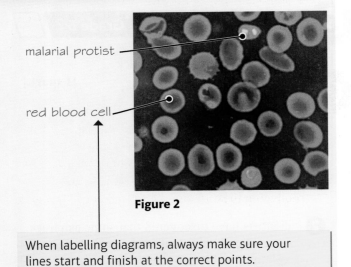

malarial protist

red blood cell

Figure 2

> When labelling diagrams, always make sure your lines start and finish at the correct points.

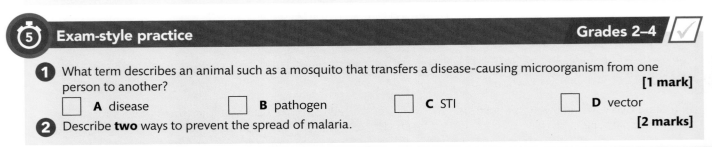 **Exam-style practice**   **Grades 2–4**

1 What term describes an animal such as a mosquito that transfers a disease-causing microorganism from one person to another? **[1 mark]**

  ☐ **A** disease   ☐ **B** pathogen   ☐ **C** STI   ☐ **D** vector

2 Describe **two** ways to prevent the spread of malaria. **[2 marks]**

Human defence systems

You need to know about the human body's defence mechanisms and how they protect us from invading pathogens. Many defences are non-specific because they protect against any pathogen. However, each type of antibody protects against a particular pathogen, so these form our specific immune system.

(10) Physical and chemical defences

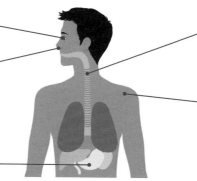

Tears, and the liquid covering the eye, contain an enzyme called **lysozyme** which kills pathogens.

The nose is lined with hairs and mucus to trap pathogens to stop them getting to the lungs.

The stomach produces **hydrochloric acid** to help kill any pathogens in food.

Sticky **mucus** in the trachea and bronchi traps pathogens. **Hair-like cilia** on the cells lining these passages move in a wave-like motion, moving mucus and trapped pathogens out of the lungs towards the back of the throat where they are swallowed.

The **skin** covers the outer surface of the body, acting as a barrier to pathogens. It secretes antimicrobial substances to kill pathogenic bacteria or inhibit their growth. Scabs form over damaged skin, keeping pathogens out while the skin repairs itself.

Figure 1 The body's non-specific defences make it difficult for pathogens to enter the body

(10) The specific immune system

When a person is infected with a pathogen, the pathogen starts to reproduce. Symptoms of the illness only appear when there are a large number of pathogens present in the body producing toxins and killing cells.

When a pathogen enters the body the **immune system** tries to destroy it. There are several ways it does this:

- **Phagocytosis** – some white blood cells engulf the pathogen and digest it.

There's more about white blood cells on page 57.

- **Antibody production** – some white blood cells produce **antibodies**. These are proteins that recognise and target specific molecules called **antigens** on the pathogen and destroy it. When the infection has passed, some white blood cells remain in the blood as **memory lymphocytes** (also known as 'memory cells'). If a person is re-infected by the same pathogen, the memory lymphocytes enable the immune system to react more rapidly, which reduces the risk of the symptoms. This is called the **secondary response**.

- **Antitoxin production** – some white blood cells produce **antitoxins**. Antitoxins are proteins that attach to the poisonous toxins produced by pathogens and neutralise them.

(5) Worked example   Grade 5

Figure 2 shows the concentration of antigens of a pathogen in the blood and the concentration of antibodies that the body produces in response.

(a) State how long it took for the body to start producing the antibody after infection. **[1 mark]**

7.5 hours

(b) Give the number of hours the person felt ill for. **[1 mark]**

32 − 10 = 22 hours

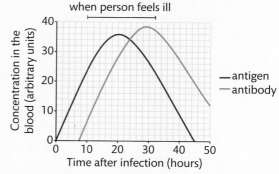

Figure 2

(5) Exam-style practice   Grades 3–4

1 State **two** ways that white blood cells attack pathogens.

[2 marks]

2 Describe **two** ways the skin provides protection from pathogens.

[2 marks]

Immunisation

You need to know how immunisation (or vaccination) can build up immunity to a disease.

 **Immunisation**

Immunisation (or **vaccination**) is the process of using dead or inactive pathogens to ensure that the immune system can recognise and quickly respond to the live pathogen if a person becomes infected.

1 Dead or inactive pathogens are injected into the body (the **vaccine**).

2 The body responds by white blood cells producing antibodies specific to antigens on the pathogen.

3 If the live pathogen infects the body in the future, white blood cells called memory lymphocytes rapidly produce large quantities of antibodies to destroy the pathogens.

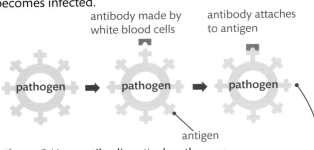

Figure 1 How antibodies attack pathogens

Go to page 37 for more about antibodies.

A different pathogen will have differently shaped antigens. The immune system will, therefore, produce differently shaped antibodies.

 Worked example **Grades 3–5**

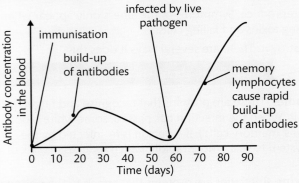

Figure 2

Figure 2 shows the build-up of antibodies after someone is immunised and then when they are infected by the actual live pathogen.

(a) Compare the changes in antibody concentration in the blood after immunisation and after infection with the live pathogen. **[2 marks]**

The antibody concentration increases after both immunisation and infection, but the increase after infection is greater and more rapid.

(b) Explain why the person might never realise they had been infected by the live pathogen. **[2 marks]**

The antibodies were produced so quickly after infection that the pathogens would have been destroyed before they had a chance to affect the body.

 Working scientifically

The more people that are immunised against a disease, then the less chance of that disease being able to spread. In the UK, young babies and children are routinely immunised against such diseases as polio, diphtheria and measles. Before the widespread use of immunisation, such potentially life-threatening diseases were much more common.

 Working scientifically

Smallpox is a disease that has killed millions of people around the world. The World Health Organization organised a global immunisation programme. In 1977, Ali Maow Maalin had the last natural case of smallpox. Smallpox is the only human disease that has been totally eradicated by science and immunisation. Millions of lives have been saved.

 Exam-style practice **Grades 3–5**

1 Why do you need a different immunisation for each disease? **[1 mark]**

☐ **A** Antibodies only last a short time.

☐ **B** Different diseases affect different parts of the body.

☐ **C** Each type of pathogen has different antigens.

☐ **D** In case the previous immunisation did not work.

2 Explain why you do **not** get a disease after you have been immunised. **[2 marks]**

 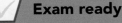

Antibiotics

You need to know how **antibiotics** can be used to treat some diseases.

(5) Antibiotics: key facts

- Antibiotics are a group of drugs that kill bacteria.
- Antibiotics work by stopping cell processes in the bacteria but not in the host organism.
- Specific bacteria should be treated using specific antibiotics.
- Antibiotics do not destroy viruses.
- Since their discovery, antibiotics have significantly reduced deaths from infectious bacterial diseases.
- However, many bacteria are now developing strains which are resistant to antibiotics. This has serious implications for treating bacterial diseases.

(10) Bacterial resistance

Bacteria can develop resistance to antibiotics by natural selection (page 26).

1. Some bacteria have mutations which make them resistant to an antibiotic.
2. Bacteria that are susceptible to the antibiotic get killed.
3. Bacteria that are resistant to the antibiotic survive and reproduce rapidly.
4. Soon all the surviving bacteria are resistant to the antibiotic.
5. Resistant strains can then spread because there are no effective treatments.

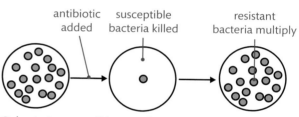

○ bacteria susceptible to antibiotic
○ bacteria resistant to antibiotic

Figure 1 Bacteria developing resistance to an antibiotic

(5) Worked example   Grade 5

Penicillin was the first antibiotic to be discovered.
The discovery was made by Alexander Fleming.
Fleming was growing bacteria in a Petri dish.
The Petri dish was contaminated by the mould *Penicillium*.
Look at Fleming's Petri dish in **Figure 2**. Suggest an explanation of how looking at this Petri dish led to Fleming discovering penicillin.   **[3 marks]**

Fleming noticed that not many bacteria were growing near the mould. He worked out that the mould must be producing a substance that killed bacteria.
He isolated the substance which is called penicillin.
This substance became the first antibiotic.

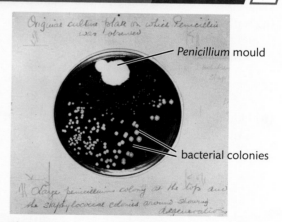

Figure 2

(10) Exam-style practice   Grade 5

1. Antibiotics do not kill viruses. Suggest an explanation why.   **[2 marks]**
2. Explain how antibiotic resistance develops in bacteria.   **[4 marks]**
3. Before prescribing an antibiotic, a doctor will often take a sample from the patient so the bacteria causing the illness can be identified. Explain the advantage of identifying the type of bacteria.   **[2 marks]**

 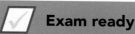

Development of drugs

You need to know how new medicines, such as antibiotics, are developed.

(10) Development of medicinal drugs

Research & development 3–6 years	Preclinical studies 1 year	Clinical trials 4–7 years	Review & approval 1–2 years
This is when potential new drugs are made or discovered.	This is when the drug is tested in the laboratory.	This is when the drug is tested on healthy human volunteers, starting with very low doses. It is tested for toxicity (is it harmful?) and efficacy (does it work?).	This is when new drugs are approved to be used on patients.
Scientists first decide what drugs are needed.	In vitro ('in glass') tests on cells and tissues (the drug is tested in Petri dishes and test tubes).	**Phase 1** The drug is tested on about 50 people to check for side effects and to see how quickly the body breaks it down.	If the drug is effective, it is sent to regulating bodies for approval.
Scientists then look for compounds that might do the job they are looking for.	Testing in animals	**Phase 2** The drug is tested on about 200 patients with the condition.	The governing body fast tracks drugs that are desperately needed. If the benefits outweigh any risks, it is approved.
Thousands of chemical compounds are then tested or modified to improve their action.	Testing in mammals	**Phase 3** If the drug is found to be safe, it is tested on about 2000 people to see how well the drug works and its optimum (the best) dose.	When the drug is available for doctors to use it is monitored for side effects indefinitely.

(5) Worked example   Grade 5

New drugs are tested using placebos and double blind trials.

(a) A placebo is designed to appear exactly the same as the drug itself, but it does **not** contain any of the actual drug. Suggest an explanation why some patients in a drugs trial are given a placebo instead of the actual drug. **[2 marks]**

The placebo acts as a 'control' (comparison). It is used to check if any effects are caused by the drug or by something else.

(b) Double blind trials are when neither the patient nor the doctor knows if the patient is getting the drug or a placebo. Suggest an explanation why double blind trials are used. **[2 marks]**

To avoid any bias by either the patient or the doctor if they know whether or not the actual drug is being used.

(2) Working scientifically

The results from testing and trialling new drugs are published. Other scientists then **peer review** the data.

This means that the other scientists check the results and the theories suggested. They may also carry out further tests to check the data provided is correct.

Peer review in this way helps to ensure that new drugs are as safe and effective as possible.

(10) Exam-style practice   Grade 5

1 Explain what is meant by peer review. **[2 marks]**

2 Look at the table above. Give the approximate time needed for a new medical drug to be developed. **[1 mark]**

3 Describe the differences between clinical trials and preclinical trials in the development of a new medicine, including the purposes of each. **[4 marks]**

Made a start | Feeling confident | Exam ready

Non-communicable diseases

You need to know that many non-communicable diseases are caused by the interaction of a number of **risk factors**. (Non-communicable diseases cannot be passed on from one person to another – see page 31.)

 (10) Non-communicable diseases

Many non-communicable diseases are caused by the interaction of different factors.

Cardiovascular disease

This is the general name for conditions affecting the heart or blood vessels, such as heart attacks or strokes. It is one of the main causes of death in the UK. It is common because there are so many risk factors:

- high blood pressure
- smoking
- drinking alcohol
- high blood cholesterol levels
- diabetes
- lack of exercise
- being overweight
- genetic factors
- unhealthy diet.

Risk factors interact to increase the risk of cardiovascular disease. The chance of getting coronary heart disease increases dramatically for someone who smokes, drinks heavily, is obese and takes little exercise.

Liver disease

Interacting risk factors include:

- genetic factors
- drinking alcohol
- drug abuse
- diabetes
- being overweight.

Lung disease

Interacting risk factors include:

- genetic factors
- smoking
- air pollution.

Cancer

Cancer is caused by changes to the genes that control cell growth, leading to uncontrolled cell division and tissue growth.

See page 15 for more about cancer.

Some people are genetically more at risk of developing cancer, but the risk is also increased by:

- sunbathing – risk factor for skin cancer
- smoking – risk factor for lung cancer
- heavy drinking – risk factor for liver and other cancers
- working with carcinogenic (cancer-causing) materials such as asbestos – risk factor for lung and other cancers
- living in unventilated buildings in areas where radioactive radon is released from the ground.

Nutritional diseases

Unhealthy diets increase the risk or severity of many diseases, such as cardiovascular disease. Unhealthy diets may consist of eating too much or too little in total, or too much or too little of particular types of food. For example:

- scurvy is caused by a lack of vitamin C
- anaemia is caused by a lack of iron
- rickets is caused by a lack of vitamin D or calcium.

(5) Worked example Grades 3–4

Explain why it is harmful to smoke, and to drink too much alcohol. **[4 marks]**

Smoking can lead to cardiovascular diseases, such as heart attacks and strokes; and to lung diseases, such as lung cancer. Drinking too much alcohol can also lead to cardiovascular diseases, such as heart attacks and strokes; and to liver disease, including liver cancer.

(10) Exam-style practice Grades 4–5

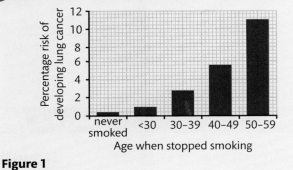

Figure 1

Figure 1 is a bar chart showing the risk of cancer for people who stop smoking.

(a) Explain what is meant by <30 on the x-axis. **[1 mark]**

(b) Give **two** conclusions that can be made from the data shown by the graph. **[2 marks]**

(c) Give the risk of getting cancer for people who have:

(i) never smoked **[1 mark]**

(ii) stopped smoking at the age of 45 years. **[1 mark]**

 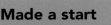

Effects of lifestyle

You need to know how lifestyle factors, acting at local, national and global levels, can affect whether or not people develop some non-communicable diseases.

(5) Risk factors

- Smokers are more likely to develop lung cancer and cardiovascular diseases.
- Heavy alcohol drinkers are more likely to suffer from cirrhosis of the liver.
- Smoking and drinking during pregnancy increases the risk of growth and development problems in embryos.
- Obese people are more likely to develop Type 2 diabetes.
- Lack of exercise and eating too many fatty foods can lead to malnutrition, obesity and coronary heart disease.

These lifestyle risk factors are having a global impact, affecting people in many different countries.

(5) Measuring obesity

BMI (Body Mass Index) is a measure of whether a person is a healthy mass (weight) for their height. It is calculated using the equation:

$$BMI = \frac{\text{mass in kg}}{(\text{height in m})^2}$$

However, factors other than weight and height can affect a person's BMI and anyone with any concerns should consult their doctor.

Waist : hip calculations – another indication of whether a person is a healthy weight is to compare measurements around their waist and hips. Generally, the hips measurement should be greater than the waist measurement.

(5) Implications

Impact of lifestyle
Having a lifestyle that includes many risk factors may not only affect an individual, but their family and the wider community as well.

Cost implications
Non-communicable diseases which are contributed to by lifestyle factors also affect the government's spending on the National Health Service.

(10) Worked example   Grade 4

1 (a) A man has a height of 1.75 m and a mass of 80.5 kg. Calculate his BMI. **[2 marks]**

$$BMI = \frac{\text{mass in kg}}{(\text{height in m})^2} = \frac{80.5}{1.75^2} = 26.3$$

> Make sure the figures used are in kg for mass and in m for height.

(b) The same man has a waist measurement of 990 mm and a hip measurement of 1.02 m. Calculate his waist : hip ratio. Give your answer to two decimal places. **[2 marks]**

$$\text{waist : hip ratio} = 0.99 : 1.02 = \frac{0.99}{1.02} : 1 = 0.97 : 1$$

> For a ratio it does not matter what units you use as long as they are the same unit. In this case, both figures are in metres (m).

2 **Figure 1** is a scatter diagram showing the correlation between BMI and blood cholesterol levels.

(a) State what conclusion can be made from the data. **[1 mark]**

There is a positive correlation between blood cholesterol levels and BMI.

(b) Name **one** type of non-communicable disease that high BMI and high blood cholesterol could lead to. **[1 mark]**

Heart disease

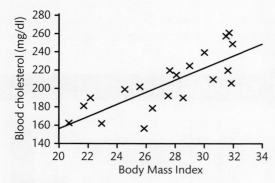

Figure 1

(10) Exam-style practice   Grades 4–5

1 Suggest why BMI measurements may **not** be a good indicator of healthy weight in a teenager. **[2 marks]**

2 Describe how poor diet affects health. **[2 marks]**

Made a start   Feeling confident   Exam ready

Cardiovascular disease

You need to know how different diseases of the cardiovascular system can be treated by lifestyle changes, life-long medication or surgery.

Diseases of the cardiovascular system

Blocked coronary arteries

The coronary arteries supply the heart muscle with blood containing oxygen and glucose.

The build-up of fatty deposits, such as cholesterol, in the coronary arteries can narrow or even block them, starving the heart muscle of oxygen. This can cause a heart attack. A heart attack can also occur when the supply of blood to the heart is suddenly blocked, for example, by a blood clot. Heart attacks are life threatening because they can seriously damage the heart muscle or cause it to die from lack of oxygen.

Faulty valves

Heart valves prevent blood from flowing backwards when the heart pumps blood. Sometimes the valves in the heart become faulty, preventing the valve from opening fully, or the valve may develop a leak. This makes it harder for the heart to pump blood around the body.

Heart failure

Heart failure occurs when the heart is unable to pump blood around the body properly.

Go to page 59 for more about the heart.

Treatment

Treatments for cardiovascular disease can include life-long medication, surgical procedures and lifestyle changes.

Treating blocked coronary arteries

- Stents can be inserted into arteries to keep them open.
- Drugs such as statins can be used to lower the blood cholesterol. Other drugs such as warfarin can be used to reduce the chances of blood clots. Patients may need to take such drugs for the rest of their lives.
- Lifestyle changes such as exercising more or eating less fatty food can help to lower blood cholesterol, and reduce the risk of blood clots forming.

Treating faulty valves

- Biological or mechanical valves can replace faulty ones.

Treating heart failure

- Heart and lung transplants can be performed.
- If the damage is extensive, the whole heart can be replaced with an artificial heart. These are sometimes used to keep patients alive while they are waiting for a biological heart transplant or to allow the heart to rest to help it recover.

Figure 1 A stent used to keep an artery open

Worked example — Grade 5

Warfarin and aspirin are two drugs that are used to reduce the risk of blood clots forming. This reduces the risk of a heart attack or stroke (a lack of blood to the brain). Warfarin is more effective than aspirin at preventing blood clots, but it also has a higher risk of causing internal bleeding. Explain how a doctor would decide which drug to give to a patient at risk from clots. **[4 marks]**

If the patient is at a high risk of a heart attack or stroke, then it might be better to give warfarin, as warfarin is more effective at preventing clots. If the patient is at a lower immediate risk of a stroke or heart attack, then it might be better to give aspirin to avoid the risk of internal bleeding.

Working scientifically

Evaluation of treatments

- Heart surgery is risky and not all surgery is successful.
- Sometimes the patient's body rejects the new heart or valve.
- Artificial hearts need a source of power, such as batteries, to make them work.
- Long-term treatment using drugs such as statins may have unwanted side effects in some people.
- Biological replacement valves can wear out.

Exam-style practice — Grades 4–5

1. Give **two** lifestyle changes that will reduce the risk of cardiovascular disease. **[2 marks]**

2. Give **two** treatments for a narrowed artery. **[2 marks]**

Photosynthesis

You need to understand the process of **photosynthesis** by which plants make their food.

(5) Photosynthesis

During the process of photosynthesis, plants and algae transfer energy from sunlight to build large complex organic molecules from simple inorganic ones. Cells in green leaves contain small structures called chloroplasts. Chloroplasts contain **chlorophyll**, a green pigment that transfers the energy from sunlight to the reaction of photosynthesis.

Photosynthesis is an **endothermic reaction**. This means that it takes in and uses energy.

The chemical equation for photosynthesis

Water is absorbed by root hair cells. Go to page 47 for more about how this happens.

Glucose is used to make lots of other substances such as sucrose. Go to page 47 for more about how sucrose is transported around the plant.

$$\text{carbon dioxide} + \text{water} \xrightarrow[\text{chlorophyll in green leaves}]{\text{light from the Sun}} \text{glucose} + \text{oxygen}$$

$$6CO_2 + 6H_2O \xrightarrow[\text{chlorophyll in green leaves}]{\text{light from the Sun}} C_6H_{12}O_6 + 6O_2$$

Carbon dioxide diffuses from the air into the leaf cells. Oxygen diffuses from the cells into the air. Go to page 10 to revise diffusion.

Light energy is absorbed by chloroplasts in plant cells.

(5) Importance of photosynthesis

Photosynthetic organisms, such as plants and algae, are the main producers of food on the planet. This food is used to make not only plants and algae grow; it is also used by all the other organisms, such as animals, in the food chains that begin with plants and algae. The mass of material in living organisms is known as **biomass**. Most biomass on Earth is therefore produced by photosynthesis.

Figure 1 Algae have a simpler structure than plants but photosynthesise in the same way

(10) Worked example — Grades 3–5

1 Explain why photosynthesis is described as an **endothermic reaction**. **[2 marks]**

During the reaction energy is taken in – in this case, in the form of light.

2 Photosynthesis produces biomass. Explain what is meant by the term **biomass**. **[2 marks]**

The mass of material in living organisms.

3 Some leaves are variegated. This means that some parts are dark green, and some parts are pale green. Suggest an explanation for which part of a variegated leaf would photosynthesise more. **[2 marks]**

The dark green part will photosynthesise more because it contains more chlorophyll so will absorb more light.

(5) Exam-style practice — Grades 2–3

1 Which of the following is produced during photosynthesis? **[1 mark]**

☐ **A** carbon dioxide ☐ **B** glucose ☐ **C** light ☐ **D** water

2 Which of the following is taken in during photosynthesis? **[1 mark]**

☐ **A** carbon dioxide ☐ **B** chlorophyll ☐ **C** glucose ☐ **D** oxygen

Rate of photosynthesis

The rate of photosynthesis is determined by three factors: temperature, light intensity and carbon dioxide concentration. You need to know how these factors affect the rate of photosynthesis.

10 Graphs of limiting factors

Limiting factors are environmental conditions that affect the rate of a process. There are three factors that affect the rate of photosynthesis.

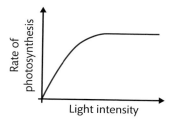 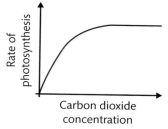 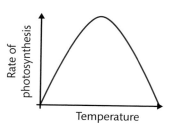

Figure 1 Graphs showing limiting factors of photosynthesis

Light provides the energy for photosynthesis, so as **light intensity** increases, so does the rate of photosynthesis. Eventually, the rate levels off because another factor has become the limiting factor.

Carbon dioxide concentration affects the rate of photosynthesis because carbon dioxide is one of the reactants for photosynthesis. As carbon dioxide concentration increases, so does the rate of photosynthesis. Eventually, the rate levels off because another factor has become the limiting factor.

Temperature affects the rate of all chemical reactions, so as temperature increases, and molecules move faster, so does the rate of photosynthesis. However, at a certain point the rate drops because high temperatures denature the enzymes (see page 7) involved in photosynthesis.

5 Worked example   Grades 4–5

The apparatus shown in **Figure 2** can be used to measure the rate of photosynthesis in pondweed.

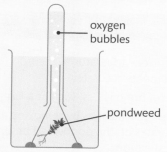

oxygen bubbles

pondweed

Figure 2

1 Describe how the apparatus in **Figure 2** can be used to work out the rate of photosynthesis. Give a reason for your answer. **[2 marks]**

Count the bubbles over a certain period of time. Pondweed gives off bubbles of oxygen as it photosynthesises.

2 A student wants to use the apparatus in **Figure 2** to investigate the effect of temperature on the rate of photosynthesis. Describe how they could do this. **[2 marks]**

Use water of different temperatures. For each temperature, count the number of oxygen bubbles given off in a set time.

Working scientifically

Commercial growers can use knowledge of limiting factors to improve yields by raising temperature, carbon dioxide and light levels. However, doing so costs money and they must find a balance between maximising photosynthesis and making a profit.

5 Exam-style practice   Grade 3

Draw **one** straight line from each limiting factor to its explanation to complete the sentences. **[2 marks]**

limiting factor

Increasing carbon dioxide concentration can increase the rate of photosynthesis because

Increasing light intensity can increase the rate of photosynthesis because

Increasing temperature can increase the rate of photosynthesis because

explanation

increasing the concentration of one of the reactants will increase the rate of reaction.

molecules move more quickly, increasing the rate of reaction.

more energy is provided for this endothermic reaction.

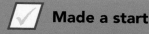 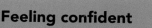

Practical: Photosynthesis

You need to know how to investigate the effect of light intensity on the rate of photosynthesis.

 **Method**

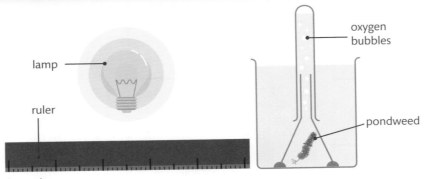

lamp

ruler

oxygen bubbles

pondweed

Figure 1 Investigating light intensity

1 Change the light intensity by altering the distance of the lamp from the pondweed.

2 Record the distance and the number of bubbles counted in one minute in a table.

Worked example — Grades 3–5

The rate of photosynthesis is measured by counting the number of bubbles given off by pondweed each minute.

Distance of pondweed from lamp (cm)	Rate of photosynthesis (bubbles/minute)
10	63
20	16
30	7
40	4
50	3

(a) Look at the table. Describe and explain the pattern shown in the results. **[4 marks]**

As the distance between the pondweed and lamp increases, the rate of photosynthesis decreases. This is because as the distance increases, the light intensity decreases, so there is less energy for photosynthesis.

(b) Explain how the accuracy of the results could be improved. **[2 marks]**

Repeat the measurements several times and calculate the means.

(c) A student repeated the experiment but placed a sheet of glass between the beaker and the lamp. The glass absorbed the heat from the lamp. Suggest a reason why the student did this. **[1 mark]**

To control the temperature.

Working scientifically

This practical investigates the effect of light intensity on the rate of photosynthesis. This means that light intensity is the **independent variable**.

The rate of photosynthesis is determined by counting oxygen bubbles in a given period of time. This is the **dependent variable**.

Key experimental skills

☑ Use of correct apparatus to record measurements accurately.

☑ Safe use of hot devices, such as a lamp.

☑ Consider ethical issues by removing any small invertebrates on the pondweed before starting the investigation.

☑ Measure rate of photosynthesis by counting oxygen bubbles.

Exam-style practice — Grade 5

1 Another way of measuring the rate of photosynthesis, other than by counting oxygen bubbles, is by measuring the volume of oxygen given off in a certain time. Evaluate the two methods. **[2 marks]**

2 Suggest a reason why it is easier to measure the rate of photosynthesis in pondweed than in a plant that does not live underwater. **[1 mark]**

Specialised plant cells

You need to know about the structural adaptations of specialised plant cells that enable them to transport substances, including food molecules which are moved by translocation.

Specialised plant cells

You need to know how the following plant cells are specialised to carry out a particular function.

Go to page 4 for specialised animal cells.

Xylem is made of columns of dead cells with **lignified** walls (contain lignin) which transport water and minerals up from the roots to the rest of the plant.

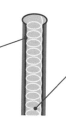

Lignin walls provide strength and support; pits in the walls allow water and mineral ions to move in and out of the xylem.

A hollow lumen (space) enables water and mineral ions to flow easily through the plant.

Root hair cells absorb water and mineral ions from the soil.

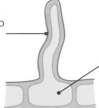

The root hair cell has a large surface area to maximise osmosis (see page 11).

Cytoplasm contains a lot of mitochondria which release energy to increase the rate of active transport (see page 13) of mineral ions.

Phloem is made of living cells which use energy to transport dissolved sucrose (sugar) from the leaves and storage regions to the other parts of the plant where it is used for growth or is stored.

Holes in the end walls allow solutions to move from cell to cell.

Some cells contain many mitochondria for active transport.

Figure 1 Specialised plant cells

Another possible answer is the holes in the end walls that allow sucrose solution to move between phloem cells.

Transport in plants

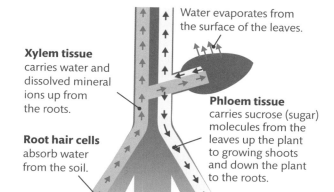

Water evaporates from the surface of the leaves.

Xylem tissue carries water and dissolved mineral ions up from the roots.

Root hair cells absorb water from the soil.

Phloem tissue carries sucrose (sugar) molecules from the leaves up the plant to growing shoots and down the plant to the roots.

Figure 2 Plant tissues involved in the transport of substances

Water and mineral ions move through plants, through **xylem** tissue, by a process called **transpiration**.

There is more about this on page 48.

Food moves through plants by a different process, called **translocation**. This occurs in **phloem** tissue. Food can move from leaves, where glucose sugar has been made by photosynthesis, to places where it is stored, for example, as starch in the roots. It can also be moved to growing regions such as new shoots or buds. The food is transported as **sucrose** (another type of sugar) dissolved in cell sap, which moves from one phloem cell to the next.

Worked example — Grades 4–5

(a) Explain **one** way that xylem tissue is adapted to its transport function. **[2 marks]**

Xylem tissue is made of dead hollow cells which form tubes for water and mineral ions to travel through.

(b) Explain **one** way that phloem tissue is adapted to its transport function. **[2 marks]**

Phloem tissue contains many mitochondria providing energy for the active transport of sucrose.

Exam-style practice — Grades 4–5

1. Explain **two** adaptations a root hair cell has to allow it to function efficiently. **[4 marks]**

2. Explain what happens in translocation. **[2 marks]**

Transpiration

You need to know how water and mineral ions move through a plant by transpiration.

 Transpiration

Transpiration is the movement of water through a plant from the roots to the leaves. Water evaporates from the surface of cells inside the leaves and diffuses out through open pores called **stomata**. This causes more water to be drawn upwards against gravity through **xylem** cells in the plant. Water is absorbed from the soil into root hair cells by osmosis.

There is more about osmosis on page 11.

As water moves up through the plant by transpiration, it carries with it dissolved mineral ions that were also absorbed from the soil by root hair cells. The movement of water is called the **transpiration stream**. This is shown in **Figure 1**.

Go to page 47 to revise root hair cells and xylem.

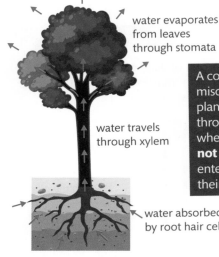

water evaporates from leaves through stomata

water travels through xylem

water absorbed by root hair cells

A common misconception is that plants take in water through their leaves when it rains. This does **not** happen. Water only enters plants through their roots.

Figure 1 The transpiration stream

 Stomata

Stomata (singular: **stoma**) are small pores, found mostly on the underside of leaves, formed by specialised cells called **guard cells**. Guard cells can swell up (by absorbing water by osmosis) which opens the stoma. At other times, the guard cells shrink slightly (because of losing water by osmosis) which closes the stoma. Stomata usually open during the daytime to allow carbon dioxide and oxygen to diffuse in and out of the leaf during photosynthesis.

The stomata also control the loss of water through transpiration. Although transpiration is important, for example, for moving mineral ions through a plant, losing too much water is harmful if plants cannot readily replace it. Since plants cannot photosynthesise at night, guard cells usually close the stomata at night to prevent water evaporating from the leaf. Stomata can also close during the day if the plant is in danger of dehydrating.

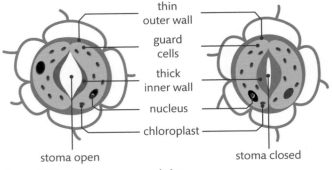

thin outer wall
guard cells
thick inner wall
nucleus
chloroplast

stoma open   stoma closed

Figure 2 Stomata can open and close

 **Worked example**   Grades 4–5

1 Explain what causes water and mineral ions to move through the xylem tissue from the roots to the leaves. **[2 marks]**

Water evaporates from the leaves which causes more water and dissolved mineral ions to be pulled up through the xylem cells from the roots.

2 Explain how stomata open and close. **[2 marks]**

Stomata open when the guard cells take in water and swell up. They close when the guard cells lose water and shrink slightly.

 **Exam-style practice**   Grade 3

1 How does water enter the roots from the soil? **[1 mark]**

☐ **A** active transport
☐ **B** evaporation
☐ **C** osmosis
☐ **D** transpiration

2 Name **three** substances that pass through the stomata. **[3 marks]**

 Made a start   **Feeling confident**   ✓ **Exam ready**

Water uptake in plants

You need to know how different environmental factors can affect the rate of transpiration.

 Factors affecting transpiration

Different environmental factors affect the rate of transpiration and therefore the rate of water uptake by a plant.

- **Temperature** – as temperature increases, water molecules have more kinetic energy. This means evaporation from the leaves increases, so transpiration is faster in higher temperatures.

- **Air movement** – as wind speed increases, the water molecules which have just left the stomata get blown away. This maintains a greater concentration gradient so water molecules diffuse out of the leaves more rapidly, increasing the rate of transpiration.

- **Light intensity** – at night, the guard cells close the stomata to retain valuable water, so transpiration stops. In bright light, the stomata open wider to allow more carbon dioxide to enter the leaf for photosynthesis, so the rate of transpiration increases.

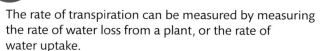 **Measuring the rate of transpiration**

The rate of transpiration can be measured by measuring the rate of water loss from a plant, or the rate of water uptake.

One way to measure the rate of water loss is by weighing a plant in a pot over a period of time. If the soil is covered so water can only evaporate from the leaves, any decrease in mass must be due to transpiration.

One way to measure the rate of water uptake is to use a potometer such as that shown in **Figure 1**. How quickly the air bubble moves is a measure of the rate of water uptake.

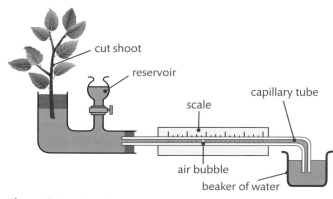

Figure 1 A potometer

 Worked example **Grades 2–4**

(a) A student uses a potometer like that in **Figure 1** to investigate the uptake of water by a plant shoot.

The bubble moves 36 mm in 10 minutes. Calculate the rate of water uptake using the following equation:

$$\text{rate of water uptake} = \frac{\text{distance moved by bubble}}{\text{time}}$$

Give your answer in mm/minute. **[2 marks]**

$$\text{rate of water uptake} = \frac{36}{10} = 3.6 \text{ mm/minute}$$

(b) The student repeats the investigation but this time puts an electric fan facing the potometer.

Explain the effect this will have on the rate of water uptake. **[2 marks]**

The rate of water uptake will increase because air movement increases the rate of transpiration.

 Exam-style practice **Grades 3–4**

1 In which weather conditions will a plant transpire mostly rapidly? **[1 mark]**

    A cold and still air   C hot and still air

    B cold and windy   D hot and windy

2 Explain why an increase in light intensity increases the rate of transpiration. **[2 marks]**

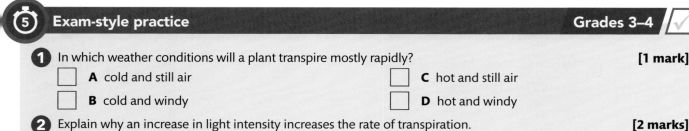

Human endocrine system

You need to know how the release and distribution of hormones is controlled by the human endocrine system.

Hormones are sometimes called chemical messengers. They are secreted by **endocrine glands**, which release hormones directly into the blood. The blood carries the hormone to a target organ where the hormone causes an effect. The effects of the hormone system are much slower than those of the nervous system as it takes time for hormones to be transported around the body by the blood. However, the effects of a hormone last longer than those of an impulse sent by the nervous system.

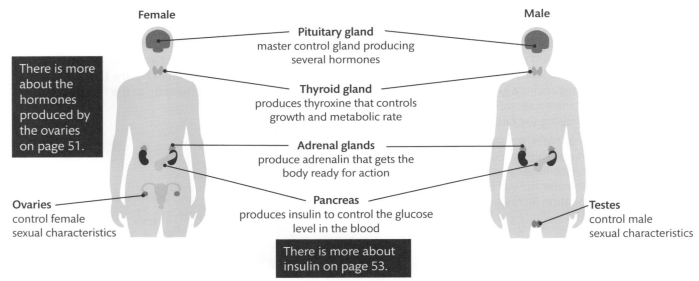

There is more about the hormones produced by the ovaries on page 51.

Pituitary gland
master control gland producing several hormones

Thyroid gland
produces thyroxine that controls growth and metabolic rate

Adrenal glands
produce adrenalin that gets the body ready for action

Ovaries
control female sexual characteristics

Pancreas
produces insulin to control the glucose level in the blood

There is more about insulin on page 53.

Testes
control male sexual characteristics

Figure 1 The endocrine (hormone) glands

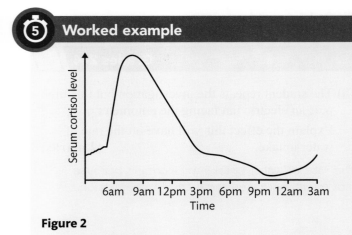

Figure 2

1 Look at **Figure 2**, a graph showing the level of serum cortisol (a hormone) in the blood. State the time of day when the serum cortisol level is at its highest and its lowest. **[1 mark]**

Highest: 8 am
Lowest: 10 pm

2 The effects of hormones are longer lasting than the effects of nerve impulses. Suggest an explanation why. **[2 marks]**

Hormones are substances which remain in the blood until they are eventually broken down, whereas nerve impulses are electrical impulses which do not last long.

1 Name the gland which produces the hormone insulin. **[1 mark]**

2 Describe what is meant by a hormone. **[3 marks]**

Made a start   Feeling confident   Exam ready

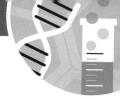

Hormones in reproduction

During puberty, hormones cause secondary sexual characteristics to develop. These include the production of sperm in males and the menstrual cycle in females. You need to know the roles of different hormones in the menstrual cycle.

10 The menstrual cycle

The **menstrual cycle** is a recurring process in which the uterus lining is prepared for pregnancy. On average, the menstrual cycle lasts 28 days, although this can vary. It starts with **menstruation** (the 'period') when the lining of the uterus breaks down. The lining then grows and thickens again ('repairs') in case an egg is fertilised (in which case the fertilised egg would embed in the thickened lining to grow). An egg is released from one of the ovaries (**ovulation**) about halfway through the menstrual cycle. If the egg is not fertilised, then towards the end of the menstrual cycle the uterus lining starts to break down, and the cycle starts again.

There are several hormones involved in this cycle.

- **Oestrogen** is secreted by the ovaries. It causes the lining of the uterus to start to build up again ('repair') after menstruation. It also stimulates another hormone which triggers ovulation.

- **Progesterone** builds up and maintains the uterus lining during the middle part of the cycle and pregnancy (if it occurs). The uterus lining is important during pregnancy because this is where the fertilised egg develops and grows. During pregnancy, progesterone

also inhibits (reduces) the production of other hormones which prevents the release of new eggs at this time. If pregnancy does not occur, then progesterone levels fall at the end of the menstrual cycle, which triggers the breakdown of the uterus lining (menstruation).

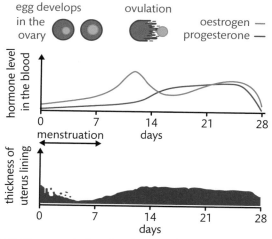

Figure 1 Changes during the menstrual cycle

5 Worked example

1 Complete the table by writing numbers 1–5 in the boxes to put the stages of the menstrual cycle in the correct order. The first one has been done for you. **[2 marks]**

Stage	Order
breakdown of uterus lining	5
maintenance of uterus lining	4
menstruation (bleeding)	1
ovulation	3
repair of uterus lining	2

2 Explain why it is important that the lining of the uterus thickens during each menstrual cycle. **[2 marks]**

If an egg gets fertilised, it will embed in the lining where the embryo will develop and grow.

5 Exam-style practice

Describe the effects of the following hormones on the uterus lining during the different stages of the menstrual cycle.
(a) oestrogen **[2 marks]**
(b) progesterone **[2 marks]**

 Made a start 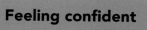 **Feeling confident** 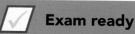 **Exam ready**

Contraception

You need to know how hormonal and barrier methods of contraception can be used to prevent pregnancy.

 Methods of contraception

Hormonal

- Oral contraceptives (the 'pill') contain the hormones oestrogen or progesterone or a combination of both. These hormones stop eggs developing and being released (ovulation) ready for fertilisation. Oral contraceptives are very effective if taken correctly. Some forms of the pill can lead to side effects such as weight gain or mood changes.
- Injections, skin patches or implants contain slow release oestrogen or progesterone or both to prevent the development and release of eggs for months or years.

Barrier

- Methods such as the condom and the diaphragm act as a physical barrier between the sperm and egg. Condoms are easy to use, but can sometimes tear or come off. Diaphragms have to be inserted just before sex and left in place afterwards for several hours.

 Working scientifically

Ethics

There are some questions that science can answer, such as: 'How can you stop a sperm fertilising an egg?'

There are some questions that science cannot answer, such as: 'When should we stop a sperm from fertilising an egg?'

Individuals have to decide whether or not to use contraception to prevent pregnancy. They also have to decide which methods of contraception to use.

Science can provide data to help you decide which methods are the most reliable, and understand the advantages and disadvantages of each method.

However, some people think that contraception is wrong.

Each person should evaluate personal, social, economic and religious implications, and make a decision about contraception based on evidence and argument.

Worked example | Grades 2–4

The table summarises four different methods of contraception.

	Contraceptive pill	Diaphragm	Patch	Condom
Reliability	very reliable	reliable	very reliable	reliable
Level of risk to health	some risk	little risk	some risk	little risk
Are effects reversible?	reversible	reversible	reversible	reversible

(a) Look at the table. State which methods of contraception are hormonal and which are barrier. **[2 marks]**

The contraceptive pill and the skin patch are hormonal methods. The diaphragm and condom are barrier methods.

(b) Use information in the table to evaluate hormonal and barrier methods of contraception. **[3 marks]**

Hormonal methods are more reliable, although there are some health risks. Barrier methods are reliable, but not as reliable as the hormonal methods, with little health risk. Both methods are reversible.

Exam focus

Always read exam questions carefully. This question asks you to 'evaluate', which means you should explain the advantages and disadvantages of each method.

Exam-style practice | Grades 3–4

1. Explain how a hormonal method of contraception works. **[2 marks]**
2. Explain how a barrier method of contraception works. **[2 marks]**

  Made a start **Feeling confident** **Exam ready**

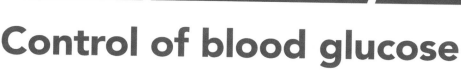

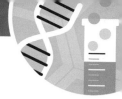

Control of blood glucose

Keeping conditions inside the body as constant as possible is important. This is called homeostasis and one example is controlling the level of glucose in the blood. You need to know how glucose levels are controlled in the human body.

5 Homeostasis

Conditions inside and outside the body are frequently changing. However, it is important for the healthy working of the body that it keeps conditions inside the body as constant as possible. Some of the conditions the body works to keep constant include:

- body temperature
- water levels in the body
- blood glucose concentration.

Maintaining a constant internal environment (i.e. the conditions inside the body) is called **homeostasis**.

10 Controlling blood glucose

After a meal, carbohydrates are digested into simple sugars, such as glucose. Glucose is important as it is used during respiration (see page 60). However, if the concentration of glucose in the blood gets too high or too low this can cause serious health problems. For example, if the blood glucose concentration gets too high, it can lead to high blood pressure. If the blood glucose concentration gets too low, it can lead to fainting. For this reason, the body uses hormones like insulin to control the blood glucose concentration.

When glucose enters the blood after a meal, the blood glucose concentration begins to rise. The **pancreas** detects the increase in blood glucose and releases the hormone **insulin**. Insulin causes glucose to move from the blood into cells. It also causes excess glucose to be converted into **glycogen** and stored in muscles and the liver. ('Excess' glucose is the amount of glucose in the blood above what is healthy.) This ensures that glucose in the blood remains at the correct concentration. If the concentration of glucose in the blood becomes too low, then the pancreas stops releasing insulin.

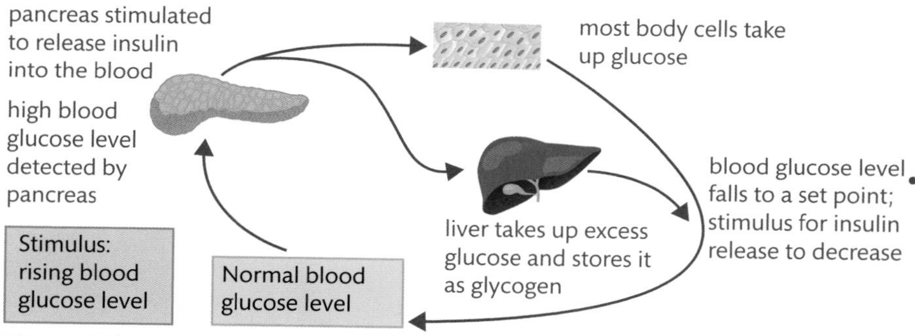
pancreas stimulated to release insulin into the blood
most body cells take up glucose
high blood glucose level detected by pancreas
liver takes up excess glucose and stores it as glycogen
blood glucose level falls to a set point; stimulus for insulin release to decrease
Stimulus: rising blood glucose level
Normal blood glucose level

Figure 1 The control of blood glucose by insulin

Page 54 explains about diabetes, when the blood glucose concentration is not controlled properly.

5 Worked example — Grades 3–4

The table shows some of the changes that happen in the body after consuming a sugar drink.

Complete the table by writing numbers 1–6 in the boxes to put the changes in the correct order. The first one has been done for you. **[3 marks]**

Change	Order
blood glucose concentration increases	2
blood glucose concentration returns to normal	6
excess glucose converted to glycogen and stored	5
glucose absorbed into blood	1
pancreas detects increase in blood glucose concentration	3
pancreas releases insulin	4

5 Exam-style practice — Grades 3–4

What term describes maintaining a constant internal environment? **[1 mark]**

☐ **A** coordination ☐ **B** homeostasis ☐ **C** response ☐ **D** stimulus

Diabetes

Type 1 and Type 2 diabetes are conditions that affect the body's ability to control blood glucose levels. You need to know about these types of diabetes and how they are controlled.

 Diabetes

Type 1 diabetes is a disease caused by the pancreas not producing enough insulin. This means that after a meal, the amount of glucose in the blood may rise to dangerously high levels. The condition can be controlled by injections of the hormone insulin.

Type 2 diabetes is a disease caused by cells in the body no longer responding to the insulin produced by the pancreas.

People with Type 2 diabetes must eat a controlled diet to prevent glucose levels in their blood changing too much. Exercise also helps to reduce the glucose levels in the blood. It is not generally possible to treat people with Type 2 diabetes with insulin injections.

Obesity is a major risk factor for Type 2 diabetes. Scientists know this because there is a correlation between the occurrence of Type 2 diabetes and different measurements of body mass such as **BMI** and **waist:hip calculations**.

(See page 42 for more about these measurements.)

BMI (Body Mass Index) is a measure of whether a person is a healthy mass for their height. It is calculated using the equation:

$$BMI = \frac{mass\ in\ kg}{(height\ in\ m)^2}$$

Another way to check if a person has a healthy mass is to compare their waist and hip measurements.

 Worked example — Grade 4

1 The hormone insulin is a protein.
Suggest a reason why people with Type 1 diabetes inject themselves with insulin rather than take insulin tablets. **[1 mark]**

The insulin protein would be digested.

If insulin was taken in by the mouth in tablets, the digestive enzymes in the stomach and intestine would break down the insulin before it got into the bloodstream and was able to do its job.

2 **Figure 1** shows the changing blood glucose concentration of two people after they each drank a sugar solution. Compare the blood glucose concentrations of the two people. Include similarities and differences in your answer. **[4 marks]**

The blood glucose concentration rises and then falls in the person with Type 1 diabetes and the person without it. At the start, the blood glucose concentration is higher in the person with Type 1 diabetes and rises higher and more rapidly than in the person without diabetes. The concentration stays high for longer in the person with diabetes.

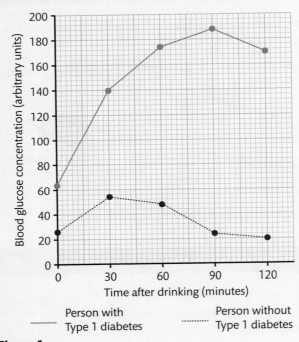

Figure 1

 Exam-style practice — Grade 5

Describe **three** differences between Type 1 and Type 2 diabetes. **[3 marks]**

  Made a start **Feeling confident** **Exam ready**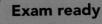

Transport in animals

You need to know how multicellular organisms have adaptations to enable the effective exchange of substances.

 Exchange surfaces

All living organisms need to exchange substances with their surroundings. For example, animals need to absorb oxygen and food from their surroundings and then transport them to their cells. Animals also need to transport waste substances like carbon dioxide and urea from their cells, and remove these substances from their bodies.

Plants need to absorb water and mineral ions through their roots before transporting them to cells that need them. When they photosynthesise, plants absorb carbon dioxide into cells in their leaves and give out oxygen.

Different substances are absorbed into, or removed from, bodies, organs, tissues or cells by the processes of diffusion, osmosis or active transport.

Go to pages 10–13 to revise these processes.

The places where organisms absorb or remove substances are called **exchange surfaces**. For small unicellular organisms their exchange surface is their cell membrane. Larger multicellular organisms have specially adapted organ systems to maximise absorption. This difference is because of their different **surface area : volume ratios**.

Small unicellular organisms have a large surface area : volume ratio so processes like diffusion can occur quickly. Larger multicellular organisms have a small outer surface area : volume ratio, which slows down the rate of diffusion. To overcome this problem, multicellular organisms have evolved to have specialised exchange surfaces and transport systems that maximise diffusion by having:

- a large surface area
- a thin membrane for a short diffusion path
- a good transport system (e.g. blood system) to maintain maximum concentration gradients.

 Worked example | **Grades 4–5**

(a) The table shows measurements for cubes of different sizes. Complete the table. **[3 marks]**

(b) Describe the trends in total surface area, volume, and surface area : volume ratio as the cubes get bigger. **[3 marks]**

As the cubes get bigger, their total surface areas and volumes increase, but their surface area : volume ratios decrease.

Length of one side (cm)	Total surface area (cm²)	Volume (cm³)	Surface area : volume ratio
1	6	1	6 : 1
3	54	27	2 : 1
5	150	125	1.2 : 1

 Surface area to volume ratio

Think of a cube with sides of length 1 cm:

- the total surface area is 6 cm² (there are six sides each of area 1 cm²)
- the volume is 1 cm³ (1 × 1 × 1)
- the ratio of surface area to volume is 6 : 1.

If another cube has sides of length 2 cm:

- the total surface area is 24 cm² (there are six sides each of area 4 cm²)
- the volume is 8 cm³ (2 × 2 × 2)
- the ratio of surface area to volume is 3 : 1.

As the cube increases in size, the surface area does not increase at the same rate as the volume. The same is true as the size of organisms increases. This means that for small organisms substances can diffuse in and out of a cell quickly and reach the whole cell. For larger organisms, the smaller surface area : volume ratio makes this impossible and transport systems and specialised exchange surfaces are needed.

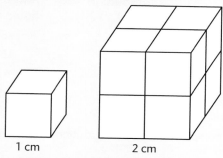

Figure 1 Cubes of different sizes have different surface area : volume ratios

Go to page 56 for more about how alveoli in the lungs are adapted for efficient gas exchange.

Go to page 47 to revise how plant root hair cells are adapted for efficient absorption of water and mineral ions.

 **Exam-style practice** | **Grades 4–5**

1 Calculate the surface area : volume ratio of a cube of side length 4 cm. **[2 marks]**

2 Explain what is meant by the term 'exchange surface'. **[2 marks]**

Alveoli

You need to know how the alveoli in the lungs are adapted for efficient gas exchange.

 The lungs

The lungs are adapted for efficient gas exchange of oxygen and carbon dioxide. This takes place between the **alveoli** (singular: **alveolus**) and their surrounding blood capillaries. There is a higher concentration of oxygen in the air we breathe into the alveoli than in the blood, so oxygen diffuses across the alveoli walls to be transported around the body by the red blood cells. Carbon dioxide is transported to the lungs in the blood plasma. There is a higher concentration of carbon dioxide in the blood than in the alveoli, so it diffuses from the blood into the alveoli to be breathed out.

For more on capillaries see page 58.

See page 57 for more about how the blood transports different substances.

Gas	Amount in inhaled air (%)	Amount in exhaled air (%)
Nitrogen	78	78
Oxygen	21	16
Carbon dioxide	0.04	4
Water vapour	variable	variable
Other gases	approx. 1	approx. 1

Table 1 A comparison of the composition of inhaled and exhaled air

 The alveoli

Alveoli, the small air sacs in the lungs, are adapted for efficient gas exchange by diffusion:

- The large number of alveoli provides a large surface area to absorb oxygen into the blood and remove carbon dioxide.
- Thin, moist membranes allow gases to diffuse quickly.
- The capillary network provides a good blood supply to transport the gases to and from the rest of the body.
- Concentration gradients for both oxygen and carbon dioxide are maintained by ventilation (breathing) and blood flow.

Go to page 10 to revise the factors affecting the rate of diffusion, and to page 55 to revise exchange surfaces.

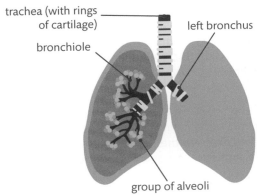

Figure 1 The lungs

trachea (with rings of cartilage), left bronchus, bronchiole, group of alveoli

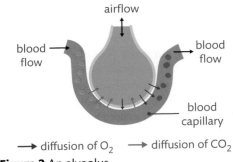

airflow — blood flow — blood flow — blood capillary

→ diffusion of O_2 → diffusion of CO_2

Figure 2 An alveolus

 Worked example — **Grade 5**

Emphysema is a lung condition that can be caused by smoking. Emphysema damages the lungs so there are fewer alveoli. Suggest an explanation for why someone with emphysema gets tired easily and is unable to do lots of exercise. **[4 marks]**

This is because fewer air sacs results in a lower surface area for gas exchange. This means less oxygen can be absorbed into the blood, and so respiration is reduced, providing less energy.

 Exam-style practice — **Grades 3–4**

1. Describe **three** ways that alveoli are adapted to their function. **[3 marks]**

2. By what process does gas exchange happen in the alveoli? **[1 mark]**

☐ **A** active transport ☐ **C** osmosis

☐ **B** diffusion ☐ **D** respiration

The blood

You need to be able to recognise the different components of blood and describe their functions.

(10) Key components of the blood

Blood is a tissue. It consists of a fluid called plasma in which red blood cells, white blood cells and platelets are suspended.

Plasma is the liquid part of the blood. It is mainly made of water but also contains dissolved carbon dioxide, dissolved food, urea (waste), hormones and heat which it transports around the body.

Platelets are cell fragments that help blood to clot. This helps to seal wounds.

Red blood cells (also called **erythrocytes**) absorb oxygen from the lungs and carry it to muscles and tissue around the body. They are adapted for this function in several ways:

- They contain the red pigment **haemoglobin** which combines with oxygen to carry it around the body.
- They have no nucleus, which increases the space available for haemoglobin.
- They have a **biconcave disc** shape to increase the surface area for oxygen to diffuse in and out.
- They are small and flexible, which allows them to pass easily through the smallest capillaries.
- They have a large surface area : volume ratio to increase the rate of diffusion of oxygen in and out.

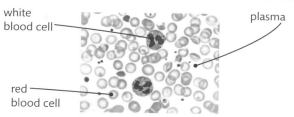

Figure 1 Blood viewed through a light microscope

White blood cells help protect us from disease:

- Some white blood cells are **phagocytes**, which ingest or surround and destroy pathogens (phagocytosis).
- Some white blood cells produce **antibodies** in response to an **antigen**. Antigens are substances that are markers on the outside of cells. White blood cells use them to determine if the cell is harmful or not. Antibodies are specialised proteins that cause the immune system to attack cells that are not from the body.
- Some white blood cells produce **antitoxins**, which neutralise harmful substances produced by infectious microorganisms. Antitoxins neutralise specific toxins.

Figure 2 Red blood cells transport oxygen

Go to page 37 to revise the immune system and sealing wounds.

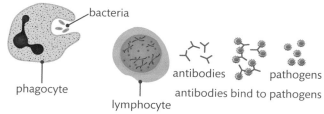

Figure 3 White blood cells destroy pathogens

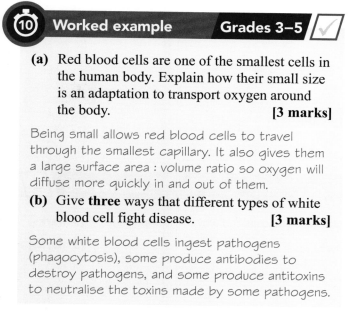

(10) Worked example | **Grades 3–5**

(a) Red blood cells are one of the smallest cells in the human body. Explain how their small size is an adaptation to transport oxygen around the body. **[3 marks]**

Being small allows red blood cells to travel through the smallest capillary. It also gives them a large surface area : volume ratio so oxygen will diffuse more quickly in and out of them.

(b) Give **three** ways that different types of white blood cell fight disease. **[3 marks]**

Some white blood cells ingest pathogens (phagocytosis), some produce antibodies to destroy pathogens, and some produce antitoxins to neutralise the toxins made by some pathogens.

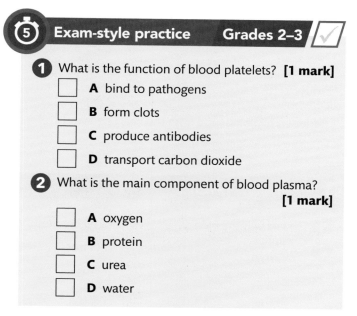

(5) Exam-style practice | **Grades 2–3**

1 What is the function of blood platelets? **[1 mark]**

- [ ] **A** bind to pathogens
- [ ] **B** form clots
- [ ] **C** produce antibodies
- [ ] **D** transport carbon dioxide

2 What is the main component of blood plasma? **[1 mark]**

- [ ] **A** oxygen
- [ ] **B** protein
- [ ] **C** urea
- [ ] **D** water

 Made a start **Feeling confident** ☑ **Exam ready**

Blood vessels

You need to know how blood is transported around the body by three different types of blood vessel.

(10) Arteries, veins and capillaries

Blood flows around the body through a series of different types of blood vessel: arteries, veins and capillaries.

Arteries carry blood at high pressure away from the heart. They have thick walls containing muscle and elastic tissue, enabling them to stretch and then return to their original shape, withstanding and maintaining the high blood pressure.

Capillaries join the ends of arteries to the ends of veins. This is where exchange of materials between the blood and body tissues occurs. Capillaries have very thin walls, usually only one cell thick, to allow oxygen, carbon dioxide, glucose and urea to easily diffuse to and from surrounding tissues.

Veins carry blood at low pressure back to the heart. They have **valves** to prevent the blood flowing backwards, and keep it flowing in one direction towards the heart. They have a large **lumen** (space inside the vessel) to maximise blood flow.

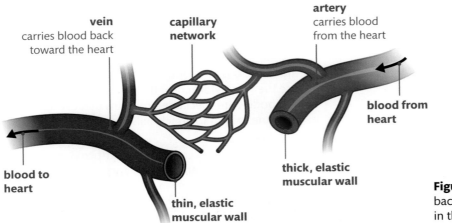

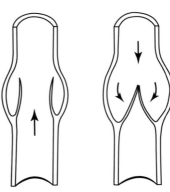

Figure 2 Veins contain valves to prevent back flow. They open to allow blood to flow in the correct direction, but close to prevent back flow

Figure 1 An artery, vein and capillaries

(5) Worked example   Grade 3

Draw **one** straight line from each type of blood vessel to its description, and then to its function.   **[3 marks]**

blood vessel	description	function
artery	large lumen	carry blood away from heart
capillary	thick muscular wall	carry blood towards heart
vein	wall one cell thick	exchange of materials

Exam focus
Remember:
Arteries carry blood <u>A</u>way from the heart and ve<u>IN</u>s carry blood <u>IN</u>to the heart.

(5) Exam-style practice   Grades 4–5

1. Explain why the blood in arteries is at a higher pressure than the blood in veins and why this is important.   **[3 marks]**

2. Explain why valves are found in veins but **not** in the other vessels.   **[3 marks]**

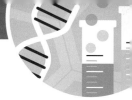

The heart

You need to know how the structure of the heart is adapted to its function within the circulatory system.

5 The heart

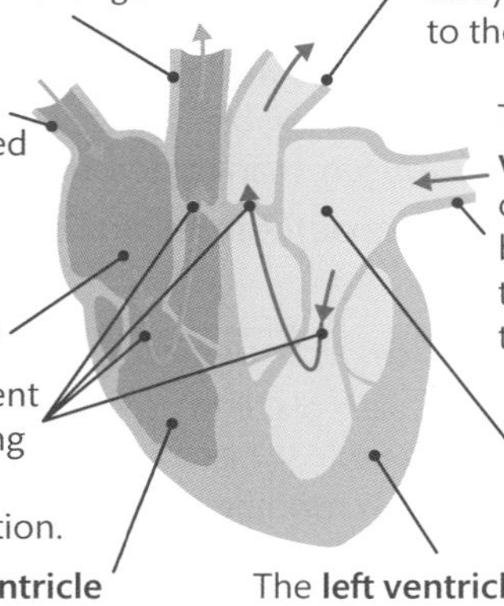
The **pulmonary artery** carries **deoxygenated blood** from the heart to the lungs.
The **aorta** carries **oxygenated blood** away from the heart to the body.
The **vena cava** brings deoxygenated blood from the body to the heart.
The **pulmonary vein** brings oxygenated blood from the lungs to the heart.
right atrium
Valves prevent blood flowing in the wrong direction.
left atrium
The **right ventricle** pumps blood to the lungs where gas exchange takes place.
The **left ventricle** has a thicker muscle wall than the right ventricle because it pushes blood all around the body.
deoxygenated blood
oxygenated blood

Figure 1 Structure of the heart

The heart is labelled as though you are looking at the front of it. This is why, for example, the left atrium and left ventricle are on the right-hand side of the diagram.

5 The double circulatory system

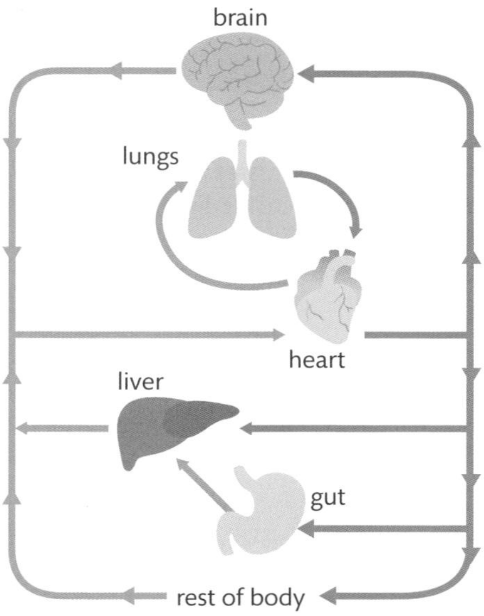
brain
lungs
heart
liver
gut
rest of body

Figure 2 The heart pumps blood around the body in a double circulatory system (so-called because blood travels through the heart twice on each complete circulation of the body)

Oxygenated blood carries oxygen. Deoxygenated blood has had the oxygen removed.

Blood entering the heart first goes into the right and left atria (singular: atrium), which contract, forcing blood into the ventricles. The left and right ventricles contract, forcing blood into the arteries. The valves ensure that blood does not flow in the wrong direction. The heart muscle also has its own supply of blood through the **coronary arteries** which supply oxygenated blood to the heart tissue.

10 Worked example — Grades 3–5

1 Give the names of the four chambers of the heart. **[2 marks]**

Left and right atria, left and right ventricles.

2 Explain why the left ventricle has a thicker wall than the right ventricle. **[2 marks]**

The right ventricle only has to pump blood to the lungs. The left ventricle has to pump blood around the whole of the rest of the body.

3 Explain the function of the heart valves and why this is important. **[2 marks]**

The valves make sure that blood flows in one direction only, so blood flows efficiently around the body.

5 Exam-style practice — Grades 3–4

1 Describe the path taken by a red blood cell from the right ventricle to the left atrium. **[3 marks]**

2 Explain why the two ventricles have thicker walls than the two atria. **[2 marks]**

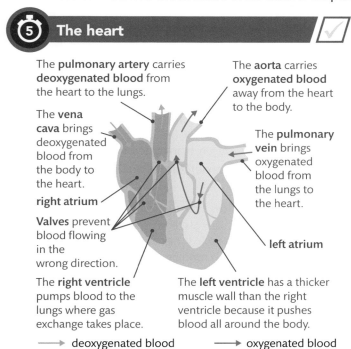

Aerobic and anaerobic respiration

Respiration is a chemical reaction that takes place continuously inside all living cells, releasing energy into and around the body. You need to know about the two types of respiration – aerobic and anaerobic.

(5) Respiration

Cellular respiration is an **exothermic reaction** that releases energy needed for **metabolic** processes (the processes that take place inside living things to maintain life – also called **metabolism**).

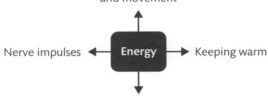

Muscle contractions and movement

Nerve impulses ← **Energy** → Keeping warm

Chemical reactions to build larger molecules

Figure 1 The energy released by respiration has several different uses

(5) Aerobic respiration

Aerobic respiration requires oxygen.

glucose + oxygen → carbon dioxide + water

$$C_6H_{12}O_6 + 6O_2 \rightarrow 6CO_2 + 6H_2O$$

Most of the reactions involving aerobic respiration happen inside mitochondria (see page 2) in cells.

The rate of aerobic respiration can be measured by how quickly oxygen is being used.

(5) Exam focus

You will be expected to recall the definitions of certain key terms in the exam. Make sure you know the meaning of all the terms used in this revision guide.

(5) Worked example | Grades 3–4

1 **(a)** State the **two** reactants of aerobic respiration. **[2 marks]**

Glucose and oxygen.

(b) State the **two** products of aerobic respiration. **[2 marks]**

Carbon dioxide and water.

2 Explain why respiration is described as an 'exothermic reaction'. **[2 marks]**

It is a chemical reaction in which energy is transferred to the surroundings.

(10) Anaerobic respiration

Anaerobic respiration does **not** require oxygen. Less energy is released by anaerobic respiration, when glucose breaks down without oxygen, than by aerobic respiration.

There are two forms of anaerobic respiration that you should know about.

Anaerobic respiration in muscles

Anaerobic respiration takes place in muscles when there is not enough oxygen available for extra aerobic respiration, such as when an animal is running away from a predator, and is already breathing as quickly as it can.

Anaerobic respiration in muscles is shown by the following equation:

glucose → lactic acid

The muscle ache felt during exercise is due to a build-up of lactic acid.

Anaerobic respiration in microorganisms and plants

Anaerobic respiration also takes place in microorganisms and plant cells, such as in plant root cells in very wet soil.

Anaerobic respiration in microorganisms such as yeast can be shown by the following equation:

glucose → ethanol (alcohol) + carbon dioxide

This type of anaerobic respiration is sometimes called **fermentation**. This is how alcoholic drinks are made.

Fermentation by yeast is also used to make bread, as the carbon dioxide released in respiration makes the dough rise.

Exam focus

Do not confuse respiration with breathing. They are **not** the same thing. Breathing means moving air in and out of the lungs. (This is sometimes also called ventilation.) Respiration means releasing energy from glucose in cells.

Exam focus

In an exam, take care you do not mistake similar scientific terms such as 'aerobic' and 'anaerobic'. Try to think of ways to remember which is which. For example, 'aerobic' sounds like 'air', which contains oxygen.

(5) Exam-style practice | Grade 4

Give **three** ways that anaerobic respiration in humans is different from aerobic respiration. **[3 marks]**

Practical: Rate of respiration

You need to know how to investigate the rate of respiration in living organisms.

(10) Method

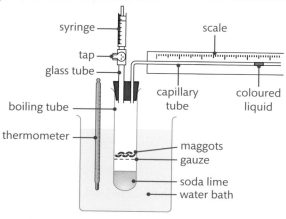

Figure 1 A simple respirometer

This apparatus can be used to investigate how temperature affects the rate of aerobic respiration:

1 Place small organisms, such as maggots, on the gauze in the boiling tube containing soda lime.

2 Put the bung in the top of the boiling tube, and place the tube in the water bath.

3 Place a drop of coloured liquid at the right hand end of the capillary tube. Note the starting position of the liquid.

4 Make a note of the temperature in the water bath.

5 Close the tap.

6 Make a note of the position of the drop of liquid after five minutes.

7 Open the tap and use the syringe to move the liquid back to the start of the scale.

8 Repeat the experiment with different temperatures of water in the water bath.

(5) Working scientifically

A **respirometer** is used to measure the rate of respiration. **Soda lime** (containing sodium hydroxide) is used to absorb any carbon dioxide present. When an organism respires aerobically, it removes oxygen from the air in the apparatus, and the carbon dioxide it gives out is absorbed by the soda lime. This causes a drop in pressure inside the boiling tube which causes the drop of liquid to move towards the organisms.

(5) Key experimental skills

☑ Use of apparatus to make and record measurements accurately.

☑ Safe use of appropriate heating techniques.

☑ Safe and ethical use of living organisms.

☑ Measure rate of respiration by measuring uptake of oxygen.

(10) Worked example   Grade 5

A student carried out the experiment above. The table shows their results.

Temperature (°C)	Distance moved by drop of liquid in 5 minutes (mm)
10	5
15	7
20	9
25	12
30	30

(a) Describe and explain the pattern shown by these results.   **[2 marks]**

As the temperature increases, the distance moved increases because the rate of respiration increases.

(b) Suggest why no temperatures higher than 30 °C were investigated.   **[1 mark]**

A higher temperature could have harmed the maggots.

(c) The student uses the results to plot a graph. Explain **two** advantages of doing that.   **[2 marks]**

To see the pattern more clearly. To see if there are any anomalies.

(d) Suggest how the accuracy of the results could be improved.   **[2 marks]**

Repeat the experiment several times and take a mean of the results at each temperature.

(5) Exam-style practice   Grades 4–5

1 Explain why temperature affects the rate of respiration.   **[2 marks]**

2 State why soda lime is used in the investigation.   **[1 mark]**

 Made a start   **Feeling confident**   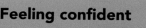 **Exam ready**

Response to exercise

You need to know how the human body responds to the increased demand for energy during exercise, and carry out calculations involving these responses.

 Responses to exercise

During exercise, the human body responds to the increased demand for energy by supplying more glucose and more oxygen to the muscles. The human body responds to exercise in different ways:

- The rate of breathing increases.
- Breaths are deeper so the volume of each breath increases.
- The heart rate increases.

Breathing increases to both take in oxygen and remove carbon dioxide more quickly. The heart beats faster so glucose and oxygenated blood are pumped to the muscles more quickly, and carbon dioxide is removed more quickly.

 Investigating the effects

There are various ways that you can investigate the effect of exercise on the human body. You can:

- measure the number of breaths per minute before and immediately after exercise
- measure the volume of each breath, using a device called a spirometer, before and immediately after exercise
- measure the heart rate by counting the pulse rate in the wrist before, during and after exercise.

 Cardiac output

During exercise, heart rate, stroke volume and cardiac output all increase.

Heart rate is the number of times the heart beats per minute. This is the same as your pulse rate. It is usually measured in beats per minute.

Stroke volume is the volume of blood pumped by the left ventricle in each heart beat. It is usually measured in ml.

Cardiac output is the total volume of blood pumped by the left ventricle per minute. It is usually measured in litres (l) per minute, and is calculated using the equation:

cardiac output (in l/min) =
        stroke volume (in l) × heart rate (in beats/min)

 Worked example **Grades 3–5**

1 A man has a heart rate of 75 beats per minute, and a stroke volume of 70 ml. Calculate his cardiac output in litres per minute. **[4 marks]**

His stroke volume = 70 ml = 0.07 litres.

His cardiac output = stroke volume × heart rate

= 0.07 × 75

= 5.25 litres per minute.

2 **Figure 1** shows changes in stroke volume and heart rate in two athletes during exercise. Give **one** difference and **one** similarity between the trends for the two athletes. **[2 marks]**

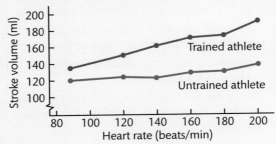

Figure 1

The similarity is that for both athletes stroke volume increases as heart rate increases.
The difference is that stroke volume increases at a faster rate for the trained athlete.

 Exam-style practice **Grades 2–4**

1 Describe how cardiac output changes during and after exercise. **[2 marks]**

2 A woman has a cardiac output of 4 litres per minute, and a heart rate of 60 beats per minute. Calculate her stroke volume in litres to two significant figures. **[3 marks]**

 Made a start **Feeling confident** **Exam ready**

Communities

A community is made up of all the living organisms within an ecosystem. You need to know how the species within a community depend on one another.

 Features of an ecosystem

A **population** is all the **organisms** of one species within an ecosystem.

A **community** consists of all the populations of different species living in the same habitat. A **habitat** is the place where organisms live.

An **ecosystem** is the interaction of a community of living organisms (**biotic factors**, page 65) with the non-living parts of their habitat (**abiotic factors**, page 64).

Plants in a community may compete for:

- light
- water
- space
- minerals.

Animals in a community may compete for:

- food
- a mate
- water
- territory.

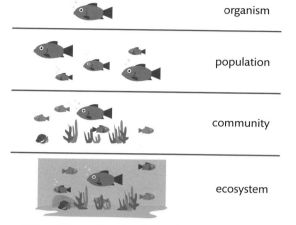

Figure 1 The different levels of organisation in an ecosystem

Worked example — Grades 4–5

Figure 2 is a food web for a grassland ecosystem. It shows interdependence and competition between species.

Figure 2

(a) Name **three** species that are competing for grass as a source of food. **[1 mark]**

Grasshopper, rabbit and mouse

(b) The grasshoppers were all killed by a disease. Explain why this might cause the population of rabbits to decrease. **[2 marks]**

The number of lizards would decrease as there would be no grasshoppers to eat.

As the number of lizards and grasshoppers decreases, the hawks would eat more rabbits, causing the population of rabbits to decrease.

Interdependence

Within a community, each species depends upon other species for the things they need, including food, shelter, pollination and seed dispersal. This is known as **interdependence**.

If a change occurs, such as the removal of a species, then the whole community could be affected. If all the species and environmental factors in a community are balanced, then the community is stable and the sizes of populations remain fairly constant.

Exam-style practice — Grades 2–3

1 Draw **one** straight line from each part of an oak woodland ecosystem to its level in the ecosystem. **[2 marks]**

part	level
all the oak trees	community
all the oak trees and the animals living in them	organism
single oak tree	population

2 What term describes **all** the interactions between the living things in an ecosystem? **[1 mark]**

- ☐ **A** competition
- ☐ **B** interdependence
- ☐ **C** pollination
- ☐ **D** predation

 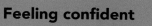

Abiotic factors

You need to know how abiotic (non-living) factors can affect the organisms in a community and their survival.

(10) Abiotic factors

Abiotic factors are non-living factors, including:

- temperature
- pH and mineral content of soil
- wind intensity and direction
- light intensity
- carbon dioxide levels (mainly affects plants)
- oxygen levels (e.g. for aquatic animals)
- moisture levels.

The oxygen content of the water in rivers, streams and lakes can be greatly reduced if it is polluted by sewage or nitrates from farming. The amount of dissolved oxygen usually determines the number and types of organisms living in that body of water. For example, mayfly larvae need water with a high oxygen content, whereas rat-tailed maggots can do well in low oxygen levels.

Figure 1 Changes in abiotic factors, such as temperature, can have a serious impact on the environment. Rising temperatures are causing sea ice in the Arctic to melt, which is having a negative effect on polar bears which are adapted to hunt and breed there.

(10) Worked example — Grades 4–5

A study was conducted into the growth of ivy plants in three different habitats. The pH of the soil was different in each habitat.

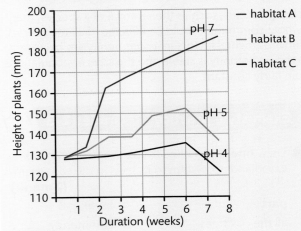

Figure 2

(a) Soil pH is an example of an abiotic factor. State what is meant by the term 'abiotic factor'. **[1 mark]**

Abiotic factors are the non-living factors that can affect the organisms in a community.

(b) **Figure 2** shows the heights of ivy plants in three habitats over an eight-week period. A student looks at the results in **Figure 2** and makes the following conclusion: *'Plants will grow better the higher the pH.'* Give **two** reasons why this is **not** a valid conclusion. **[2 marks]**

The data is only about ivy and we do not know how other plants will grow. The highest pH is pH 7 (which is neutral) and we do not know how the ivy will grow at pHs above pH 7.

(1) Exam focus

In the exam, you could be expected to extract and interpret information from charts, tables and graphs. Use specific data to help describe or explain any patterns shown.

(5) Exam-style practice — Grades 2–3

1 Which of the following is **not** an abiotic factor? **[1 mark]**

- [ ] **A** competition
- [ ] **B** light
- [ ] **C** temperature
- [ ] **D** water

2 Swallows are birds that migrate from Europe to Africa for the winter. Suggest **one** abiotic factor that causes them to migrate. **[1 mark]**

✓ **Made a start** ✓ **Feeling confident** ✓ **Exam ready**

Biotic factors

You need to know how biotic (living) factors can affect a community and its survival.

10 Biotic factors

Communities can be affected by **biotic factors** such as:

- **predation**
- **competition**
- **associations**.

Predation

Predators depend on their prey for food. Predators also control the sizes of the prey populations.

Competition

Living things compete for the resources they need. For example, plants compete for light and water, and animals compete for food, mates or territory. Competition can occur both between members of the same species, and between different species.

Associations

There are other interactions between organisms apart from predation or competition. Some species form close relationships in which both benefit. This is called **mutualism**. **Figure 1** shows oxpecker birds on a rhinoceros. The birds eat parasitic insects and ticks on. The birds gain food and the rhinoceros gets the ticks removed.

Parasitism is an association in which only one of the species (the parasite) benefits and the other (the host) is harmed. **Figure 2** shows a parasitic flea feeding on the blood of its host.

Figure 1 Oxpecker birds and rhinoceros in a mutualistic association

Figure 2 Fleas are parasites, feeding on the blood of their host but not killing it

5 Worked example Grades 2–4

1 Draw **one** straight line from each biotic factor to an example of it. **[3 marks]**

biotic factor	example
competition	bees feeding from flowers while they pollinate them
mutualism	lions eating antelopes
parasitism	tapeworm living in the gut of a pig
predation	tree shading grass

2 Mistletoe is a plant that grows on different tree species. The mistletoe extracts water and nutrients from the tree and sometimes even kills it. Explain what type of association this is. **[3 marks]**

This is an example of parasitism. The mistletoe is the parasite that benefits from the association. The tree is the host that is harmed.

10 Exam-style practice Grades 4–5

1 Give **one** biotic factor affecting an Arctic ecosystem. **[1 mark]**

2 State which of the following factors are biotic, and which are abiotic. **[2 marks]**

temperature
carbon dioxide levels
new pathogens
wind intensity
food availability
predators

3 Suggest an explanation for how the introduction of the grey squirrel to the UK has caused the red squirrel to become endangered. **[2 marks]**

Practical: Population studies

The size of a population in a habitat can be measured using quadrats. You need to know how quadrats can also be used along a belt transect to investigate the effect of an abiotic factor on the distribution of a species.

(10) Using a belt transect and quadrats

This method describes the process of **sampling** the plants as you move away from the trunk of a large tree. One abiotic factor that would change is the light intensity, which would be greater further away from the trunk.

1 Set up a line, called a **belt transect**, from the base of the tree trunk to beyond the shade of the tree, using a tape measure (or string marked out with the required distances).

2 Place a **quadrat** against the transect line, ensuring the corner of the quadrat is lined up with 0 on the tape measure.

3 Count how many plants of each different species are within the quadrat and record your findings in a suitable table.

4 Move the quadrat 1 metre along the transect; count and record your findings of plants of each species.

5 Repeat the steps above until you have results for every metre until you are beyond the shade of the tree.

6 Go back to the tree trunk, set up a new transect line in a different direction and repeat the steps given above.

(5) Maths skills

In some investigations you may need to calculate the **mean** number of plants of a particular species per quadrat.

The mean is calculated by: $\dfrac{\text{total number of plants}}{\text{number of quadrats}}$

The mean is one type of average. Two other types of average are:

- the **mode**, which is the most common value in a range of values
- the **median**, which is the middle value when all the values are put in order.

(10) Worked example — Grades 4–5

The table shows the number of buttercups found in four different areas of a field.

Quadrat number	1	2	3	4
Number of buttercups	6	2	5	7

(a) Calculate the mean number of buttercups per quadrat. **[1 mark]**

$$\text{mean} = \dfrac{\text{total number of buttercups}}{\text{number of quadrats}}$$

$$= \dfrac{20}{4} = 5$$

(b) Using your answer from **(a)**, estimate the population of buttercups in the field.
The quadrat used has an area of $0.25\,\text{m}^2$ and the field has an area of $100\,\text{m}^2$. **[2 marks]**

$$\dfrac{100}{0.25} = 400 \text{ quadrats for the whole field}$$

$5 \times 400 = 2000 \text{ buttercups in the field}$

There is an average of 5 buttercups per quadrat.

Working scientifically

To ensure the data collected is accurate:

- place the quadrats down at specified coordinates
- identify all the different species present
- count the number of individual plants of each species, not the number of flowers, for example.

(5) Key terms

✓ A **quadrat** is a square frame, often $0.25\,\text{m}^2$. Quadrats are used to sample the distribution of plants (or sometimes animals). They are either placed in a line (belt transect) or placed randomly to compare two different areas.

✓ A **belt transect** is a series of quadrats in a line across a habitat.

✓ **Sampling** means using information from several places to make **estimates** of the results for the whole area. The more samples taken, the more accurate the estimates will be.

✓ **Random** coordinates can be taken from random number tables. Placing quadrats at random coordinates avoids **bias**.

(5) Exam-style practice — Grade 4

Some students investigated the plants growing under a large tree. They used a belt transect from the base of the tree trunk to an area that was no longer under the tree. They found more plants growing as they went further away from the tree trunk. Suggest an explanation for this. **[3 marks]**

First, work out the number of quadrats it would take to cover the whole field.

Biodiversity

Biodiversity refers to the variety of plant and animal species within a habitat, in a larger area or on Earth. You need to be able to discuss the benefits of, and threats to, **biodiversity**, both locally and on a global scale.

5 Advantages of biodiversity

The greater the number of species in a community, the greater the biodiversity.

An ecosystem (page 63) is much more stable if there is greater biodiversity because organisms can depend upon multiple species for food and shelter. This gives them a greater chance of survival compared with relying on just one species.

Working scientifically

Many human activities have major negative impacts on biodiversity, leading to some species becoming extinct and many others becoming endangered. The future of the human species on Earth relies on maintaining a good level of biodiversity. Measures are now being taken to protect and maintain biodiversity.

5 Key threats to biodiversity

- deforestation
- pollution, e.g. eutrophication
- climate change
- destruction of habitats
- landfill
- changes in agricultural methods
- increasing human population
- over-exploitation, e.g. fishing
- introduction of **non-indigenous** (non-native) species

5 Eutrophication

Eutrophication is a problem involving extra nutrients entering the water in rivers and lakes. This can be caused by sewage pollution or by mineral ions from artificial fertilisers put on fields to help crop plants grow (see page 71).
The extra nutrients cause excessive growth of algae, which reduces the light entering the water, causing the death of water plants. As the plants die, they decay due to the action of bacteria, which in turn use up oxygen from the water, killing fish and other water animals.

Fish farming can also contribute to eutrophication. If fish are kept in large cages in open water, then waste from the large number of fish can enter the natural ecosystem, damaging it.

10 Worked example — Grades 4–5

1. Give the meaning of the term 'biodiversity'. **[1 mark]**

   The variety of all the different species in an ecosystem.

2. Explain how deforestation is leading to a decrease in biodiversity. **[2 marks]**

   As habitats are destroyed, the populations of trees and other plants are being reduced, and also the different animal species that live on them.

3. The harlequin ladybird was introduced in the USA as a predator to control whitefly on crops.
   The harlequin ladybird is an aggressive competitor of other ladybird species. It has now appeared in the UK. Suggest an explanation why scientists are concerned about the appearance of this ladybird in the UK. **[3 marks]**

   The harlequin ladybird will compete with native UK species, for example, for food. It may out-compete UK species, leading to them dying out, and reducing biodiversity.

5 Exam-style practice — Grade 3

Eutrophication can lead to a reduction in biodiversity. Complete the table by writing numbers 1–6 in the boxes to put the stages in the correct order. The first one has been done for you. **[2 marks]**

Stage	Order
algae at the water surface block light from plants below	
bacteria causing plant decay use up oxygen in water	
excess nutrients enter a river or lake	1
lack of oxygen kills fish and other water animals	
nutrients cause excessive growth of algae	
water plants die and decay	

Maintaining biodiversity

It is important to reverse the negative effect the growing human population has had on biodiversity and to improve the stability of ecosystems. You need to know about some of the methods used, and the difficulties involved, with conserving species and maintaining biodiversity.

10 Maintaining biodiversity

- **Captive breeding programmes** increase the population of endangered species until they are no longer vulnerable and can be released to re-establish wild populations.
- **Reducing the rate of deforestation** in some areas, and **increasing the rate of reforestation** by replanting in other areas, reduces the negative impacts on the climate, habitats and food supply which aids organisms' survival.
- **Reducing carbon dioxide emissions** slows down global warming which is already reducing the populations of Arctic and Antarctic animals.
- **Recycling waste** reduces the use of landfill and saves energy. Landfill sites produce 'landfill gas', a mixture of greenhouse gases which contribute to climate change. Dumping waste at landfill also wastes land and destroys ecosystems.
- **Protecting and regenerating habitats** prevents harm to the ecosystem. Coral reefs are protected to prevent further damage and to allow the coral to recover.
- **Reintroducing field margins and hedgerows** to the edges of fields of crops increases biodiversity in these areas, especially where farmers grow only one type of crop.

Figure 1 A giant panda, born and raised in a captive breeding programme, being released into the wild

5 Working scientifically

Running programmes to maintain biodiversity effectively can be very expensive – national parks and protected habitats all cost money to maintain.

Some revenue can be generated by opening protected areas to the public and charging them for entry.

Governments may offer incentives to businesses to reduce their carbon emissions and reduce their waste, or they may tax heavily polluting industries.

Farmers may be offered benefits for replanting hedgerows such as an increased price for their crops and livestock.

5 Worked example · Grade 5

Explain why it is important to prevent organisms from becoming extinct. **[3 marks]**

Species should be preserved so future generations can see them. Extinctions can have a dramatic effect on food chains, causing other species to become endangered.

Most species directly or indirectly impact our food supply.

Another suitable answer is that certain plants are sources of vital medicines. It may be difficult or even impossible to find replacements.

5 Exam-style practice · Grades 1–2

1 Which of the following would increase biodiversity? **[1 mark]**

- [ ] **A** deforestation
- [ ] **B** disposing of waste in landfill sites
- [ ] **C** reforestation
- [ ] **D** replacing hedgerows with fences

2 Explain how captive breeding programmes can help increase biodiversity in the wild. **[2 marks]**

 Made a start Feeling confident · Exam ready

Carbon cycle

You need to know how materials in the natural world are recycled to provide the building blocks for future organisms. The **carbon cycle** is one example of how substances are cycled through an ecosystem.

⏱10 The carbon cycle

Most of the different substances that living organisms are made of, such as carbohydrates, proteins, lipids and DNA, contain the element **carbon**. Without carbon, life as we know it could not exist. There is only a certain amount of carbon on the Earth, and carbon atoms are constantly being recycled through both the biotic (living) and abiotic (non-living) parts of ecosystems.

Carbon dioxide (CO_2) is removed from the atmosphere by photosynthesis (see page 44) in plants and algae. The plants and algae use the carbon to make glucose which is later converted to other substances as they grow, such as starch, protein and lipids. When animals eat plants, they take in these substances and convert them to other carbon-containing compounds in their own bodies. When animals and plants respire (see page 60), carbon is returned to the atmosphere as carbon dioxide again.

There are other processes in the carbon cycle. For example, dead animals and plants, or their waste, are decayed by **decomposers**, returning carbon dioxide to the atmosphere. Sometimes, over millions of years, the remains of dead organisms form fossil fuels such as coal and oil. When these fuels are burned, carbon returns to the atmosphere as carbon dioxide again.

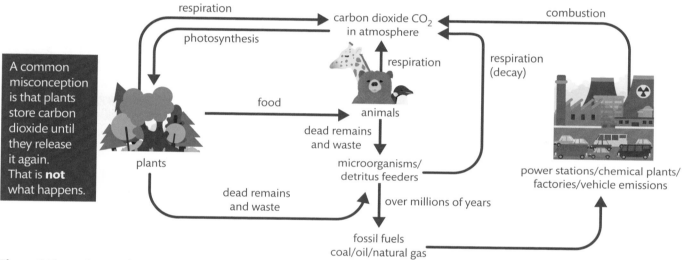

Figure 1 The carbon cycle

⏱5 Decomposers

Decomposers are microorganisms, such as certain bacteria or fungi, that **decay** (decompose) dead remains and waste (**detritus**). As the decomposers respire, they release carbon dioxide into the atmosphere. Decay also releases mineral ions, such as nitrates, into the soil for new plant growth.

Go to page 71 to see how nitrates are involved in the nitrogen cycle.

⏱5 Worked example | Grade 5

Explain how microorganisms help to provide plants with the mineral ions they need. **[2 marks]**

Microorganisms feed on dead plant and animal matter. As they break down the waste they return mineral ions to the soil.

⏱5 Exam-style practice | Grades 2–3

1 Draw **one** straight line from each chemical change in the carbon cycle to the name of the process. **[2 marks]**

chemical change	process
carbon dioxide used to make glucose	growth
glucose broken down making carbon dioxide	photosynthesis
glucose converted to other compounds such as proteins	respiration

2 What term describes microorganisms that cause decay? **[1 mark]**

☐ **A** competitors   ☐ **C** parasites

☐ **B** decomposers   ☐ **D** predators

✓ **Made a start**   ✓ **Feeling confident**   ✓ **Exam ready**

Water cycle

The water cycle is another example of a substance that is cycled through ecosystems.

 The water cycle

The water cycle is important because every living organism on Earth depends on water to survive. Without water, all living organisms would die very quickly. The water cycle brings fresh water to people, animals and plants all around the world. There are four main stages to the water cycle.

1 **Evaporation** – (heat) energy from the Sun causes water in the oceans, lakes and rivers to evaporate, forming water vapour in the atmosphere.

2 **Condensation** – as water vapour cools high up in the atmosphere it condenses to form clouds.

3 **Precipitation** – as clouds become more condensed water falls as rain, snow or hail.

4 **Collection** – water may fall straight into rivers, lakes and oceans ready for the process to begin again, or it may be absorbed into the soil and taken up by vegetation to eventually evaporate from the leaves (by **transpiration**). Water that is not absorbed will flow across the ground (surface run-off) until it reaches a river or other area of water.

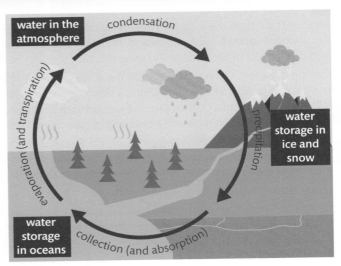

Figure 1 The water cycle

Plants also produce more water when they respire.

 Worked example | **Grades 3–4**

1 Describe **three** ways water enters the atmosphere in the water cycle. **[3 marks]**

Some water evaporates from rivers, lakes and seas. Water is produced when living organisms respire and is given out, for example, when animals breathe. Water is lost from plant leaves during transpiration.

2 Describe **one** advantage and **one** disadvantage of producing potable water by the desalination of sea water compared with other methods. **[2 marks]**

One advantage is that desalination is a way of obtaining potable water in some places where fresh water is scarce. One disadvantage is that desalination plants are expensive to build and run.

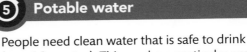 **Potable water**

People need clean water that is safe to drink (**potable water**). This can be a particular problem in areas of drought. Potable water can be obtained in different ways including:

- from springs and wells
- treating previously used water
- from sea water (**desalination**).

Desalination is the removal of salts from sea water usually by some form of distillation.

There is more about desalination on page 104.

Another advantage of desalination is that the water produced is safe to drink and does not contain pathogens or toxins. Another disadvantage is that desalination plants use a lot of energy to run which can cause pollution such as carbon emissions.

 Exam-style practice | **Grades 3–4**

1 Suggest **two** reasons why water might **not** be potable. **[2 marks]**

2 Explain what is meant by the term '**precipitation**'. **[3 marks]**

Nitrogen cycle

Plants take in **nitrate ions** for healthy growth. You need to know how **nitrogen** compounds such as nitrates are cycled through ecosystems in the nitrogen cycle.

 ## Fertilisers and crop rotation

Growing the same type of crop plant in the same soil for many years reduces the levels of nitrates and other mineral ions. **Fertilisers** and **crop rotation** can restore the levels:

- **Natural fertilisers** such as compost or manure slowly decompose in the soil to release nitrates and other minerals. **Artificial fertilisers**, which may be liquid or powder, contain nitrates and other minerals that can be quickly taken up by plants.

- **Crop rotation** means that different crop plants, with different mineral requirements, are grown each year. Often one of the crops in the rotation is peas, beans or clover. Their roots have swellings called **root nodules** which contain **nitrogen-fixing bacteria**. The bacteria provide the plant with nitrates and also increase nitrate levels in the soil.

Go to page 67 to revise how excessive use of artificial fertilisers can cause eutrophication.

Figure 1 Root nodules

 ## The nitrogen cycle

Plants and animals need nitrogen to make compounds such as proteins, but they cannot use nitrogen gas as it is too unreactive. Different types of soil bacteria are involved in making nitrates available for uptake by plants.

Nitrates are also added to fields during thunderstorms. The energy in lightning can make nitrogen gas in the air react with oxygen, leading to the formation of nitrates in the rain.

Go to pages 47 and 48 to revise how mineral ions are taken into, and transported through, plants.

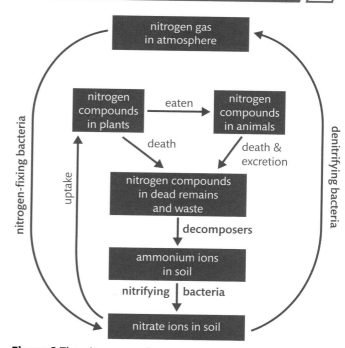

Figure 2 The nitrogen cycle

 ## Worked example Grade 5

A farmer uses the following four-year crop rotation: wheat, turnips, barley, clover.
The farmer grows clover because it contains nitrogen-fixing bacteria in root nodules.
The farmer does **not** harvest the clover, but ploughs it back into the soil. Explain how this benefits the farmer. **[3 marks]**

The nitrogen-fixing bacteria convert nitrogen gas from the air into nitrogen compounds such as nitrates. These will improve plant growth in the future.

Exam-style practice Grade 5

(a) Name the type of bacteria that converts nitrates to nitrogen gas. **[1 mark]**

(b) Name **two** types of bacteria involved in converting nitrogen compounds in compost and manure into nitrates. **[2 marks]**

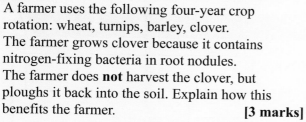

Look at **Figure 2** to help you.

Atoms, elements and compounds

You need to be able to apply your knowledge of atoms, elements and compounds to name substances and write balanced chemical equations.

 Elements and compounds

Everything is made of atoms. An **atom** is the smallest part of an **element** that can exist on its own.

Elements

There are about 100 different naturally-occurring elements. All elements are listed on the **periodic table**. Each element is made of atoms that have the same atomic number (number of protons). Each type of atom can be represented by an atomic symbol, e.g. Na for an atom of sodium.

An element is a pure substance that cannot be chemically broken down into anything simpler. The atoms of a particular element are chemically identical to each other.

Compounds

Compounds form when two or more elements chemically combine in fixed proportions. The name or symbol of a compound is made from the elements reacting together. For example, sodium and chlorine form sodium chloride.

Compounds can be split back into their elements by a chemical reaction. In a chemical reaction, a new substance is always made. Chemical reactions often involve an energy change.

Go to page 74 to revise the structure of the atom.

When metals react, their name stays the same. When a non-metal reacts with a metal, the name of the non-metal changes and ends in **-ide**.

If a compound is made of a metal, a non-metal and oxygen, then the ending becomes **-ate**. For example, a compound made from sodium, chlorine and oxygen would be sodium chlorate.

 Key skills

- ☑ Identify the names and symbols of the first 20 elements in the periodic table, and the elements in Groups 1 and 7.
- ☑ Name compounds from given formulae or chemical equations.
- ☑ Write word equations and produce balanced chemical equations for given reactions.

Go to page 75 to find out about protons and atomic number.

Atoms do not have the same properties as the substances that they make.

 Worked example | **Grade 4**

1 Name the compounds formed by the combination of the following elements.
(a) Cu and F   [1 mark]

Copper fluoride

(b) Cu, O and F   [1 mark]

Copper fluorate

2 Write a word equation for the reaction between magnesium and oxygen.   [1 mark]

magnesium + oxygen → magnesium oxide

To write a word equation, put the reactants (starting substances) on the left, then an arrow leading to the products (ending substances) on the right.

The name of the metal comes first in the name of a compound.

 Exam-style practice | **Grade 4**

1 State why aluminium is an element.   [1 mark]

2 Give the correct atomic symbol for aluminium.   [1 mark]

3 **Figure 1** shows a section of the periodic table.
(a) Name the labelled element in Group 1.   [1 mark]
(b) (i) Give the name and symbol of the element in the blue box.   [1 mark]
     (ii) Write a word equation showing this element reacting with chlorine.   [1 mark]

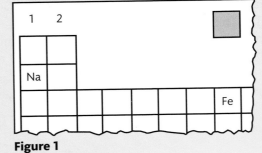

Figure 1

 Made a start   **Feeling confident**   **Exam ready**

The model of the atom

The work of many scientists has led to our current model of the atom. You need to know the theories (outlined below) that have developed over time due to the discovery of subatomic particles.

(10) Developing the model of the atom

1800s

1930s

1. Dalton thought that atoms were like solid balls (spheres). He said that atoms could not be split. Atoms of the same element were identical, but different from atoms of another element. As technology improved, more experiments happened. This led scientists to discover particles inside the atom. So, Dalton's model had to be changed and developed to accommodate these new discoveries.

2. As particles were found inside an atom, ideas had to change. J. J. Thomson suggested the **plum pudding model**, where atoms were like a positively charged 'pudding' with electrons like 'plums' in the cake.

3. Rutherford, Geiger and Marsden tested the plum pudding model by aiming a beam of positively-charged alpha particles at a very thin sheet of gold foil (scattering experiment). Some of the alpha particles were deflected and a few repelled by positively-charged particles (the nucleus). Most alpha particles passed through unaffected, showing that the nucleus was only a very small part of the atom. This evidence gave rise to the **nuclear model**.

4. Bohr adapted the nuclear model. Using theoretical calculations alongside experimental observations, he suggested that electrons travel in circular orbits around the nucleus. Further research showed that the nucleus was actually made of smaller particles with equal amounts of positive charge. These became known as protons. About 20 years after the nuclear model became accepted, Chadwick discovered that neutrons also existed in the nucleus.

(5) Scientific theory

You need to know how scientific theories change over time. New experimental evidence may lead to a scientific model being changed or replaced. The **scientific method** is a systematic, logical approach used to discover how science works. It may be modified but ultimately it is used to gather evidence from experiments, observations and calculations to solve a problem.

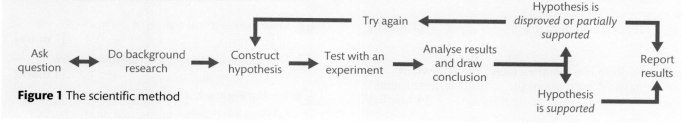

Figure 1 The scientific method

(2) Worked example — Grade 5

State the difference between the plum pudding model of the atom and Dalton's model of the atom. **[2 marks]**

The plum pudding model had positive and negative particles. Dalton's model did not have any charged particles.

(5) Exam-style practice — Grade 5

1 State the name of the particle found by Chadwick. **[1 mark]**

2 Describe the main difference between Dalton's model of the atom and the model of the atom that is used today. **[2 marks]**

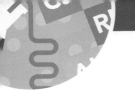

Subatomic particles

You need to know about the size and structure of atoms.

10 Structure of an atom

Everything is made of atoms. Atoms contain subatomic particles, some of which are charged. **Figure 1** is a diagram of a lithium atom. It shows the subatomic particles and where they are found in the atom.

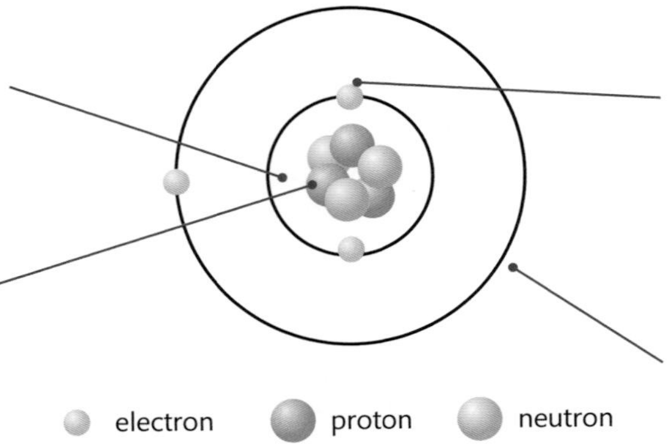
In the centre of the atom is a very tiny **nucleus**. This is where most of the mass of the atom is found. Protons and neutrons are found in the nucleus. All the atoms of the same element have the same number of protons.
The **atomic number** is the number of protons the atom contains. The number of electrons in an atom is equal to the number of protons in its nucleus.
The tiny negatively-charged electrons are found in electron shells surrounding the nucleus. They are attracted to the positively-charged protons.
Atoms are electrically neutral as they have an equal number of protons and electrons and neutrons are not charged.
electron
proton
neutron

Figure 1 The nuclear model of the atom

2 Size of an atom

The atom is the smallest part of an element. Atoms have a radius of about 0.1 nanometres (nm) (1×10^{-10} m). A nanometre is equal to one-billionth of a metre (1×10^{-9} m). The nucleus of an atom has a radius of about 0.00001 nm (1×10^{-14} m).

You do not need to remember the sizes but you do need to know that the nucleus is about a thousandth of the radius of the atom.

Subatomic particle	Location	Relative mass	Relative charge
Proton	Nucleus	1	+1
Neutron	Nucleus	1	No charge
Electron	Shells	0 (negligible)	–1

5 Worked example — Grade 5

1 Convert the following units.

(a) 7 nm to m **[1 mark]**

7×10^{-9} m

(b) 3×10^{-9} m to nm **[1 mark]**

3 nm

2 Sodium is a metal element. Explain where most of the mass of the sodium atom is found. **[4 marks]**

An atom is made of mainly space and the electrons have negligible mass. So, most of the mass is found in the nucleus as this is made of protons and neutrons which each have a relative mass of 1.

Maths skills

You need to know how to convert nanometres to metres using standard form.

1 nm = 1×10^{-9} m

10 Exam-style practice — Grade 4

1 State the electrical charge of the nucleus of an atom. **[1 mark]**

2 Name the subatomic particles found in the nucleus of an atom. **[1 mark]**

3 Look at **Figure 2**, a diagram of a helium atom.

(a) Give the number of each subatomic particle shown in **Figure 2**. **[3 marks]**

(b) Explain why an atom of helium has no overall charge. **[2 marks]**

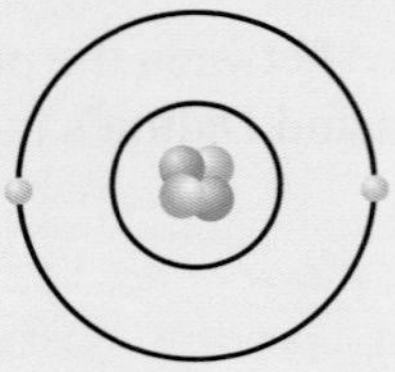

Figure 2

Size and mass of atoms

You need to be able to calculate the numbers of protons, neutrons and electrons in atoms when you are given the atomic number and mass number.

5 Representing atoms

The sum of the number of protons and neutrons in an atom is its **mass number**. Almost all the mass of an atom is in the nucleus.

The **atomic number** is the number of protons in an atom's nucleus. Atoms contain the same number of protons and electrons.

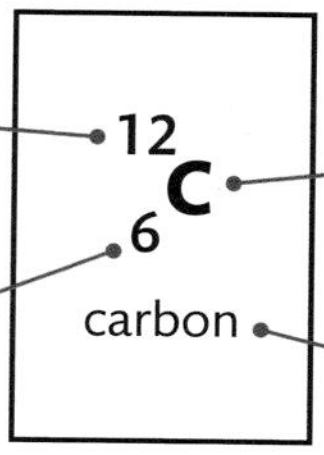

The **atomic symbol** is the short-hand name for the element.

This is the **name** of the element.

10 Worked example — Grade 5

(a) Name the **three** subatomic particles in an atom of aluminium and give their relative charge and relative masses. **[3 marks]**

Protons have a relative mass of 1 and a charge of +1.
Electrons have a very small relative mass and a charge of −1.
Neutrons have a relative mass of 1 and a charge of 0.

(b) An atom of aluminium is represented by $^{27}_{13}\mathrm{Al}$. Calculate the number of protons, electrons and neutrons in an atom of aluminium. **[3 marks]**

number of protons = atomic number = 13
number of electrons = number of protons = 13
number of neutrons = mass number − atomic number
= 27 − 13 = 14

(c) An unknown element X, has 8 electrons and 9 neutrons. Give the atomic symbol of element X. **[2 marks]**

number of electrons = number of protons = 8
mass number = protons + neutrons = 17
Therefore atom symbol is $^{17}_{8}\mathrm{X}$.

1 Maths skills

You need to know how to use mass number and atomic number to work out the number of protons, neutrons and electrons.

For sodium:

number of protons = atomic number = 11
number of electrons = number of protons = 11
number of neutrons = mass number − atomic number
= 23 − 11 = 12

Exam focus
When giving the mass of an atom in an exam you do not need to state the units.

mass number minus atomic number

In an atom, the number of electrons is equal to the number of protons.

10 Exam-style practice — Grade 5

(a) The current model of the atom has three subatomic particles. Complete the table.

Subatomic particle	Relative mass	Relative charge
	$\frac{1}{1836}$	
neutron		
	1	

[1 mark]
[1 mark]
[1 mark]

(b) Use the periodic table to complete the table. **[2 marks]**

Particle	Number of protons	Number of neutrons	Number of electrons
fluorine	9		9
fluoride	9		10

Isotopes and relative atomic mass

Isotopes are atoms of the same element that have different numbers of neutrons. They have the same chemical properties but different physical properties.

 Isotopes

Isotopes are atoms with the same atomic number but a different mass number. This means they have the same number of protons and electrons but a different number of neutrons. Isotopes of an element have the same chemical properties. Isotopes of the same element are usually identified by their mass number, e.g. hydrogen-3.

Isotopes of hydrogen

	Hydrogen ^1_1H	Deuterium ^2_1H	Tritium ^3_1H
Number of protons	1	1	1
Number of electrons	1	1	1
Number of neutrons	0	1	2

Atoms can be represented in this way. The top number is the mass number. The bottom number is the atomic number.

Radioactive isotopes

Some radioactive isotopes have useful applications. For example, cobalt-60 is used in cancer treatment.

Fluorine-18 is used as a tracer for detecting cancers and in cardiac and brain imaging.

 Worked example — Grade 4

1 Two isotopes of lithium are ^7_3Li and ^8_3Li. Describe the similarities and differences between them, referring to the number of subatomic particles in each isotope. **[3 marks]**

The atoms of both isotopes possess the same number of protons and electrons – three of each.

They have a different number of neutrons – ^7_3Li has four neutrons and ^8_3Li has five neutrons.

2 Copper (Cu) is an element listed in the periodic table. Use the relative atomic mass of copper in the periodic table to suggest why it has more than one isotope. **[3 marks]**

The relative atomic mass is not a whole number. This suggests that there is more than one isotope in a sample of copper.

 Relative atomic mass

The relative atomic mass (A_r) is the average mass of one atom of an element compared to $\frac{1}{12}$ of the mass of an atom of carbon-12.

The average takes into account that there could be more than one isotope in the sample. This can mean that the relative atomic mass may not be a whole number.

Chlorine has two isotopes, Cl-35 and Cl-37. In the periodic table, chlorine (Cl) has a relative atomic mass of 35.5 showing that there is slightly more of the lighter isotope. In fact, there is about 75% Cl-35 and 25% Cl-37 in a sample of chlorine so the average is 35.5.

 Exam-style practice — Grades 3–4

Look at the atomic symbols below. The letters are **not** the symbols for these elements.

^6_3R ^7_3M $^{23}_{11}T$ $^{39}_{19}Z$ $^{85}_{37}V$

(a) Give the definition of an isotope. **[2 marks]**

(b) State which atoms in the list above are isotopes of each other. **[1 mark]**

 Made a start **Feeling confident** **Exam ready**

Developing the periodic table

You need to be able to describe the development of the periodic table over time, in terms of the scientific theories and instruments available.

Mendeleev's periodic table

In the late 1800s, Mendeleev arranged the elements in a table. He used his knowledge of the atomic mass of the elements as well as the reactions of the elements and their compounds.

The elements were listed mainly by increasing mass but were grouped based on their properties. He left gaps for elements that he thought were not discovered yet and made predictions about them.

In some cases, he changed the order of the elements to fit the chemical pattern better. For example, he placed iodine after tellurium although the relative atomic mass of iodine is slightly lower. He thought that the masses must be wrong. In fact, they are correct – tellurium has a high abundance of isotopes of high mass.

Mendeleev also left gaps to keep the pattern, predicting that new elements would be discovered to fill the gaps. Over the next 20 years more elements were discovered and their properties were found to match Mendeleev's predictions.

Row	Group							
	1	2	3	4	5	6	7	8
1	H	-	-	-	-	-	-	-
2	Li	Be	B	C	N	O	F	-
3	Na	Mg	Al	Si	P	S	Cl	-
4	K	Ca	?	Ti	V	Cr	Mn	Fe, Co, Ni, Cu
5	(Cu)	Zn	?	?	As	So	Br	-
6	Rb	Sr	Yt	Zr	Nb	Mo	?	Ru, Rh, Pd, Ag

Figure 1 Part of the periodic table made by Dmitri Mendeleev

 Exam focus

To answer a multiple-choice question, you need to apply the following principles.

- You must put a cross in only **one** box. If you do not cross any boxes or cross more than **one** box, you will score zero.
- Read all of the answers before selecting which one to cross; several answers may seem correct at first until you have read through all of the options.
- If you are unsure, eliminate the answers you know are wrong and then make a considered decision on the options left.

Working scientifically

To develop new scientific ideas, predictions need to be tested. If the evidence supports the prediction, a scientific idea will develop.

The development of the periodic table is an example of how scientific ideas develop. Many scientists suggested possible arrangements of the elements but others rejected them as they weren't supported by evidence.

Worked example — Grade 4

In Mendeleev's periodic table, the elements lithium, sodium and potassium were all placed into Group 1.

Explain why he grouped them together. **[2 marks]**

Because they have similar properties – for example, react with water to give alkaline solutions.

Exam-style practice — Grade 5

Look at **Figure 1**.

(a) Name **three** elements Mendeleev put into his Group 4. **[1 mark]**

(b) Which property did Mendeleev use to arrange his periodic table? **[1 mark]**

☐ **A** atomic mass ☐ **B** atomic number ☐ **C** atomic size ☐ **D** atomic charge

(c) Suggest an explanation for the use of question marks in Mendeleev's table. **[1 mark]**

(d) In the modern periodic table, iodine is in Group 7 after tellurium in Group 6, even though iodine has a lower relative atomic mass. Give a reason why atoms are not ordered by increasing mass in the modern periodic table. **[2 marks]**

 Made a start Feeling confident 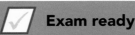 Exam ready

The periodic table

The modern periodic table is based on Mendeleev's work, but the elements are arranged in order of increasing atomic number rather than atomic mass. You will be given a copy of the periodic table in your exam.

⏱10 Groups and periods ✓

The periodic table is called this because similar properties occur at regular intervals. Originally, the atomic number simply gave the number of where the atom was placed. It was only later realised that this was also the number of protons in the nucleus. An element's position in the periodic table shows how it reacts and how reactive it is likely to be.

alkali metals Hydrogen is a non-metal but has the same electronic configuration as the alkali metals and so is often put in the top middle area of the periodic table. halogens noble gases

1	2											3	4	5	6	7	0
							1 H Hydrogen 1									4 He Helium 2
7 Li Lithium 3	9 Be Beryllium 4											11 B Boron 5	12 C Carbon 6	14 N Nitrogen 7	16 O Oxygen 8	19 F Fluorine 9	20 Ne Neon 10
23 Na Sodium 11	24 Mg Magnesium 12											27 Al Aluminium 13	28 Si Silicon 14	31 P Phosphorus 15	32 S Sulfur 16	35.5 Cl Chlorine 17	40 Ar Argon 18
39 K Potassium 19	40 Ca Calcium 20	45 Sc Scandium 21	48 Ti Titanium 22	51 V Vanadium 23	52 Cr Chromium 24	55 Mn Manganese 25	56 Fe Iron 26	59 Co Cobalt 27	59 Ni Nickel 28	63.5 Cu Copper 29	65 Zn Zinc 30	70 Ga Gallium 31	73 Ge Germanium 32	75 As Arsenic 33	79 Se Selenium 34	80 Br Bromine 35	84 Kr Krypton 36
85 Rb Rubidium 37	88 Sr Strontium 38	89 Y Yttrium 39	91 Zr Zirconium 40	93 Nb Niobium 41	96 Mo Molybdenum 42	98 Tc Technetium 43	101 Ru Ruthenium 44	103 Rh Rhodium 45	106 Pd Palladium 46	108 Ag Silver 47	112 Cd Cadmium 48	115 In Indium 49	119 Sn Tin 50	122 Sb Antimony 51	128 Te Tellurium 52	127 I Iodine 53	131 Xe Xenon 54
133 Cs Caesium 55	137 Ba Barium 56	139 La Lanthanum 57	178 Hf Hafnium 72	181 Ta Tantalum 73	184 W Tungsten 74	186 Re Rhenium 75	190 Os Osmium 76	192 Ir Iridium 77	195 Pt Platinum 78	197 Au Gold 79	201 Hg Mercury 80	204 Tl Thallium 81	207 Pb Lead 82	209 Bi Bismuth 83	[210] Po Polonium 84	[210] At Astatine 85	[222] Rn Radon 86
[223] Fr Francium 87	[226] Ra Radium 88	[227] Ac Actinium 89	[261] Rf Rutherfordium 104	[262] Db Dubnium 105	[266] Sg Seaborgium 106	[264] Bh Bohrium 107	[277] Hs Hassium 108	[268] Mt Meitnerium 109	[271] Ds Darmstadtium 110	[272] Rg Roentgenium 111							

Elements with atomic numbers 112–116 have been reported but not fully authenticated.

Elements with similar properties are found in vertical columns known as **groups**. The group number is given on the periodic table above each column. All elements in the same group have the same number of electrons in their outer shell, for example, oxygen is in Group 6 and has six electrons in its outer shell.

Rows of elements are called **periods**. All elements in the same period have the same number of electron shells with electrons in. For example, sodium is in Period 3 and has electrons in the first three electron shells. Across a period, the number of outer-shell electrons increases by 1. For example, in Period 2, lithium has the electronic configuration of 2.1, beryllium has configuration 2.2 and boron 2.3.

⏱5 Worked example Grade 5 ✓

When lithium metal is added to water it fizzes, producing lithium hydroxide and hydrogen gas. Predict the reaction between sodium and water and name the products formed. **[2 marks]**

Sodium would react with water by fizzing. Hydrogen and sodium hydroxide would be produced.

Find sodium and lithium in the periodic table above or on page 239 and compare their positions with the answer. When counting rows, remember that the first row (or period) only contains two elements, H and He.

⏱10 Exam-style practice Grade 5 ✓

① An element has an electronic configuration of 2.8.5.
  (a) State which group the element is in. **[1 mark]**
  (b) State which period the element is in. **[1 mark]**
  (c) Name another element which would react in a similar way to this element. **[1 mark]**

② An element has 12 electrons.
  (a) State which group the element is in. **[1 mark]**
  (b) State which period the element is in. **[1 mark]**

③ Explain the arrangement of the first 20 elements in the periodic table. You should answer in terms of atomic structure. **[1 mark]**

 Made a start 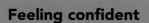 Feeling confident   Exam ready

Electronic configuration

You need to be able to recognise and represent the electronic configurations of the first 20 elements of the periodic table.

 10 Electronic configuration

Negatively-charged electrons are held in electron shells surrounding the positively-charged nucleus of an atom.

Electrons occupy the lowest available electron shell first, starting with the innermost electron shell. The innermost electron shell is very small and can only hold two electrons. Each subsequent shell can hold up to eight electrons.

The electronic configuration of an atom can be represented by a diagram or by listing the number of electrons in each shell, starting with the innermost shell.

- The atomic number is the same as the number of electrons in an atom.
- The number of electrons in the outermost electron shell is the same as the element's group number in the periodic table. The exception to this is elements in Group 0, which have complete outer shells.
- The number of electron shells is the same as the element's period number in the periodic table.

Examples of electronic configuration

Element	fluorine	neon	sodium
Electronic configuration	 2.7	2.8	2.8.1
Group	7	0	1

Although electrons repel each other, and should be spread evenly around the shell, it is helpful to pair the electrons up so that you can clearly see how many are in each shell.

Go to page 74 for more about the properties of electrons.

 5 Worked example **Grade 5**

(a) Give the electronic configuration of nitrogen (atomic number 7). **[1 mark]**

2.5

(b) Complete the diagram to show the electronic configuration of nitrogen. **[2 marks]**

(c) The electronic configuration of lithium is 2.1 and of sodium is 2.8.1. State and explain which group lithium and sodium are placed in. **[2 marks]**

Both atoms have 1 electron in their outer shell so they should be in Group 1.

Nitrogen is in Group 5 so it has five electrons in its outer electron shell.

The number of electron shells is equal to the period the element is in (2). The number of electrons in the outer shell is equal to the group (5).

 5 Exam-style practice **Grade 5**

The electronic configurations of four elements are:

A 2.5 **B** 2.7 **C** 2.8.8 **D** 2.8.8.1

Use the periodic table to answer these questions.
Identify which element(s), **A**, **B**, **C** or **D**:

(a) is a Group 0 gas

(b) are two elements in the same period

(c) is found in Group 1

(d) is in Period 3. **[4 marks]**

Go to page 239 to see the periodic table.

 Made a start   **Feeling confident** **Exam ready** **79**

Metals and non-metals

You need to know about the electronic configuration for the first 20 elements, reactivity and properties of metals and non-metals.

 Differences between metals and non-metals

An element can be classified as a metal or non-metal. Metals are found on the left and centre of the periodic table (**Figure 1**). There are more metal elements than non-metal elements.

- Metals lose electrons when they react, forming positive ions.
- Non-metals gain or share electrons when they react, forming negative ions or covalent compounds (page 85).

As you move down the periodic table, the number of electron shells increases. Also, the more electron shells that a metal has, the more easily it can lose electrons and react. For non-metals, the opposite is true and the more electron shells there are, the less able the element is to gain electrons. The outer electrons are further from the positive charge of the protons in the nucleus, so less energy is needed to remove them.

Go to pages 82–84 to revise ionic bonding and compounds.

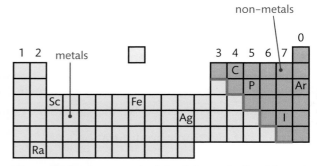

Figure 1 Metals are on the left of the periodic table and non-metals are on the right

 Worked example | **Grade 4**

1. Predict the electronic configurations of the following elements. **[3 marks]**

    (a) Magnesium (atomic number 12)

    2.8.2

    (b) Silicon (atomic number 14)

    2.8.4

    (c) Chlorine (atomic number 17)

    2.8.7

2. The atomic number of potassium is 19.

    (a) Give the electronic configuration of potassium. **[1 mark]**

    2.8.8.1

    (b) State and explain the group and period that potassium is placed in. **[2 marks]**

    Group 1 because it has one electron in its outer shell. Period 4 because it has four occupied shells.

You are expected to predict the electronic configurations for the first 20 elements in the periodic table (hydrogen to calcium).

You could be asked to show electronic configurations as diagrams or numerically, as shown in the worked example.

If the question asks for the diagram, this would be the answer.

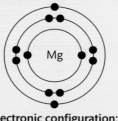

Electronic configuration: 2.8.2

 Exam-style practice | **Grade 3**

1. (a) Describe what the green zig-zag line in **Figure 1** shows. **[1 mark]**
   (b) State whether carbon (C) is a metal or a non-metal. Give a reason for your answer. **[1 mark]**

2. State and explain which element, A or B below, is a metal and which is a non-metal. Use the electronic configurations below to help you. **[3 marks]**
   Element A: 2.2
   Element B: 2.6

Chemical bonds

You need to be able to apply knowledge about the types of chemical bonds to the physical and chemical properties of substances.

(5) Types of bonding

You need to know about three types of chemical bond: ionic, covalent and metallic.

Chemical bonding occurs because atoms need a full outer shell of electrons to become stable.

Atoms can join together by **transferring** electrons (page 82) or by **sharing** electrons (page 85).

(5) Ions

An **ion** is an atom or group of atoms with a positive or negative charge. Ions form when atoms lose or gain electrons, to make a full outer shell (page 79). For example, a chlorine atom (electronic configuration 2.8.7) gains one electron to become a chloride ion, Cl^- (2.8.8), and a sodium atom (2.8.1) loses one electron to become a sodium ion, Na^+ (2.8).

(10) Comparing types of bonding

Type of bonding	ionic bonding	covalent bonding	metallic bonding
Occurs between	metals and non-metals	non-metal elements only or compounds of non-metals	metal elements only
Diagram	chloride ion (Cl^-) — sodium ion (Na^+)	H — O — H	delocalised electrons
Description of bonding	Electrostatic force of attraction between oppositely charged ions.	Shared pair of electrons between atoms.	Positive ions are surrounded by delocalised electrons.
Examples	NaCl and MgO	CO_2 and H_2O	Cu and Al

(10) Worked example — Grade 5

State and explain which type of bonding occurs in each of the following substances. **[3 marks]**

(a) Sodium chloride

Ionic bonding because sodium is a metal and chlorine is a non-metal.

(b) Magnesium metal

Metallic bonding because there are only metal atoms present.

(c) Hydrogen gas

Covalent bonding because hydrogen is a non-metal.

(5) Exam-style practice — Grade 2

(a) State the bonding found in:
  (i) sodium **[1 mark]**
  (ii) sodium chloride **[1 mark]**
  (iii) chlorine **[1 mark]**
(b) State the **two** types of bonding which involve metals. **[2 marks]**

Ionic bonding

You need to know how to describe ionic bonding and represent it using dot and cross diagrams.

Ionic bonding ✓

An ion is an atom (or group of atoms) with a positive or negative charge.

Metal atoms lose electrons to form positively-charged ions, called **cations**. Non-metal atoms gain electrons to form negatively-charged ions, or **anions**.

Positive and negative ions attract each other, forming ionic bonds.

The ions formed from the metals in Groups 1 and 2 and the non-metals in Groups 6 and 7 have the electronic configuration of a Group 0 element.

⑩ Worked example   Grade 5 ✓

Figure 1 shows the electronic configurations of sodium and fluorine.

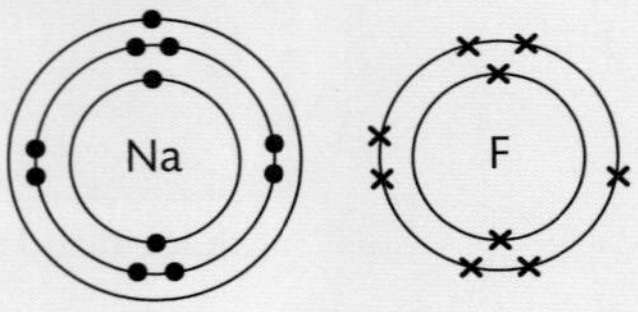

Figure 1

(a) Electrons are transferred from sodium atoms to fluorine atoms. Describe how fluorine atoms and sodium atoms form sodium fluoride.   **[2 marks]**

Sodium atoms lose one electron to form ions with a +1 charge. Fluorine atoms gain one electron to form ions with a −1 charge.

(b) Draw each of the ions formed during the reaction. Give the charge on each of the ions formed.   **[3 marks]**

sodium ion   fluoride ion

(c) Give the compound formula of sodium fluoride.   **[1 mark]**

NaF

(d) Sodium reacts in a similar way with chlorine to make sodium chloride. Chlorine has an atomic mass of 35. Determine the number of protons, neutrons and electrons in the chloride ion.   **[1 mark]**

Chloride has 17 protons, 18 electrons and 18 neutrons.

⑤ Electron transfer ✓

Ionic bonds are formed by the transfer of electrons from metal atoms to non-metal atoms, so both gain a stable arrangement of electrons. Electron transfer is represented by dot and cross diagrams.

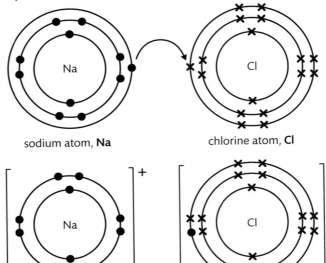

sodium atom, **Na**   chlorine atom, **Cl**

sodium ion, **Na⁺**   chloride ion, **Cl⁻**

Figure 2 The dot and cross diagrams show the formation of sodium chloride, an ionic compound. Go to page 83 to revise ionic compounds.

Fluorine is in Group 7 so it needs to gain one electron to have a full outer shell. Because a fluorine atom gains an electron the fluoride ion is negatively charged.

The outer-shell electrons are the only ones involved in chemical bonding. So, in dot and cross diagrams, we often only draw the outer-shell electrons and not the inner shell electrons.

Use the periodic table to work out the number of protons from the atomic number. Once you have this number you can use the atomic mass given in the question to determine the number of neutrons. Go to page 75 to revise calculating the number of protons, neutrons and electrons.

⑤ Exam-style practice   Grade 5 ✓

Potassium will react with fluorine to make potassium fluoride. Draw each of the ions formed during this reaction. Give the charge on each of the ions formed.   **[3 marks]**

✓ **Made a start**   ✓ **Feeling confident**   ✓ **Exam ready**

Ionic compounds

You need to be able to identify ionic compounds from different types of diagrams.

5 Giant ionic structures

Ionic compounds contain many ions, which are held together by strong electrostatic forces of attraction. Ionic compounds form giant structures called **lattices**. The **electrostatic forces of attraction** between the ions are strong due to the attraction between the oppositely charged ions.

Ionic lattices are three-dimensional structures. The forces of attraction act in all directions throughout the lattice. Ionic compounds can be represented by:

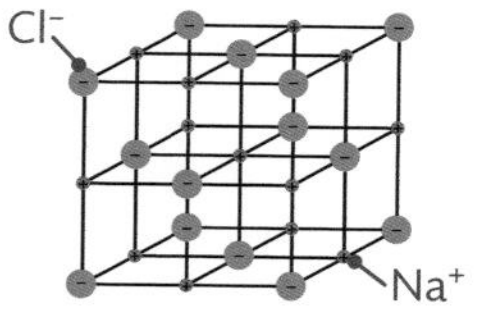

Figure 1 A ball and stick diagram

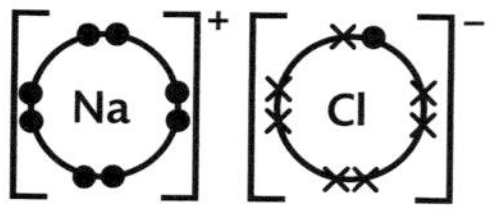

Figure 2 A dot and cross diagram

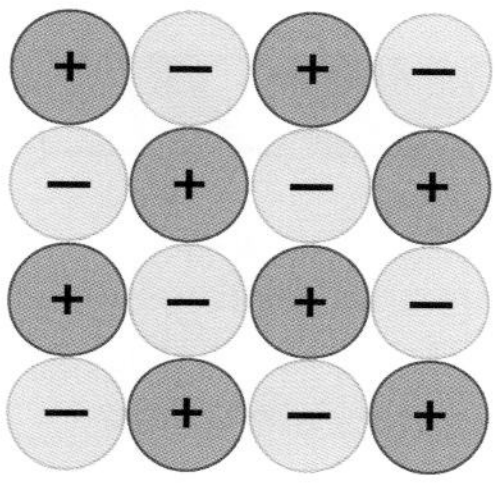

Figure 3 A two-dimensional diagram

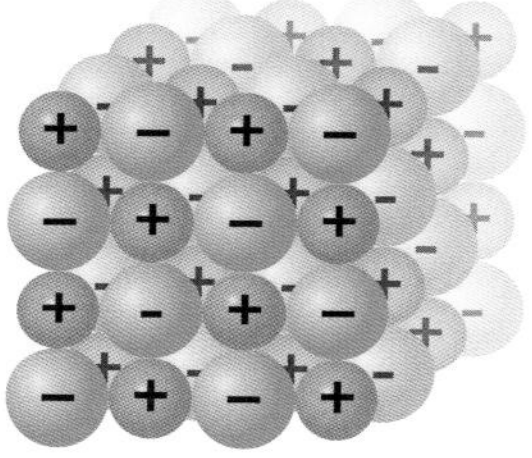

Figure 4 A three-dimensional diagram

To help you work out the ionic formula follow these steps:

1. Write the formula of the metal ion and the non-metal ion side by side. You must include the charges.

   Mg^{2+} Cl^{1-}

2. Then circle the number on the charge and cross them down to make the subscript.

   $Mg^{②+}$ ⟷ $Cl^{①-}$

3. Cancel down to get the smallest ratio. Re-write the formula without the charges and remember that if the number is 1, then you don't need to include it in the formula.

   $MgCl_2$

If an ion is made up of several atoms (such as OH^-), and there are two or more in a compound, use brackets ( ) to show that the subscript number applies to the whole ion, such as $Ca(OH)_2$.

1 Exam focus

In the exam, you could be asked to draw dot and cross diagrams for ionic compounds formed between metals in Groups 1 and 2 and non-metals in Groups 6 and 7. Make sure you know the charges on the ions formed.

10 Worked example — Grade 5

Using **Table 1**, deduce the formulae of the ionic compounds below.

Negative ions (anions)	Formula of ion	Charge
Hydroxide	OH^-	1−
Nitrate	NO_3^-	1−
Sulfate	SO_4^{2-}	2−
Carbonate	CO_3^{2-}	2−
Halide	Cl^-, Br^-, I^-	1−
Oxide	O^{2-}	2−

This charge is the charge on the ion. This will not be written in the formula of an ionic compound but must be written when the ion is being considered on its own.

Table 1

(a) Magnesium chloride **[1 mark]**

$MgCl_2$

(b) Potassium oxide **[1 mark]**

K_2O

(c) Sodium carbonate **[1 mark]**

Na_2CO_3

(d) Calcium carbonate **[1 mark]**

$CaCO_3$

10 Exam-style practice — Grades 2–5

1. State how many elements are in sodium chloride, NaCl. **[1 mark]**
2. Give the name and formula of a compound made of only potassium and bromine. **[2 marks]**
3. Describe the structure and bonding of the ionic compound sodium chloride. **[2 marks]**
4. Use **Figure 1** to answer the following questions.
   (a) State the type of bonding shown. **[1 mark]**
   (b) Give **one** limitation and **one** advantage to using this type of model. **[2 marks]**

For more on limitations of models see page 85.

Properties of ionic compounds

You can use the structure and type of bonding in an ionic compound to explain its properties.

 Properties of ionic compounds

The type of bonding in a compound affects its properties. Scientists can design new materials with tailored properties using their understanding of structure and bonding.

Structure	3D lattice structure
Melting point	high
Boiling point	high
Electrical conductivity	conducts when molten (l) or dissolved in water (aq)
Solubility in water	often soluble

> Go to pages 82 and 83 to revise ionic bonding and the structure of ionic compounds.

> Ionic compounds have high melting and boiling points because a large amount of energy is required to break the strong electrostatic forces that hold the oppositely charged ions together in all directions within the giant lattice structure.
> Go to page 99 for more about state changes.

> Ionic compounds can conduct electricity when melted (molten) or dissolved in water (aqueous) because the ions are free to move, allowing charge to flow.

 Worked example Grade 5

Figure 1 shows the structure of sodium chloride.

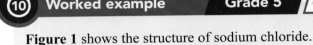

chloride ion (Cl⁻)
sodium ion (Na⁺)

Figure 1

1 (a) State the type of bonding present in sodium chloride. **[1 mark]**

Ionic bonding

(b) Describe the bonding given in part **(a)**. **[2 marks]**

Strong electrostatic forces of attraction between oppositely charged ions.

2 Explain why sodium chloride can conduct electricity when molten or in aqueous solution, but not when solid. **[2 marks]**

The ions must be free to move for sodium chloride to conduct electricity. This happens when it is liquid or dissolved in water, but not when it is solid.

3 Explain why sodium chloride has a high melting point (801 °C). **[2 marks]**

Sodium chloride is made of oppositely charged ions. These are held together by strong electrostatic forces of attraction. These forces need large amounts of energy to overcome them.

 **Exam focus**

In your exam, you may need to explain why ionic compounds have high melting points and boiling points (in terms of forces between ions), and whether or not they conduct electricity (when they are solids, molten or in aqueous solution).

 **Exam-style practice** Grade 4

1 Chlorine reacts with sodium to produce sodium chloride (NaCl).

(a) Write a word equation for the reaction. **[1 mark]**

(b) Describe the structure of sodium chloride. **[2 marks]**

2 Magnesium oxide has a similar structure to sodium chloride. Use your understanding of ionic compounds to answer the following questions about magnesium oxide.

(a) Describe the structure of magnesium oxide. You may use a diagram. **[2 marks]**

(b) Give a reason why magnesium oxide can conduct electricity when molten. **[2 marks]**

(c) Predict whether the boiling point of magnesium oxide is high or low. **[1 mark]**

Covalent bonding

You need to be able to identify and draw covalent bonds for simple molecules, polymers and giant covalent structures.

2 Models

Models are simplified versions of the world. They help to explain observations and make predictions. Molecules are 3D and are best represented in computer models which can show their shape and size. But you need to represent them in 2D on a page. So, you can use dot and cross diagrams, ball and stick diagrams and displayed formula. Each one has its benefits and drawbacks depending on what you are trying to show.

5 Forming covalent bonds

A covalent bond is a strong bond, which forms between atoms that share a pair of electrons. Covalent bonds are found in simple molecules (page 86), polymers (page 91) and giant covalent structures (page 87).

Covalent bonds form between non-metal atoms, which combine together by sharing outer-shell electrons. The shared pair of electrons holds the two atoms together. When atoms bond together in this way, they are called a molecule.

This is a dot and cross diagram. It usually shows the outer-shell electrons only as they are the particles that are involved in the bonding. This model does not show the relative shape and size of the molecule.

Only the electrons in the outermost shell can be shared.

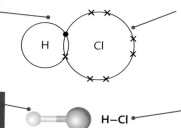

This is a ball and stick model. It shows the shape and size of the molecule but not the position of the electrons.

This is a displayed formula. It shows the atoms and the bonds in a molecule but not the shape, size or electrons.

Figure 1 The covalent bonding in hydrogen chloride can be displayed in different ways

10 Worked example   Grade 3

Methane, CH$_4$, is a hydrocarbon found in natural gas.

(a) Draw a dot and cross diagram to show the bonding in methane. **[4 marks]**

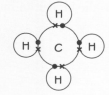

(b) Draw the displayed formula of methane. **[1 mark]**

(c) Describe the bonding and structure of methane. **[2 marks]**

Covalent bonding between the atoms in simple molecules

2 Exam focus

For the exam, you need to know how to do the following:

☑ Draw dot and cross diagrams for H$_2$, O$_2$, HCl, H$_2$O, CO$_2$ and CH$_4$.

☑ Show a single covalent bond as a line between two atoms.

☑ Describe the limitations of dot and cross, ball and stick, 2D and 3D models to represent covalent molecules.

☑ Deduce the molecular formula of a substance from a given diagram.

10 Exam-style practice   Grade 5

1 The diagram shows a water molecule. State what the lines represent. **[1 mark]**

2 The diagram shows a molecule of carbon dioxide. Determine how many bonds there are between the carbon atom and one of the oxygen atoms. **[1 mark]**

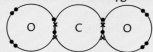

3 Draw a dot and cross diagram to show the bonding in chlorine, Cl$_2$. **[2 marks]**

Properties of simple molecular substances

Simple molecules, such as carbon dioxide and water, consist of two or three atoms bonded together. You need to use your knowledge of forces and bonding to predict the properties of simple molecular substances.

 Structure of simple molecular substances

Simple molecules, sometimes referred to as simple covalent molecules, have strong covalent bonds **within** the molecule.

Simple molecular substances have weak intermolecular forces **between** the molecules. The intermolecular forces increase with the size of the molecules, so larger molecules have stronger intermolecular forces.

Go to page 85 to revise covalent bonds.

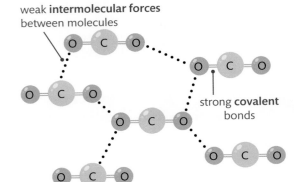

weak **intermolecular forces** between molecules

strong **covalent** bonds

Figure 1 Carbon dioxide consists of simple molecules

 Properties of simple molecular compounds

Simple molecular substances are usually liquids or gases at room temperature. When you are melting or boiling simple molecular substances **no** strong covalent bonds are broken. Only the weak intermolecular forces need to be overcome. This does not take much energy. This means that they have low melting and boiling points. Larger molecules have higher melting and boiling points because there are stronger intermolecular forces to overcome.

Simple molecular substances do not conduct electricity. There are no ions or electrons that are free to move.

Although small molecules are soluble in water, as molecules get bigger they become less soluble. So, many simple molecules are insoluble in water.

 Worked example | **Grade 5**

1 Explain why chlorine is a gas at room temperature. Use your knowledge of structure and bonding in your answer.
[3 marks]

Chlorine forms simple molecules with the formula Cl_2. When chlorine turns into a gas no strong covalent bonds are broken, just the weak forces of attraction between the molecules. This does not require a lot of energy and so the melting and boiling points are low. This means that chlorine is a gas at room temperature.

2 Figure 2 shows the structures of two alkane molecules.

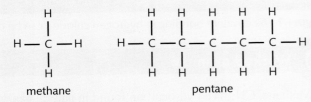

methane   pentane

Figure 2

Using ideas about intermolecular forces, explain which alkane has the higher boiling point.
[2 marks]

Intermolecular forces increase with the size of molecules. As pentane is a larger molecule it will have a higher boiling point.

The covalent bonds are not broken when a substance melts or boils; only the intermolecular forces are.

 Exam-style practice | **Grade 3**

1 (a) Give the molecular formula of hydrogen.
[1 mark]

(b) Draw a dot and cross diagram of a hydrogen molecule.
[2 marks]

2 State the type of bonding that occurs within a simple molecular compound.
[1 mark]

3 Explain, in terms of forces, what must happen for a simple molecular substance to boil.
[2 marks]

 Made a start  **Feeling confident** 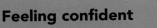 **Exam ready**

Giant covalent structures

You need to be able to recognise a giant covalent structure from a diagram that shows its structure and bonding.

 ## Two types of giant covalent structures

Giant covalent structures are covalently bonded solids that contain many atoms. The atoms form a 3D network of covalent bonds called a giant covalent structure. Examples of giant covalent structures include graphite and diamond.

Each carbon atom in graphite forms three covalent bonds. Carbon has electronic configuration 2.4, so each carbon atom in graphite has one electron that delocalises, like in a metal (page 92). Each carbon atom in diamond forms four covalent bonds.

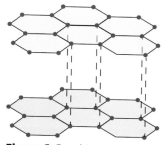

For more on the structure of graphite see page 89.

The layers can slide so graphite is slippery.
The delocalised electrons can move so graphite is a conductor of electricity.

Figure 1 Graphite

The atoms are held in place so diamond makes hard crystals.

For more on the structure of diamond see page 88.

Figure 2 Diamond

Giant covalent structures have very high melting and boiling points because a lot of energy is required to break the many strong covalent bonds. Giant covalent structures are insoluble in water.

Some giant covalent structures can conduct electricity and others cannot. As there are no mobile charged particles in diamond, it is unable to conduct electricity. Graphite contains charged particles (electrons) that can move, so it can conduct electricity.

 ## Worked example — Grade 5

Exam focus

Make sure you look at any diagrams, images or photos provided in the exam. If you're unsure of the answer to the question, a diagram can help.

Figures 1 and **2** show the structures of two forms of carbon. Using **Figures 1** and **2** and your knowledge of structure and bonding, explain why:

(a) graphite is very soft   **[2 marks]**

Graphite contains strong covalent bonds between the carbon atoms in each layer. However, between the layers there are only weak forces of attraction, so the layers can slide over each other.

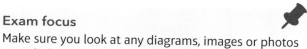
Graphite is soft as the layers can slide. This is because they are only held together by weak forces of attraction.

(b) diamond is very hard.   **[2 marks]**

The atoms in diamond are bonded together in a three-dimensional structure, so the structure is more difficult to break.

All the carbon atoms in diamond are held together by strong covalent bonds, which require a large amount of energy to break.

Exam-style practice — Grades 3–5

1 State the number of covalent bonds each carbon atom forms in graphite.   **[1 mark]**

2 State the number of covalent bonds each carbon atom forms in diamond.   **[1 mark]**

3 Name the structure found in both graphite and diamond.   **[1 mark]**

4 Give **three** properties of graphite.   **[3 marks]**

5 Suggest an explanation for why diamonds are suitable for cutting tools.   **[2 marks]**

 Made a start   **Feeling confident**   **Exam ready**

Diamond

Diamond is a rare and expensive form of carbon. You need to explain its many useful properties in terms of its structure and bonding.

⑤ Structure of diamond

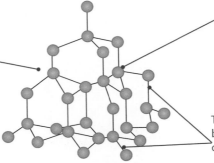

Diamond is a giant covalent structure of carbon **atoms**.

Each carbon atom is bonded to **four** other carbon atoms.

There are strong covalent bonds between each of the atoms in all different directions.

Figure 1 Structure of diamond

⑤ Properties and uses of diamond

The properties of diamond, such as high melting point, are related to its giant covalent structure. A lot of energy is required to break the strong covalent bonds between the carbon atoms in diamond.

State at room temperature	solid
Appearance at room temperature	colourless and transparent
Hardness	very hard
Melting and boiling points	very high
Electrical conductivity	does not conduct
Solubility in water	insoluble

The unique structure and properties of diamond make it suitable for many different uses. For example, it is used in **cutting tools**. Diamond is one of the hardest naturally-occurring substances. It can be used to cut a wide range of materials. Its high melting point prevents the tools from melting under the heat generated by cutting (**Figure 2**).

Figure 2 Cutting discs are coated in tiny diamonds

⑤ Worked example — Grade 5

Diamond is a hard material used for cutting tools. State the element in diamond, its structure and bonding. Use this information to explain why diamond is not used as an electrode. **[4 marks]**

Diamond is made of carbon atoms only. They are bonded covalently in a giant covalent structure. Diamond does not have any free-moving delocalised electrons or ions. This means that diamond cannot conduct electricity and so cannot be used as an electrode.

⑩ Exam-style practice — Grades 3–4

1 What type of bonding is present in diamond? **[1 mark]**

☐ **A** Ionic

☐ **B** Covalent

☐ **C** Metallic

☐ **D** Intermolecular forces of attraction

2 What is the structure of diamond? **[1 mark]**

☐ **A** Lattice

☐ **B** Metallic crystal

☐ **C** Simple molecule

☐ **D** Giant covalent structure

3 (a) Give the symbol of the element in diamond. **[1 mark]**

(b) State **three** properties of diamond. **[3 marks]**

(c) Give **one** industrial use of diamond. **[1 mark]**

4 Explain why diamond cannot be used as a lubricant. **[2 marks]**

☑ **Made a start** ☑ **Feeling confident** ☑ **Exam ready**

Graphite

Graphite is another form of carbon. It is a non-metal that can conduct electricity as it has free-moving delocalised electrons. You need to know about the structure and properties of graphite and how they relate to its many uses.

5 Structure of graphite

Graphite is made up of covalently bonded carbon **atoms**.

Each carbon atom has three covalent bonds and one delocalised electron. The delocalised electrons are anywhere in the layers of the carbon atoms.

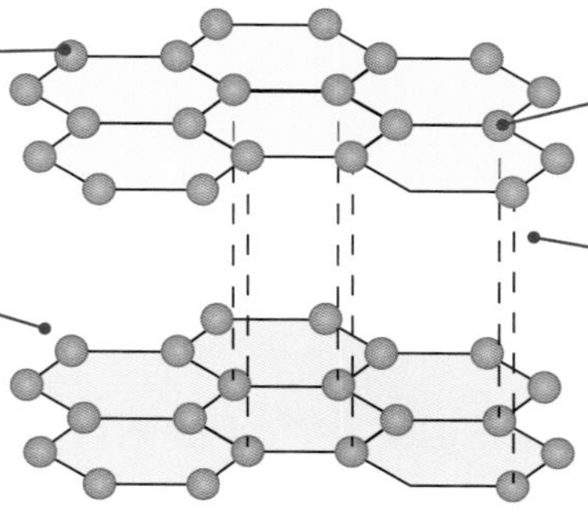

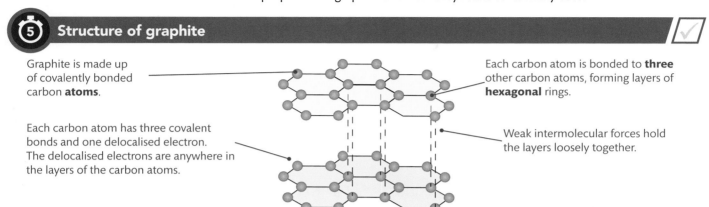

Each carbon atom is bonded to **three** other carbon atoms, forming layers of **hexagonal** rings.

Weak intermolecular forces hold the layers loosely together.

Figure 1 Structure of graphite

5 Properties and uses of graphite

Like diamond, graphite is made up of many strong covalent bonds, which require a lot of energy to be broken. This means that graphite has high melting and boiling points.

State at room temperature	solid
Appearance at room temperature	grey/black
Hardness	soft
Melting and boiling points	very high
Electrical conductivity	good conductor
Solubility in water	insoluble

Graphite is a good conductor because its delocalised electrons enable it to conduct electricity.

The structure and properties of graphite make it suitable for many different uses.

- **Pencil lead** – the forces between the layers are weak, so the layers easily slide onto paper, leaving a mark.
- **Lubricant** – graphite is slippery, which makes it a perfect dry lubricant for machine parts and metal locks.
- **Electrodes for electrolysis (and batteries)** – graphite has a high melting point and conducts electricity, making it a suitable electrode.

5 Worked example — Grade 5

1 Graphite is used in electrodes. Explain why graphite conducts electricity. Use your knowledge of its structure in your answer. **[3 marks]**

There are delocalised electrons in the structure that can move and carry the charge.

2 Explain how the structure and bonding in graphite gives it a high melting and boiling point. **[3 marks]**

Graphite has a giant covalent structure. There are many strong covalent bonds which must be overcome to separate the atoms. This would take a lot of (heat) energy.

10 Exam-style practice — Grade 5

(a) Give **two** properties that make graphite suitable for use as electrodes in electrolysis. **[2 marks]**

(b) Describe the structure and bonding of graphite. **[2 marks]**

(c) Why is graphite slippery and soft? **[1 mark]**

☐ **A** It is made of layers.

☐ **B** It is an ionic compound.

☐ **C** It is made of simple molecules.

☐ **D** It is a metal.

(d) Give **two** uses for graphite. **[2 marks]**

Graphene and fullerenes

Graphene and fullerenes are carbon structures based on covalently bonded rings of carbon atoms. You need to know about the structure and properties of graphene and fullerenes and how these relate to their uses.

 **Graphene**

Structure and properties

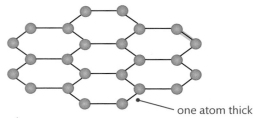

Figure 1 Graphene
one atom thick

Graphene is a single layer of graphite formed from carbon atoms, each bonded to three other carbon atoms in a hexagonal ring arrangement. Graphene is 2D and has a giant covalent structure where each carbon atom is held by covalent bonds. This arrangement gives graphene the following properties:

- good conductor of electricity (due to the delocalised electrons)
- strong (due to lots of covalent bonds to break)
- low density so it is lightweight
- flexible (only one atom thick)
- transparent (as only one atom thick).

Uses of graphene

Potential uses of graphene include: display screens, electrical circuits and solar cells. It can also be used in medical, chemical and industrial processes. Graphene is a relatively recent discovery and scientists are learning more about its uses each day.

 Worked example Grade 5

Explain, in terms of structure and bonding, the properties of Buckminsterfullerene. **[6 marks]**

Buckminsterfullerene is made of carbon atoms only. It forms a structure like a football made of 60 carbon atoms. Each atom is held in place by strong covalent bonds. The resulting simple molecule is large but only has weak forces of attraction between the molecules.

Buckminsterfullerene has lower melting and boiling points compared to larger fullerenes.

Use scientific terminology to show your understanding.

 Fullerenes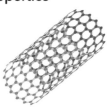

Structure and properties

Figure 2 Fullerene

Fullerenes are hollow cages or tubes made of carbon atoms. Just like in graphene, each carbon is bonded to three other carbon atoms, but unlike graphene, fullerenes have a three-dimensional structure. Cylindrical fullerenes (**carbon nanotubes**) form tubes based on hexagonal rings of carbon. These structures are giant covalent molecules where the carbon atoms are held by strong covalent bonds. Fullerenes have the following properties:

- good conductor of electricity (due to the delocalised electrons)
- high tensile strength
- high melting and boiling points (due to the high number of strong covalent bonds to break).

The first fullerene to be discovered was a sphere containing 60 carbons (named Buckminsterfullerene).

Buckminsterfullerene is held together by strong covalent bonds with a simple molecular structure.

Figure 3 Buckminsterfullerene C_{60}

Uses of fullerenes

Fullerenes are useful for nanotechnology, electronics and in drug delivery systems for fighting cancers. Tube fullerenes (nanotubes) are used for reinforcing structures, for example tennis racket frames, as they are very lightweight but very strong.

 **Exam-style practice** Grade 4

1. Name the element common to diamond, graphite, fullerenes and graphene. **[1 mark]**
2. Compare and contrast the structures of graphene and carbon nanotubes. **[3 marks]**

 Made a start **Feeling confident** **Exam ready**

Polymers

You need to know that simple polymers consist of large molecules containing chains of carbon atoms, and to be able to describe their structure and bonding.

10 Polymers

Polymers are very large molecules. The atoms in a polymer molecule are joined together by strong covalent bonds in long chains. There are variable numbers of atoms in the chains of a particular polymer. One example of a polymer is poly(ethene).

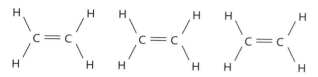

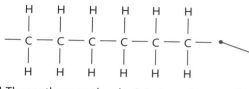

Figure 1 Three ethene molecules join to make part of a poly(ethene) molecule

> Go to page 85 for more about covalent bonds.

The intermolecular forces between the large surfaces of polymer molecules are strong compared with the intermolecular forces between small molecules, so polymers melt at higher temperatures. Polymers are solids at room temperature.

> Polymers have fairly high melting points due to the intermolecular forces between their large molecules.

Repeat units

Polymer molecules consist of lots of identical, repeat units in a chain.

The word poly means 'many' so poly(ethene) is made from many ethene molecules joined together.

Figure 2 Ethene and the repeat unit of poly(ethene)

> The line is a strong covalent bond. This shows that polymers make giant covalent molecules. The strong covalent bonds mean that the polymer is not biodegradeable as a lot of energy is needed to break the bonds.

Figure 3 Uses of poly(ethene)

5 Worked example — Grade 3

Poly(ethene) is an example of a polymer.

(a) State the bonding present in poly(ethene).
[1 mark]

Covalent bonding

(b) Give the structure of poly(ethene). [1 mark]

Giant covalent molecule

(c) Explain why poly(ethene) is flexible. [1 mark]

The polymer chains can slide over each other.

5 Exam-style practice — Grade 5

1. Describe the bonding that joins the atoms together in a polymer molecule. **[3 marks]**

2. Give the symbol of the main element that forms polymer chains. **[1 mark]**

3. Explain why poly(ethene) does not conduct electricity. **[2 marks]**

Metals

Metals have very strong bonds due to the presence of free-moving delocalised electrons. You need to be able to recall the structure and arrangement of metal particles. You also need to be able to describe the properties of metals.

⑤ Structure of metals

Most metals have one, two or three electrons in their outer shell. These electrons are said to be 'delocalised', which means they are not in fixed positions but instead are free to move throughout the metal structure. As the electrons can move, they are shared within the structure, giving rise to strong metallic bonds. The metallic bonds are formed from the strong attraction between positively-charged nuclei and the negatively-charged electrons.

Layers of ions can slide easily over each other and so metals are flexible (malleable) and can be drawn into wires (ductile).

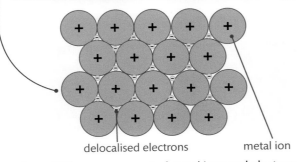

delocalised electrons   metal ion

Figure 1 The arrangement of metal ions and electrons in metallic bonding

⑩ Worked example   Grades 3–5

❶ Describe the structure of a solid metal. **[6 marks]**

Positively-charged metal ions in a regular arrangement. The ions are touching and vibrating but not flowing. Between the ions are free-moving delocalised, negatively-charged electrons.

❷ Give **two** properties of metals.   **[2 marks]**

Metals are good conductors of electricity and they are ductile.

❸ A blacksmith hammers iron into different shapes. Explain why iron is malleable.   **[3 marks]**

Metals such as iron are malleable because their atoms are in layers which can slide easily over each other; this makes them easy to bend and shape.

Metals often have high density, and high melting and boiling points. But there are exceptions. For example, the Group 1 metals have low density, so the first three float on water. Also, mercury has a low melting point and is a liquid at room temperature, whereas most metals are solids.

⑤ Properties of metals

Metals form giant structures called lattices. The particles are held in layers by strong metallic bonds. There are free-moving delocalised electrons around all the particles.

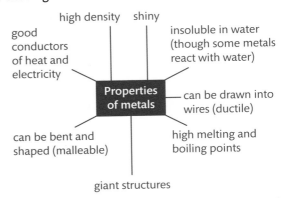

When we compare properties of metals to non-metals we find that they are opposite to each other.
Most non-metals have low boiling points and are poor conductors of electricity (insulators).

⑤ Metals as conductors

Metals are good conductors of electricity because they have delocalised electrons within their metallic structure. This model for the structure of a metal can be used to explain the difference in conductivity of metals. Often, the more electrons available in the outer shell, the better the conductivity. This is because there are more delocalised electrons available to carry the charge.

Remember, it is only the electrons in the outer shell that are free to move throughout the metallic structure.

⑩ Exam-style practice   Grades 4–5

❶ Which of these statements best describes metallic bonding?   **[1 mark]**

- [ ] **A** transfer of electrons
- [ ] **B** sharing electrons
- [ ] **C** attraction of positive nuclei and electrons
- [ ] **D** atoms form hexagonal rings

❷ Give the term used to describe materials that allow energy transfer to take place within the material.   **[1 mark]**

❸ Explain why metals have high melting and boiling points.   **[2 marks]**

 Made a start   **Feeling confident**   **Exam ready**

Relative formula mass

The relative formula mass of a compound is found by adding together the relative atomic masses of all the atoms in the compound.

(5) Relative formula mass

The **relative formula mass** (M_r) is the sum of the relative atomic masses (A_r) of all the atoms in the formula of a substance. The relative atomic mass can be found on the periodic table. For example, to find the M_r of sodium hydroxide (NaOH), you add together the A_r values of all the atoms in its formula:

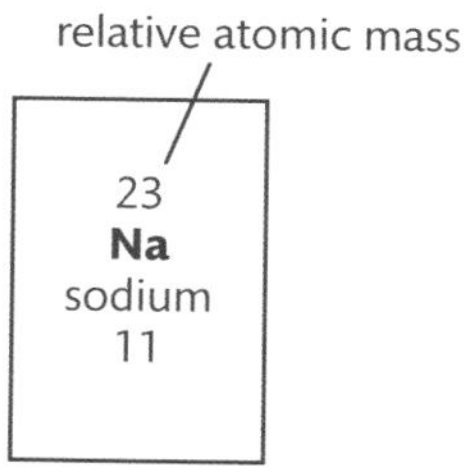

A_r of Na is 23

A_r of O is 16

A_r of H is 1

so the M_r of NaOH is 23 + 16 + 1 = 40.

relative atomic mass

23
Na
sodium
11

In a balanced chemical equation, the sum of the M_r of the reactants is equal to the sum of the M_r of the products. You can even calculate a relative formula mass for an ionic compound. For this, use the smallest whole number ratio of the ions, which is actually the formula used in balanced symbol equations.

Go to page 76 to revise relative atomic mass.

(10) Worked example — Grades 3–4

1 Use the periodic table to find the relative atomic mass for sodium, Li. **[1 mark]**

7

2 Calculate the relative formula mass for calcium hydroxide, Ca(OH)$_2$. (A_r values: H = 1; O = 16 and Ca = 40) **[2 marks]**

Ca(OH)$_2$ is made of one atom of calcium and two atoms of oxygen and two atoms of hydrogen.

So, the relative formula mass = 40 + 2 × (16 + 1)
= 74

3 Calculate the relative formula mass of hydrogen chloride, HCl. (A_r values: H = 1; Cl = 35.5) **[2 marks]**

HCl = H + Cl
= 1 + 35.5
= 36.5

4 Calculate the relative formula mass of water (H$_2$O). (A_r values: H = 1; O = 16) **[2 marks]**

H$_2$O = (2 × H) + O
= (2 × 1) + 16
= 18

The relative formula mass has no units.

The brackets mean two lots of the atoms in the bracket. This is because the calcium ion has a +2 charge and there needs to be two hydroxide ions (OH$^-$) to balance the charge in the compound.

Calcium hydroxide solution is better known as limewater. It goes from colourless to cloudy when it comes into contact with carbon dioxide gas. So, limewater is used as a chemical test for carbon dioxide. See page 107 for more information.

You can also look at the periodic table to find the relative atomic mass of each atom.

(10) Exam-style practice — Grade 4

1 **Figure 1** represents a molecule of methane.
(a) State how many of each type of atom is present in methane. **[1 mark]**
(b) Calculate the relative formula mass of methane.
(A_r values: C = 12; H = 1) **[2 marks]**

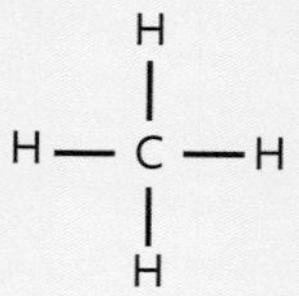

Figure 1

2 Calculate the relative formula mass of carbon dioxide, CO$_2$.
(A_r values: C = 12; O = 16) **[2 marks]**

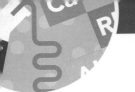

Empirical formulae

You need to be able to work out (deduce) the empirical formula of a compound from its molecular formula, and work out the molecular formula of a compound from its empirical formula and relative molecular mass.

5 Formulae

Atoms of different elements combine, in specific ratios, to form compounds.

The empirical formula gives the simplest whole-number ratio of atoms in an element or compound.

The molecular formula of a compound gives the numbers of each atom present in one molecule of the compound.

Experimental data can be used to identify the empirical formula of a compound.

Both of these numbers can be divided by 6. This will give the smallest whole-number ratio and so the empirical formula.

10 Worked example — Grade 5

1. A hydrocarbon has a molecular formula of C_6H_6. Determine the empirical formula. **[1 mark]**

CH

2. A compound has a molecular formula of $C_{12}H_{16}O_8$. Deduce its empirical formula. **[1 mark]**

$C_3H_4O_2$

3. The relative molecular mass of a compound is 84 and the empirical formula is CH_2. Calculate the molecular formula of the compound. **[3 marks]**

Carbon = 12; hydrogen = 1

so $CH_2 = 12 + 2 = 14$

$\frac{84}{14} = 6$

The molecular formula is C_6H_{12}

4. A compound contains 40 g carbon, 6.72 g hydrogen and 53.28 g of oxygen. Calculate the empirical formula of the compound. **[3 marks]**

	C	H	O
Mass	40	6.72	53.28
Divide by A_r	/12	/1	/16
Ratio	= 3.33	= 6.72	= 3.33
Divide by smallest	/3.33	/3.33	/3.33
	= 1	= 2	= 1

Empirical formula = CH_2O

5 Experimental determination of empirical formula

1. Using a top pan balance, take the mass of an empty crucible and lid. Add a 5 cm length piece of magnesium ribbon and reweigh.
2. Set up the equipment as shown in **Figure 1**.
3. Heat the crucible strongly. Using tongs, lift the lid occasionally to allow more oxygen to react with the magnesium. Do not look directly at the reacting magnesium. It makes a very bright light that can damage your eyesight.
4. Lift the lid again slightly. If the magnesium does not begin to glow brighter, then the reaction is complete. Turn off the heat and allow the crucible, its contents and the lid to cool.
5. Reweigh the crucible. Calculate the increase in mass of the crucible.

The increase in mass of the crucible is due to oxygen combining with the magnesium to make magnesium oxide. The equations for this reaction are:

magnesium + oxygen → magnesium oxide

$2Mg(s) + O_2(g) \rightarrow 2MgO(s)$

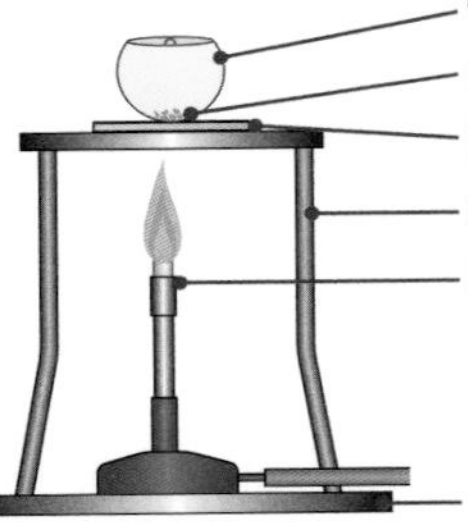
crucible
magnesium
pipe-clay triangle
tripod
Bunsen burner
heat-resistant mat

Figure 1 Apparatus for heating magnesium

Each number (of atoms) is divided by the highest common factor, 4, to give the simplest whole-number ratio of atoms.

To calculate the molecular formula, first work out the mass of the atoms in the empirical formula.

Next, divide the relative molecular mass by the empirical mass. Here, this gives 6.

So the molecular formula is the empirical formula × 6.

The empirical formula of a compound shows the smallest whole-number ratio of atoms in the compound.

To get a whole-number ratio.

To calculate the empirical formula, first divide the mass of the element by the relative atomic mass (A_r, from the periodic table) to find the ratio.

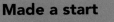

Balancing equations

You need to be able to balance a chemical equation given the masses of reactants and products, using the law of conservation of mass.

5 Balancing equations

Chemical reactions can be represented by balanced chemical equations. In a balanced chemical equation, there must always be the same number of each type of atom on either side of the arrow. This is because no atoms are lost or made in a chemical reaction.

Chemical equations can only be balanced by putting numbers in front of the formulae of elements or compounds. So, $2H_2O$ means two molecules of H_2O (water, **Figure 1**). You cannot change the formulae of elements or compounds to balance an equation.

If you tried to balance an equation by adding a 2 to the end of the formula, you would end up with a new substance – hydrogen peroxide H_2O_2 (**Figure 2**).

Water is a compound that makes up about 70% of the human body but hydrogen peroxide is a bleach! So, the position of the 2 really matters.

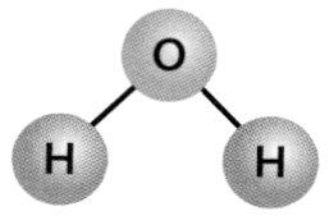

Figure 1 H_2O is a molecule with one oxygen and two hydrogens

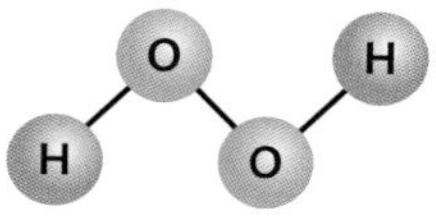

Figure 2 Hydrogen peroxide, H_2O_2

5 Worked example — Grade 5

Balance the following equations.

(a) $CH_4 + 2O_2 \rightarrow CO_2 + 2H_2O$ **[1 mark]**

Carbon: 1 → 1 ✓
Oxygen: 2 → 3 ✗
Hydrogen: 4 → 2 ✗

(b) $2Na + 2H_2O \rightarrow 2NaOH + H_2$ **[1 mark]**

Sodium: 1 → 1 ✓
Hydrogen: 2 → 3 ✗
Oxygen: 1 → 1 ✓

Balanced chemical equations show that there are the same number and type of atom on each side of the equation, they have just re-arranged.

Work out how many atoms of each element are present on each side of the equation. You need to have the same total number of each type of atom in front of the arrow as there are after the arrow.

Adding a 2 before H_2O balances the hydrogen atoms. There are now 4 oxygen atoms on the right side of the reaction and 2 on the left. Adding a 2 before O_2 then balances the oxygen atoms.

Adding a 2 in front of Na, H_2O and NaOH balances the hydrogen and oxygen atoms. There are now two sodium atoms on the left and right sides of the reaction, four hydrogen atoms on both sides and two oxygen atoms on both sides.

2 State symbols

You can add state symbols to show whether a chemical is a solid (s), liquid (l), gas (g) or dissolved in water (aq).

State symbols are only written in balanced chemical equations and they are lower case in brackets after the formula of the chemical.

10 Exam-style practice — Grade 5

1. Carbon (C) can react with oxygen (O_2) to make carbon monoxide (CO).
   (a) Write a word equation for this reaction. **[1 mark]**
   (b) Write a balanced chemical equation for this reaction. **[2 marks]**
2. Give **one** reason why a balanced equation is more useful than a word equation for describing a reaction. **[1 mark]**
3. Give a reason why chemical equations should always balance. **[1 mark]**
4. Balance the following chemical equation:
   $Na + O_2 \rightarrow Na_2O$ **[1 mark]**

Conservation of mass

A closed system does not allow substances to get in and out. But it will let energy transfer between the system and the surroundings. So, in a closed system, the mass of the products equals the mass of the reactants. Some chemical reactions seem to involve a change in mass. This is usually because one of the reactants or products is a gas.

(5) Change in mass

In a non-enclosed system, substances can get in and out, and energy can transfer between the system and its surroundings. The mass will appear to change if a gas is a reactant or product because:

1. A gaseous product escapes while the reaction takes place. The product mass will be lower than the reactant mass.

2. Gases from the air enter a reaction. They have not been measured with the reactants so the mass will appear to increase.

Change in mass can be calculated using the law of conservation of mass (page 97). For example, after heating 6.2 g of copper carbonate (**Figure 1**), the product (copper oxide) has a mass of 4 g. This means that 2.2 g of gas was produced and lost to the air during the reaction.

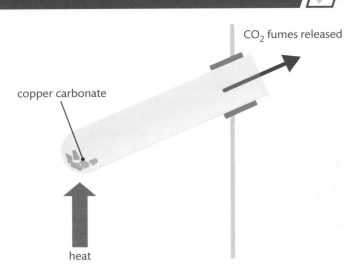

CO$_2$ fumes released

copper carbonate

heat

Figure 1 Heating copper carbonate will cause it to decompose and release carbon dioxide. If the gas is not collected, there will appear to be a loss of mass during the reaction.

When a substance undergoes thermal decomposition, the mass of the products may appear to have decreased as the gas produced can escape, leaving only the metal oxide as the product.

(5) Worked example   Grade 5

For each of the following reactions, explain how and why the mass may appear to change during each reaction.

(a) magnesium + oxygen → magnesium oxide **[2 marks]**

The mass appears to increase because oxygen from the air is gained by the magnesium in the reaction to form the product, magnesium oxide.

(b) calcium + hydrochloric → calcium + hydrogen
         acid   chloride   **[2 marks]**

The mass appears to decrease because hydrogen gas is given off in the reaction and lost to the air.

When a metal is heated, it may react with oxygen from the air. The mass of the magnesium oxide will be greater than the mass of just the magnesium.

Think about the conditions required for the law of conservation of mass (page 97).

(10) Exam-style practice   Grade 5

1. When heated, zinc carbonate thermally decomposes to produce zinc oxide and carbon dioxide.

   (a) Write the word equation for this reaction. **[1 mark]**

   (b) A student decomposed 50 g of zinc carbonate in an unsealed container. After the reaction, there was only 32 g of product. Give a reason why. **[1 mark]**

   (c) Suggest what would happen to the mass if the reaction took place in a closed system. **[1 mark]**

2. When ethanol, C$_2$H$_5$OH, burns it reacts with oxygen from the air to produce carbon dioxide and water. Balance the chemical equation. **[1 mark]**

   C$_2$H$_5$OH + _____ O$_2$ → _____ CO$_2$ + _____ H$_2$O

 Made a start   Feeling confident   Exam ready

Calculating masses in reactions

The law of conservation of mass lets scientists make predictions about chemical reactions.

(10) Conservation of mass and balanced chemical equations

The law of conservation of mass states that in a closed system, the mass of the products equals the mass of the reactants. This means that no atoms are lost or made during a chemical reaction – only their arrangement changes. For example, hydrogen and oxygen react to form water (**Figure 1**). The total number of hydrogen and oxygen atoms is unchanged in the reaction. There are four hydrogen atoms and two oxygen atoms before the arrow (reactants) and after the arrow (products).

For mass to be conserved the reaction must take place in a **closed system** where none of the reactants or products can escape.

You can write the law as an equation and use it to find missing masses in chemical reactions:

mass of A + mass of B → mass of AB

total mass of reactants = total mass of products

The law of conservation of mass applies to changes of state (page 99). This includes precipitation, when a solid product settles out of liquid reactants, and sublimation. **Sublimation** is the process by which a solid turns directly into a gas.

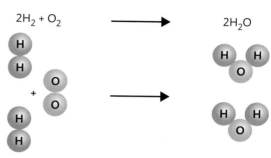

Figure 1 Hydrogen reacts with oxygen to form water in a balanced chemical equation

(10) Worked example | Grade 3

1 112 g of iron reacts with oxygen to produce 160 g of iron oxide. Calculate the mass of oxygen used in this reaction. **[2 marks]**

iron + oxygen → iron oxide

112 g + ? = 160 g

mass of oxygen = 160 − 112 = 48 g

2 Magnesium and chlorine react to produce magnesium chloride in the following reaction.

$Mg + Cl_2 \rightarrow MgCl_2$

Show that mass is conserved in this reaction.

(Atomic masses: Mg = 12; Cl = 35.5) **[3 marks]**

$Mg + Cl_2 \rightarrow MgCl_2$

24 + (2 × 35.5) → 24 + (2 × 35.5)

95 → 95

Total mass of the atoms on both sides of the equation is 95, so mass is conserved.

Exam focus

In the exam, you may need to use the law of conservation of mass to work out the unknown mass of a substance in a reaction.

1. Write the word equation for the reaction.
2. Write the masses provided in the question under the correct substances.
3. Rearrange the masses to calculate the missing substance. Don't forget to include units in your answer.

Conservation of mass can be shown by adding up the relative atomic mass (see pages 76 and 93) of each of the atoms on either side of a balanced chemical equation.

The total mass of the atoms on the left-hand side (the reactants) will always equal the total mass of the atoms on the right-hand side in a balanced equation.

(10) Exam-style practice | Grades 3–4

1 When iodine is heated, it sublimes (changes from the solid state to the gas state). If 50 g of iodine is heated, state the mass of the iodine vapour produced. **[1 mark]**

2 When heated, magnesium carbonate thermally decomposes, producing magnesium oxide and carbon dioxide.

   (a) Write a word equation for this reaction. **[1 mark]**

   (b) If 84 g of magnesium carbonate is used and 40 g of magnesium oxide is produced, calculate the mass of carbon dioxide produced in the reaction. **[2 marks]**

 Made a start 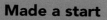 **Feeling confident** **Exam ready**

Concentrations of solutions

Many chemical reactions take place in solution. The concentration of a solution depends on the mass of solute and the volume of solution.

5 Calculating concentrations

A solution is made by dissolving a solute (usually a solid) in a solvent (usually a liquid). The concentration of a solution is how much solute is dissolved into the solvent.

Concentration can be calculated using the formula given below:

$$\text{concentration (g dm}^{-3}) = \frac{\text{mass (g)}}{\text{volume (dm}^3)} \qquad c = \frac{m}{v}$$

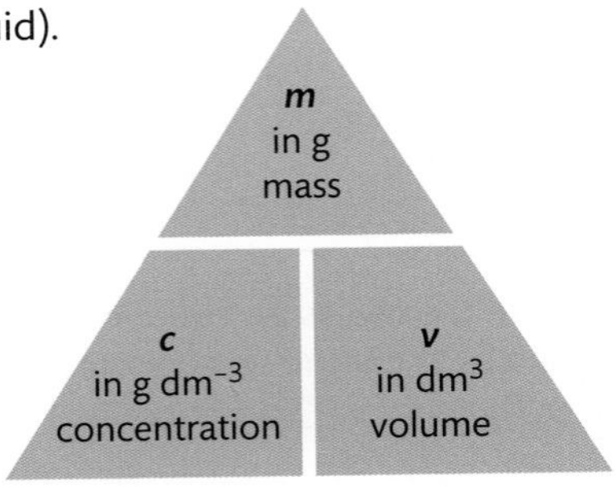

To find the mass of solute, you need to rearrange the formula:

mass (g) = concentration (g dm^{-3}) × volume (dm^3)

If the mass of solute is increased but the volume of solvent stays the same, the concentration of the solution will increase.

If the volume of solvent is increased but the mass of solute stays the same, the concentration of the solution will decrease.

10 Worked example — Grades 3–4

1 Calculate the mass of solute needed to be dissolved in 1.5 dm^3 of a solvent to produce a concentration of 3 g dm^{-3}. **[3 marks]**

mass = concentration × volume

= 3 × 1.5 = 4.5 g

Use the formula triangle to rearrange the calculation for mass.

2 58 g of sodium hydroxide was dissolved in water. Calculate the volume of solution used to produce a concentration of 16.11 g dm^{-3}. **[3 marks]**

$v = \frac{m}{c} = \frac{58}{16.11} = 3.6\ dm^3$

You can use the units as a clue to work out the formula. The units of concentration are g dm^{-3}. This tells you that concentration = mass ÷ volume.

3 Calculate the concentration of a 125 cm^3 sodium hydroxide solution (NaOH), made from 2 g of sodium hydroxide. **[3 marks]**

$\frac{125}{1000} = 0.125\ dm^3$

You need to divide by 1000 to change the units from cm^3 to dm^3.

$\frac{m}{v} = c$

$\frac{2}{0.125} = 16\ g\ dm^{-3}$

Remember to give the correct units.

2 Maths skills

You need to know how to convert units from cm^3 to dm^3 and vice versa.

1 dm^3 = 1000 cm^3 (multiply by 1000)

1 cm^3 = 0.001 dm^3 (divide by 1000)

10 Exam-style practice — Grade 4

1 A student dissolves 60 g of sodium chloride into 1500 cm^3 of water.

(a) Give 1500 cm^3 in dm^3. **[1 mark]**

(b) Use your answer to part **(a)** to calculate the concentration of the solution of sodium chloride in g dm^{-3}. **[2 marks]**

2 Calculate the mass of calcium chloride needed to produce a solution with a concentration of 10 g dm^{-3} when dissolved into 5 dm^3 of water. **[3 marks]**

States of matter

You need to be able to predict the states of substances at different temperatures and explain changes of state using the particle model.

(10) Changing state

The three states of matter, solid, liquid and gas, can be represented by the **particle model**. This simple model shows the changes (interconversions) that occur when energy is supplied or removed from the particles. When the substances are heated the energy can overcome the forces **between** the particles. The density, arrangement and movement of particles change when a substance changes state.

Particles in a substance **gain energy** when the substance turns from a solid to a liquid (**melting**) or from a liquid to a gas (**boiling or evaporating**).

- The distance between particles increases.
- Some of the forces between the particles are overcome.
- The particles have more energy so move faster.

Particles in a substance **lose energy** when the substance turns from a gas to a liquid (**condensing**) and from a liquid to a solid (**freezing**).

- The distance between particles decreases.
- The forces between the particles pull them closer.
- The particles have less energy so move more slowly.

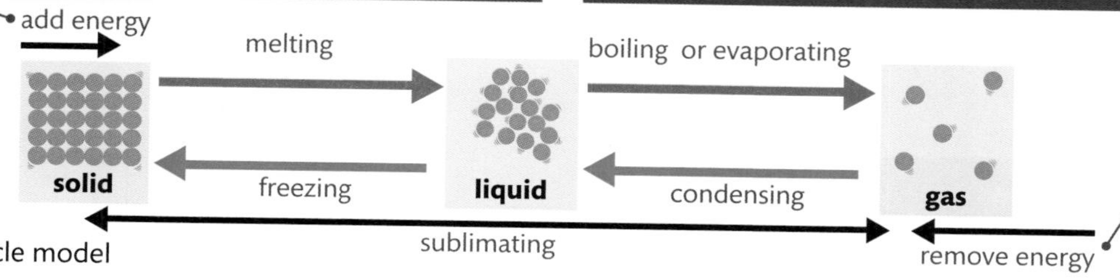

Figure 1 The particle model

The amount of energy needed to change state from a solid to a liquid and from a liquid to a gas varies. The energy must be great enough to overcome the forces of attraction **between** the particles. The strength of the forces varies according to the type of bonding and structure of the substance. The stronger the forces between the particles, the higher the **melting point** and **boiling point** of the substance.

(2) Physical and chemical change

Physical changes do not affect the chemical composition of a substance. Changing the state of matter, for example freezing a liquid into a solid, is an example of a physical change. No new substances have been made. In a chemical change, a new substance is formed.

(5) Worked example — Grade 5

Explain, in terms of particles and energy, how a liquid evaporates. **[3 marks]**

The particles in a liquid have different energies. An increase in energy causes the forces of attraction between some particles to break. These particles will escape from the surface of the liquid and form a gas.

(2) State symbols

Symbols are used in a chemical equation to represent states of matter:

- (s) for solids, e.g. ice
- (l) for liquids, e.g. water
- (g) for gases, e.g. steam
- (aq) for aqueous solutions, e.g. NaCl in water.

For example:

$2Na(s) + 2H_2O(l) \rightarrow 2NaOH(aq) + H_2(g)$

Go to page 95 for more about state symbols.

(5) Exam-style practice — Grade 5

1. Look at the table. For each of the compounds, identify whether they are a solid, liquid or gas at room temperature (25 °C). **[3 marks]**
2. Predict the state of LiCl at 900 °C. **[1 mark]**

Compound	Melting point (°C)	Boiling point (°C)
LiCl	610	1382
CCl_4	−23	77
OCl_2	−20	4

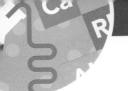

Pure substances

You need to be able to tell the difference between pure and impure substances using melting and boiling points.

5 What is a pure substance?

In everyday language, a pure substance is a substance that has had nothing added to it, for example, pure milk. In chemistry, pure means a substance that contains only one type of particle. For example, pure water has only water molecules in it.

Mixtures are more than one substance not chemically joined. So, impure substances are mixtures. Mixtures can be separated by physical means, such as filtering. Pure substances cannot be separated by physical methods, such as filtration. Impurities in a substance will affect its properties. The values for melting point, boiling point and density obtained for a sample can be compared with data to identify its purity.

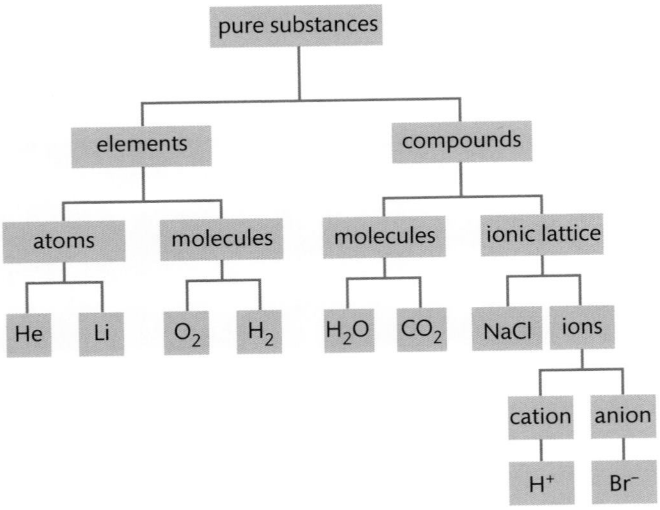

Figure 1 Examples of pure substances

10 Worked example — Grade 5

The table shows the boiling points of three samples of water.

Sample	Boiling point (°C)
A	98–99
B	100
C	101–104

(a) Use the table to determine which of the samples is pure and which is a mixture. **[3 marks]**

A and C are mixtures and B is pure.

(b) State and explain which sample is pure water. **[2 marks]**

Sample B is pure water because it boils at 100 °C, which is the boiling point of water.

(c) It is important that medicines are as pure as possible to reduce the chance of side effects. Explain **one** method that could be used to check the purity of a medicine. **[6 marks]**

Measure the melting point of a sample and compare it to the known melting point of the medicine. If it is the same, then it is pure. If the melting point is a range near to this value, then it is a mixture containing the medicine. The bigger the range the more impure the sample.

Other possible methods involve measuring the boiling point or the density, and then comparing them with known data. You could also use chromatography to see how many substances are present. See page 102 for more on chromatography.

1 Working scientifically

Melting point apparatus can be used to investigate the purity of a sample. The sample is heated along with a thermometer until it begins to melt. The temperature range over which it melts is recorded. The narrower the temperature range the more pure the sample is likely to be.

If a substance is pure, every sample of that substance will have the same properties, including:

- melting point
- boiling point
- density.

10 Exam-style practice — Grade 3

The melting point of pure water is 0 °C and the boiling point is 100 °C.

(a) Give the definition of the term 'melting point'. **[2 marks]**

(b) Ice on the road can be melted by adding salt. Explain whether adding ice to water increases or decreases the melting point. **[2 marks]**

(c) Describe the effect on the boiling point of water if salt is added to the water. **[2 marks]**

Look at the table in the Worked example.

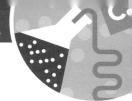

Mixtures

You need to know the different types of mixtures and how they can be separated using physical methods.

10 Separating mixtures

A mixture contains two or more substances that are not chemically joined together, which means they can be separated by physical methods. The chemical properties of the substances in the mixture are unchanged as they haven't reacted with each other.

- **Filtration** separates an insoluble solid from a liquid. A mixture is passed through filter paper in a filter funnel. The liquid (filtrate) can pass through the gaps in the filter paper but the solid (residue) cannot.
- **Simple distillation** separates a solvent from a solution. A mixture is heated and the liquid evaporates, condenses and is collected.
- **Fractional distillation** separates a mixture of liquids. It is covered in more detail on page 138.
- **Crystallisation** separates a soluble solid from a liquid. A mixture is heated until the solvent evaporates, leaving a crystallised solid behind.
- **Paper chromatography** separates a mixture of several liquids. It is covered in more detail on page 102.

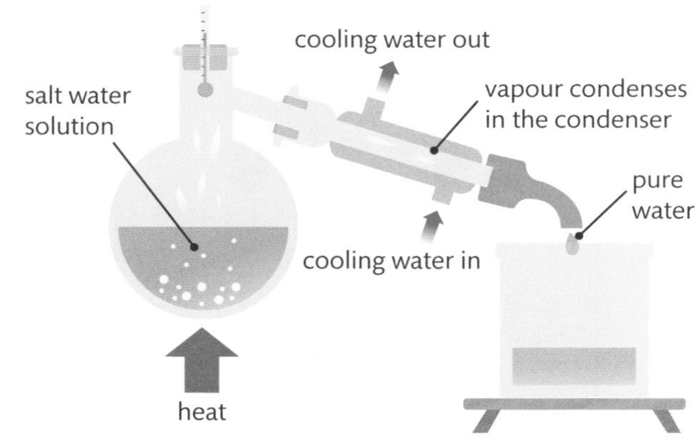

Figure 1 Simple distillation

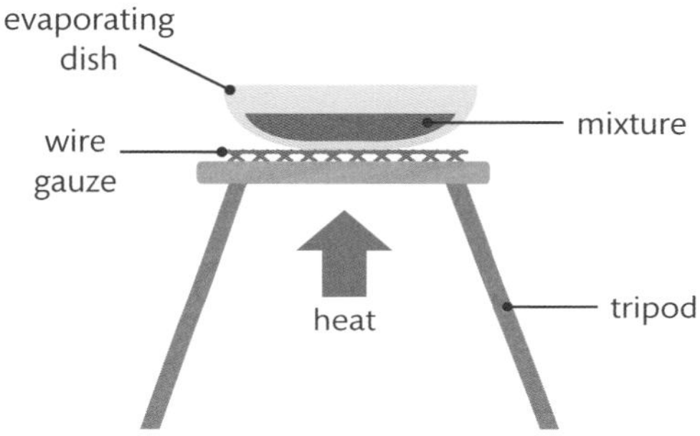

Figure 2 Crystallisation

5 Worked example — Grade 5

A student is given a mixture containing a liquid that evaporates at 65 °C, a soluble solid and a second liquid that evaporates at 98 °C. Describe the steps the student should follow to separate the soluble solid. **[4 marks]**

Step 1: The two liquids can be separated by fractional distillation. The liquid with a boiling point of 65 °C will evaporate first and be collected in the beaker.

Step 2: The remaining mixture should be heated in an evaporating dish to evaporate the liquid that boils at 98 °C. It is then left to cool to allow crystals to form.

10 Exam-style practice — Grade 4

1 Draw one straight line from each mixture to its method of separation. **[3 marks]**

mixture	**separation method**
sugar and water	filtration
ink and water	simple distillation
sand and water	crystallisation

2 Name the apparatus labelled **W**, **X** and **Y** in **Figure 3**. **[3 marks]**

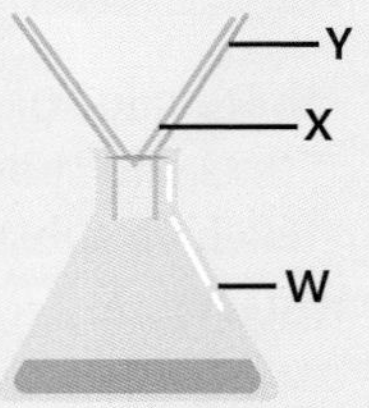

Figure 3

Chromatography

Chromatography is a technique used to separate the parts of a mixture so they can be identified. You need to understand how chromatography works and be able to calculate R_f values using chromatograms.

 ## Paper chromatography

Chromatography is usually used to separate coloured substances, such as inks, food colourings and dyes. Chromatography is important in the manufacturing of pharmaceutical drugs. The process can be used to assess the purity of drugs and medicines, enabling scientists to reduce the risk of unnecessary side effects. Go to page 103 to revise how to set up chromatography apparatus to produce a chromatogram.

Paper chromatography involves two phases:

- A **stationary phase**, which is contained in the paper and does not move.
- A **mobile phase**, which moves through the stationary phase and carries the dissolved components of the mixture.

The different dissolved components of the mixture travel at different rates through the paper.

R_f values

The **R_f value** is the ratio of the distance moved by a substance (from the centre of its spot on the base line) to the distance moved by the solvent.

The R_f value of a particular substance will always be the same if the same type of chromatography paper and solvent are used. This means that R_f values can be used to identify unknown substances.

The more soluble a substance, the further it will travel up the chromatography paper and the higher the R_f value will be.

Mixtures separate into several spots in different positions on the chromatogram.

Pure compounds produce a single spot on the chromatogram.

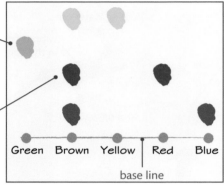

Figure 1 A chromatogram of different food colourants

Maths skills

R_f values can be worked out using the formula:

$$R_f = \frac{\text{distance moved by substance}}{\text{distance moved by solvent}}$$

In paper chromatography:

- a pencil is used to draw the base line because ink may run into and interfere with the chromatogram
- the base line should sit above the solvent level so that the substance does not dissolve in the solvent
- if the solvent or samples are harmful, wear eye protection.

 ## Worked example   Grade 5

Substance **X** travels 78 mm from the base line while the solvent travels 150 mm.

(a) Calculate the R_f value for this substance. Give your answer to two significant figures. **[3 marks]**

$$R_f = \frac{78}{150}$$

$$R_f = 0.52$$

(b) Substance **A** has an R_f value of 0.49, substance **B** has an R_f value of 0.52 and substance **C** has an R_f value of 0.76. State which substance is the same as the original substance, **X**. **[1 mark]**

B

 ## Exam-style practice   Grade 3

A scientist uses a separation technique to investigate the colours in food colourants. **Figure 1** shows the results.

(a) State the name of the separation technique. **[1 mark]**

(b) State the number and type of colours found in the brown food colouring. **[3 marks]**

(c) Give the definition of the term 'R_f value'. **[2 marks]**

 Made a start   Feeling confident   Exam ready

Practical: Investigating inks

The aim of this practical is to find out the composition of inks, using paper chromatography and simple distillation.

⏱ Paper chromatography

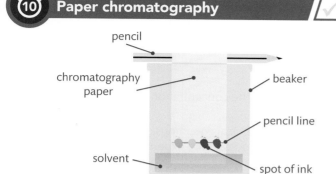

Figure 1 Paper chromatography apparatus

1 Use a ruler to draw a horizontal pencil line (the base line) 2 cm from the bottom of the chromatography paper.

2 Using glass capillary tubes, put a small spot of each of the known colourings on the pencil line, 1 cm apart. Make sure each spot is no more than 5 mm in diameter.

3 Using another glass capillary tube, put a small spot of the unknown mixture on the paper.

4 Label each spot in **pencil**.

5 Tape the top edge of the chromatography paper to the pencil so that the paper hangs with the base line at the bottom.

6 Pour water into the beaker so that the water level will be **below** the base line.

7 Rest the pencil on the top edge of the beaker. The bottom edge of the paper should just dip into the water.

8 Allow the solvent to run until it is near the top of the paper, then use a ruler to measure the distance the solvent has moved up the paper (from the base line) and the distance the spot has moved (from the base line).

⏱ Worked example — Grade 5

Describe the main stages of how paper chromatography separates substances. **[3 marks]**

Choose a mobile phase that the substances can dissolve in. The mobile phase is run through the mixture on a stationary phase made of paper. The substances move at different rates over the paper.

⏱ Simple distillation of inks

Simple distillation is a method that can be used to separate pure water from inks.

The apparatus is set up as shown in **Figure 2**.

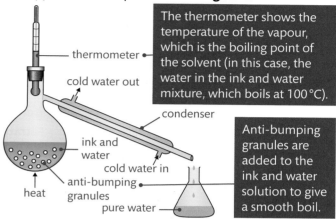

The thermometer shows the temperature of the vapour, which is the boiling point of the solvent (in this case, the water in the ink and water mixture, which boils at 100 °C).

Anti-bumping granules are added to the ink and water solution to give a smooth boil.

Figure 2 Simple distillation apparatus

1 Pour some ink and water into a round-bottomed flask.

2 Attach a condenser to the top and connect it to a cold water supply.

3 Heat the flask using a Bunsen burner until the solution boils gently, then maintain the temperature.

4 Collect a sample of the distilled solvent in the conical flask.

⏱ Working scientifically

Hazard symbols can be found on the containers of some substances. They give you information about the risks and how to use the substances safely. You could be asked to list the risks and suggest ways to ensure that you are using the substances safely.

For example, substances that are flammable should be used away from naked flames. Swapping a Bunsen burner for a water bath is a much safer option.

Flammable	Irritant	Corrosive
🔥	!	🧪

⏱ Exam-style practice — Grade 5

Simple distillation can be used to separate a solvent (water) from a solution of ink and water.

(a) State the name of the equipment that causes the solvent (water) vapour to turn back to a liquid. **[1 mark]**

(b) Describe **one** hazard and **one** suitable precaution for the hazard for the distillation experiment. **[2 marks]**

(c) Describe how a thermometer can be used in a distillation to identify the liquid being collected. **[1 mark]**

Potable water

You need to know how potable water (drinking water) is produced.

(15) Potable water

Potable, or drinking water, is not pure as it still contains dissolved substances (at safe levels), such as minerals. The origin of the term 'potable' is the Latin word *potare* which means to drink.

Making water potable

For water to be suitable as safe drinking water, it must be treated to kill microbes. The concentration of dissolved salts must be low enough to not cause harm.

The processes used to produce potable water depend on the water source and the local conditions. If supplies of fresh water are limited, desalination of salt water may be required. Desalination processes are expensive because they require large amounts of energy.

Type of water	Source	Treatment processes
waste water and groundwater	rainwater, which collects underground or in lakes and rivers	**Filtration** – The waste water or groundwater is filtered through layers of gravel, then sand, to remove any solid waste. **Sedimentation** – Smaller particles are allowed to settle out to the bottom of a tank. **Chlorination** – The final stage of water treatment is to use chlorine to kill any microbes present in the water.
sea water	from the oceans	**Distillation** – The sea water is heated until it evaporates, leaving the salt behind. The water vapour is then condensed to give fresh water.

Go to page 101 for more information on distillation.

Pure water only contains water particles. Potable water is safe to drink and may be pure but it can also be a mixture (rain water) or even a formulation (tap water). Pure water, often produced by distillation, must be used when scientists carry out analyses. Otherwise dissolved salts in the water will affect the results.

(5) Worked example — Grades 3–4

1 State the **three** main steps to make potable water from fresh water. **[3 marks]**

Filtration, sedimentation and chlorination

2 Explain why it is more expensive to make water from salt water compared to fresh water. **[2 marks]**

The sea water has to be heated, so more energy is needed.

3 Describe how waste water is treated to produce potable water. **[2 marks]**

Solid particles are removed by filtering and sedimentation and then chlorine is added to kill microbes.

(10) Exam-style practice — Grade 4

1 Name **one** method that can be used to produce potable water from salt water. **[1 mark]**

2 Name **one** substance that can be used to kill microbes in rainwater. **[1 mark]**

3 Give **one** reason why unprocessed sea water is not used as drinking water. **[1 mark]**

4 Name the main source of potable water in the UK. **[1 mark]**

5 Give **three** sources of water that can be used to produce potable water. **[3 marks]**

Made a start   Feeling confident   Exam ready

The pH scale and neutralisation

You need to know how to use the pH scale to measure how acidic or alkaline a solution is.

 Acids, bases and alkalis

Acids

An acid is a substance that produces hydrogen (H^+) ions when dissolved in water.

Acids have a pH of less than 7.

Bases and alkalis

Bases are substances that react with acids to make neutral substances called salts.

Alkalis are soluble bases. Copper oxide is a base but not an alkali, whereas sodium hydroxide is a base and an alkali because it dissolves in water.

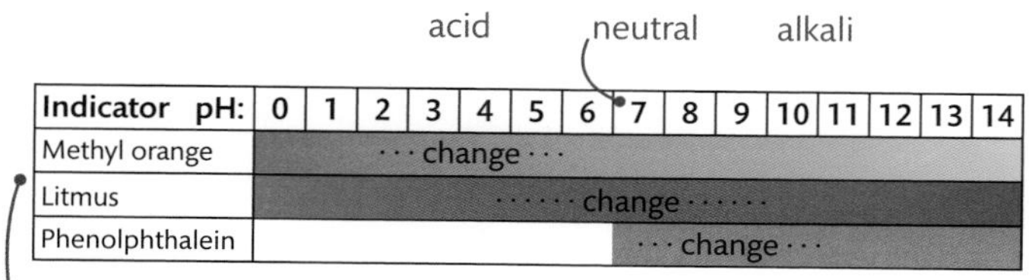

Indicator pH:	0	1	2	3	4	5	6	7	8	9	10	11	12	13	14
Methyl orange			· · · change · · ·												
Litmus				· · · · · · change · · · · · ·											
Phenolphthalein									· · · change · · ·						

acid · neutral · alkali

Figure 1 Colours of indicators in acids and alkalis

The pH of a solution can only be measured using a pH probe or universal indicator and comparing the colour to a chart.

 Worked example **Grades 4–5**

Vinegar has a pH of about 2.5.

(a) State what pH is a measure of. **[1 mark]**

How acidic or alkaline a substance is.

(b) Explain, using the pH value of vinegar, what type of substance vinegar is. **[2 marks]**

Its pH is lower than 7 so vinegar is an acid.

(c) State what ion is responsible for the pH at 2.5. **[1 mark]**

H^+

An alkali is a substance that produces hydroxide (OH^-) ions when dissolved in water.

Aqueous solutions of alkalis have a pH greater than 7.

Neutralisation reactions

A solution with pH 7 is neutral. When acids and bases react, a neutralisation reaction occurs.

The hydrogen ions from the acid react with the hydroxide ions from the alkali to produce water:

$$H^+(aq) + OH^-(aq) \rightarrow H_2O(l)$$

Indicators change colour to show if a chemical is an acid or an alkali. To measure the pH, use a pH probe or use universal indicator.

 Working scientifically

If there is the same concentration (e.g. $3.65\,g\,dm^{-3}$) of a strong acid, such as HCl, and a strong alkali, such as NaOH, that react in a 1:1 ratio, then it takes the same volume of NaOH to neutralise a particular volume of HCl (e.g. $25\,cm^3$).

$$NaOH + HCl \rightarrow NaCl + H_2O$$
$$1 \quad : \quad 1$$

mass = volume (dm^3) × concentration ($g\,dm^{-3}$)
$= (25 \div 1000) \times 3.65$
$= 0.09125$ grams of HCl

volume of NaOH = grams ÷ concentration
$= 0.09125 \div 3.65$
$= 0.025\,dm^3$
$= 25\,cm^3$

 Maths skills

Divide by 1000 to convert from cm^3 to dm^3.

 Exam-style practice **Grade 4**

1 Write a word equation for the neutralisation reaction between hydrochloric acid and sodium hydroxide. **[1 mark]**

2 An unknown solution is tested using phenolphthalein. The indicator changes to a bright pink colour.
  (a) Identify the type of solution being tested. **[1 mark]**
  (b) Name the type of ion present in the solution tested. **[1 mark]**

 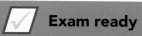

Practical: pH change

You need to know how to investigate the change in pH when adding an alkali to a fixed volume of acid.

⏱ Neutralisation reactions

During a neutralisation reaction in which alkali is added to an acid, the pH of the solution will change from a low pH to a high pH.

When hydroxide ions are added to an acid they react with the hydrogen ions and reduce their concentration, causing the pH to increase.

A graph can be plotted to show how the pH changes as more alkali is added.

A universal indicator or a pH probe can be used to measure the approximate pH of a solution. Universal indicator changes colour to show the pH of a substance. pH can also be measured using a pH probe.

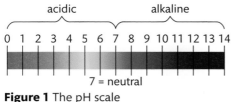

This is the point at which the amount of acid is equal to the amount of alkali.

Figure 1 The pH scale

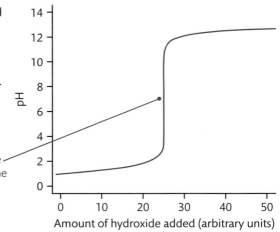

Figure 2 A pH curve

⏱ Worked example — Grade 5

A student was asked to investigate how the pH changes when calcium hydroxide powder is added to hydrochloric acid. The student has a measuring cylinder, a beaker, a glass rod, universal indicator paper and a colour chart, a spatula and a white tile.

1 Describe how the reaction between calcium hydroxide powder and hydrochloric acid can be used to investigate the pH change during the reaction. **[6 marks]**

1 Measure volume of the dilute hydrochloric acid, using the measuring cylinder, add to the beaker.

2 Place small pieces of the indicator paper onto a white tile.

3 Use the glass rod to transfer a drop of the solution in the beaker onto one piece of the universal indicator paper.

4 Compare the colour to a pH chart and record its value.

5 Add a level spatula of calcium hydroxide powder to the beaker and mix.

6 Repeat steps 3 to 5 until there are no further changes in pH, recording how many spatulas of calcium hydroxide are added.

2 Suggest a piece of equipment that could be used to improve the accuracy of the pH reading. **[1 mark]**

A pH probe.

② Maths skills

You could be asked to draw a graph of pH data from an experiment. To show the relationship between two variables, you need to draw a scatter graph with a smooth curve drawn between the points. Remember, the variable that you change – the **independent variable** – goes on the x-axis; the variable that you measure – the **dependent variable** – goes on the y-axis.

⏱ Exam-style practice — Grade 5

Spatula measures of sodium oxide were added to hydrochloric acid and the pH changes were recorded. The table shows the results.

(a) Plot a graph of the results. **[3 marks]**

The x-axis should be the number of spatulas of sodium oxide (independent variable) and the y-axis should be the pH (dependent variable). Make sure that your graph takes up more than half of the graph paper and you draw a smooth curve of best fit.

(b) Describe the pattern shown in the data. **[2 marks]**

(c) Draw a cross on your graph to show when the solution was neutral. **[1 mark]**

No. of spatulas	pH
0	2.2
1	2.6
2	3.0
3	3.2
4	3.4
5	3.6
6	3.7
7	3.9
8	4.2
9	4.4
10	5.0
11	9.6
12	10.6
13	11.0

You could be asked to suggest other ways to improve the accuracy (how close to the truth your values are) of the experiment – a measuring cylinder with a bigger scale, a burette or a pipette are all more accurate ways to measure the volume of a liquid; using a balance would enable the exact mass of the alkali added each time to be determined.

| Made a start | Feeling confident | Exam ready |

Salt production

You need to know how salts are formed and the conventions used for naming them.

Forming salts

Salts are made by a reaction between an acid and a base. Bases are chemicals that react with acids and alkalis are bases that can also dissolve in water. When an acid is neutralised by an alkali, such as a soluble metal hydroxide, or by a base, the products are always a salt and water.

acid + metal oxide → salt + water

acid + metal hydroxide → salt + water

If a metal carbonate is neutralised, then carbon dioxide is also produced.

acid + metal carbonate → salt + water + carbon dioxide

Test for CO₂

Limewater (aqueous calcium hydroxide) turns cloudy if carbon dioxide is passed through it.

Worked example   Grade 4

(a) When calcium carbonate is added to hydrochloric acid, a neutralisation reaction occurs. Write a word equation for the reaction.   **[1 mark]**

calcium carbonate + hydrochloric acid →
calcium chloride + water + carbon dioxide

(b) Describe a chemical test to show that carbon dioxide has been made.   **[3 marks]**

Pass the gas through limewater/a solution of calcium hydroxide and it will go cloudy.

1. Identify the metal reacting. It is calcium.
2. Work out the salt name ending from the acid. The acid is hydrochloric acid, so the second part of the name of the salt is chloride.
3. Name the salt. It is calcium chloride.
4. Complete the equation.

Naming salts

A salt has a name with two parts; the first part is just the name of the metal reacting.

For example, if the base is magnesium hydroxide, the first name of the salt is magnesium.

The second part comes from the type of acid reacting:

Acid reacting	Second part of salt name
sulfuric	sulfate
nitric	nitrate
hydrochloric	chloride

So, magnesium hydroxide and sulfuric acid would produce a salt called magnesium sulfate (and water).

If magnesium carbonate reacted with nitric acid, then magnesium nitrate would be produced (with water and carbon dioxide).

Working scientifically

When producing a balanced chemical equation, you will need to work out the formula of the salt produced. The overall charge on a compound of the salt is 0, so any charges must be balanced.

Charges on common ions

Ion	Charge
carbonate	CO_3^{2-}
sulfate	SO_4^{2-}
nitrate	NO_3^-
chloride	Cl^-

Exam-style practice   Grades 4–5

1. Name the salt produced in the reaction between potassium hydroxide and nitric acid.   **[1 mark]**

2. Name the type of reaction that produces a salt.   **[1 mark]**

3. Name the acid reactant used to produce the salt copper chloride.   **[1 mark]**

4. Write a word equation for the reaction of sodium carbonate and hydrochloric acid.   **[1 mark]**

5. Balance the chemical equation for the neutralisation of sodium hydroxide by sulfuric acid.   **[1 mark]**

____NaOH + H₂SO₄ → ____H₂O + Na₂SO₄

Reactions of acids with metals

When acids and some metals react, a salt and hydrogen gas are produced.

(5) Metals reacting with acids

Acids react with some metals to produce salts and hydrogen. The following reaction takes place between a metal and an acid:

metal + acid → salt + hydrogen

When reacting acids with metals, hydrochloric acid makes chlorides and sulfuric acid makes sulfates.

(5) Worked example   Grades 4–5

1 Calcium is a reactive metal and can react with acids.

(a) Give the name of the salt made when calcium reacts with hydrochloric acid. **[1 mark]**

Calcium chloride

(b) Write a word equation for calcium reacting with nitric acid. **[2 marks]**

calcium + nitric acid → calcium nitrate + hydrogen

(c) Give the formula of the salt that is made when calcium reacts with sulfuric acid. **[1 mark]**

$CaSO_4$

2 When reactive metals react with an acid, a gas is made.

(a) Give the observation that suggests a gas is made. **[1 mark]**

Fizzing/bubbling/effervescence

(b) Explain how to test the gas to show it is hydrogen. **[2 marks]**

Collect the gas in a test tube, put a lighted splint into the test tube and listen for a pop.

(5) Testing for hydrogen gas

A lit splint will make a squeaky pop noise when held near a test tube of hydrogen gas.

You only need to write the name of the salt.

The reactants (starting substances) are on the left of the arrow and the products (substances that are made) are on the right of the arrow. Remember that the products are a salt and hydrogen.

You must give the formula not the name.

(10) Exam-style practice   Grade 5

1 Write a word equation for the reaction between magnesium and hydrochloric acid. **[2 marks]**

2 State the formula of the gas produced when a metal reacts with acids. **[1 mark]**

3 Suggest the reactants used to make magnesium sulfate. **[2 marks]**

4 Predict the name of the salt produced when calcium reacts with nitric acid. **[1 mark]**

 Made a start   **Feeling confident**   **Exam ready**

Soluble salts

You need to be able to describe the preparation of a soluble salt.

5 Making a soluble salt

A soluble salt can be made by reacting an acid with solid insoluble bases, such as metals, metal oxides, hydroxides or carbonates.

1. Add solid base, e.g. metal oxide, to the acid until no more reaction takes place.

↓

2. Filter to remove excess solid.

↓

3. Heat gently, then leave to crystallise into a solid salt. Soluble salts can be dissolved in water.

↓

4. Remove the crystals and pat dry with absorbent paper.

Working scientifically

When using a Bunsen burner you should take the following precautions:

- Wear eye protection.
- Stand at a reasonable distance away from the flame.
- Place the Bunsen burner on a heat-resistant mat.

Remember, the solid is added in excess to the acid so that all the acid reacts, as the excess solid can then be filtered to remove it, leaving only the products (the salt and water).

5 Different types of reactants

Some metals are too reactive, or not reactive enough, to be used to produce soluble salts. This is why metal oxides, hydroxides or carbonates are used.

- Sodium chloride – sodium is too reactive, so sodium hydroxide or sodium carbonate is used instead.
- Copper chloride – copper does not react with dilute hydrochloric acid so copper oxide or copper carbonate is used instead.

Crystallisation is a separation technique used to separate solids from liquids by evaporating the solvent. See page 101 for more information on separation techniques.

5 Worked example — Grade 4

1 A student reacts sodium carbonate with dilute sulfuric acid.

Describe how the student could make sure that all of the acid had reacted. **[1 mark]**

Keep adding sodium carbonate until the fizzing stops.

2 Name the separating technique used to get a pure dry sample of a soluble salt from a solution. **[1 mark]**

Crystallisation

10 Exam-style practice — Grades 4–5

1 Describe how you would remove the excess solid when producing a soluble salt by reacting an acid with an insoluble metal hydroxide. **[1 mark]**

2 Which reactants are used to **safely** produce sodium sulfate? **[1 mark]**

☐ **A** sodium hydroxide and hydrochloric acid

☐ **B** sodium and sulfuric acid

☐ **C** sodium hydroxide and sulfuric acid

☐ **D** sodium and water

3 Name the soluble salt produced when copper oxide reacts with nitric acid. **[1 mark]**

Practical: Making salts

You need to know how to prepare a sample of pure, dry soluble copper sulfate from an insoluble oxide.

⑩ Making a salt

❶ Pour 200 cm³ sulfuric acid into a beaker and warm it gently. This increases the rate of reaction and allows more of the product to dissolve.

❷ Stir in copper(II) oxide powder until no more reacts and you can see some black copper(II) oxide left. The liquid will turn blue, as the copper sulfate is being made.

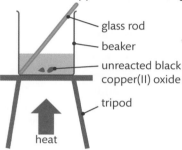

glass rod
beaker
unreacted black copper(II) oxide
tripod
heat

Figure 1 Adding copper(II) oxide to sulfuric acid

❸ Allow the apparatus to cool.

❹ Set up funnel and filter paper apparatus.

❺ Filter the solution.

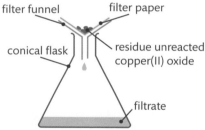

filter funnel   filter paper
conical flask   residue unreacted copper(II) oxide
filtrate

Figure 2 Filtration

❻ Collect the filtrate in a conical flask.

❼ Transfer the filtrate to an evaporating basin, then gently heat until at least half of the solvent has evaporated. This will make a hot saturated solution and, as it cools, crystals of copper sulfate will form.

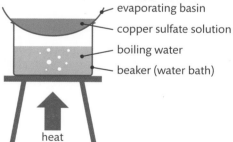

evaporating basin
copper sulfate solution
boiling water
beaker (water bath)
heat

Figure 3 Crystallisation

❽ Leave the filtrate somewhere warm to crystallise for 24 hours.

❾ Remove crystals from evaporating dish, put onto filter paper and pat dry. The crystals can then be weighed if required.

⑩ Worked example   Grade 5

❶ A salt can be made by reacting an acid and an alkali. Name this type of reaction.   **[1 mark]**

Neutralisation

❷ **(a)** Write a word equation for the reaction between sulfuric acid and copper(II) oxide.   **[1 mark]**

sulfuric acid + copper(II) oxide →
                    copper sulfate + water

(b) Explain why the following steps are important in the production of the salt copper sulfate.   **[4 marks]**

Warming the acid: speeds up the reaction

Adding excess copper oxide: ensures all the acid reacts

The mixture is filtered: removes any excess copper oxide

The filtrate is heated to begin evaporation: encourages the formation of crystals

(c) Describe what you would observe during the reaction of copper oxide and sulfuric acid.   **[2 marks]**

The black solid copper oxide would disappear, and a blue solution would form.

② Working scientifically

A water bath may be used instead of a Bunsen burner during the crystallisation process. To allow large crystals to form, crystallisation must occur slowly. If the solution is heated fast until it all evaporates, only a powdery solid will be left. The initial use of the water bath speeds up the evaporation process but heating is gentle so still permits large crystals to form.

⑩ Exam-style practice   Grade 5

❶ Give a safe method for preparing a pure dry sample of a salt from dilute hydrochloric acid and copper oxide.   **[5 marks]**

❷ Name the salt produced in question **1**.   **[1 mark]**

Titration

You need to know how to carry out an acid–alkali titration to prepare a pure sample of a soluble salt.

⏱ Titration method

1 Fill the burette with acid; record the initial reading.

2 Use the pipette and pipette filler to add a measured volume of alkali to the conical flask.

3 Add a few drops of indicator, swirl to mix; place the conical flask on a white tile.

4 Slowly add small portions of the acid from the burette into the conical flask, swirling to mix.

5 When the indicator just changes colour (permanently) stop adding the acid, as the end point has been reached. Record the final reading to calculate how much acid is used.

6 Repeat steps 1 to 5 until you get concordant results.

> 'Concordant' refers to two or more results within 0.1 cm³ of each other.

⏱ Preparing a soluble salt from a titration

7 Once you have achieved concordant results, measure out the same volume of alkali and the volume of acid determined by the titration and mix together. This time you do not need to add indicator as this would make the salt coloured and not pure.

8 Heat the solution gently in an evaporating dish until you have salt crystals.

9 Dry the crystals between two pieces of filter paper.

> Look at page 101 for the evaporation technique.

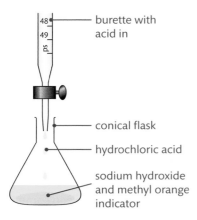

burette with acid in
48
49
ps
conical flask
hydrochloric acid
sodium hydroxide and methyl orange indicator

Figure 1 Preparing a soluble salt using titration

⏱ Worked example

The results of a titration to determine how much sulfuric acid is required to neutralise sodium hydroxide are given in the table.

	Titration 1/ rough titration	Titration 2	Titration 3	Titration 4
Initial reading (cm³)	0.00	25.00	0.10	20.00
Final reading (cm³)	22.20	44.30	19.30	43.00
Volume used (cm³)	22.20	19.30	19.20	23.00
Tick if result used		✓	✓	

(a) Complete the table to give the volume used in titration 2. **[1 mark]**

(b) Complete the final row to show which values should be used to calculate the mean. **[1 mark]**

(c) Calculate the mean. **[2 marks]**

$$\frac{(19.30 + 19.20)}{2} = 19.25 \, cm^3$$

> The volume used is calculated by subtracting the initial reading from the final reading.

> The mean should always be calculated from the two (or three) most concordant results. It should not include any trial or rough titration values.

⏱ Exam-style practice

1 State the **two** products made when an acid reacts with an alkali. **[2 marks]**

2 Give the reason why an indicator is not added to a reaction between an acid and an alkali when a pure dry sample of the salt is being collected. **[1 mark]**

Solubility rules

You need to know the rules of solubility to be able to predict which mixed solutions will produce precipitates.

Solubility rules

Soluble in water	Insoluble in water
all nitrate salts	
all common sodium, potassium and ammonium salts	
most sulfates	lead sulfate, barium sulfate and calcium sulfate
most chlorides	silver chloride and lead chloride
carbonates and hydroxides with sodium, potassium or ammonium ions	most carbonates and hydroxides

Worked example   Grades 4–5

1 A student mixed lead nitrate and ammonium sulfate solutions together in a test tube.

(a) Write a word equation for the reaction.   **[1 mark]**

lead nitrate + ammonium sulfate →
          lead sulfate + ammonium nitrate

(b) Explain any observations the student would make.   **[2 marks]**

The student would see a precipitate form, because lead sulfate is insoluble.

2 For each of the following pairs of solutions predict, using solubility rules, whether or not a precipitate will be formed when they are mixed. Name any precipitates.

(a) sodium carbonate and calcium nitrate   **[1 mark]**

Calcium carbonate precipitate formed

(b) potassium chloride and ammonium sulfate   **[1 mark]**

No precipitate

(c) magnesium chloride and ammonium nitrate   **[1 mark]**

No precipitate

(d) calcium chloride and silver nitrate   **[1 mark]**

Silver chloride precipitate formed

3 Give the state symbol that would be used for a precipitate in a balanced equation.   **[1 mark]**

(s)

Preparation of insoluble salts

1 Mix together two solutions that will produce the precipitate you want (e.g. silver nitrate and sodium chloride to give silver chloride).

2 Filter the reaction mixture to separate out the insoluble salt. The residue in the filter paper is the solid that you are trying to collect.

3 Wash the residue with a small amount of distilled water and allow the water to filter away.

4 Allow the residue to dry between some filter paper.

Exam focus
You need to be able to name the precipitate formed when named solutions are mixed together. Remember you are looking at the products of the reaction, not the reactants, when working out solubility.

Exam focus

You are expected to recall the rules for solubility given at the top of the page.

Try to invent a mnemonic to help you remember them.

Exam-style practice   Grade 5

1 State what is meant by the term 'soluble'.   **[1 mark]**

2 **(a)** Draw and label the equipment used to separate an insoluble salt from a solution.   **[4 marks]**

(b) Give a reason why the residue is washed with distilled water.   **[1 mark]**

Electrolysis

You need to understand the process of electrolysis.

⏱ 5 Key terms ✓

- ✓ **electrolysis** – using electricity to decompose a compound
- ✓ **electrolyte** – the liquid that is being broken down by electricity; it is an ionic compound that is (l) or (aq)
- ✓ **electrode** – a solid electrical conductor, usually metal or carbon
- ✓ **anode** – the positively-charged electrode (remember **A**node **A**dd +)
- ✓ **cathode** – the negatively-charged electrode

Inert (unreactive) materials are often used for the electrodes, so that they don't interfere with the electrolysis reaction.

⏱ 5 The process ✓

In electrolysis, electrical energy from a direct current supply decomposes (breaks down) electrolytes. Electrolytes are ionic compounds where the ions are free to move. So, they are either molten liquids or dissolved in water (aqueous solutions).

Ionic compounds cannot conduct when solid as the ions are in fixed positions.

Electrolysis causes the charged ions to move towards oppositely charged electrodes. Opposite charges attract. So, positive ions (metal ions and hydrogen ions) are always attracted to the negative electrode (cathode). Negative ions (non-metal ions) are always attracted to the positive electrode (anode).

The ions are discharged at the electrodes, producing elements.

⏱ 2 Working scientifically 🧪⚗ ✓

Electrolysis is used to extract reactive metals from their ore if they cannot be extracted by reduction with carbon.

⏱ 10 Worked example Grade 5 ✓

Figure 1 shows an electrolysis cell.

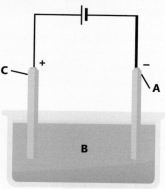

Figure 1

(a) Use words from the box to identify **A**, **B** and **C**. **[3 marks]**

| anode cathode cell electrolyte |

A: cathode

B: electrolyte

C: anode

(b) Give a reason why electrodes are normally made from inert substances. **[1 mark]**

Electrodes are normally made from inert materials so that they don't react with the electrolyte or with the products of electrolysis.

(c) State which electrode non-metal ions are attracted to. **[1 mark]**

Anode (positive electrode)

⏱ 5 Exam-style practice Grade 4 ✓

1 Draw one straight line from each term to the correct definition. **[4 marks]**

electrolyte   electrode with a positive charge
electrode   electrode with a negative charge
anode   solid, electrical conductor
cathode   liquid used for electrolysis

2 Metals form positive ions. Identify the electrode the metal ions will travel to. **[1 mark]**

Electrolysis of molten ionic compounds

You need to know how molten ionic compounds separate during electrolysis and be able to state the reactions that occur at each electrode.

Reactions at electrodes

Ionic compounds are made of positive metal ions and negative non-metal ions. When an ionic compound has melted, the ions can move in the liquid. When current is passed through the molten ionic compound, the ions move and carry the charge.

The positive metal ions will always travel to the negatively-charged cathode, where they gain electrons (reduce) to form the metal element.

At the anode, the non-metal ions will lose electrons (oxidise) forming the non-metal element.

Worked example — Grade 5

(a) State the name of the chemical reaction where electricity is used to decompose molten lead bromide. **[1 mark]**

Electrolysis

(b) Write a word equation for the reaction where electricity is used to break zinc chloride into its elements. **[1 mark]**

zinc chloride → zinc + chlorine

(c) Explain why sodium chloride must be molten or in solution for electrolysis. **[2 marks]**

The ions must be free to move and carry the charge.

(d) Describe what happens at the positive electrode during the electrolysis of sodium chloride. **[3 marks]**

The chloride ions lose one electron each to form chlorine (gas).

Equations

Electrolysis can be described in word equations. The reactant is the name of the ionic compound and the products are the elements that it is made from.

For example, the electrolysis of molten sodium chloride is:

sodium chloride → sodium + chlorine

You can also use balanced chemical equations. Remember that non-metals make diatomic (two atom) molecules. Metals do not make molecules and so the equation may need to be balanced.

The electrolysis of molten sodium chloride would be:

$$2NaCl \rightarrow 2Na + Cl_2$$

This means two atoms of sodium. There would be molten shiny metal at the cathode (negative electrode).

Chlorine molecules are made and a green gas would be seen at the anode (positive electrode).

Ionic compounds must be molten or in solution to have free ions. If the compound is dissolved in an aqueous solution, different products may form at the electrodes (page 115).

The negative non-metal ion is attracted to the positive electrode where it becomes **oxidised** (loses electrons).

Exam focus

You could be asked to draw a labelled diagram of the apparatus you would use for electrolysis in the exam. Go to page 116 to see what you should include in the diagram.

Exam-style practice — Grade 5

1. Lead is produced by the electrolysis of molten lead bromide.

   (a) Draw a diagram of the apparatus that you could use for the electrolysis of lead bromide. **[4 marks]**

   (b) Write a balanced chemical equation for the electrolysis of molten lead bromide ($PbBr_2$). **[2 marks]**

   (c) Suggest what you would observe at the anode. **[2 marks]**

2. For each of the following ionic compounds, predict the products of electrolysis at the anode (positive electrode) and cathode (negative electrode). Assume each substance is molten.

   (a) lead iodide **[2 marks]**

   (b) zinc bromide **[2 marks]**

   (c) magnesium oxide **[2 marks]**

   (d) lithium chloride **[2 marks]**

 Made a start **Feeling confident** **Exam ready**

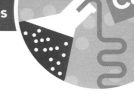

Electrolysis of aqueous solutions

You need to be able to describe what happens to aqueous solutions during electrolysis (where an ionic substance is dissolved in water).

5 Ions

A small number of water molecules break into H^+ and OH^- naturally. So, in an ionic solution there are lots of neutral water molecules, a few ions from the ionic compound and a small number of H^+ and OH^- ions from water.

When electricity flows through the ionic solution, the positive ions from the ionic compound and the hydrogen ions are both attracted to the negative electrode. The negative ions from the ionic compound and the OH^- ions go to the positive electrode.

There is only one product formed at each electrode.

At the positive electrode, either oxygen or a Group 7 element known as a halogen (see page 125) is made. If the ionic compound contains Cl^-, Br^- or I^-, it is known as a halide. Halides will make halogens i.e. Cl_2, Br_2 and I_2.

At the negative electrode, either hydrogen or a metal is made. If the ionic compound contains a metal above hydrogen in the reactivity series (see page 117), then hydrogen is made. If not, then the metal is produced.

10 Worked example — Grade 4

Figure 1 shows apparatus for the electrolysis of concentrated sodium chloride solution.

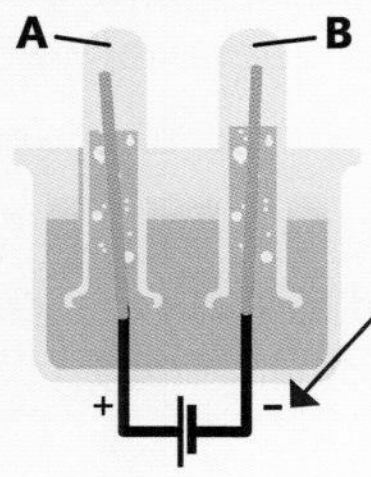

Figure 1

(a) Name gases **A** and **B**. **[2 marks]**

A: chlorine

B: hydrogen

(b) State what substance is found in the solution in the beaker after the reaction has taken place. **[1 mark]**

Sodium hydroxide

(c) State and explain the pH value of the resulting solution. **[2 marks]**

pH in the range 10–14

Sodium hydroxide dissolves to form an alkaline solution.

5 Electrolysis of water

A small proportion of water molecules dissociate into ions, allowing it to conduct electricity. During the electrolysis of water (acidified with a little dilute sulfuric acid) hydrogen and oxygen are released at the electrodes:

- OH^- ions are attracted to the anode where they lose electrons and form oxygen gas and water
- H^+ ions are attracted to the cathode where they gain electrons and form hydrogen gas.

The overall balanced equation for the process is:

$2H_2O(l) \longrightarrow 2H_2(g) + O_2(g)$

The volume of hydrogen given off is twice the volume of oxygen given off.

Exam focus

If you are asked to draw the apparatus for electrolysis, make sure you include a power source as shown here.

Chlorine is a halogen and so will be discharged at the anode.

As sodium is more reactive than hydrogen, hydrogen will be discharged at the cathode.

As hydrogen and chlorine have been discharged at the electrodes, Na^+ and OH^- are left in the solution, forming NaOH.

Sodium hydroxide is an alkali. So, any pH above 10 but less than 14 can be accepted. See page 105 to revise the pH scale.

10 Exam-style practice — Grade 5

Electrolysis can be used to show that aqueous copper chloride contains ions.

(a) State and explain what happens when an electrical current passes through the solution. **[4 marks]**

(b) State the products of this electrolysis. **[2 marks]**

(c) Write a balanced chemical equation for the electrolysis of copper(II) chloride. **[3 marks]**

Practical: Electrolysis of copper sulfate

You need to know what happens during the electrolysis of copper sulfate using inert electrodes and copper electrodes.

② Apparatus ✓

- ☑ 50 cm³ copper sulfate solution
- ☑ 100 cm³ beaker
- ☑ electrodes (2 × carbon (inert) and 2 × copper (active))
- ☑ two crocodile/4 mm plug leads
- ☑ low-voltage power supply
- ☑ blue litmus paper
- ☑ tweezers

⑤ Electrolysis of copper sulfate ✓

① Half fill a beaker with copper sulfate solution.

② Put the carbon (inert) electrodes into the solution. **The rods must not touch each other**. Attach crocodile leads to the rods. Connect the rods to the direct current (red and black) terminals of a low-voltage power supply.

③ Switch on the power supply (4 V).

④ The negative electrode has a mass increase and an orange-brown coloured solid forms on the surface of the electrode. The positive electrode effervesces (you can see bubbles and hear fizzing).

⑤ Use tweezers to hold a piece of damp blue litmus paper in the solution next to the positive electrode.

⑥ Repeat the experiment with copper (active) electrodes. You might want to weigh both electrodes before and after the electrolysis. Don't forget to pat them dry before you weigh them.

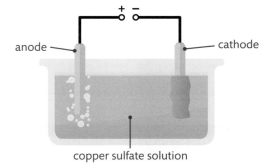
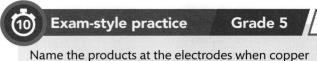

Figure 2 Electrolysis apparatus

⑩ Exam-style practice Grade 5 ✓

Name the products at the electrodes when copper sulfate solution is electrolysed with inert electrodes. **[2 marks]**

⑩ Worked example Grade 5 ✓

Figure 1 shows apparatus for the electrolysis of copper sulfate solution.

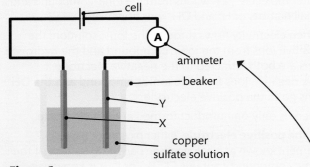

Figure 1

(a) Give the names of the electrodes **X** and **Y**. **[1 mark]**

X is the anode; Y is the cathode.

(b) Name an inert element that can be used for the electrodes. **[1 mark]**

Carbon

(c) Describe the observations when copper electrodes are used instead of inert electrodes. **[3 marks]**

The anode gets smaller/has a lighter mass.

The cathode get bigger/has greater mass.

Residue (black solid) forms under the anode.

The ammeter is used to show that current is flowing and the electrolysis is happening.

② Working scientifically 🧪⚗️ ✓

If the electrodes are not involved in the chemistry of the electrolysis, they are called inert. Carbon rods are often used as inert electrodes as they are cheap. When copper salt solutions are electrolysed with inert electrodes, the negative electrode gets heavier as copper metal is made on the surface of the electrode.

Sometimes, the electrodes are involved in the chemistry of the electrolysis. These electrodes are called active electrodes. When copper salt solutions are electrolysed with copper electrodes, the mass of the positive electrode decreases and the mass of the negative electrode increases by nearly the same amount. The difference in the mass is due to the impurities in the metal. This is how copper is purified so that it can be used for electrical wires.

☑ **Made a start** ☑ **Feeling confident** ☑ **Exam ready**

The reactivity series

You need to understand how the reactivity of metals with water or dilute acids or salt solutions relates to how easy it is for the metal to form a positive ion (cation). You should be able to deduce an order of reactivity of metals based on experimental results.

Reactivity of metals

Metals are found on the left and centre of the periodic table. They have metallic bonds and form giant metallic structures. Metals are shiny, malleable, ductile and are conductors. When metals react, they lose their outer-shell electrons to form cations (positive ions). The easier the metal finds it to lose its outer-shell electrons, the more reactive the metal is.

> For more on ion formation, see page 82.

The reactivity series places metals in order from the most reactive to the least reactive metal. Hydrogen and carbon are often included in the reactivity series as reference points. If a metal is above hydrogen in the reactivity series, it will react with acids. When hydrogen reacts it loses an electron in the same way that metals do. If a metal is below carbon in the reactivity series, it can be extracted from its compound using smelting. Carbon is used to extract metals from their ores based on their reactivity – the reactivity of carbon needs to be known to predict these reactions (see page 118).

A more reactive metal will displace (take the place of) a less reactive metal from a compound of the less reactive metal. The reactivity of metals can also be compared using their reactions with water and dilute acids.

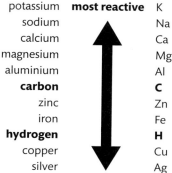

Figure 1 The reactivity series

	most reactive	
potassium		K
sodium		Na
calcium		Ca
magnesium		Mg
aluminium		Al
carbon		**C**
zinc		Zn
iron		Fe
hydrogen		**H**
copper		Cu
silver		Ag
gold	least reactive	Au

Reacting metals with acids and water

The alkali metals all react vigorously with cold water (see page 124). Calcium and magnesium have less vigorous reactions with water. Less reactive metals, such as zinc and iron, need dilute acids to react. The reactivity can be compared by seeing how vigorously the hydrogen gas is released. The more vigorous the reaction, the more reactive the metal.

metal + acid → salt + hydrogen

metal + water → metal hydroxide + hydrogen

Worked example — Grade 5

A student investigates the reactivity of four different metals with salt solutions. The table shows the observations.

	Cu	Mg	Zn	Ag
$CuSO_4$	no reaction	**colour change**	**colour change**	no reaction
$AgNO_3$	**colour change**	**colour change**	**colour change**	no reaction
$ZnSO_4$	no reaction	**colour change**	no reaction	no reaction
$MgSO_4$	no reaction	no reaction	no reaction	no reaction

> You should be able to work out the most reactive to the least reactive metals by either how many reactions they took part in or how vigorous their reactions were.

(a) Deduce the order of reactivity of zinc, copper and magnesium. **[1 mark]**

magnesium (most reactive)   zinc   copper (least reactive)

(b) Describe what the results suggest about the reactivity of silver in relation to the other metals given. **[1 mark]**

It is the least reactive of the four metals tested.

(c) Write a word equation for the reaction between copper sulfate and magnesium. **[2 marks]**

copper sulfate + magnesium → magnesium sulfate + copper

Exam-style practice — Grades 4–5

1 **Figure 2** shows four metals reacting with dilute hydrochloric acid. State and explain which is the most reactive metal. **[2 marks]**

2 Explain how metal reactivity is related to cation formation. **[3 marks]**

3 Write a word equation for the reaction of calcium with water. **[2 marks]**

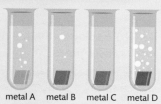

metal A   metal B   metal C   metal D

Figure 2

 Made a start   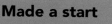 Feeling confident   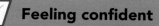 Exam ready

Extraction of metals and reduction

You need to know how carbon is used to extract metals from their ores, found in the Earth's crust. Ores are naturally-occurring rocks that contain enough metal so that it is economic to extract it.

 Extracting metals

Only very unreactive metals like gold are found uncombined in nature. These are known as native metals. Most metals are found as compounds, known as minerals. They are usually metal oxides or metal sulfides. When it is economically viable to extract the metal from the mineral, the rock is known as an ore. Aluminium is a reactive metal and found as aluminium oxide in an ore called bauxite. The method used to extract metals from their ore depends on their reactivity and the cost of the extraction process required. Metals that are less reactive than carbon can be extracted from their oxides by reduction (known as smelting); this process involves heating the metal oxide with carbon.

The extraction process removes the oxygen from the metal oxide. This means the metal is reduced. At the same time, the carbon is oxidised to form carbon dioxide.

Metals extracted by reduction with carbon include zinc, iron, tin, lead and copper.

Unreactive metals, such as gold, are found in the Earth's crust as uncombined elements, so chemical separation is unnecessary. However, physical processes and chemical reactions may be needed to remove other elements that could contaminate the gold.

Some metals, such as aluminium, are so reactive that their oxides cannot be reduced by carbon. Go to page 119 for more about extracting these types of metals.

> For example: iron oxide + carbon → iron + carbon dioxide.

> Metals such as zinc, iron and copper are present in ores as their oxides.

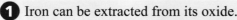

 Worked example — **Grade 5**

1 Iron can be extracted from its oxide.

(a) Name this type of process. [1 mark]

Reduction

(b) Explain how oxygen can be removed from iron oxide to make iron. [2 marks]

Heat the iron oxide with carbon to reduce the iron and remove the oxygen.

(c) Explain why aluminium must be extracted using electrolysis. [2 marks]

Aluminium is above carbon in the reactivity series so carbon cannot remove oxygen from aluminium oxide.

2 The following equation is an example of a reduction reaction used to extract a metal from its ore.

$$2CuO + C \rightarrow 2Cu + CO_2$$

(a) Write the word equation for the reaction taking place. [1 mark]

copper oxide + carbon → copper + carbon dioxide

(b) Explain why this reduction reaction can take place. [1 mark]

Copper is less reactive than carbon.

> The iron loses the oxygen it is combined with and is **reduced**.

> It may seem obvious that the iron oxide is heated but you need to always state the conditions used in a reaction. Although carbon is given in the answer, any element that is more reactive than iron could be used to extract it from its oxide.

> Only metals below carbon in the reactivity series can be extracted from their oxides using this process. As aluminium is further up the reactivity series than carbon, a different process is required.

 Exam-style practice — **Grade 5**

1 Lead oxide reacts with carbon to form the products lead and carbon dioxide.

(a) Write a word equation for the extraction of lead from lead oxide. [1 mark]

(b) State the name of the process used to extract lead from lead oxide. [1 mark]

(c) Explain why carbon can be used to extract lead from lead oxide. [2 marks]

2 Explain why calcium cannot be reduced from calcium oxide using carbon. [2 marks]

Electrolysis to extract metals

You need to know how reactive metals can be extracted from their compounds using electrolysis. Metals that are more reactive than carbon cannot be extracted by smelting so electrolysis is used instead.

5 Reactive metals

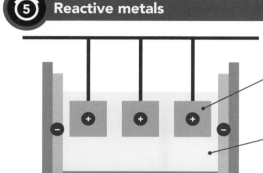

Oxygen is made at the anode. The oxygen reacts quickly with the carbon of the anode to make carbon dioxide.

Aluminium oxide is dissolved in molten cryolite.

Molten aluminium is made at the cathode.

The electrolysis of metals involves large amounts of energy as the metal compound must be in a molten state. Energy is also needed to produce the electrical current.

Bauxite is an aluminium ore that is mined and then refined to extract the aluminium oxide. The aluminium oxide is then reduced using electrolysis to make pure aluminium.

Aluminium oxide is dissolved in another aluminium-containing ore called cryolite. This reduces the melting temperature of the aluminium oxide and makes the electrolysis cheaper.

Figure 1 Electrolysis of aluminium

10 Worked example   Grades 4–5

1 (a) (i) State the method used for extraction of aluminium from its ore.   **[1 mark]**

Electrolysis

(ii) Explain why this method is used.   **[1 mark]**

Because aluminium is more reactive than carbon so reduction using carbon cannot be used.

(b) Name the substance used for the electrodes in the electrolysis of aluminium.   **[1 mark]**

Graphite (a form of carbon)

(c) Write a word equation for the extraction of aluminium from aluminium oxide.   **[1 mark]**

aluminium oxide → aluminium + oxygen

(d) Oxygen is produced at the anodes. Explain why the positive electrodes need replacing regularly.   **[2 marks]**

The oxygen produced reacts with the carbon electrodes to produce carbon dioxide. This results in the electrodes gradually wearing away.

2 Copper can be extracted from its ore using reduction with carbon. Copper can also be extracted and purified using electrolysis. Compare and contrast the two methods of extraction.   **[4 marks]**

Reduction with carbon requires a lot of energy to be provided in the form of high temperatures, which is expensive. It usually involves burning fossil fuels, which are a limited resource. Burning fossil fuels and reduction also produce carbon dioxide, which enhances the greenhouse effect. Additionally, reduction can only be used for metals lower in the reactivity series than carbon and metal products are impure and may need further processing. Electrolysis is very expensive as it requires a lot of energy to melt the metal and to provide electricity for the electrolysis process. It also involves burning fossil fuels, which are limited and cause global warming. Electrodes often need replacing. However, it can be used to extract any metal and metal products are pure.

10 Exam-style practice   Grade 5

1 Magnesium can be extracted from magnesium chloride using electrolysis. Explain why large amounts of energy are used in the extraction process.   **[2 marks]**

2 The melting point of aluminium oxide is over 2000 °C. Name the substance used to produce an electrolyte at a lower temperature.   **[1 mark]**

Metal oxides

You need to be able to state the properties of metal oxides and give equations for their formation.

2 Formation of metal oxides

Metal oxides are formed when a metal reacts with oxygen.

metal + oxygen → metal oxide

Metal oxides are examples of a giant ionic lattice structure. They are always solid at room temperature. They have high melting and boiling points.

5 Naming metal oxides

When metals react to form oxides, they gain oxygen so they are **oxidised**:

- copper + oxygen → copper oxide
- calcium + oxygen → calcium oxide
- lead + oxygen → lead oxide.

5 The reactivity series

The reactivity of a metal is related to its reactivity towards water and acids to form the metal cation. The more reactive the metal, the more easily it can be oxidised (page 117).

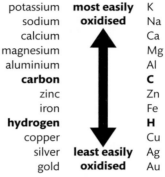

potassium	**most easily oxidised** ↑	K
sodium		Na
calcium		Ca
magnesium		Mg
aluminium		Al
carbon		**C**
zinc		Zn
iron		Fe
hydrogen		**H**
copper		Cu
silver		Ag
gold	↓ **least easily oxidised**	Au

Figure 1 The reactivity series: the more reactive a metal, the more easily it will be oxidised

10 Worked example — Grade 5

A student investigates magnesium oxide, a metal oxide.

(a) State what type of bonding is present in magnesium oxide. **[1 mark]**

Ionic bonding

(b) Balance the chemical equation below for the formation of magnesium oxide.

$Mg + O_2 \rightarrow MgO$ **[1 mark]**

$2Mg + O_2 \rightarrow 2MgO$

There are 2 atoms of magnesium needed.

Oxygen forms diatomic molecules.

You will need two MgO to balance the equation. This means there are the same number and type of atom on each side of the equation.

(c) The student notices that shiny magnesium metal ribbon left out in air quickly develops a cloudy surface, whereas gold jewellery remains shiny. Explain what causes the observed change and why gold does not behave in the same way. **[2 marks]**

The magnesium surface reacts fast with oxygen in the air to form magnesium oxide, which changes the appearance of the metal. Gold is much lower in the reactivity series than magnesium, so it does not oxidise in air.

5 Exam-style practice — Grade 5

(a) Write a word equation to identify the product formed in the reaction of iron and oxygen. **[1 mark]**

(b) State the bonding in the product of this reaction. **[1 mark]**

(c) Describe the bonding in the product of this reaction. **[2 marks]**

Recycling and life-cycle assessment

You need to know how a life-cycle assessment (LCA) is used to assess the environmental impact of a product, and the advantages of recycling metals to preserve metals and protect the environment.

⑤ Stages of an LCA

An LCA studies the environmental impact at several stages in the life of a product, including:

- extraction and processing of the raw material
- manufacture and packaging
- use during its lifetime
- disposal by incineration, landfill or recycling.

During each stage, energy is used, pollution is produced and waste is created.

LCAs are used to compare products with the same use but that are made from different materials, for example, paper cups and drinking glasses. In each case, the stages above need to be evaluated to identify which product has the least environmental impact.

⑤ Worked example — Grade 5

The table shows the energy used and waste created during the production of two different types of carrier bag. The figures shown are per 1000 carrier bags produced.

Bag type	Raw material	Electricity used (kWh)	Waste (g)
conventional high-density polyethylene (HDPE)	crude oil (finite resource)	6.15	418.4
cotton	plant (sustainable resource)	11.00	1800.0

Evaluate the environmental impact of the two different carrier bags. Use data from the table and your own knowledge in your answer. **[6 marks]**

HDPE bags require less energy, almost half, than cotton bags to make. The waste from HDPE bags is much less than cotton bags — about a quarter.

> The question says that you need to use the data from the table. You could quote the numbers, but it is better if you use the data to give a comparison.

HDPE is from a finite resource and will run out. Plastic is non-biodegradable and this will cause environmental problems. The cotton bag is renewable and sustainable, as well as biodegradable.

Although the HDPE uses less energy and makes less waste, I believe that cotton is better for the environment to make a bag from.

⑤ Recycling

Recycling reduces waste; however, energy is required to transform something into a new product, so pollution will still be created. The amount of energy required for recycling depends on the material and the final product. The levels of energy consumed and pollution produced by recycling are usually less than when the same product is made from raw materials.

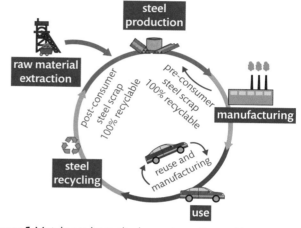

Figure 1 Metals can be melted, recast or reformed into new products. Scrap steel can be added to iron from the blast furnace to reduce the amount of iron that needs to be extracted.

> The data illustrates the environmental impact of the production of the different bags. It doesn't indicate the environmental impact of people reusing the bags.

② Working scientifically

Some parts of the LCA are subjective and based on the opinion of the person writing it. LCAs can be biased and used to misrepresent the actual cost to the environment.

⑩ Exam-style practice — Grade 4

1. Plastic bottles can be both reused and recycled. Give **two** advantages of reusing a plastic bottle rather than recycling it. **[2 marks]**

2. State the purpose of life-cycle assessments (LCAs). **[2 marks]**

3. Describe how recycling produces pollution, and the environmental impact of this pollution. **[4 marks]**

> When you are evaluating, it is important to consider the advantages and disadvantages and then state your considered opinion.

 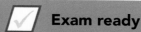

Reversible reactions

Many reactions, such as burning a fuel, go only in one direction. They make new chemical products that cannot be turned back easily into the reactants. Other chemical reactions are easily reversible – the products of the reaction can react to form the original reactants.

⏱ 5 Types of reaction

An **irreversible reaction** is shown by

A + B → C + D

The products, C and D, do not react to form the reactants, A and B.

A **reversible reaction** is indicated by a two-headed arrow (⇌). This symbol means that the reaction can happen in both directions.

A reversible reaction can be shown as:

A + B ⇌ C + D

In a closed system (one from which no substances can escape), both forward and back reactions can happen and equilibrium will be reached. **Equilibrium** occurs when the rate of the forward reaction is equal to the rate of the reverse reaction. The reactions continue in both directions, but the overall concentrations remain the same – dynamic equilibrium (see page 123).

⏱ 2 A reversible reaction

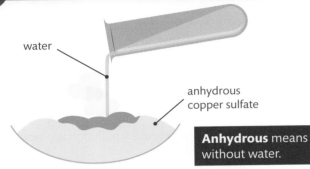

water

anhydrous copper sulfate

Anhydrous means without water.

Figure 1 When water is added to white anhydrous copper sulfate, blue hydrated copper sulfate forms. When hydrated copper sulfate is heated, it loses water and anhydrous copper sulfate forms.

The reaction between anhydrous copper sulfate and water is reversible.

hydrated copper sulfate ⇌ anhydrous copper sulfate + water
blue **white**

⏱ 10 Worked example — Grades 4–5

1 Complete the word equation below, producing sulfur trioxide, to show that the reaction is reversible. **[1 mark]**

sulfur dioxide + oxygen ⇌ sulfur trioxide

2 The thermal decomposition of ammonium chloride, into ammonia and hydrogen chloride, is reversible. Write a word equation to show the reaction. **[2 marks]**

ammonium ⇌ ammonia + hydrogen
chloride   chloride

> The marks are awarded for correctly using the information from the question to write the word equation **and** for correctly showing the reaction is reversible.

3 When water is added to a sample of blue anhydrous cobalt chloride, pink hydrated cobalt chloride forms.

(a) Write a word equation to show the reaction which took place. **[1 mark]**

anhydrous   + water ⇌ hydrated
cobalt chloride   cobalt chloride

(b) Devise an experiment to show that this reaction is reversible. **[2 marks]**

Heat the hydrated cobalt chloride to drive off the water. The cobalt chloride will change colour from pink back to blue showing that the reaction has reversed.

⏱ 5 Working scientifically

The direction of a reversible reaction can be altered by changing the conditions, such as temperature, concentration and, if gases are involved in the reaction, pressure.

Some reactions involve a colour change or a change of state. For example, when solid white ammonium chloride is heated, it forms two colourless gases. When these gases are cooled, solid white ammonium chloride reforms.

⏱ 10 Exam-style practice — Grade 5

1 The reaction between hydrogen and nitrogen is reversible. State what is meant by the term 'reversible'. **[2 marks]**

2 When hydrated copper sulfate is heated it changes colour from blue to white, producing anhydrous copper sulfate. When water is added, hydrated copper sulfate is reformed.

(a) Describe the observation that shows this reaction is reversible. **[1 mark]**

(b) Write a word equation to show the reaction taking place. **[2 marks]**

Made a start | Feeling confident | Exam ready

Dynamic equilibrium and the Haber process

You need to understand dynamic equilibrium reactions and know about the conditions that affect them.

Reaching dynamic equilibrium

Dynamic equilibrium is reached in a reversible reaction when the forward reaction occurs at exactly the **same rate** as the reverse reaction. For equilibrium to be achieved the reaction must take place in sealed apparatus (**closed system**).

1 At the start of the reaction there are no products.

2 As the reaction proceeds in the forward direction (to the right), reactants are being used up and products are formed.

3 Some of the newly formed products react. Their reaction moves in the reverse direction (to the left), favouring the production of the reactants.

4 The reaction reaches equilibrium when the rate of the forward reaction is equal to the rate of the reverse reaction. The reactions continue in both directions, but the concentration of each substance stays the same overall.

The amount of reactants and products at any one time are not equal but the proportions of each reactant and product remain constant. There is usually more of one than the other.

The Haber process

Ammonia is an important raw material in the manufacture of fertilisers, explosives, plastics and cleaning products.

Ammonia is manufactured by reacting nitrogen and hydrogen in the Haber process:

$$N_2(g) + 3H_2(g) \rightleftharpoons 2NH_3(g)$$

> Go to page 138 to revise fractional distillation.

Nitrogen is extracted from the air by fractional distillation and hydrogen can be made from a reaction between steam and natural gas.

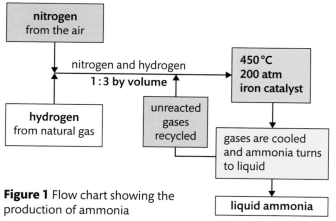

Figure 1 Flow chart showing the production of ammonia

Conditions for the Haber process

The reaction for producing ammonia is reversible. The conditions used are a compromise between yield (the amount of product made) and speed – manufacturers need to produce enough ammonia in a suitable length of time. So, a compromise known as the optimum is used.

Temperature: 450 °C
Usually, the higher the temperature, the faster the reaction, **but** because the Haber reaction is exothermic in the forward direction, too high a temperature will reduce the yield.

Pressure: 200 atmospheres
Increasing pressure increases the yield of ammonia, **but** increasing pressure means increased cost, as the reaction vessel must be built strong enough to withstand the high pressure.

Catalyst: iron
A catalyst is used to speed up the rate of the reaction; it does not affect the yield but will make the production of ammonia quicker.

Exam-style practice · Grade 4

Ammonia is produced using the Haber process.

(a) State the conditions needed for the Haber process. **[3 marks]**

(b) Describe the process used to collect the ammonia. **[1 mark]**

(c) Explain why the unreacted gases are recycled in the Haber process. **[2 marks]**

Worked example · Grade 4

State what is meant by the term 'dynamic equilibrium'. **[1 mark]**

A dynamic equilibrium can only happen with a reversible reaction in a closed system. The forward and reverse reactions continue to happen at the same rate. The concentrations of all of the substances remain the same overall.

Group 1

You need to know the electronic configurations of Group 1 elements, such as sodium and potassium, and the trends in their chemical properties.

5 Properties of Group 1 elements

Group 1 elements are known as the **alkali metals** due to the fact that they form alkaline solutions when they react with water. They are soft metals with low melting points.

All Group 1 elements have one outer electron.
When they react, they lose this outer-shell electron and form a positively-charged ion.

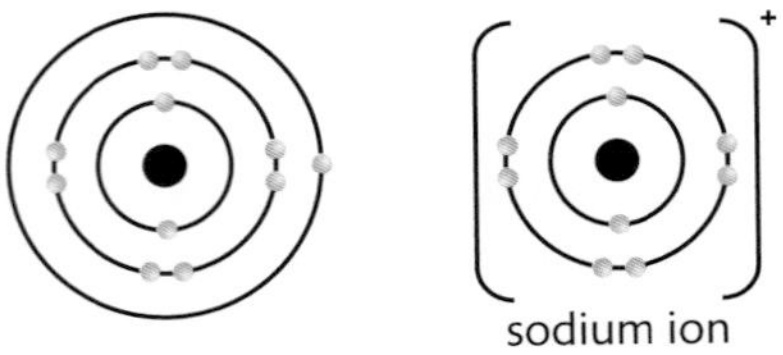

Figure 1 Sodium has the electronic configuration 2.8.1

10 Worked example — Grade 5

1 Write a word equation to show the reaction of lithium with water. **[2 marks]**

lithium + water → lithium hydroxide + hydrogen

2 Write the balanced chemical equation for the reaction between water and sodium. **[1 mark]**

$2Na(s) + 2H_2O(l) \rightarrow 2NaOH(aq) + H_2(g)$

Alkali metals react vigorously with water to produce an alkaline solution containing a metal hydroxide that turns universal indicator purple. Hydrogen gas is also produced. You should know the test for hydrogen – a lit splint produces a squeaky pop.

3 The size of the atom increases down Group 1. Explain how this affects the reactivity of the metals. **[3 marks]**

Reactivity increases down the group. The outer electron is further from the positively-charged nucleus and so can be lost more easily.

10 Exam-style practice — Grade 5

1 Describe the pattern in reactivity of elements down Group 1. **[1 mark]**

2 Lithium reacts with water. Give **three** observations that will be seen. **[3 marks]**

3 Look at the table for the reactions of Group 1 metals with water. Suggest how rubidium will react with water. **[1 mark]**

2 Observations as they react with water

The first three Group 1 metals are lithium, sodium and potassium. The following table shows how these metals react with water.

Element	Reaction with water
Li	floats and moves around the surface of the water, fizzes
Na	floats and moves around the surface of the water, fizzes rapidly, may ignite, metal melts into a ball
K	floats and moves around the surface of the water, catches fire with a lilac flame, may be a small explosion

increasing reactivity ↓

Working scientifically

To gain full credit for balancing equations you must first give the correct formulae for the reactants and products.

You should know that Group 1 elements are shown as monoatomic atoms and the formula for water is H_2O.

5 Reactivity of Group 1 elements

Group 1 metals react with non-metals to make ionic compounds. The elements are more reactive as you go down the group. This is because the atoms get bigger so the electrons are further from the nucleus and it is easier for the atoms to lose their outer-shell electrons and become 1+ ions.

Alkali metals react with water to make a metal hydroxide and hydrogen. The first three metals float on water, move around the surface and potassium bursts into lilac flames.

As you go down Group 1:

- reactivity increases
- metals become softer
- density increases
- melting point decreases.

Exam focus

You need to be able to predict the properties of other alkali metals by using your knowledge of the trends you have learned for the reactions of lithium, sodium and potassium.

Group 7

You need to know the electronic configurations of the first Group 7 elements and their physical properties and reactivity.

(5) Bonding

Fluorine, chlorine, bromine and iodine are all Group 7 elements and are also known as the **halogens**. They have seven electrons in their outer shell. They either gain electrons by reacting with a metal to form an ionic compound, or they share electrons with non-metals to form a covalent bond.

The halogens exist as **diatomic molecules** (pairs of atoms), sharing electrons in a covalent bond (see page 85).

Damp blue litmus paper will turn red and then be bleached, turning white, if held in chlorine gas.

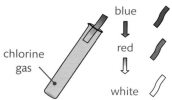

Figure 1 Testing for chlorine gas

(10) Worked example — Grade 4

1 The size of the atoms increases down Group 7. Explain how this affects the reactivity of Group 7 elements. **[3 marks]**

The reactivity decreases as you go down the group. The atoms get bigger. This means the outer-shell electrons are further away from the positive nucleus. So, it is more difficult for the bigger atoms to attract the extra electron. This means the reactivity is less.

2 Astatine is at the bottom of Group 7. Predict its physical appearance at room temperature (20 °C). **[2 marks]**

Dark grey or black solid

3 Describe the trend in boiling point in Group 7. **[2 marks]**

As you go down the group, the boiling point increases.

Larger molecules have greater intermolecular forces which need more energy to overcome and boil the substance.

(2) Properties

Group 7 elements are all non-metals. They have similar properties:

- low melting and boiling points
- brittle when solid
- poor conductors of heat and electricity
- molecules each contain two atoms (diatomic)
- coloured vapours – at room temperature:
  - Cl_2 is a green gas
  - Br_2 is a brown liquid
  - I_2 is a grey solid which sublimes to form a mauve (violet) gas when warmed.

As you go down Group 7:

- reactivity decreases
- relative molecular mass increases
- melting and boiling points increase.

When a substance sublimes it changes from a solid to a gas without passing through the liquid phase.

(5) Reactions

Halogens react vigorously with metals to form halide ions with a charge of –1. The vigour of these reactions decreases as you go down the group. For example:

iron + chlorine → iron(III) chloride

$$2Fe(s) + 3Cl_2(g) \rightarrow 2FeCl_3(s)$$

They react with non-metals to form simple molecules (page 86). For example, chlorine, bromine and iodine form hydrogen halides, which dissolve in water to form acidic solutions.

(10) Exam-style practice — Grade 5

1 (a) State the electronic configuration of chlorine. **[1 mark]**

(b) Explain why chlorine readily forms ionic compounds with metals. **[2 marks]**

(c) Suggest how the reaction between fluorine and calcium is different from the reaction between chlorine and calcium. **[1 mark]**

2 (a) Suggest the pH of a solution of a hydrogen halide. **[1 mark]**

(b) Give the observations when damp blue litmus paper is put in a sealed test tube of chlorine gas. **[2 marks]**

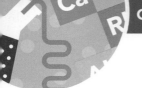

Group 7 reactivity

The trend in reactivity of the halogens can be explained using displacement reactions and their electronic configuration.

10 Displacement reactions

A more reactive halogen will **displace** (push out) a less reactive halogen from its salt in aqueous solution.

Chlorine is more reactive than iodine, so will displace it from an aqueous solution of its salt.

chlorine + sodium iodide → sodium chloride + iodine

Bromine is less reactive than chlorine, so it cannot displace chorine – no reaction takes place.

	Chloride	Bromide	Iodide
Chlorine	no reaction	bromine forms (turns orange)	iodine forms (turns brown)
Bromine	no reaction	no reaction	iodine forms (turns brown)
Iodine	no reaction	no reaction	no reaction

Table 1 Investigating halogen displacement. The table shows the observations when halogens are mixed with solutions of halides.

5 Electronic configuration

The **reactivity** of a halogen depends on its **electronic configuration**. All Group 7 elements have seven outer electrons and easily gain one more to make a full outer shell. The closer the outer shell is to the nucleus, the more strongly the nucleus can attract the outer electrons. Therefore, chlorine attracts an extra electron more easily than bromine.

These are the halide ions and can only be found in compounds, e.g. sodium chloride, sodium bromide and sodium iodide. These substances are ionic compounds known as halide salts. Often they are used in aqueous solution (dissolved in water).

The halogens are the elements. They are diatomic covalent molecules. For this displacement reaction the halogens are often used in a solution. This is safer than using the pure halogen.

10 Worked example — Grade 5

1 Give the electronic configuration of:

(a) a fluorine atom **[1 mark]**

2.7

(b) a chlorine atom. **[1 mark]**

2.8.7

2 Using your understanding of displacement reactions with halide ions, describe the relative reactivity of the halogens down the group. Use this trend to predict the reactions of astatine. **[3 marks]**

A more reactive halogen (one higher up the group) will displace a less reactive halogen (lower in the group) from its salt in solution. So, for example, chlorine displaces iodine.

As astatine is at the bottom of Group 7, it is the least reactive of the halogens and so would be displaced from its halide by all of the other halogens. It would be unable to displace any of the other halogen halides due to its lack in reactivity.

You will be given a copy of the periodic table in the exam. You may be asked to **predict** the properties of elements in Groups 0, 1 and 7 based on trends or patterns seen in the group.

Electronic configurations can also be shown as diagrams:

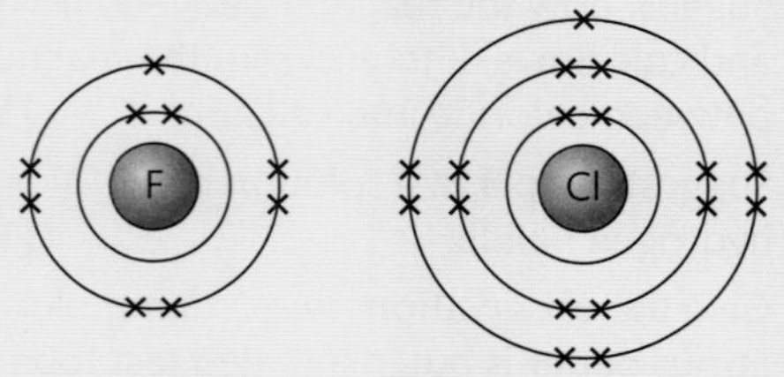

(a) Fluorine atom **(b)** Chlorine atom

5 Exam-style practice — Grade 4

1 Write a word equation for the reaction between potassium iodide and bromine. **[2 marks]**

2 Explain why chlorine displaces iodine from potassium iodide. **[2 marks]**

3 Suggest the name of the halogen that is made when lithium iodide is reacted with bromine. **[1 mark]**

Group 0

You need to know the electronic configurations of Group 0 elements and the trends in their physical and chemical properties.

(10) Electronic configuration

The elements in Group 0 are also known as **noble gases**. They do not react chemically and are described as inert. This is due to their stable electron arrangement. They all have a full outer shell – eight electrons in their outermost shell (except helium which has two). They do not easily form molecules but exist as **monatomic** (single) atoms.

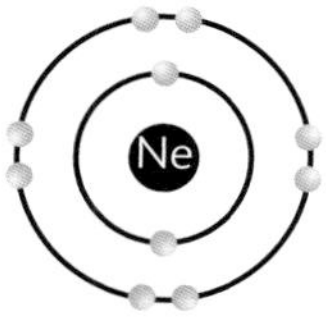

Figure 1 Neon has the electronic configuration 2.8

(5) Physical and chemical trends

Trends are observed in the properties of Group 0 elements.

He
Ne
Ar
Kr
Xe

- The relative atomic mass increases. There are more protons and neutrons in each atom down the group.
- The size of the atoms increases due to the number of electron shells increasing.
- The boiling points increase. As the atoms get bigger they have more electrons, which leads to increased intermolecular forces between the atoms.

Go to page 79 to revise electronic configuration.

(10) Worked example — Grade 5

1 Give the meaning of the term 'monatomic'. **[1 mark]**

A single atom.

2 Explain why Group 0 elements are used as the atmosphere for some chemical reactions. **[2 marks]**

Group 0 elements are inert so they do not affect chemical reactions.

3 State and explain how the boiling point of Group 0 elements changes down the group. **[3 marks]**

The boiling point increases down the group.
As the size of the atoms increases down the group, there are more electrons leading to increased intermolecular forces between the atoms.

4 The radius of a neon atom is 154 pm. Predict whether the radius of a xenon atom will be larger or smaller than a neon atom. **[1 mark]**

Look at the periodic table to see where xenon is compared to neon.

The radius of a xenon atom will be larger than the radius of a neon atom.

This is because xenon has three more occupied electron shells than neon.

(2) Uses of noble gases

The inertness of noble gases makes them useful where an unreactive or non-flammable atmosphere is required.

Helium is used to fill balloons and airships, as it has a very low density (so a lot of lifting power) as well as being non-flammable.

Noble gases are often used to exclude air; for example argon, the most readily available noble gas, is used in welding to prevent the hot metal from oxidising and in laboratories to protect highly reactive compounds. Argon and krypton are used in some high-end lighting to prevent lamp filaments oxidising or evaporating.

Noble gases are also used in gas discharge lamps, like car headlamps (xenon) and neon lights. (In fact, not only neon but all the noble gases, though colourless, produce coloured discharges.)

(1) Exam focus

Make sure you know the trends in Group 0, Group 1 and Group 7 of the periodic table. You need to be able to predict the properties of the elements in these groups.

(5) Exam-style practice — Grade 5

1 Explain how electronic configuration shows that an atom belongs to Group 0. **[1 mark]**

2 **(a)** Explain the trend in relative atomic mass down Group 0. **[2 marks]**

(b) Describe how the number of outer electrons affects the reactivity of the noble gases. **[1 mark]**

3 Draw the electronic configuration of an argon atom. **[2 marks]**

Calculating rate of reaction

You need to be able to find the rate of a reaction using formulae.

 Determining a value

The rate of reaction measures how much product is made per second in a particular reaction. It can also be how much reactant is used per second. It can be calculated using formulae.

The rate of a reaction can be found by measuring the mass of a solid, or volume of a gas, produced over a fixed period of time during a reaction. Alternatively, it may be found by measuring the quantity of the reactant used over time.

Depending on whether the product or the reactant is being measured, either of the following formulae can be used:

> If mass is measured (in grams) during the reaction, the unit for rate is g/s.

$$\text{mean rate of reaction} = \frac{\text{quantity of reactant used}}{\text{time}}$$

> If volume is measured during the reaction, the unit for rate is cm^3/s.

$$\text{mean rate of reaction} = \frac{\text{quantity of product formed}}{\text{time}}$$

> Time is always measured in seconds.

 Worked example | **Grade 5**

A student investigates the reaction between zinc powder and hydrochloric acid. Hydrogen and a solution of zinc chloride are produced.

(a) Write the word equation for this reaction. **[1 mark]**

zinc + hydrochloric acid → zinc chloride + hydrogen

(b) Name apparatus suitable for collecting the gas produced in the reaction. **[1 mark]**

A gas syringe could be used to collect the hydrogen gas released.

(c) The table shows the results of the experiment. Calculate the mean rate of the reaction using the data in the table. **[2 marks]**

Results							
Time (s)	0	10	20	30	40	50	60
Volume of gas (cm^3)	0	20	40	58	72	80	80

$$\text{mean rate} = \frac{\text{volume of gas}}{\text{time}} = \frac{80}{50} = 1.6 \, cm^3/s$$

> Consider the reaction being described; it is sometimes worth writing out an equation to see what reaction is taking place.

> The rate of reaction changes throughout the course of a reaction. It is usually quickest at the start and it slows down as the reactants are used up.
>
> The results show that the reaction had finished by 50 seconds as no more gas was produced.

 Exam-style practice | **Grade 5**

Figure 1 is a graph showing rate of reaction.

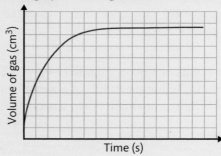

Figure 1

(a) A student calculated the rate of reaction for the plotted line. Identify the units needed. **[1 mark]**

(b) The reaction reaches completion after 2 minutes, producing $120 \, cm^3$ of gas. Calculate the mean rate of reaction. **[2 marks]**

Factors affecting rate of reaction

For a reaction between two particles to occur, the particles must collide with enough energy to react. If a change causes more collisions, or gives particles more energy, then rates of reaction increase. You need to know about five main factors that can affect the rate of a reaction.

(5) Measuring the rate

Depending on the type of reaction taking place, the rate of reaction can be measured by:

- collecting the gas given off during a reaction (with a gas syringe or by displacement of water and collecting the gas in an upturned measuring cylinder)
- mass change (with a balance)
- colour change (disappearing cross).

(2) Working scientifically

You need to know how to change the conditions of an experiment to alter the reaction rate. Variables can affect the rate of a reaction. You can control variables to ensure that a reaction occurs efficiently within a reasonable timeframe.

(5) Factors affecting rate of reaction

Pressure of reacting gases: Increasing pressure gives a higher rate of reaction: gas particles are more likely to collide as they are being squashed into a smaller volume, so the rate of collision increases.

Temperature: The higher the temperature the higher the rate of reaction; particles gain kinetic energy and so move faster, increasing the rate of collision.
Each collision also has more energy.

> More successful collisions in the same time increases the rate of reaction

Factors affecting rates of reactions

Surface area of solid reactants: A larger surface to volume ratio on a solid gives a higher rate of reaction. Reactions take place on the surface of a solid, so a greater surface area to volume ratio means that there is a greater rate of collision as more particles are exposed at any time.

Concentration of reactants in solution: The higher the concentration the higher the rate of reaction; there are more particles present in the reaction mixture, so a greater rate of collision.

Catalysts: Using catalysts increases the rate of a reaction. They provide an alternative pathway which requires lower activation energy. So, although there is the same rate of collisions (number of collisions in a given time), some of the lower energy collisions will give a product.

(5) Worked example · Grade 5

A student investigated a reaction between marble chips and acid. 2 g of cubic marble chips with average measurements of 2 mm × 2 mm × 2 mm were reacted with 20 cm³ of hydrochloric acid.

(a) Calculate the volume of one marble chip. Include the units. **[3 marks]**

Volume = 2 x 2 x 2 = 8 mm³

> Volume measurements are always to the power of 3.

(b) Calculate the surface area of one marble chip. Include the units. **[2 marks]**

Surface area = 6 x 2 x 2 = 24 mm²

> There are six faces on a cube.

> Area units are always to the power of 2.

(c) Calculate the surface area to volume ratio. **[2 marks]**

24 : 8 becomes 3 : 1

(10) Exam-style practice · Grade 5

A student investigated the reaction between marble chips and hydrochloric acid. Their results are shown in the table below.

Time (s)	20	38	52	75	90	110	130	150
Mass of reactants (g)	1.02	0.69	0.46	0.21	0.10	0.10	0.10	0.10

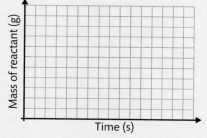

(a) On the axes provided, plot the results of the investigation. Draw a line of best fit. **[4 marks]**

(b) State **two** ways of increasing the rate of the reaction other than changing the temperature. **[2 marks]**

> The ratio should be simplified and has no units as it is comparing the values not the measurements.

Practical: Monitoring rate of reaction – colour change

You need to know how to investigate the way changes in concentration affect the rates of reactions. This includes measuring the volume of a gas produced and the change in colour.

Apparatus

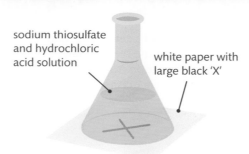

sodium thiosulfate and hydrochloric acid solution

white paper with large black 'X'

This reaction can be summarised in the following equations:

sodium thiosulfate + hydrochloric acid →
        sodium chloride + water + sulfur dioxide + sulfur

$Na_2S_2O_3(s) + 2HCl(aq) \rightarrow 2NaCl(aq) + H_2O(l) + SO_2(g) + S(s)$

The solid sulfur makes the liquid become cloudy (or turbid).

Working scientifically

To make this experiment more accurate (closer to true values) use a light sensor. Time how long it takes for no light to be detected by the sensor.

Method

1. Prepare the sodium thiosulfate solution in a conical flask. Use a measuring cylinder to add water.
2. Place the conical flask on top of the black cross.
3. Use a measuring cylinder to measure the dilute hydrochloric acid.
4. Pour the acid into a conical flask. At the same time, swirl the flask gently and start the stop clock.
5. Look down through the top of the flask. Stop the clock when you can no longer see the cross. Record the time in seconds.
6. For reliability, repeat this process three times for each concentration of sodium thiosulfate. Calculate the mean time taken for each concentration.

Reliability can be thought about in two ways:
Repeatability – each time you repeat the experiment you get similar results.
Reproducibility – other groups get similar results to you.

Only take a mean from similar results. Any results that do not follow the pattern are anomalous and would make your mean less accurate (less close to true values).

Worked example

Grade 5

The table shows the effect of changing concentration of sodium thiosulfate on the rate of reaction.

Increased concentration means there are more acid particles present so more chance of successful collisions. As a result, the rate of the reaction would increase as the concentration increases.

Concentration of sodium thiosulfate (g dm⁻³)	Time taken for cross to disappear (s)			
	1	2	3	Mean
3.95	202	206	206	205
7.91	127	125	128	127
11.86	76	72	74	74

(a) Calculate the mean for the highest concentration in the table. **[2 marks]**

$\frac{(76 + 72 + 74)}{3} = 74$

(b) Using the data in the table, state **one** conclusion the student could make about the effect of concentration on the rate of the reaction. **[2 marks]**

Increasing the concentration of sodium thiosulfate caused the rate of reaction to increase.

Exam-style practice

Grade 5

Hydrochloric acid reacts with sodium thiosulfate to make a sulfur precipitate.

(a) Use collision theory to explain how increasing the temperature would affect the rate of this reaction. **[3 marks]**

(b) Give the independent, dependent and control variables for the investigation into the effect of temperature on the rate of reaction. **[3 marks]**

Made a start   Feeling confident   Exam ready

Practical: Monitoring rate of reaction – gas production

You need to know how to investigate the rate of a reaction by measuring the gas produced over a period of time.

5 Investigating the rate of reaction between marble chips and acid

Rate of reaction is affected by several factors, including temperature, concentration of solute, and surface area to volume ratio of solid reactants. In this reaction, you will investigate how the rate is affected by surface area (the size of the marble chips used) and concentration (the concentration of the hydrochloric acid).

Marble is a rock made of mainly calcium carbonate, $CaCO_3$. It is an insoluble base.

5 Methods of gas collection

There are two methods you can use to collect a gas produced during a reaction.

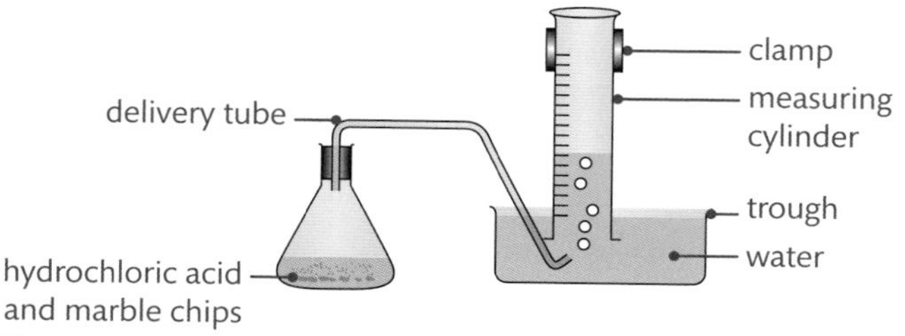
clamp
measuring cylinder
delivery tube
trough
water
hydrochloric acid and marble chips

Figure 1 Upturned measuring cylinder over water; this is called collecting the gas by displacement

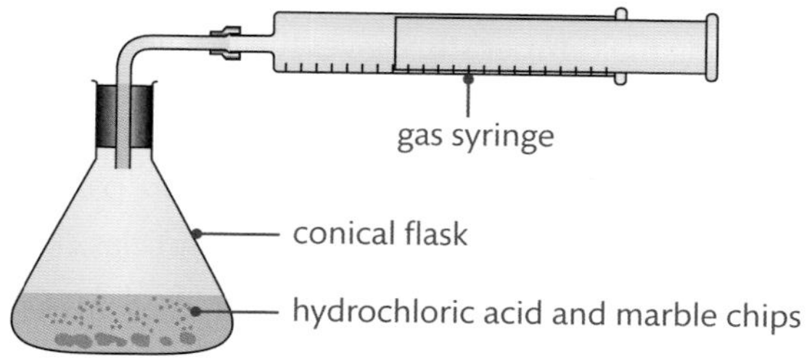
gas syringe
conical flask
hydrochloric acid and marble chips

Figure 2 Gas syringe

10 Method

1. Measure the volume of acid required and add to the conical flask.
2. Measure the mass of large marble (calcium carbonate) chips and add to the conical flask. Quickly insert the bung to prevent any loss of gas.
3. Measure the total volume of gas produced every 20 seconds and record. Continue until there are at least five data points so that a graph with a line of best fit can be plotted.

In part **(b)**, 1 mark is awarded for showing a less steep gradient at the start – as the reaction is slower. The second mark is for recognising that the same total volume of gas would be produced during the reaction.

Exam focus

Size of marble chips and concentration are examples of **independent variables** because you change them in your investigation. The independent variable should always be the first column in a results table and plotted on the *x*-axis.

The **dependent variable** is the variable that you measure and record during the experiment. It should always be on the *y*-axis in a graph. Here, it is the volume of gas produced.

5 Worked example — Grade 5

A student investigated how concentration of acid affects the rate of reaction with marble chips. The graph below shows the results obtained with **concentrated** hydrochloric acid.

(a) Label the axes and give the units for each. **[2 marks]**

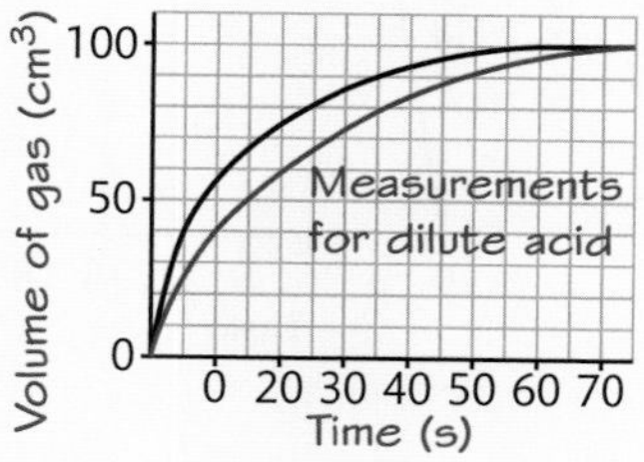
Volume of gas (cm³)
100
50
0
0 20 30 40 50 60 70
Time (s)
Measurements for dilute acid

(b) The student repeated the experiment using **dilute** hydrochloric acid. Sketch on the graph to show how the rate of the reaction would change. **[2 marks]**

5 Exam-style practice — Grade 5

Describe how surface area of a solid affects rate of reaction. **[2 marks]**

Made a start | Feeling confident | Exam ready

Collision theory and activation energy

You need to know how factors such as temperature, concentration, surface area and pressure (of gases) can be altered to affect the rate of a reaction, using collision theory.

5 Collision theory

For a reaction to happen, reacting particles must **collide** with **enough energy** to react.

Activation energy is the minimum amount of energy required for a reaction to take place.

Activation energy can only change if a catalyst is added. A catalyst provides an alternative reaction pathway with a lower activation energy so more collisions are successful and the rate of reaction increases.

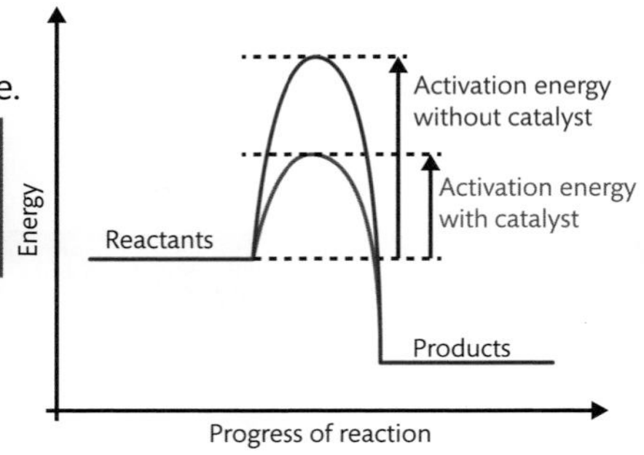

Factors affecting rate of reaction

The rate of reaction is directly proportional to the frequency of collisions. This means that increasing factors that make collisions more frequent will increase the rate of reaction.

- Increasing the **temperature** gives the reacting particles more energy, so they are moving faster and more likely to collide and more likely to have at least the activation energy when they do collide.

Go to page 129 for more about factors that affect rate of reaction.

- Increasing the **concentration** results in more particles in the reaction mixture, so there is a higher chance of collisions.
- Increasing the **pressure** pushes the gas particles closer together, so they are more likely to collide.
- Increasing the **surface to volume ratio** of solid reactants results in increased frequency of collisions.

10 Worked example — Grade 5

A student investigates the volume of gas produced in the reaction between magnesium ribbon and hydrochloric acid. **Figure 1** shows the student's results.

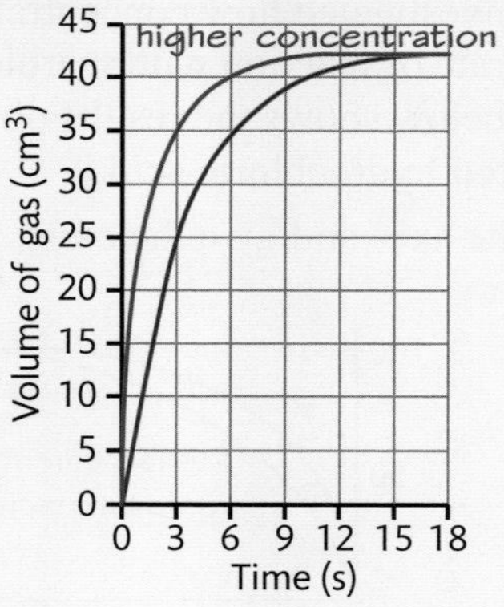

Figure 1

The student then repeats the experiment using a more concentrated solution of hydrochloric acid with the same mass of magnesium.

(a) Draw the new line of best fit on the graph for the higher concentration of acid. **[2 marks]**

If the concentration of the acid is increased, the rate of reaction will be faster, as there will be more chance of successful collisions occurring. Therefore, the line will be steeper at the start of the reaction. As there is the same number of magnesium particles in the reaction mixture, the reaction will still produce the same volume of gas, so the curve should plateau at the same volume.

(b) The student repeats the experiment using powdered magnesium, rather than magnesium ribbon. Use collision theory to explain why the rate of reaction will increase with powdered magnesium. **[2 marks]**

Magnesium powder has a larger surface area than magnesium ribbon. This will help more collisions between the acid and magnesium particles.

5 Exam-style practice — Grade 5

1 A student investigated the reaction between zinc powder and sulfuric acid.
State and explain what will happen to the rate of reaction if the temperature of the reaction mixture is increased. **[3 marks]**

2 The reaction to make hydrogen chloride gas from hydrogen gas and chlorine gas is given below:
hydrogen + chlorine → hydrogen chloride
Explain in terms of collision theory how increasing the pressure affects the rate of reaction. **[2 marks]**

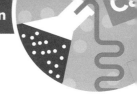

Reaction profiles

You need to know how reaction profiles, also known as energy level diagrams, are used to compare the energy of reactants and products to determine the type of reaction taking place.

5 A reaction profile

A reaction profile provides information on:
- the energy of the reactants
- the energy of the products
- the amount of activation energy needed for the reaction
- whether the reaction is exothermic or endothermic.

Go to page 135 for more information about exothermic and endothermic reactions.

The minimum amount of energy required for a reaction to start.

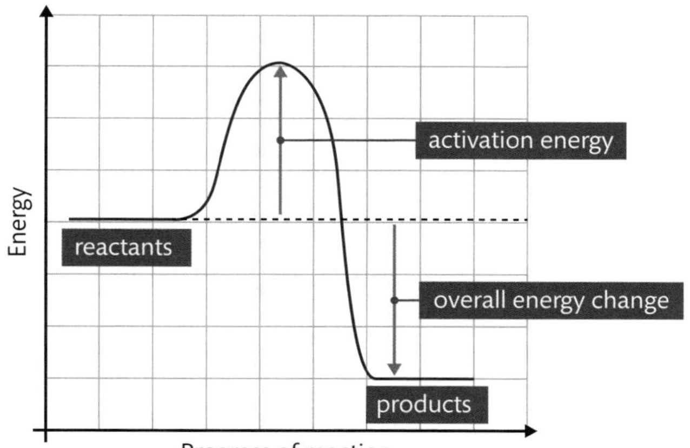

Figure 1 A reaction profile for an exothermic reaction

10 Worked example — Grade 5

The reaction between sodium hydrogen carbonate and citric acid is endothermic. Draw a reaction profile to show the reaction. Include the following labels on the diagram:
- activation energy
- overall energy change. **[4 marks]**

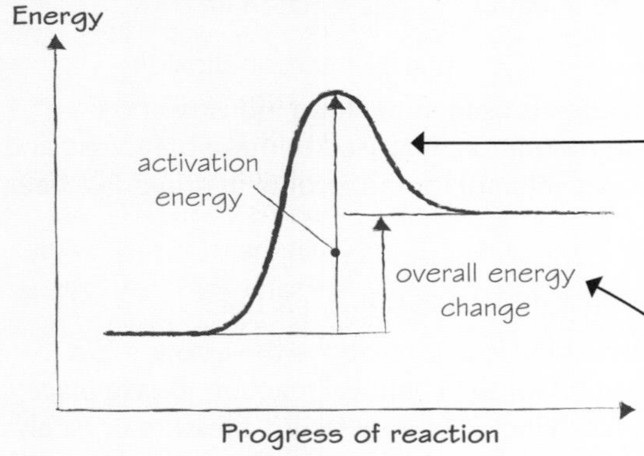

This reaction is endothermic, which means that the products will have more energy than the reactants because energy is being taken in from the surroundings.

The curve is drawn from the reactants to the products. In an endothermic reaction, the reactants must have less energy than the products. This is because energy is gained by the system. The peak of the curve must be higher than the energy level of the products. This shows the activation energy required by the reaction.

The overall energy change is the difference between the reactants and the products. In this case, energy is being taken in by the reaction between sodium hydrogen carbonate and citric acid.

5 Exam focus

In the exam, you could be asked to do the following:
- Draw reaction profiles for exothermic and endothermic reactions.
- Label the activation energy and the overall energy change of a reaction.
- Use reaction profiles provided to identify the type of reaction taking place. This means say whether the reaction is exothermic or endothermic.

10 Exam-style practice — Grade 5

1. Cooling packs used to treat sports injuries involve an endothermic reaction. Draw and label a reaction profile for this type of reaction. **[4 marks]**
2. The diagram below shows the reaction profile for the combustion of methane.

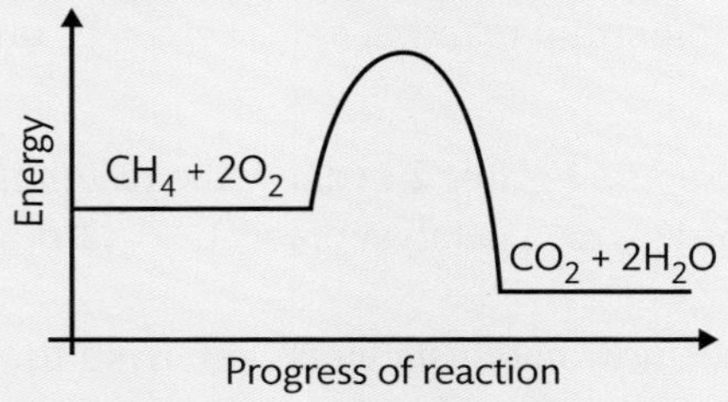

(a) Use the diagram to state if the reaction is exothermic or endothermic. **[1 mark]**

(b) Explain your answer. **[1 mark]**

(c) Label the activation energy of the reaction on the diagram. **[1 mark]**

Catalysts

You need to know what a catalyst is and how it affects the rate of a chemical reaction.

⑤ Reaction pathways

A **catalyst** is a substance that speeds up the rate of a reaction without changing the products that are made. At the end of the reaction, the catalyst is unchanged chemically. It is not used up in the reaction, so there is the same mass of catalyst at the end as you started with. Catalysts increase the rate of reaction by providing a different pathway for the reaction. The pathway provided has a lower activation energy, so more particles will have enough energy to react, and the reaction will be faster. Different catalysts are needed for different reactions. For example, enzymes are biological catalysts.

The activation energy is lower for a catalysed reaction so its reaction profile peaks at a lower energy level.

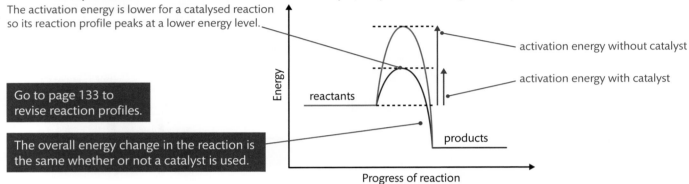

activation energy without catalyst

activation energy with catalyst

Go to page 133 to revise reaction profiles.

The overall energy change in the reaction is the same whether or not a catalyst is used.

Figure 1 A reaction profile diagram showing the effect of a catalyst

⑩ Worked example — Grade 5

1 Hydrogen peroxide decomposes **slowly** to produce water and oxygen.

hydrogen peroxide → water + oxygen

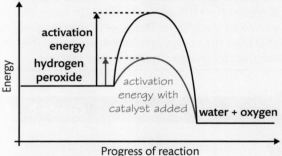

Figure 2

(a) Look at **Figure 2**. In terms of energy, identify the type of reaction taking place. Does the reaction show an exothermic or endothermic reaction? **[1 mark]**

Exothermic

(b) Complete **Figure 2** to show the reaction profile with a catalyst present. **[2 marks]**

2 Describe how catalysts work, referring to their effect on the activation energy of a reaction. **[2 marks]**

A catalyst provides an alternative pathway for the reaction, which requires less energy.

② Working scientifically

Enzymes are biological catalysts and are found in living organisms. Yeast is a fungus and makes an enzyme that can work as a biological catalyst. The word equation for this reaction is:

glucose $\xrightarrow{yeast}$ ethanol + carbon dioxide

This reaction is used in the food industry and is called fermentation. It is used to make bread rise and to produce ethanol for the alcohol in drinks like beer.

You can identify a catalyst in a reaction:

- if something is written above the arrow, it is a condition for the chemical reaction to take place; this could include temperature, pressure or catalysts
- if a substance is the same on both sides of the reaction, i.e. it's not part of the reaction
- if you are told a reaction speeds up, but the same reaction occurs, when a substance is added.

⑤ Exam-style practice — Grade 5

1 The Haber process makes ammonia. It can be summarised by the word equation:

hydrogen + nitrogen $\xrightarrow{iron}$ ammonia

Name the catalyst used in this reaction. **[1 mark]**

2 Name the catalysts used in biological systems. **[1 mark]**

Made a start   Feeling confident   Exam ready

Exothermic and endothermic reactions

You need to know the difference between exothermic and endothermic reactions and be able to identify the type of reaction when given details about temperature changes.

(5) Classifying reactions

During a reaction, energy is transferred from the reactants to the surroundings, or from the surroundings to the reactants. **Exothermic** reactions **release** energy (usually by heat) to the surroundings. The temperature of the surroundings **increases**. Examples include: oxidation, metal displacement, neutralisation and combustion.

Endothermic reactions **take in** energy from the surroundings. The temperature of the surroundings **decreases**. Examples include: thermal decomposition, photosynthesis, salts dissolving in water, electrolysis and citric acid reacting with sodium hydrogencarbonate.

(5) Bond energy

Breaking bonds is an endothermic change and making bonds is an exothermic change:

- A reaction is **endothermic** if more energy is needed to break bonds in reactants than is released when making products.
- A reaction is **exothermic** if more energy is released when making products than is needed to break bonds in reactants.

(10) Worked example   Grade 5

1 Exothermic and endothermic reactions can be used for everyday purposes.

   (a) State the type of reaction that hand warmers and self-heating cans use.   **[1 mark]**

   Exothermic

   (b) State the type of reaction that headache cooling pads and sports injury packs use.   **[1 mark]**

   Endothermic

2 A student was investigating the best reaction for use in hand warmers. The table below shows the results and costs for the energy changes in three different chemical reactions.

Reaction	Temperature change (°C)	Cost (£)
A	+6	3.50
B	−3	2.00
C	+17	25.00

   (a) Identify the most suitable reaction.   **[1 mark]**

   Reaction A

   (b) Explain the reason for your answer.   **[2 marks]**

   Because the reaction releases thermal energy and is cheaper than reaction C.

(5) Exam-style practice   Grade 4

1 A student reacts two substances and measures the energy change as the reactants become the products during the reaction. The products have less energy than the reactants.
Name this type of reaction.   **[1 mark]**

2 Ammonium nitrate dissolving in water is an example of an endothermic change. Describe how the temperature of the mixture will change during this reaction.   **[1 mark]**

Temperature changes

You need to know how to investigate variables that affect temperature changes in reacting solutions, including acid with metals or carbonates, salts dissolving in water, precipitation reactions, neutralisation reactions and displacement of metals. When these reactions occur in solution, the temperature change can be measured to reflect the energy change that has occurred.

(2) Apparatus ☑

- ☑ dilute hydrochloric acid
- ☑ sodium hydroxide solution
- ☑ polystyrene cup and lid with small hole
- ☑ 250 cm³ beaker
- ☑ measuring cylinder
- ☑ thermometer

(5) Maths skills ☑

You might need to draw a graph of the results. The independent variable (volume of sodium hydroxide added) should be on the x-axis and the dependent variable (temperature) on the y-axis.

You will need at least five points to draw a line of best fit. It should show the trend in the data and does not need to go through every point.

(2) Working scientifically ☑

Control variables are the things you need to keep the same during the experiment, to make sure the results are valid (answer the question asked). In this reaction, the concentration and volume of hydrochloric acid must be kept the same.

(10) Method ☑

1. Using a measuring cylinder add 20 cm³ dilute hydrochloric acid into a polystyrene cup.

2. Stand the cup inside a beaker. This will make it more stable and will insulate it.

3. Use a thermometer to measure the temperature of the acid. Record the temperature.

4. Measure 5 cm³ of sodium hydroxide solution.

5. Pour the sodium hydroxide into the cup. Loosely fit the lid and gently stir the solution with the thermometer through the hole. When the reading on the thermometer remains constant record the temperature in your table.

6. Continue the process until an equal volume of sodium hydroxide has been added.

7. Repeat this experiment two more times and record your findings in a table similar to the one below.

Total volume of NaOH added (cm³)	Increase in temperature (°C)			
	1	2	3	Mean
0	0	0	0	0
5	8	6	5	6.3
10	17	19	19	18.3

(5) Worked example ⬛ Grade 5 ☑

A student uses the apparatus in **Figure 1** to measure the temperature change when hydrochloric acid reacts with calcium carbonate.

(a) Describe an improvement to the apparatus to reduce the heat lost to the surroundings. **[2 marks]**

Use a polystyrene cup instead of the beaker and loosely place a lid on top of the cup.

(b) Describe the observation that the student would make to determine whether the reaction is exothermic. **[1 mark]**

The reading on the thermometer would increase.

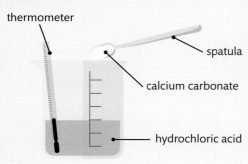

thermometer
spatula
calcium carbonate
hydrochloric acid

Figure 1

(5) Exam-style practice ⬛ Grade 3 ☑

A student measures the temperature change when water is added to anhydrous cobalt chloride and hydrated cobalt chloride is formed. Calculate the mean temperature change. **[2 marks]**

	Trial 1	Trial 2	Trial 3	Mean
Temperature change (°C)	−6.0	−8.0	−5.0	

Crude oil and hydrocarbons

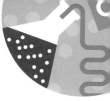

Organic chemistry is the study of the structure, properties and reactions of the large variety of compounds that contain carbon. The main sources of these organic compounds are living or once-living organisms. You need to know the general formula for alkanes, as well as their physical and chemical properties.

5 Crude oil

Crude oil is a mixture of a very large number of compounds. It formed millions of years ago from the remains of biomass (mainly plankton) buried in mud. Crude oil can be found in rocks and trapped under the seabed of oceans. Due to the time it takes to create crude oil, it is a finite resource. This means if we continue using crude oil as fast as we are, it will run out.

Crude oil is an important source of useful substances. It is used for a variety of fuels, including petrol and diesel, and as a feedstock for the production of many substances, including plastics, soaps and detergents, healthcare products such as aspirin, synthetic fibres for clothes and furniture, rubbers and paints.

Exam focus

You need to know that carbon atoms can form rings as well as chains but you do not need to know the names or structures of any ring molecules.

5 Hydrocarbons

Most of the compounds in crude oil are hydrocarbons – compounds consisting of hydrogen and carbon only. Most of these hydrocarbons belong to a homologous series (family of compounds) called the alkanes. These are formed from chains of carbon atoms. Some molecules may be found as rings of carbon atoms (**Figure 1**).

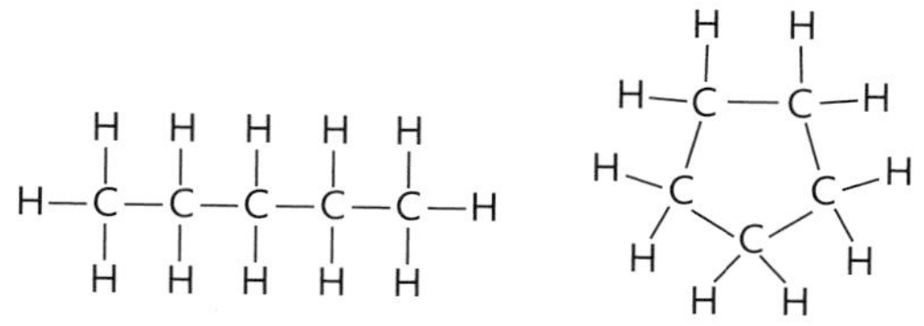

straight-chain hydrocarbon **ring formation**

Figure 1 Hydrocarbon molecules contain carbon atoms joined together in straight chains or in rings

5 Alkanes

Alkanes share the general formula C_nH_{2n+2} where *n* is equal to the number of carbon atoms. Each successive alkane differs by $-CH_2-$ in its molecular formula from its neighbouring compound. Alkanes are saturated; this means they have no double bonds between carbon atoms.

Name	Molecular formula
methane	CH_4
ethane	C_2H_6
propane	C_3H_8
butane	C_4H_{10}

5 Properties of hydrocarbons

In a homologous series, such as the alkanes, a gradual change in physical properties, such as their boiling points, can be seen as the chain length increases.

You don't need to remember the boiling points, only how they change (trend). As the hydrocarbon chain gets bigger, the boiling point increases because the intermolecular forces of attraction are larger between bigger molecules.

Alkane	Boiling point (°C)
methane	–164
ethane	–89
propane	–42
butane	–0.5
pentane	36
hexane	39

Compounds in a homologous series have similar chemical properties.

See page 139 for further properties of hydrocarbons.

5 Worked example Grade 5

1 Give the molecular formula for an alkane with eight carbon atoms. **[2 marks]**

C_8H_{18}

Using the general formula C_nH_{2n+2}
if C = 8 then H = (8 × 2) + 2 = 16 + 2 = 18

2 Describe how the hydrocarbon chain length affects the boiling point. **[2 marks]**

As chain length increases, there are stronger forces of attraction between the molecules. This means more energy is needed to overcome these forces for the chemical to change state, so the boiling point increases.

3 State what is meant by the term 'hydrocarbon'. **[2 marks]**

A compound that contains only hydrogen and carbon.

5 Exam-style practice Grade 5

1 Crude oil is a finite resource. State what is meant by the term 'finite'. **[1 mark]**

2 State what is meant by the term 'homologous series'. Give an example. **[3 marks]**

3 Give the molecular formula of hexane, which has 6 carbon atoms. **[1 mark]**

Fractional distillation

You need to know how fractional distillation is used to separate mixtures of liquids, such as crude oil.

⏱ Fractions

Crude oil is a mixture of hydrocarbons, which can be separated into fractions. Each fraction contains hydrocarbon molecules with a similar number of carbon atoms and similar boiling points.

The fractions are then processed to produce fuels such as gases, petrol, kerosene, diesel oil, fuel oil and bitumen.

The fractions are also processed to be used as the raw materials for the petrochemical industry to produce products such as lubricants, solvents, detergents and polymers.

See page 137 for more about crude oil.

The fractionating column has a **temperature gradient**. The temperature is controlled so that the hottest part of the column is actually at the bottom, not the top as you might expect.

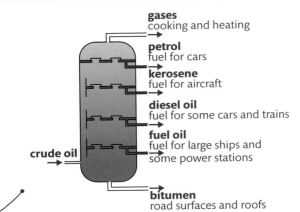

gases cooking and heating
petrol fuel for cars
kerosene fuel for aircraft
diesel oil fuel for some cars and trains
fuel oil fuel for large ships and some power stations
crude oil
bitumen road surfaces and roofs

Figure 1 The fractional distillation column used to separate crude oil, the fractions and their uses

⏱ Worked example — Grades 5–6

1 Crude oil can be separated into fractions. State the property of the fractions that makes this possible. **[1 mark]**

They have different boiling points.

2 Crude oil is a mixture of hydrocarbons. Explain how fractional distillation is used to separate crude oil into useful fractions. **[3 marks]**

Crude oil mixture is heated until it is vapourised. Each fraction has a different boiling point. So each fraction condenses at a different temperature.

3 Describe how the molecules in a fraction are similar to each other. **[1 mark]**

They all contain a similar number of carbon atoms.

4 Give **one** use for the diesel oil produced during fractional distillation. **[1 mark]**

Diesel oil can be used in engines (of cars, buses, tractors, etc).

Key words to include in your answer when writing about the process of fractional distillation are 'evaporate' and 'condense'.

② Exam focus

You should be able to explain how crude oil is separated into simpler, more useful substances. Learn the steps involved in fractional distillation and the uses of the fractions produced.

⏱ Exam-style practice — Grade 5

1 Fuel oil has many uses. It is separated from crude oil by fractional distillation.

Using **Figure 1** to help you, describe the steps involved in the fractional distillation of crude oil. **[4 marks]**

2 **Figure 2** shows a laboratory experiment used to separate crude oil by fractional distillation.

Describe what processes are taking place at **X** and **Z**. **[2 marks]**

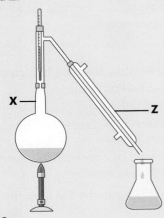

Figure 2

Made a start | Feeling confident | Exam ready

Properties of hydrocarbons

You need to know how the size of hydrocarbon molecules affects their properties.

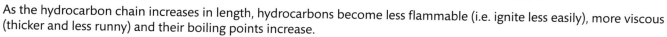

5 Properties of hydrocarbons

As the hydrocarbon chain increases in length, hydrocarbons become less flammable (i.e. ignite less easily), more viscous (thicker and less runny) and their boiling points increase.

Members of a homologous series (family of compounds) have similar chemical properties, for example, when a hydrocarbon burns in plenty of oxygen, **complete combustion** takes place. The hydrocarbon fuel is oxidised. This exothermic process releases thermal (heat) energy.

When complete combustion of hydrocarbon fuel occurs, the same products are always produced.

hydrocarbon fuel + oxygen → carbon dioxide + water

10 Worked example — Grade 5

1 Petrol is a fuel produced from crude oil.

Write a word equation to show the complete combustion of petrol. **[2 marks]**

petrol + oxygen → water + carbon dioxide

2 Suggest how the following properties of methane (CH_4) and decane ($C_{10}H_{22}$) differ. **[3 marks]**

(a) **flammability** – methane is more flammable than decane

(b) **viscosity** – methane is less viscous than decane

(c) **boiling point** – methane has a lower boiling point than decane

You need to consider the length of the hydrocarbon chain to determine how the properties will change from one hydrocarbon to another. Decane is longer than methane.

The type of hydrocarbon given is not important. If complete combustion of a hydrocarbon is taking place, the products will always be **water** and **carbon dioxide**.

The term **complete combustion** means there is enough oxygen for the fuel to fully oxidise. The carbon in the hydrocarbon will become carbon dioxide and the hydrogen will become water.

5 Incomplete combustion

When there is only a limited amount of oxygen available, fuel cannot burn completely, and instead **incomplete combustion** occurs. This reaction produces a mixture of water, carbon monoxide and carbon (soot).

butane + oxygen → carbon monoxide + carbon + water

$$C_4H_{10}(l) + 4O_2(g) \rightarrow 3CO(g) + C(s) + 5H_2O(g)$$

This reaction releases less energy than complete combustion, and the products can cause health and environmental issues (carbon monoxide is toxic and carbon (or soot) can cause breathing problems).

Butane is the fuel in this chemical reaction.

Exam focus

Remember to read the question carefully. For **in**complete combustion, there is not enough oxygen for the fuel to burn completely and the products formed are more harmful.

2 Key terms

- ☑ **Viscous** describes the thickness of a liquid: the more viscous a liquid, the thicker and less runny it is (like treacle).
- ☑ **Flammable** is used to describe materials that will catch fire more easily.
- ☑ **Oxidation** is a chemical reaction where a substance gains oxygen.

5 Exam-style practice — Grades 5–6

1 Name the products of the complete combustion of a hydrocarbon. **[1 mark]**

2 Write the word equation for the incomplete combustion of the hydrocarbon propane. **[1 mark]**

3 Describe how the viscosity of hydrocarbons changes with increasing molecular size. **[1 mark]**

4 Give a reason why combustion is classified as an oxidation reaction. **[1 mark]**

Atmospheric pollutants

You need to know about the different ways in which atmospheric pollutants can be formed when fuels burn. Chemical pollutants are substances in the environment at unnaturally high levels which can cause harm.

(5) Pollution from combustion of fuels

Hydrocarbons are often used as fuels. When they burn in lots of oxygen, only carbon dioxide and water are made. This is **complete combustion**.

If there is not enough oxygen present, then **incomplete combustion** happens. This still makes carbon dioxide and water, but it also makes products that can cause health issues and atmospheric pollution, such as carbon monoxide (CO) and soot (carbon, C).

Hydrocarbon fuels contain impurities, such as sulfur, which can cause atmospheric pollution when burned.

Due to the high temperature and pressure in a car engine, the oxygen and nitrogen in the air can react to make oxides of nitrogen. This is an atmospheric pollutant.

> Dry air is about 80% nitrogen and 20% oxygen.

(5) Oxides of nitrogen

When fuels are burned in engines, the temperature is so high that it can cause the oxygen and nitrogen in the air to react together, producing **oxides of nitrogen**.

Effects of oxides of nitrogen:
- Cause a photochemical smog.
- Increase the acidity of rain.
- Irritate eyes, nose, throat and lungs.

(5) Acid rain

Sulfur in some hydrocarbon fuels gives sulfur dioxide gas when the fuel is burned. When sulfur dioxide enters the atmosphere, it reacts with oxygen and water vapour to make **acid rain**. Acid rain has a pH lower than natural rainwater (pH 5.5).

Effects of acid rain:
- Acidifies lakes and rivers, which may harm or kill aquatic life as it reduces the pH levels of the water.
- Damages statues made of marble and limestone (carbonates) and buildings. The acid rain reacts with the carbonates to make a salt, water and carbon dioxide.
- Corrodes metals. The acid rain can react with some metals making hydrogen and a salt.
- Acidifies soil, preventing healthy crops from growing and killing trees. The acid rain lowers the pH of soils and this changes the amount of minerals in the soil.

(10) Worked example   Grades 5–7

1 State what is meant by 'incomplete combustion'.
[1 mark]

When a fuel burns in a limited supply of oxygen, not all the carbon in it is converted to carbon dioxide.

2 Incomplete combustion of carbon-containing fuels causes harmful products to be released. Explain the problems caused by these products.
[4 marks]

Carbon monoxide is produced. It is a toxic gas which is colourless and odourless and so cannot be detected easily.

Carbon or soot is produced, which causes breathing problems. It also blackens buildings and settles in chimneys, presenting a fire hazard.

> Carbon monoxide combines with haemoglobin in red blood cells. This reduces the amount of oxygen the blood can carry so people become drowsy and have headaches. At very high levels, it can be fatal (kill you).

> Inhalation of carbon particulates has been linked to respiratory problems including asthma and cardiovascular issues.

(5) Exam-style practice   Grade 5

1 Write a balanced chemical equation for the formation of sulfur dioxide from sulfur.
[1 mark]

2 State what is meant by the term 'pollutant'.
[1 mark]

3 Name **three** pollutants that may be produced when a fuel is burned.
[3 marks]

 Made a start   **Feeling confident**   **Exam ready**

Comparing fuels

You need to be able to evaluate the advantages and disadvantages of using different fuels for cars, for example, petrol and hydrogen.

 Renewable and non-renewable fuels

A **non-renewable fuel** is one that is being used faster than it is being formed, so will run out eventually. Petrol, kerosene and diesel oil are non-renewable fossil fuels obtained from crude oil. Methane is a non-renewable fossil fuel found in natural gas. Hydrogen is a fuel that can be used in cars, and can be made from both renewable and non-renewable sources by the following processes:

- the reaction of natural gas with steam (non-renewable)
- cracking of crude oil (non-renewable)
- electrolysis of water (renewable).

Fuel	Advantages	Disadvantages
hydrogen	👍 only water is made when hydrogen is burned (combusted); this is not a pollutant 👍 high amount of energy per gram of hydrogen 👍 unlimited supply as made by electrolysis of water	👎 is explosive and can be difficult and expensive to store and transport safely 👎 need a lot of electricity to make hydrogen from water; often this electricity is from fossil fuels which are finite and cause pollution
petrol	👍 easy to transport and store safely 👍 has been used for a long time, so well tested	👎 finite resource 👎 when it is used it causes pollution which can lead to acid rain, smog and contribute to global warming

 Worked example **Grades 4–5**

Compare the use of hydrogen and petrol as fuels in cars. **[4 marks]**

Petrol is non-renewable and will run out. However, when hydrogen is made from electrolysis of water, it is a renewable source.

When petrol is combusted, pollutants are made. These include carbon dioxide, which has been linked to climate change. If there is a limited amount of oxygen, then toxic carbon monoxide gas can be made as well as soot which causes particulate pollution. However, when hydrogen is burned there are no pollutants made, only harmless water.

Petrol is a liquid and easier to store and transport than hydrogen, which is a gas.

All fuels have advantages and disadvantages. It is important that you can compare these fuels and explain which one you think is best and why.

Exam focus

You could also be asked to **evaluate** different fuels. In this case, you need to discuss both the advantages and disadvantages **and also** give a statement to conclude whether or not the advantages outweigh the disadvantages.

 Exam-style practice **Grade 4**

Using hydrogen as a fuel does not create pollution. Suggest **two** disadvantages with using hydrogen as a fuel. **[3 marks]**

 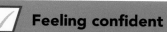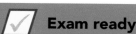

Cracking and alkenes

You need to understand how and why hydrocarbons can be cracked to produce smaller, more useful alkane and alkene molecules.

(10) Cracking

Fractions from crude oil are mixtures of hydrocarbons with similar chain length. There is a greater demand for smaller hydrocarbons found in the lighter fractions than the larger hydrocarbons found in heavier fractions. Cracking is a way to break down long hydrocarbons from the heavier fractions to make smaller, more useful hydrocarbons.

Cracking produces shorter alkane molecules and alkenes. Shorter alkanes can be used for fuels, such as petrol. Alkenes can be used to make polymers. For example, poly(ethene), the plastic used in carrier bags, is formed from ethene, which is an alkene.

Cracking uses a catalyst such as aluminium oxide and a high temperature.

(1) Alkenes

Alkenes are unsaturated hydrocarbons – they have a double bond between two carbon atoms, shown as C=C.

> You do not need to remember the exact numbers. But you are expected to know that the demand for the smaller hydrocarbons is greater than the amount obtained from fractional distillation. Also, the amount of larger fractions is greater than the demand for them. So, cracking is used to make more smaller hydrocarbons and use some of the bigger fractions.

(2) Demand for hydrocarbons

Fractions	Approximate %	
	Typical supply from crude oil	**Global demand**
Gases	2	4
Petrol	16	27
Kerosene	13	8
Diesel oil	19	23
Fuel oil and bitumen	50	38

Table 1 Global supply and demand for the fractions of crude oil

(5) Worked example   Grade 7

1 Hydrocarbons can be cracked to produce shorter hydrocarbons. Complete the equation to show the cracking of dodecane ($C_{12}H_{26}$).
[1 mark]

> The total number of C and H atoms in the products must equal the total number of C and H in the hydrocarbon (on the left) being cracked.

$$C_{12}H_{26} \rightarrow C_5H_{12} + C_4H_8 + C_3H_6$$

2 **Figure 1** shows how alkanes can be cracked in the laboratory.

(a) Explain why aluminium oxide is used.
[1 mark]

To speed up the reaction (it is a catalyst).

(b) State the type of chemical reaction that cracking is. **[1 mark]**

Thermal decomposition

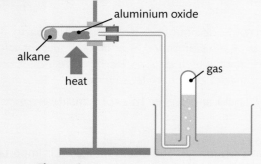

Figure 1

> Heat energy is used to break down the hydrocarbon into simpler substances.

(5) Exam-style practice   Grades 5–6

Look at **Table 1**.

(a) Name the fractions that are in greater demand than can be supplied. **[1 mark]**

(b) State the difference in percentage of fuel oil and bitumen produced and percentage demanded by the global market. **[1 mark]**

(c) Excess hydrocarbons from one fraction may be cracked to produce more useful fractions. State and explain which fraction is most likely to be produced by cracking. **[2 marks]**

Earth's early atmosphere

You need to know how Earth's atmosphere has developed over time.

(15) Evolution of Earth's atmosphere

Scientists think that Earth formed about 4.6 billion years ago. To begin with, Earth was a ball of molten rock. Many scientists believe that Earth's early atmosphere was formed from the gases given out by volcanoes.

Although Earth was a volatile place with a lot of volcanic activity, lots of changes happened in its first billion years that changed the atmosphere, allowing life to begin.

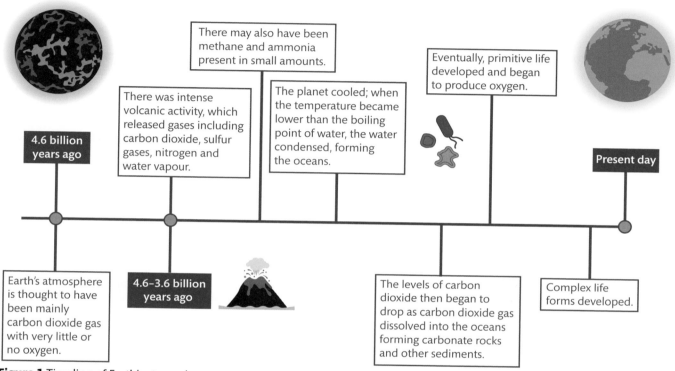

There may also have been methane and ammonia present in small amounts.

There was intense volcanic activity, which released gases including carbon dioxide, sulfur gases, nitrogen and water vapour.

The planet cooled; when the temperature became lower than the boiling point of water, the water condensed, forming the oceans.

Eventually, primitive life developed and began to produce oxygen.

4.6 billion years ago

Present day

Earth's atmosphere is thought to have been mainly carbon dioxide gas with very little or no oxygen.

4.6–3.6 billion years ago

The levels of carbon dioxide then began to drop as carbon dioxide gas dissolved into the oceans forming carbonate rocks and other sediments.

Complex life forms developed.

Figure 1 Timeline of Earth's atmosphere

(2) Working scientifically

There are many different theories about the composition of Earth's early atmosphere and the events that happened in its evolution. However, there is very limited evidence to support these theories because Earth formed such a long time ago.

(5) Worked example   Grade 5

❶ Describe how the oceans formed on Earth.
                                              [2 marks]

The water vapour condensed and formed the oceans.

❷ Give the process that produced the gases in the Earth's early atmosphere.   **[1 mark]**

Volcanic activity

(5) Exam-style practice   Grade 5

The current atmosphere of Mars is very similar to Earth's early atmosphere.

The approximate proportions of the gases in the atmosphere of Mars are given below.

Gas	Percentage composition
carbon dioxide	95.0
nitrogen	X
oxygen	0.5
argon	1.0

(a) Give the approximate value of X.   **[1 mark]**

(b) Suggest a reason why there is only a small percentage of oxygen on Mars.   **[2 marks]**

Oxygen and carbon dioxide levels

Earth's early atmosphere is thought to have been mainly carbon dioxide with little or no oxygen. You need to know how the oxygen and carbon dioxide levels have changed over time.

5 Increasing O_2 levels

Over billions of years there have been dramatic changes to the levels of carbon dioxide and oxygen in Earth's atmosphere. About 2.7 billion years ago, primitive plants started to produce oxygen, increasing the levels present in the atmosphere.

Over the next billion years, plants evolved, causing the levels of oxygen to increase further (to about 20 per cent). This increase in oxygen allowed animals to evolve.

The process by which plants and algae produce oxygen is called **photosynthesis**. It can be represented by the following equation:

carbon dioxide + water $\xrightarrow{\text{light}}$ glucose + oxygen

5 Decreasing CO_2 levels

Atmospheric carbon dioxide levels were decreased by:

- primitive plants photosynthesising
- carbon dioxide gas dissolving in the oceans.

Carbon dioxide gas is readily soluble in water.

When plants and animals die, the carbon inside them becomes trapped. Under specific conditions of temperature and pressure their remains become fossil fuels.

10 Worked example — Grade 5

1 **(a)** Describe **two** processes that caused atmospheric levels of carbon dioxide to change from around 95% to around 0.04%. **[2 marks]**

CO_2 was absorbed by plants for photosynthesis. It was also dissolved in the oceans.

(b) Determine the ratio of carbon dioxide in Earth's early atmosphere to carbon dioxide in Earth's current atmosphere. **[2 marks]**

early : current

2375 : 1

2 **(a)** Name the process carried out by plants and algae that increases the levels of oxygen in the atmosphere. **[1 mark]**

Photosynthesis

(b) Complete the word equation for this process.
carbon dioxide + water → **[1 mark]**

carbon dioxide + water → glucose + oxygen

Exam focus

If you know the chemical formula of a substance, you can write it in your answer to save time. Make sure that you write it correctly: you will not get a mark for CO2 or CO².

Maths skills

To work out the ratio of the gas levels divide both values by the lowest value.

95 ÷ 0.04 = 2375

0.04 ÷ 0.04 = 1

5 Exam-style practice — Grade 6

1 State the approximate percentage of Earth's atmosphere today that is oxygen. **[1 mark]**

2 Describe how the levels of carbon dioxide reduced from the early atmosphere to today. **[2 marks]**

Made a start | Feeling confident | Exam ready

Gases in the atmosphere

You need to know the proportions of the most abundant gases in the atmosphere today.

 Earth's atmosphere

The composition of Earth's atmosphere has stayed mostly the same for the past 200 million years, but the exact proportions of each gas varies constantly. Scientists can use software to measure the effects humans are having on the atmosphere to develop solutions to reduce the impact.

- ■ nitrogen (approximately 80%)
- ■ oxygen (approximately 20%)
- ■ all others, including carbon dioxide, water vapour and noble gases (less than 1%)

Figure 1 The proportions of gases in the atmosphere today

Oxygen
A glowing splint will relight if it comes into contact with a test tube of oxygen.

Maths skills

To convert from a percentage to a fraction you must divide the percentage of oxygen by the total percentage of the atmosphere: $20 \div 100 = \frac{1}{5}$.

 Maths skills

You are expected to be able to convert data provided as percentages, ratios and fractions. For example, the ratio of nitrogen to oxygen in the atmosphere is:

divide by 20 $\begin{array}{c} 80:20 \\ 4:1 \end{array}$

Ratios are a comparison of values. They are shown in their simplest form. This is done by dividing both values by the same factor.

Exam focus
You may need to draw graphs in the exam.

- Choose a sensible scale to work with.
- Ensure the plotted graph covers more than half of the grid provided.
- Label the axes to identify what they are showing and give units if applicable, with the independent variable (the one you choose) on the *x*-axis and the dependent variable (the one you measure during the experiment or survey) on the *y*-axis.

 Worked example Grade 5

The table shows the approximate proportions of gases in the atmosphere today.

Gas	Approximate composition (%)
nitrogen	80
oxygen	20
other gases	< 1

(a) Using the data in the table, determine approximately what fraction of gas in Earth's atmosphere is oxygen. **[1 mark]**

$\frac{1}{5}$

(b) Using the grid below, draw a graph to represent the data in the table. **[3 marks]**

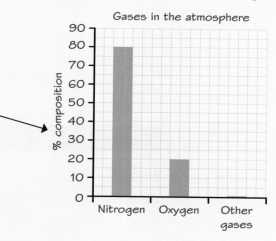

① Give the percentage of the Earth's atmosphere that is nitrogen gas. **[1 mark]**

② Show that the fraction of oxygen in the atmosphere is approximately one fifth. **[1 mark]**

 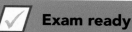

Greenhouse gases

You need to know about the effects greenhouse gases have on the temperature of Earth.

 Production of greenhouse gases

Greenhouse gases in the atmosphere, such as carbon dioxide, water vapour and methane, maintain the temperature of Earth by trapping solar energy from the Sun. Theories suggest that greenhouse gases were made by volcanic activity as Earth formed. Today, greenhouse gases are mainly produced by burning fossil fuels, livestock farming (cows), and gases made at landfill sites.

Trapping solar energy

Energy from the Sun reaches Earth. Some of this energy is absorbed by Earth and some is reflected back.

Greenhouse gases in Earth's atmosphere, such as carbon dioxide, methane and water vapour, absorb some of this reflected radiation. This natural process is called the greenhouse effect and keeps Earth warm.

Go to page 147 to revise how human activity is increasing the amount of greenhouse gases in Earth's atmosphere.

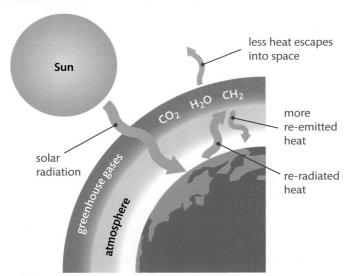

Figure 1 Trapping solar energy

 Worked example **Grade 5**

1 State what is meant by the term 'greenhouse gas'. **[2 marks]**

It is a gas that traps heat energy in the atmosphere, so it is maintaining the temperature of Earth's surface.

2 The greenhouse gases methane, water vapour and carbon dioxide are all produced by natural and artificial processes. For each gas, give a natural source and an artificial source. **[6 marks]**

Methane: Natural source – produced when organic material, such as plants, rots

Artificial source – agriculture, e.g. cattle and rice fields

Water vapour: Natural source – evaporation from water bodies, e.g. lakes and rivers

Artificial source – burning fossil fuels

Carbon dioxide: Natural source – respiration of plants and animals, forest fires

Artificial source – combustion of fossil fuels

 Exam-style practice **Grades 4–5**

1 Name **three** greenhouse gases. **[1 mark]**

2 Describe how greenhouse gases maintain Earth's temperature. **[2 marks]**

3 Describe how greenhouse gases were produced in Earth's early atmosphere. **[1 mark]**

 Made a start **Feeling confident** **Exam ready**

Human contribution to greenhouse gases

You need to be able to evaluate how some human activities are causing climate change.

(10) Carbon dioxide and climate change

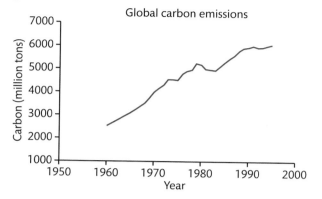
Global carbon emissions

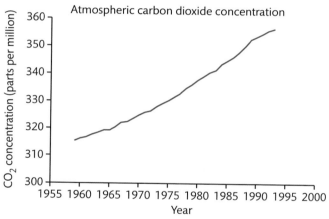
Atmospheric carbon dioxide concentration

Temperature variation from mean

Figure 1 Carbon emissions, carbon dioxide concentration and average global temperature

Figure 1 shows a good correlation between the variables, but is the data collected accurate? You may need to consider these effects:

- The carbon dioxide concentrations were measured near an active volcano.
- The temperature measurements are usually taken in towns and cities, which are warmer than rural areas. In the past, instruments were less sensitive and some concentrations are estimated from ice core samples.

(5) Working scientifically

Scientists think that human activity is causing global temperatures to rise and resulting in global climate change. This idea is based on peer-reviewed evidence.

Peer review is a process where scientists evaluate the reliability of other scientists' investigations and results in order to help validate the research.

(2) Greenhouse gases

Burning fossil fuels and dumping waste in landfill releases carbon dioxide and methane. Deforestation and rising human population also increase carbon dioxide (CO_2) emissions, and livestock farming produces methane (CH_4).

(2) Worked example Grade 6

Explain why many scientists are concerned about the use of fossil fuels in cars. **[3 marks]**

Fossil fuels are non-renewable. When they are combusted they cause pollutants and have been linked to climate change.

Burning fossil fuels may cause increasing carbon dioxide levels. Increasing carbon dioxide levels increase the greenhouse effect which leads to global warming, a part of climate change.

(5) Exam-style practice Grade 5

1 Give **two** human activities that are causing carbon dioxide levels to increase. **[2 marks]**

2 Give a reason why other gases should be investigated as well as carbon dioxide. **[2 marks]**

Global climate change

Increased levels of carbon dioxide and methane in the atmosphere due to human activity are a cause of global warming, leading to potential effects on our climate.

5 Climate change

Weather is the daily conditions in an area, such as temperature, humidity, rainfall and wind.
Climate is the average weather taken over a long time, often decades.

The **global climate** is the average climate across the whole world.

Effects of global climate change include:

- changes in natural habitats, making them inhospitable for some plants and animals
- unpredictable weather patterns, making it increasingly difficult for farmers to grow crops
- flooding and other extreme weather events that destroy buildings and cause deaths.

Human activities releasing greenhouse gases include:

- methane from livestock farming
- carbon dioxide from burning fossil fuels.

5 Impact on the population

Climate change has potential impacts on the human population. These are some examples:

Water and ice

Higher temperatures lead to sea ice and glaciers melting. As glaciers melt, there could be avalanches and habitats could be destroyed or flooded, which could destroy entire species. Communities that use melt water may see their supply of freshwater decrease. Areas that rely on winter tourism may suffer from a lack of snow.

Sea level increases

Seawater expands as it warms up, leading to an increase in sea level. Melt water running into the sea from glaciers and the Antarctic ice cap also leads to sea level rises. This puts coastal land, towns and cities at risk of flooding.

5 Worked example — Grade 5

The effects of climate change can be reduced. Describe **two** ways that governments can reduce the impact of climate change on their communities. **[2 marks]**

Governments could help their citizens to adapt to new conditions such as building flood defences.

They could also provide irrigation systems to help crops grow.

People could be relocated from the coast to inland and educated on different crops to farm.

Climate change can cause drought and/or flooding.

1 Exam focus

For the carbon dioxide already in our atmosphere, it could be removed using carbon capture and storage schemes, or by planting more trees.

5 Exam-style practice — Grade 5

1. Describe **two** impacts of climate change. **[2 marks]**
2. Give the major cause of climate change. **[1 mark]**
3. Look at the pie chart opposite.
   Which of these human activities produces the most methane? **[1 mark]**

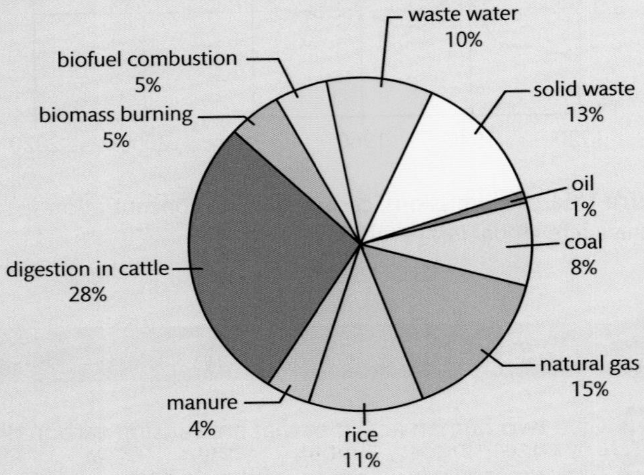
waste water 10%
solid waste 13%
oil 1%
coal 8%
natural gas 15%
rice 11%
manure 4%
digestion in cattle 28%
biomass burning 5%
biofuel combustion 5%

Key concepts in physics

You need to be able to recall and use SI units for quantities, as well as using multiples of these units.

 Quantities and their units

Physics relies on measuring things. For everything that we measure, there is an agreed unit that we measure in.

The following are units from the SI system that you should know:

length	metre, m
mass	kilogram, kg
time	second, s
current	ampere, A
temperature	kelvin, K
amount of substance	mole, mol

 Multiples and sub-multiples of units

Measurements in physics very often involve either very large or very small numbers. Multiples or sub-multiples of units are used for these.

You should know the following conversions:

giga (G) = $\times 10^9$ centi = $\times 10^{-2}$

mega (M) = $\times 10^6$ milli = $\times 10^{-3}$

kilo (k) = $\times 10^3$ micro (μ) = $\times 10^{-6}$

nano (n) = $\times 10^{-9}$

 Standard form

The universe is thought to be 13 799 000 000 years old. It is useful to express very large or very small numbers like this using standard form.

For example:

30 000 000 = 3×10^7. This means that the '3' at the start of the number is followed by 7 zeros.

If the number is very small, for example 0.0003, it would be written as:

3×10^{-4}, indicating that the '3' has been moved 4 spaces to the right of the decimal point.

In standard form and to three significant figures the age of the universe is 1.38×10^{10} years.

 Significant figures

It is often not sensible to write an answer to many decimal places. For example, a calculation may give an answer to many more decimal places than you could realistically measure.

It is more useful to quote to a certain number of significant figures. 0.0342 is 0.03 to one significant figure. 5.975 is 6.0 to two significant figures.

 Worked example   Grade 4

1 A journey from home to school takes a quarter of an hour.

Calculate the number of seconds the journey takes. **[2 marks]**

quarter of an hour = 0.25 hours

1 hour = 60 minutes; 1 minute = 60 seconds

1 hour = 60 × 60 seconds

0.25 hours = 0.25 × (60 × 60) = 900 seconds

2 The length of a table is 1.652 m. Write the length in millimetres to two significant figures. **[1 mark]**

1.652 m = 1.652 × 1000 mm = 1652 mm

To two significant figures = 1700 mm

Start by converting one hour into seconds. Then you can multiply your answer by the number of hours in the question, in this case 0.25.

 Exam-style practice   Grade 4

1 The average radius of an atom can be measured indirectly and is about 0.000 000 000 1 m.

In standard form, this measurement is:

☐ **A** 1.0×10^{-9} m

☐ **B** 1.0×10^{-10} m

☐ **C** 1.0×10^{-11} m

☐ **D** 1.0×10^{-12} m   **[1 mark]**

2 A human hair is about 0.1 mm thick.

(a) Write this measurement in metres, m. **[1 mark]**

(b) The number of human hairs that can be laid side by side in a space of 10 mm is:

☐ **A** 10

☐ **B** 100

☐ **C** 1000

☐ **D** 10 000   **[1 mark]**

When using a value to calculate a result, convert to the correct units first, before making the calculation.

Two significant figures means only showing the first two digits that are not zero, and rounding up.

 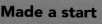

Scalar and vector quantities

You need to know the difference between a scalar quantity and a vector quantity.

[2] Definitions ☐

Scalars are quantities that have only a **magnitude** (a size).

Vectors are quantities with both a magnitude and a direction.

You can add scalar quantities in the same way you add numbers. When adding vectors, you need to consider the direction.

[2] Vector quantities ☐

- ✓ velocity (m/s)
- ✓ displacement (m)
- ✓ acceleration (m/s^2)
- ✓ force (N)
- ✓ weight (N)
- ✓ gravitational field strength (N/kg)

Remember that for both scalar and vector quantities, you must always include the unit.

[2] Scalar quantities ☐

- ✓ distance (m)
- ✓ speed (m/s)
- ✓ charge (C)
- ✓ density (kg/m^3)
- ✓ efficiency
- ✓ energy (all types) (J)
- ✓ frequency (Hz)
- ✓ mass (kg)
- ✓ power (W)
- ✓ pressure (Pa)
- ✓ temperature (°C)
- ✓ time (s)
- ✓ wavelength (m)
- ✓ volume (m^3)
- ✓ area (m^2)

Efficiency does not have a unit. It is a ratio that can be written as a fraction, decimal or percentage.

[10] Adding vectors 🖩 ☐

Vector quantities can be represented by arrows. The length of the arrow represents the magnitude. The direction of the arrow represents the direction of the vector quantity.

If two vectors act in a straight line, they can be added (same direction) or subtracted (opposite direction).

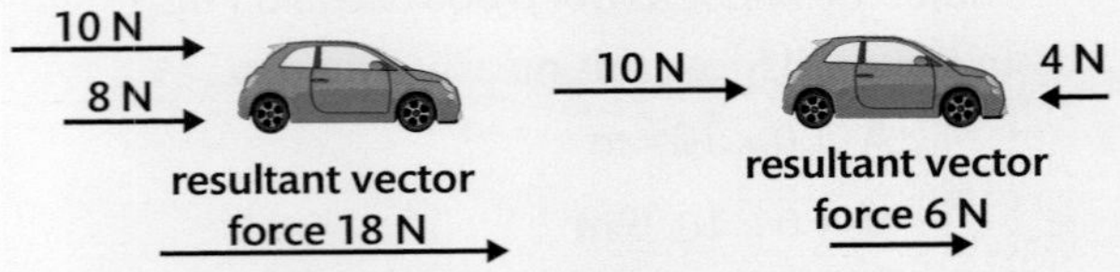

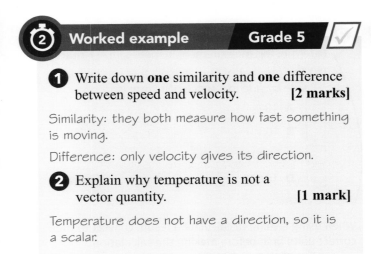

Figure 1 Finding the resultant vector

If two vectors have the same magnitude (length) but are in opposite directions, they add up to zero.

Figure 2 Resultant vector equals zero

[2] Worked example — Grade 5 ☐

1 Write down **one** similarity and **one** difference between speed and velocity. **[2 marks]**

Similarity: they both measure how fast something is moving.

Difference: only velocity gives its direction.

2 Explain why temperature is not a vector quantity. **[1 mark]**

Temperature does not have a direction, so it is a scalar.

[5] Exam-style practice — Grade 4 ☐

1 Use words from the box to complete the sentences below. **[3 marks]**

direction	scalar	vector

Displacement has size and ....

This means displacement is a ....

Distance only has size, so distance is a ....

2 Which of the following measurements is a vector?

☐ **A** 12.0 m/s

☐ **B** 12.0 kg

☐ **C** 12.0 km in a direction of 120°

☐ **D** 120 °C **[1 mark]**

Distance and speed

Distance and displacement mean different things in physics. You need to understand the difference between them.

 Distance, displacement, speed and velocity

Distance is how far an object has travelled. Distance only has a magnitude. It is a scalar quantity (page 150).

Displacement is the distance travelled in a straight line, in a particular direction. Displacement has direction as well as magnitude, so it is a vector quantity (page 150). The displacement at the end of a journey is usually less than the total distance travelled because of turns or bends in the journey.

Speed is how fast an object is travelling.

Velocity is how fast an object is travelling in a given direction.

The green line shows the path you took and is the distance you actually walked.

The magnitude of the displacement is a lot less than the distance. You walked for 110 metres, but ended up only 50 metres from where you started.

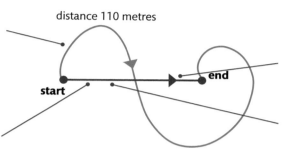

distance 110 metres

The arrow shows the direction of the displacement.

displacement 50 metres to the right

Figure 1 Going for a walk

 Worked example | **Grade 5**

Mahad lives 2 km from the shop. Mahad walks from home to the shop, in a straight line. The diagram shows the position of his home, the shop and a park.

home   shop

(a) Draw a line on the diagram to show Mahad's displacement from home when he reaches the shop. **[2 marks]**

home   shop

(b) Mahad meets some friends and they decide to walk back to Mahad's house through the park. Draw another line on the diagram to show the route home. **[2 marks]**

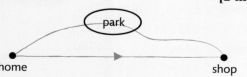

home   shop

(c) Explain why the distance Mahad walks on the route home is different from his displacement. **[2 marks]**

Displacement is a straight line with a direction. Distance follows the curved path.

Use a ruler to draw a straight line from the start point to the finish point. Make sure you put an arrow on the line to show the direction.

Make sure your path goes through the shop, the park and the home.

Exam focus

The question has two marks, so you need to make two points in your explanation.

Exam focus

You need to be able to add or subtract vectors. Always include the unit in your answer.

 Exam-style practice | **Grade 5**

For each of the journeys given below, find:
- the total distance travelled
- the displacement.
  (a) travel 200 km left **[2 marks]**
  (b) go up 180 m in a lift, then back down 80 m **[2 marks]**
  (c) run 350 m to the shops, then the same distance back to your home. **[2 marks]**

 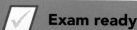

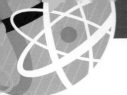

Speed and velocity

You need to know the difference between speed and velocity, and how to calculate them. Speed only has magnitude so is a scalar quantity. Velocity has magnitude and direction so is a vector quantity.

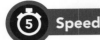

5 Speed

Speed is a measure of the distance an object has moved in a specific amount of time.

distance travelled (m) = average speed (m/s) × time (s)

As most moving objects do not have a constant speed, this equation gives the average speed over a time.

You need to know typical examples of everyday speeds.

	walking	running	cycling	wind	cars on a motorway	sound waves
Approximate speed (m/s)	1.5	3	6	0–20	20–30	330

The speed of sound can vary.

5 Velocity

Velocity is speed in a particular direction.

Unlike speed, velocity has a direction. This can be shown as:

- a word, such as 'north' or 'left'
- a positive (+) or negative (–)
- an arrow.

Even at constant speed, the velocity changes if an object changes direction.

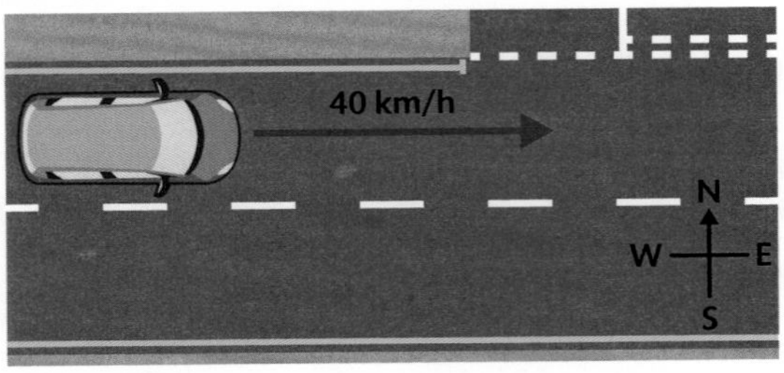

Figure 1 A car has a velocity of 40 km/h east

10 Worked example — Grade 5

1 Which of these speeds would be normal for a person cycling? **[1 mark]**

- [ ] **A** 0.6 m/s
- [ ] **B** 1.2 m/s
- [x] **C** 6.0 m/s
- [ ] **D** 12.0 m/s

2 Train A travels in a straight line due east and covers 440 km in 2 hours.

(a) Calculate the average speed of train A in km/h.
Use the equation:

$$\text{average speed} = \frac{\text{distance}}{\text{time}}$$ **[2 marks]**

$\text{speed} = \frac{440}{2} = 220\,\text{km/h}$

(b) Write down its average velocity. **[1 mark]**

220 km/h east

(c) Train B travels at half the speed of train A.
Calculate the average speed of train B. **[2 marks]**

$\text{Train B speed} = \frac{220}{2} = 110\,\text{km/h}$

Write down the equation and check the units as you put the numbers in.

Velocity is a vector, so you must include a direction in your answer.

10 Exam-style practice — Grade 5

1 A runner runs in a straight line for 700 s at an average speed of 3 m/s. Calculate the distance she travels.
Use the equation:
distance travelled = average speed × time
[2 marks]

2 The table shows the distances travelled in certain amounts of time by three cars.

(a) Calculate the speed of car B. **[2 marks]**

(b) Which car has the fastest average speed? **[1 mark]**

Car	A	B	C
Distance	600 m	200 m	20 m
Time	25 s	10 s	0.5 s
Speed	24 m/s		40 m/s

Distance–time graphs

Distance–time graphs show the distance an object travels over a period of time. You need to be able to interpret these types of graph to work out the speed of an object moving in a straight line.

5 Distance–time graphs

A line on a **distance–time graph** shows how far an object moves over time.

- A straight line that is angled compared to the time axis shows an object that is moving with a constant speed.
- The gradient of a straight line on a distance–time graph is found by calculating the change in distance divided by the change in time.
- The gradient is the speed of the object.
- When the line on the graph is horizontal, it has a gradient of zero. This means the object is **stationary**.

10 Worked example   Grade 5

1 **Figure 1** shows the journey of a horse and its rider.

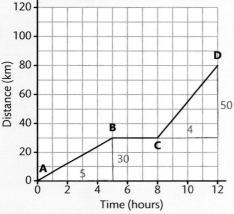
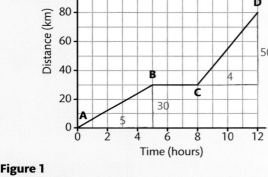

Figure 1

Describe the journey in as much detail as possible.
[4 marks]

A–B the horse travels 30 km in 5 hours

The speed (gradient) = 30 ÷ 5 = 6 km/h

B–C the horse is stationary for 3 hours

C–D the horse moves a further 50 km in 4 hours

Its speed is 50 ÷ 4 = 12.5 km/h

> When asked to describe a graph in detail, you should describe the different sections of the graph, giving the times for each section, the distance travelled and the speed.

2 **Figure 2** shows the journeys of a cyclist and a motorcyclist.

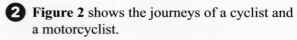
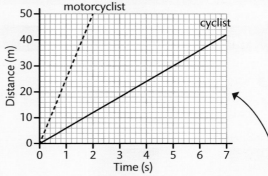

Figure 2

(a) Describe the motion of the cyclist. **[1 mark]**

The cyclist is travelling at a constant speed.

(b) Calculate the average speed of the cyclist.
Use the equation

$$\text{speed} = \frac{\text{distance}}{\text{time}}$$
[2 marks]

$$\text{speed} = \frac{42}{7} = 6 \text{ m/s}$$

Maths skills
Calculating the speed is the same as finding the gradient of the straight line.

(c) Compare the speed of the motorcyclist with the speed of the cyclist. **[3 marks]**

The motorcyclist travels at an average speed of 25 m/s and the cyclist travels at an average speed of 6 m/s. The motorcyclist is faster.

10 Exam-style practice   Grade 5

1 Look at **Figure 2**. Without performing any calculations, explain how the graph for the cyclist would be different if the cyclist travelled at half the speed shown. **[2 marks]**

2 Two new Mars exploration vehicles are tested in the lab for the first time. Vehicle A moves 12 m in 6 s at a constant speed. Vehicle B covers the same distance in 10 s.
(a) Draw a distance–time graph to show these movements. **(b)** Which vehicle has a higher average speed? **[3 marks]**

Made a start | Feeling confident | Exam ready

Uniform acceleration

Acceleration is the measure of how quickly an object's velocity changes. Acceleration is a vector quantity. **Uniform** means the acceleration stays the same size and direction. You need to know how to calculate acceleration for the exam.

5 Calculating acceleration

The **average acceleration** of an object can be worked out using this equation, which you need to remember:

$$\text{acceleration (m/s}^2\text{)} = \frac{\text{change in velocity (m/s)}}{\text{time taken }(x)}$$

$$a = \frac{(v - u)}{t}$$

For uniform acceleration, you can also use this equation, but you do not need to remember it:

$$v^2 - u^2 = 2 \times a \times x$$

x is the distance

v is the end velocity in m/s

u is the start velocity in m/s

10 Worked example — Grade 5

1 The lorry in **Figure 1** accelerates from stationary to a speed of 20 m/s. It takes 10 s to reach this speed.

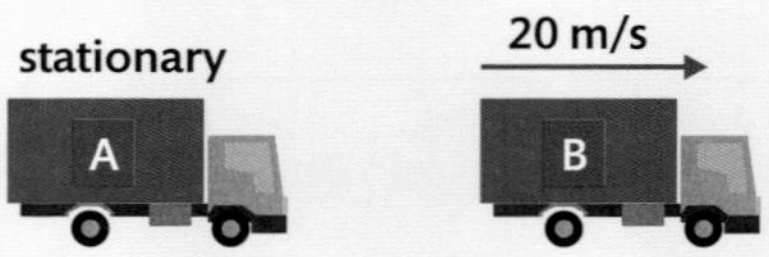

Figure 1

Calculate the acceleration of the lorry.
Use the equation **[2 marks]**

$$a = \frac{(v - u)}{t}$$

$$a = \frac{(20 - 0)}{10} = 2\,\text{m/s}^2$$

2 A train travelling at 50 m/s must slow down to 20 m/s before it reaches a bend.

It takes 90 s to slow down.
Find the acceleration of the train.

Use the equation $a = \frac{(v - u)}{t}$ **[2 marks]**

$$a = \frac{(v - u)}{t} = \frac{20 - 50}{90} = -0.33\,\text{m/s}^2$$

3 A ball is dropped and hits the floor at 6 m/s.
Calculate how long it takes to fall. **[3 marks]**

$$t = \frac{(v - u)}{a} = \frac{6 - 0}{10} = 0.6\,\text{s}$$

2 Acceleration examples

You need to know some typical accelerations and the forces needed to achieve them.

Action	Acceleration (m/s²)	Force needed (N)
Train leaving platform	0.5	50 000
Person starting to run	1	70
Car	4	4000
Object in free fall in Earth's atmosphere	10	equal to the weight of the object

Exam focus

This equation appears on your equation sheet.

Write *s*, *u*, *v*, *a* and *t* in the margin and make a note of what numbers you know as you read the question.

It is decelerating, so the answer will be negative.

Ensure you get the start and end velocities the right way around. This gives a negative answer, indicating deceleration.

10 Exam-style practice — Grades 5–6

1 An apple falls from a branch onto the ground. The time taken for the apple to fall is 1.5 s. Calculate the speed of the apple when it hits the ground. (Acceleration in free fall = g = 10 m/s²) **[2 marks]**

2 A jet is stationary at one end of a runway. The jet can take off when it reaches a velocity of 65 m/s. It can accelerate at 5 m/s². Calculate the time it takes the jet to reach its take-off velocity. **[2 marks]**

3 A car is travelling at 20 m/s. The driver accelerates suddenly and the speed increases to 30 m/s. The car travels 100 m during this time. Calculate the acceleration of the car. **[2 marks]**

Made a start | Feeling confident | Exam ready

Velocity–time graphs

Velocity–time graphs show how the velocity of an object changes over time. You need to know how to calculate a constant acceleration from the gradient of a velocity–time graph and distance travelled from the area under the velocity–time graph.

5 Distance and acceleration

- The acceleration for a given section is equal to the gradient of the line. If the line is straight, the acceleration is constant.
- The distance travelled is the area under the line.

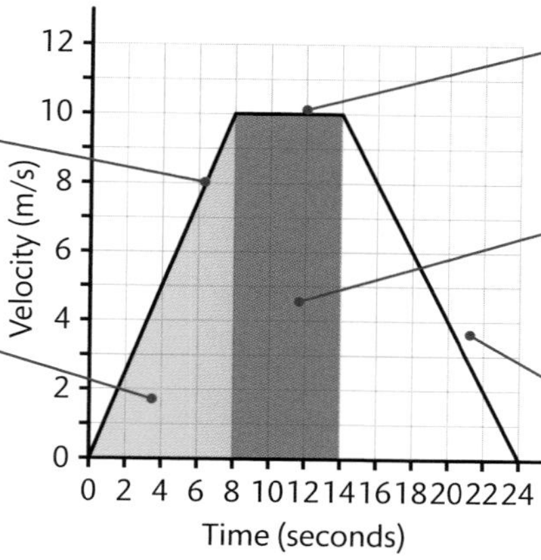

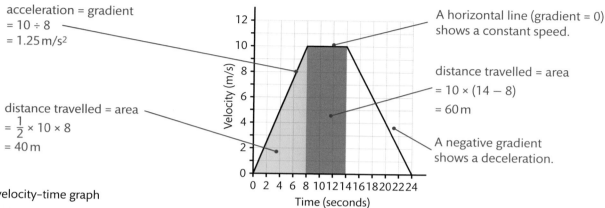

acceleration = gradient
= 10 ÷ 8
= 1.25 m/s²

distance travelled = area
= $\frac{1}{2}$ × 10 × 8
= 40 m

A horizontal line (gradient = 0) shows a constant speed.

distance travelled = area
= 10 × (14 – 8)
= 60 m

A negative gradient shows a deceleration.

Figure 1 A velocity–time graph

10 Worked example — Grade 5

1 **Figure 2** shows the velocity of a bus.

Calculate:

(a) the acceleration of the bus between:

(i) 0 and 8 s. Use the equation:

$$\text{acceleration} = \frac{(v - u)}{t}$$ **[2 marks]**

$$\text{acceleration} = \frac{v - u}{t} = \frac{16 - 0}{8} = 2\ \text{m/s}^2$$

(ii) 14 and 24 s **[2 marks]**

$$\text{acceleration} = \frac{0 - 16}{10} = -1.6\ \text{m/s}^2$$

(b) the distance travelled by the bus between 8 s and 14 s. **[2 marks]**

distance = area under graph = rectangle
= (14 – 8) × 16 = 6 × 16
= 96 m

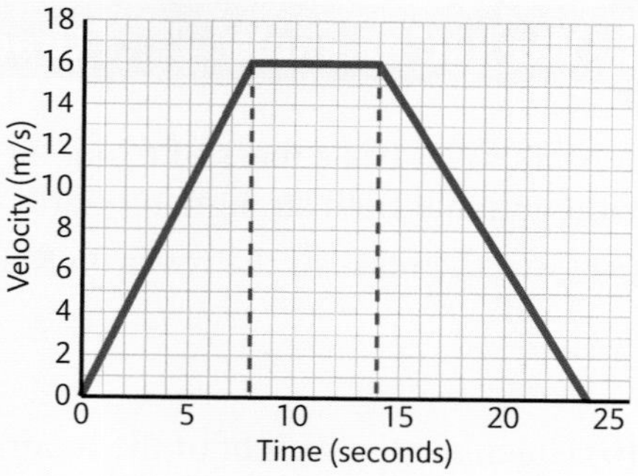

Figure 2

5 Worked example — Grade 5

2 **Figure 3** shows the velocity–time graphs for the motion of three different objects.

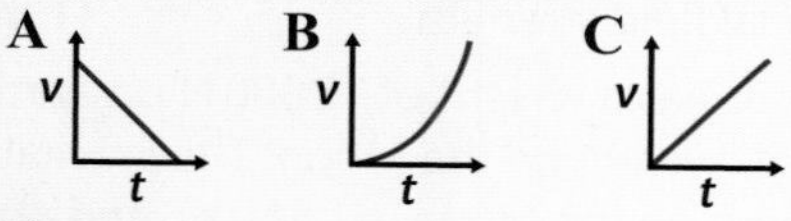

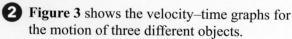

Figure 3

Describe the motion of each object. **[3 marks]**

A is decelerating at a uniform rate (or accelerating at a uniform negative rate).

B is increasing in velocity with non-uniform acceleration.

C is accelerating at a uniform rate.

10 Exam-style practice — Grade 5

Figure 4 shows the velocity of a golf cart over 45 seconds.

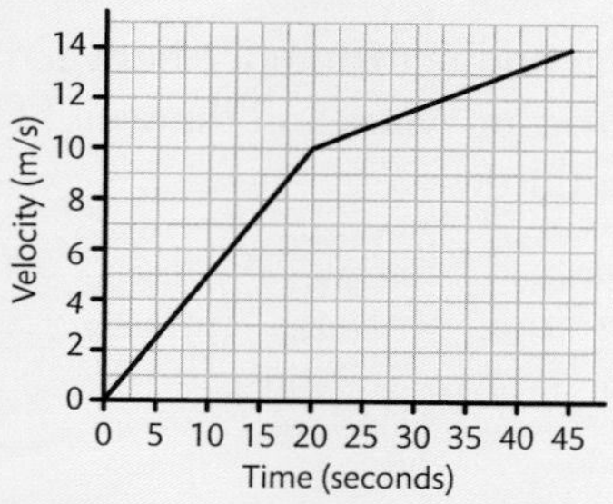

Figure 4

(a) Describe the motion of the golf cart without any calculations. **[2 marks]**

(b) Calculate the acceleration of the golf cart at 10 s. **[2 marks]**

Gravity

You need to know the relationship between gravity, weight and mass.

⑩ Mass, weight and gravity

The weight of an object is dependent on its mass and the strength of gravity due to the planet or moon it is near. The weight of an object may change but its mass remains constant.

Mass (m)
- the amount of matter in an object
- measured in kilograms, kg

Weight (W)
- the force of gravity acting on a mass; near a planet, the force acts downwards, towards the centre of the planet
- measured in newtons, N
- measured using a calibrated spring-balance (newtonmeter)

Gravitational field strength (g)
- the strength of gravity at any one point
- measured in N/kg

You need to know the equation:
weight (N) = mass (kg) × gravitational field strength (N/kg)

$W = m \times g$

⑤ Acceleration in free fall

There is another situation near the surface of Earth where gravity is important: free fall. For example, a skydiver falling towards the ground from an aircraft accelerates towards the ground. The force due to gravity causes this acceleration. We can calculate this force using force = mass × acceleration (see page 157).

This force is the same size as the skydiver's weight, and the acceleration in free fall is 10 m/s^2 near the surface of Earth, so the calculation is very similar to the weight:
force (N) = mass (kg) × 10 m/s^2

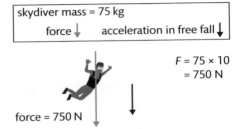

skydiver mass = 75 kg

force ↓   acceleration in free fall ↓

$F = 75 \times 10$
$= 750$ N

force = 750 N

Figure 1 This skydiver accelerates in free fall

⑩ Worked example — Grades 4–5

A Mars rover has a mass of 67 kg on Earth. Gravitational field strength on Earth = 10 N/kg.

(a) Give the mass of the rover on Mars. **[1 mark]**

Mass does not change so on Mars it is still 67 kg.

(b) Calculate the weight of the rover on Mars. The gravitational field strength, g, on Mars is 3.7 N/kg. Use the equation $W = m \times g$ **[2 marks]**

67 × 3.7 = 248 N

(c) Comment on the difference between the weight of the rover on Mars and the weight of the rover on Earth. **[2 marks]**

The gravitational field strength on Earth is greater than that on Mars. The rover will weigh more on Earth than on Mars.

⑤ Weight and mass

Weight and mass are directly proportional.

weight ∝ mass

If one object has twice the mass of another, it will also have twice the weight for the same gravitational field strength. Mass is constant. Weight depends on the gravitational field strength at the point where the object is.

⑩ Exam-style practice — Grades 4–5

1 State the equipment used to measure the weight of an object. **[1 mark]**

2 State the relationship between weight and gravitational field strength. **[1 mark]**

3 A spacecraft has a weight of 12 000 N on Earth. Calculate its weight on the Moon. The gravitational field strength on the Moon is 1.6 N/kg, and on the Earth is 10 N/kg.

Use the equation $W = m \times g$ **[2 marks]**

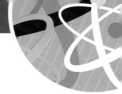

Newton's laws of motion

Newton's three laws of motion explain how forces affect the motion of objects. You need to consider resultant forces when using Newton's laws.

5 Newton's first law

If all the forces acting on an object are balanced (the resultant force = 0), the object will remain at a constant velocity or at rest.

What does it mean?

This means that once an object is moving, it keeps moving at the same velocity as long as no overall (resultant) force acts upon it.

To make the object speed up, slow down, or change direction, you need to apply a resultant force.

If an object has no resultant force, then all the forces are balanced. It will continue to move with constant velocity, or remain stationary.

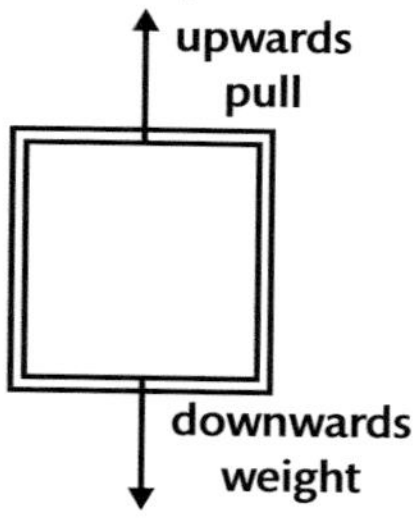

Figure 1 Balanced forces acting on a lift

The vertical and horizontal forces add up to zero. We say they are balanced or in **equilibrium**.

You also need to remember this in a different way: if an object is stationary or moving at a constant velocity, then there is no resultant force acting on it.

5 Newton's third law

When two objects interact they exert an equal and opposite force on each other.

What does it mean?

When one object applies a force to another, it experiences the same force itself but in the opposite direction. Note that the two forces:

- are the same size
- act in exactly opposite directions
- act on different objects, so they do not cancel out.

2 Worked example — Grade 5

An empty lorry accelerates at 2 m/s^2. A force of 2000 N is needed to do this. The lorry is then filled with heavy objects. Describe the force needed to accelerate the loaded lorry, compared to the empty lorry. **[2 marks]**

Force = mass × acceleration
If the acceleration is the same and the mass has increased, the force needed will be larger.

5 Newton's second law

If the forces acting on an object are unbalanced, the object's acceleration will be:

- in the direction of the resultant force
- directly proportional to the resultant force.

You need to remember the equation that results from this law: force, F (N) = mass, m (kg) × acceleration, a (m/s^2)

What does it mean?

An unbalanced force makes an object accelerate. It might speed up, slow down (decelerate) or change direction.

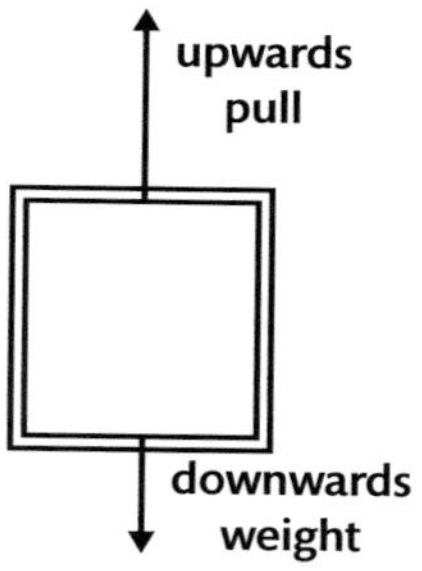

Figure 2 Unbalanced forces acting on a lift. There is a resultant force in the upwards direction so the lift accelerates upwards.

10 Exam-style practice — Grade 5

1 Which phrase completes the statement of Newton's first law of motion?

If the resultant force on an object is zero, the object will:

☐ **A** accelerate
☐ **B** decelerate
☐ **C** keep moving at a constant velocity
☐ **D** stay at rest or keep moving at a constant velocity **[1 mark]**

2 A tennis ball has a mass of 0.06 kg.
The ball accelerates at 500 m/s^2.
Calculate the force producing this acceleration.
State the unit.
Use the equation
$F = m \times a$ **[2 marks]**

Practical: Investigating acceleration

You need to know how to investigate the effect of force and mass on acceleration.

(5) Two experiments

Experiment 1 – Effect on acceleration of changing force

① Increase the force on the trolley (**Figure 1**) by moving masses from the trolley to the hanging masses.

② The interrupt card passes through the light gate. A data logger calculates the acceleration.

Experiment 2 – Effect on acceleration of changing mass

① Increase the mass of the trolley by fixing masses to it.

② Measure the acceleration. Keep the force (hanging mass) the same.

The masses accelerate as well as the trolley, so this keeps the total mass the same.

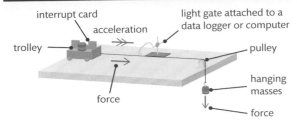

Figure 1 Apparatus for measuring acceleration

(10) Worked example — Grades 4–5

(a) In Experiment 1, how would you expect increasing the force to change the acceleration?

✓ **A** Increase

☐ **B** Stay the same

☐ **C** Decrease **[1 mark]**

(b) State **one** other force acting on the trolley. Explain what could be done to reduce the effect of this force on your results. **[2 marks]**

Friction – lift the ramp so the trolley runs slightly downhill to make up for friction.

(c) A graph is plotted using the results from Experiment 1.

(i) What shape of graph would you expect to see, A, B or C? **[1 mark]**

 ☐ **A** ☐ **B**  ✓ **C**

(ii) Write down the equation that explains your answer to part (i). **[2 marks]**

$F = m \times a$

(2) Interrupt card

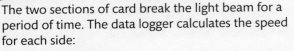

The two sections of card break the light beam for a period of time. The data logger calculates the speed for each side:

$$\text{speed} = \frac{\text{card length}}{\text{time}}$$

It also measures the time between interruptions:

$$\text{acceleration} = \frac{\text{difference in speeds}}{\text{time between interruptions}}$$

Doing the experiment on an air track would be ideal, but there will still be friction in the pulley.

(10) Exam-style practice — Grade 5

① In Experiment 1, explain how you would find the size of the force accelerating the trolley and what the size of this force depends on. **[3 marks]**

② Suggest and explain **one** safety precaution that should be taken in these experiments. **[2 marks]**

 Made a start   **Feeling confident**   **Exam ready**

Stopping distance

Stopping distance is the distance over which a vehicle stops. It is the total of the thinking distance and the braking distance. You need to know about factors that affect the stopping distance of a vehicle.

(15) Calculating stopping distance

To calculate the stopping distance of a car, you need to account for the driver's **reaction time** (thinking distance) and the braking distance.

stopping distance = thinking distance + braking distance

- **Thinking distance** – the distance travelled while the driver is reacting. This occurs before they start to brake.
- **Braking distance** – the distance it takes the car to stop once the brakes have been applied.

Revise the factors affecting braking distance on page 160.

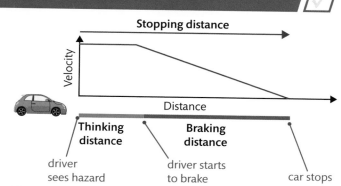

Figure 1 A graph showing the stopping distance of a car

(2) Factors affecting thinking distance

Thinking distance increases at higher speeds and when reaction time is slowed. Typical reaction times vary from 0.2 s to 0.9 s. Factors that can slow reaction time include:

- drinking alcohol
- taking drugs/medicine
- being tired
- poor visibility, e.g. due to fog
- distraction, e.g. using a mobile phone.

(5) Measuring reactions

Method 1
Reaction times can be measured using a stop clock. One person presses start and the other has to hit the stop button as quickly as possible.

Method 2
One person holds a ruler vertically while the other holds their finger and thumb at the bottom of the ruler. When the ruler is dropped they have to catch it. The slower their reactions, the more of the ruler passes through their fingers.

(5) Worked example — Grade 5

After a traffic accident, police officers investigating the accident test the drivers involved for alcohol and drugs. Explain why they do this. **[3 marks]**

A driver's reaction time is increased if they have drunk alcohol or taken drugs. An increased reaction time increases a vehicle's stopping distance and can be the cause of an accident.

You need to use the equation that relates speed, distance and time. Go to page 152 to revise how to use this equation.

(10) Exam-style practice — Grades 4–5

1. A driver's reaction time is 0.6 s. At a speed of 22 m/s (50 mph) the thinking distance is approximately 13 m. Estimate the thinking distance at a speed of 31 m/s (70 mph). **[1 mark]**

   ☐ **A** 9 m   ☐ **C** 19 m

   ☐ **B** 13 m   ☐ **D** 31 m

2. The table shows results from an investigation into reaction time using a stop clock.

	Result 1	Result 2
Concentrating	0.31 s	0.35 s
Distracted	0.60 s	0.64 s

   (a) Compare the results and explain what they show. **[2 marks]**

   (b) Use your answer to suggest why a car driver should avoid distractions. **[2 marks]**

Factors affecting braking distance

You need to know how to calculate braking distance and the factors that affect it.

 Factors affecting braking distance

Factors such as greater speed and greater mass increase the kinetic energy, which means there is more work for the brakes to do. The vehicle therefore travels further before it stops.

Go to page 159 to revise stopping distances.

The following factors affect the braking distance:

- mass of the vehicle
- speed of the vehicle
- condition of the vehicle's brakes
- condition of the road (loose, wet, icy, rough)
- the condition of the tyres on the vehicle.

The braking distance of a car travelling at 9 m/s is about 6 m. When the car travels faster at 31 m/s the braking distance is up to 96 m. That is why when travelling faster, or in conditions that make the braking distance longer, drivers need to leave larger gaps between them and the vehicle in front. Cars decelerate (slow down) in emergencies at approximately 3–5 m/s². Rapid deceleration can cause the car to skid and the driver to lose control.

The energy of braking

Brakes use friction to do work and stop the vehicle. This energy is transferred to thermal energy in the brakes. If the brakes overheat, they may not function as well.

The forces of deceleration

A vehicle can also be stopped suddenly in an accident. This can involve much larger decelerations and higher forces than normal braking. The high forces can cause serious injuries to people.

 Worked example — Grade 5

Figure 1 is a graph showing the effect of speed on stopping distance for a car.

1 (a) Calculate the stopping distance when the car is travelling at a speed of 25 m/s. **[2 marks]**

```
thinking + braking = stopping
distance   distance   distance
17  +  46  =  63 m
```

(b) The car accelerates so it is now travelling at 30 m/s. Will the stopping distance be higher or lower than that calculated in part (a)? Give a reason for your answer. **[2 marks]**

Higher because the thinking distance and braking distance increase with speed.

2 A driver applies the brakes over a long period of time while driving down a hill. Explain why this could be dangerous. **[2 marks]**

Friction causes brakes to heat up as they are used. As the brakes get hotter they apply less friction so the brakes are not as effective.

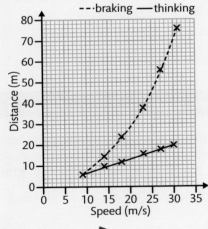

Figure 1

As the speed increases, the thinking distance increases in direct proportion to speed.

The braking distance depends on speed squared, because the kinetic energy of the vehicle depends on speed squared.

 Exam-style practice — Grades 4–5

1 Brakes on road cars work best at temperatures up to 300 °C. Brakes on racing cars work best at temperatures up to 1400 °C. Give a reason for this difference. **[2 marks]**

2 Explain the effect that doubling the speed of a vehicle has on braking and thinking distances. **[2 marks]**

Made a start   Feeling confident   Exam ready

Gravitational potential energy

You need to be able to calculate the change in gravitational potential energy of an object when it is raised or lowered in Earth's gravitational field.

 Calculating GPE

The gravitational potential energy (GPE) of an object, measured in joules (J), depends on its mass, its height and the **gravitational field strength**.

It can be calculated using the equation:

change in = mass × gravitational field × change in
GPE (J)   (kg)   strength (N/kg)   vertical height (m)

$\Delta GPE = mg\Delta h$

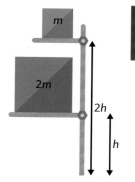

The gravitational field strength on Earth is 10 N/kg.

Figure 1 Both of these boxes go through the same change in gravitational potential energy when they are lifted from the ground. The bottom box has twice the mass of the top box, but is only lifted to half the height.

 Kinetic energy

work done = change in GPE   GPE $\longrightarrow$ kinetic energy

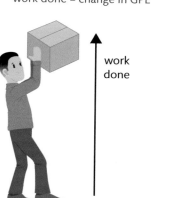
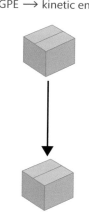

work done

Figure 2 Lifting and dropping a box

To lift the box, the change in GPE is equal to the work done in lifting it. When dropped, the GPE is transferred to kinetic energy as the box falls. The kinetic energy upon hitting the ground is equal to the change in GPE the box had at the top. For more about work done, see page 184.

 Worked example   Grades 4–5

A lift full of people has a mass of 550 kg. ($g = 10$ N/kg).

(a) Determine the total weight of the lift and people. **[2 marks]**

weight = mass × gravitational field strength =
550 × 10 = 5500 N

(b) Calculate the GPE gained by the lift if it moves upwards 20 m. **[2 marks]**

$\Delta GPE = mg\Delta h$ = 550 × 10 × 20 = 110 000 J

(c) State how the answer would be different if the lift had carried fewer people. **[1 mark]**

Change in GPE would have been smaller.

The change in GPE depends on mass. If there are fewer people, there will be less mass so the change in GPE will be smaller.

 **Exam-style practice**   Grades 4–5

1 A cyclist of mass 70 kg goes training by cycling up a hill that is 300 m higher than the starting point. The cyclist returns to the starting point using a different route. What is the cyclist's overall change in gravitational potential energy? **[1 mark]**

☐ **A** 0J   ☐ **C** 210 000 J

☐ **B** 21 000 J   ☐ **D** 420 000 J

2 Calculate the change in gravitational potential energy for a 70 kg rock climber who climbs 100 m up a cliff. ($g = 10$ N/kg) **[2 marks]**

3 Use the idea of energy transfer to explain:

(a) why the speed of a ball increases as it falls **[2 marks]**

(b) why something dropped from a greater height will hit the ground at a faster speed. **[2 marks]**

4 A crane lifts a crate 20 m and the crate gains 1000 J of GPE. Calculate how much more GPE the crate will gain if it is lifted a further 40 m. **[2 marks]**

 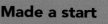

Kinetic energy

All moving objects have kinetic energy. You should be able to calculate the kinetic energy of a moving object.

② Calculating *KE*

kinetic energy (J) = 0.5 × mass (kg) × (speed)^2 (m/s)^2

$KE = \frac{1}{2} \times m \times v^2$

Doubling the mass will double the kinetic energy.

As the speed is squared, doubling the speed will make the kinetic energy four times larger.

⑩ Worked example — Grades 4–5

(a) A vehicle of mass 1000 kg travels at 20 m/s. Calculate its kinetic energy. **[2 marks]**

$KE = \frac{1}{2} \times 1000 \times 20 \times 20 = 200\,000\,J$

(b) Calculate the kinetic energy at 40 m/s and 60 m/s. **[3 marks]**

At 40 m/s: 200 000 × 4 = 800 000 J

At 60 m/s: 200 000 × 9 = 1 800 000 J

(c) A car requires more fuel to do the same journey when fully loaded with passengers than with no passengers. Explain why. **[3 marks]**

It will have greater mass, so a higher kinetic energy (for the same speeds). At higher masses, the engine has to do more work to reach the same speed. Chemical energy stored in the fuel is transferred to the kinetic energy store of the car, so the increase in energy stored means more fuel is used.

② Energy transfers

If you do 500 J of work to move something (see page 184), you transfer 500 J of kinetic energy. It will also take 500 J of work to stop it from moving. If it stops due to friction, then it has done 500 J of work against friction.

500 J work done

500 J kinetic energy

Figure 1 Moving a trolley

But where does the transferred energy 'go'? If the trolley stops due to friction, the friction causes the surfaces of the wheels and ground to heat up as they rub together. The energy is dissipated (transferred as thermal energy) into the surroundings.

Maths skills

40 m/s is twice the original speed. The kinetic energy will be 2^2 = 4 times larger.

60 m/s is three times the original speed. The kinetic energy will be 3^2 = 9 times larger.

Or you could calculate the KE the same way as you did in part (a):

$\frac{1}{2} \times 1000 \times 40 \times 40 = 800\,000\,J$

$\frac{1}{2} \times 1000 \times 60 \times 60 = 1\,800\,000\,J$

⑧ Exam-style practice — Grades 4–5

1 The table shows the mass, speed and kinetic energy of three different objects.

Object	Mass of object (kg)	Speed (m/s)	Kinetic energy (J)
A	5	10	250
B	10	20	
C	5	30	2250

(a) Complete the table for object B. **[2 marks]**

(b) Deduce which object, A, B or C, has the highest kinetic energy. **[1 mark]**

2 (a) Calculate the kinetic energy of a 1200 kg car travelling at 20 m/s. **[2 marks]**

(b) Determine how much work the brakes will have to do to stop the car. **[1 mark]**

3 A car and a van are driving on a straight road. The van has twice the mass of the car, but the car travels at twice the speed. Compare their kinetic energies. **[2 marks]**

Made a start   Feeling confident   Exam ready

Conservation of energy

A system is an object or group of objects. A closed system is one where no energy or mass is transferred into or out of the system. When there are energy changes in a closed system there is no net change to the total energy in that system.

 Principle of conservation of energy

Energy is either transferred usefully, stored or dissipated. Energy cannot be created or destroyed.

This means the total amount of energy in any closed system remains constant. Where energy appears to be 'lost', it is usually being wasted. Energy can be transferred by heating, forces and an electric current.

Catching a ball
kinetic → thermal
A moving object hitting an obstacle transfers kinetic energy to thermal energy.

Archer shooting an arrow upwards towards a distant target
chemical (from muscles) → potential energy from stretching the bow string → kinetic (as arrow flies) → gravitational potential energy (as arrow goes up) → kinetic (as arrow falls back down) → thermal
Some energy would be wasted as thermal energy due to work done against the target as the arrow hits it.

A boat constantly accelerating
chemical → kinetic and thermal
The boat gains kinetic energy as it accelerates, and thermal energy due to more work being done against the resistance of water on the boat.

Energy transfers
(Wasted forms of energy are highlighted.)

Vehicle braking
kinetic → thermal
The friction in the brakes transfers to thermal energy.

Electric kettle
electrical → thermal
Energy is transferred by heating to boil the water.

 Reducing energy losses

Kinetic energy is transferred to thermal energy when work is done against friction in moving parts. Friction can be reduced by lubricating moving parts, reducing the amount of energy wasted.

Thermal energy is often a wasted energy in electrical circuits. The wasted energy can be reduced by using low currents or decreasing the resistance of the circuit.

Thermal energy is wasted in many buildings as it can be conducted through the walls. The lower the thermal conductivity and the thicker the walls, the less energy wasted. Many types of building insulation are thick and contain trapped air. Air has poor thermal conductivity, which reduces the rate of wasted thermal energy being transferred from the building.

 Exam-style practice   Grades 4–5

1 Describe the energy transfers for:
   (a) a horse running at constant speed   **[1 mark]**
   (b) a rocket launching upwards at constant speed   **[1 mark]**
   (c) a car moving at constant speed.   **[1 mark]**
2 Identify how energy is wasted in a coal-fired power station and suggest how it can be reduced.   **[2 marks]**
3 Explain how wearing a thick woolly jumper reduces the amount of thermal energy being transferred to the surroundings.   **[3 marks]**

 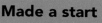 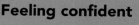

Efficiency

Efficiency is a measure of how much of an energy transfer is used usefully. The more efficient something is, the less energy it wastes. You need to be able to calculate efficiency and comment on how efficient something is.

② Calculating efficiency

You can calculate efficiency using the equation:

$$\text{efficiency} = \frac{\text{useful energy transferred by device (J)}}{\text{total energy supplied to device (J)}}$$

Efficiency can also be calculated as a percentage:

$$\text{efficiency (\%)} = \frac{\text{useful energy transferred by device}}{\text{total energy supplied to device}} \times 100$$

Energy is normally measured in joules. As long as the units for both output and input are the same the calculation will work, for example, if both output and input energy are in megajoules, MJ.

② Efficiency: key facts

- ✓ Efficiency does not have any units.
- ✓ The first equation will give you a result between 0 and 1.
- ✓ The closer to 1 (or 100%), the more efficient the process and the less energy is wasted.
- ✓ If something is 65% efficient, 65% of the energy is used usefully and 35% is wasted.

If your answer is higher than 100% or 1, you have substituted the numbers into the equation the wrong way round.

⑩ Worked example — Grade 5

A power station produces 150 000 kJ of electrical energy per second and transfers energy from burning coal at a rate of 380 000 000 J per second.

(a) Assuming all other energy is wasted (dissipated), state how much energy is wasted. **[2 marks]**

380 000 kJ – 150 000 kJ = 230 000 kJ

(b) Calculate the efficiency of the power station. **[2 marks]**

$$\text{efficiency} = \frac{150\,000}{380\,000} = 0.39$$

(c) A load of coal, when burned, can provide up to 250 kJ of energy. Calculate how much energy can be transferred as electricity. **[2 marks]**

useful energy transferred by the device
= efficiency × total energy supplied to the device
= 0.39 × 250 kJ = 97.5 kJ

Remember, watts are joules per second (page 185), so the rate of use of chemical energy in coal can be given in watts. Convert this to kJ so the units match.
380 000 000 J ÷ 1000 = 380 000 kJ

All of the 380 000 kJ that is taken in must be given out. 150 000 kJ comes out as electrical energy every second, so whatever is left must be the 'wasted' energy. This energy is dissipated (transferred to the surroundings).

The calculation uses the values for useful energy transferred in one second divided by total energy supplied in one second, so the units of time cancel.

You need to use the efficiency from the previous answer and rearrange the equation for useful energy output.

Efficiency measures the proportion of energy that is used usefully.

⑩ Exam-style practice — Grades 4–6

1 A TV uses 400 J of energy and wastes 150 J. Calculate its efficiency. **[1 mark]**

2 A house's central heating is 85% efficient. State what '85% efficient' means. **[1 mark]**

3 Appliance A has an input of 100 J per second. Appliance B has an input of 50 J per second. Explain which is more efficient if they both give out thermal energy at a rate of 35 J per second. **[2 marks]**

4 A heater transfers 2000 J of thermal energy. Find the input energy if it is 60% efficient. **[2 marks]**

5 The table shows the energy inputs and outputs of a filament bulb and a light-emitting diode (LED) in 1 second.

Component	Energy input (J)	Energy of light produced (J)	Thermal energy produced (J)
Filament bulb	40	8	32
LED	10	8	2

Suggest **two** reasons why filament bulbs should be replaced by LEDs. **[2 marks]**

 Made a start **Feeling confident** **Exam ready**

Renewable energy resources

Renewable energy resources provide alternative sources of energy that will not run out or that are easy to replace. They are used for heating, transport, or to generate electricity. You need to know the advantages and disadvantages of renewable energy resources.

Most renewable resources do not produce carbon dioxide when generating electricity and so do not contribute to global warming. They help to reduce overall emissions of carbon dioxide.

(15) Comparison of renewable resources

Renewable resource	Advantages	Disadvantages
Sun – can directly warm buildings and water supplies, or sunlight can be used to generate electricity using solar panels	👍 low maintenance costs (no moving parts) 👍 works anywhere	👎 only works when the sun shines 👎 solar cells have low power output
Biofuels – fuel for transport or electricity is made from vegetable oil, alcohol, wood, methane or waste	👍 reliable 👍 high power output	👎 fuel crops can drive up the cost of food 👎 environmental impact if forests cleared to make room for crops
Wind – wind turbines generate electricity	👍 can be placed in isolated locations 👍 free energy once installed, but some maintenance costs	👎 danger to birds if badly placed 👎 noisy 👎 spoil landscape 👎 only work when it is windy 👎 cannot be used in storms
Hydroelectricity – water movement rotates turbines to generate electricity	👍 reliable 👍 high power output 👍 small waterwheels work in some isolated locations 👍 free energy once installed, but some maintenance costs	👎 building dams can flood valleys, which destroys habitats
Tides – the daily movement of the ocean is used to generate electricity	👍 reliable 👍 high power output 👍 free energy once installed, but has maintenance costs	👎 flooding river estuaries can destroy habitats

(5) Worked example — Grade 5

A scientific base near the North Pole wants to power their camp using only solar cells. In the middle of winter, there is no direct sunlight – nights last 24 hours. Give the advantages and disadvantages of the idea of using solar cells.

[5 marks]

It is a good idea in summer because solar cells are portable so they are easily moved and can be set up anywhere. It will not work in winter as it does not get light and so no electricity would be produced through the winter. The power outputs of solar cells are quite low.

(10) Exam-style practice — Grades 4–5

1 Sugar cane is worth more as ethanol for fuel than as food. Suggest two problems this could cause. Tick **two** boxes. **[2 marks]**

- ☐ **A** The cost of sugar cane as a food could increase.
- ☐ **B** Sugar cane has a low power output compared to other fuels.
- ☐ **C** Sugar cane is a non-renewable resource.
- ☐ **D** There is an environmental impact when trees are cleared to grow crops.

2 Wind and hydroelectricity are renewable energy sources. Discuss the reliability of each power source. **[2 marks]**

3 Biofuels can be used to generate electricity. State **one** advantage and **one** disadvantage of using biofuels to generate electricity. **[4 marks]**

 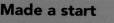

Non-renewable energy resources

Non-renewable energy resources, such as fossil fuels and nuclear power (nuclear energy from atoms), are used to generate electricity. You need to be able to compare the ways in which renewable and non-renewable resources are used.

2 Non-renewable resources

People use fossil fuels directly by:

- burning coal, oil or natural gas to heat their homes or cook food
- using petrol or diesel in their cars.

People use fossil fuels or nuclear power indirectly when using electricity. Most electricity in the UK is still generated using non-renewable resources such as natural gas, but an increasing proportion of electricity is being generated by renewable resources such as wind and solar.

2 Three issues around supply

1. If non-renewable energy resources run out, people will have to find other ways to produce energy.
2. Oil has many other uses, such as producing plastics. If oil runs out, people would have to find alternatives for these other uses.
3. Burning fossil fuels produces carbon dioxide that is released into the atmosphere. Increased levels of carbon dioxide in the atmosphere contribute to climate change.

5 Comparing nuclear and fossil fuels

	Nuclear power	Fossil fuels
Advantages	👍 Other than steam, no gases are emitted. There is no effect on climate change or health. 👍 Small amounts of fuel produce large amounts of energy. 👍 Nuclear fuel will last much longer than fossil fuels and nuclear power stations do not release carbon dioxide. 👍 No direct effect on global climate change or on health during normal operation.	👍 The fuels are relatively low cost. 👍 Fossil fuel power stations can be started up very quickly (especially gas). It is easy to adapt to changing power demands.
Disadvantages	👎 The nuclear waste stays radioactive for thousands of years and has to be safely stored. 👎 Transport of radioactive fuel and waste is dangerous and costly. 👎 When its useful life is complete, a nuclear power plant has to be carefully decommissioned (taken apart and its contents safely disposed of), which is a costly process. 👎 Accidents can release radioactive substances into the environment. 👎 Nuclear power stations take a very long time to start up and shut down. 👎 As a result of accidents, such as at Fukushima in Japan in 2011, many people oppose investment in nuclear power.	👎 Carbon dioxide, a greenhouse gas, is produced, which contributes to climate change. 👎 Burning fossil fuels produces more pollution, not just carbon dioxide but sulfur dioxide, carbon soot and smoke. 👎 Sulfur dioxide and smoke can cause breathing problems. 👎 Coal is a much less efficient fuel and large amounts need to be transported.

2 Worked example — Grade 5

Suggest whether using an electric car is more environmentally friendly than using a petrol car. **[2 marks]**

The electricity for electric cars is generated from either renewable or non-renewable sources. If the source is non-renewable, greenhouse gases and smoke are still produced, but at a power plant, so pollution around busy roads is reduced.

10 Exam-style practice — Grade 5

1. Compare the advantages and disadvantages of nuclear and coal-fired power stations. **[4 marks]**
2. The UK is moving to using more renewable rather than non-renewable resources. Suggest **four** reasons for this trend. **[4 marks]**

Made a start / Feeling confident / Exam ready

Types of wave

All waves are either transverse or longitudinal. You need to know the differences between these two types of wave. Some waves require a medium (a substance, such as air, water or metal) to travel through. Light and other electromagnetic waves do not require a medium.

Longitudinal waves

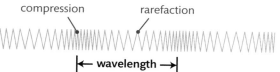

Figure 1 Longitudinal waves

For **longitudinal waves**, vibrations of the particles in the wave are parallel to the direction of movement of the wave (or energy transfer).

There are no **peaks** or **troughs**. Instead, the wave has **compressions**, where particles are close together and **rarefactions**, where the particles are more spread out.

A **wavelength** is measured from the centre of one compression to the next.

Examples:

- sound (in any medium)
- seismic waves that travel through the solid crust in earthquakes and cause side-to-side movements
- a Slinky being pushed and pulled.

The speed of sound in air can be determined by making a sudden noise such as a clap at a distance from an object that reflects sound, such as a large wall. Measuring the distance to the wall and using a stop watch to time how long it takes for the echo to be heard gives the quantities needed for the calculation. The wave has travelled the distance to the wall twice (to the wall and back to your ears) so:

$$\text{wave speed (m/s)} = \frac{\text{distance to wall (m)} \times 2}{\text{time (s)}}$$

Transverse waves

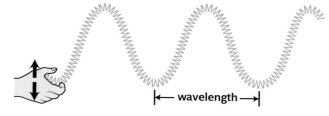

Figure 2 Transverse waves

For **transverse waves**, the vibrations are at right angles to the direction of the wave (or energy transfer).

Examples:

- ripples on water
- a Slinky being shaken
- seismic waves that travel through the crust and mantle and cause up-and-down movements in earthquakes
- light (and all electromagnetic waves).

The speed of ripples on water can be measured by laying a ruler flat on the bottom of a ripple tank so the ripples pass over it (see page 169).

Measuring the time it takes for a ripple to travel the length of the ruler means wave speed can be calculated.

$$\text{wave speed} = \frac{\text{distance}}{\text{time}}$$

Another way of doing this is to set the frequency of the ripples using a signal generator attached to the motor and then measure the distance between the ripples.

wave speed = frequency × wavelength

Waves transfer energy

Place a piece of paper on a Slinky and create the two types of wave. Notice that the paper moves back and forth or up and down, but it does not move along the wave. This shows that waves do not transport material from one place to another. They only transfer energy by vibrations in the material.

Worked example — Grade 5

A seagull floats on the sea. As waves pass, the gull bobs up and down but not forwards. Explain what this shows about ocean waves. **[2 marks]**

Ocean waves are transverse as they transfer energy at right angles to the direction of the wave. It also demonstrates that the water itself is not travelling as the wave travels.

Exam-style practice — Grades 4–5

1. A student wants to investigate the speed of sound. They stand 50 m away from a large building. The student claps their hands and uses a stop watch to time how long it takes for an echo to be heard. Explain how they could use their results to determine the speed of sound. **[3 marks]**

2. A student is trying to measure the speed of sound in air, using the method described in question **1**. They stand in the playground and measure the time it takes for the echo to reach them from the side of the sports hall. Give the most significant source of error in this experiment and suggest how it could be improved. **[2 marks]**

3. Explain why sound cannot pass through a vacuum. **[2 marks]**

✓ **Made a start** ✓ **Feeling confident** ✓ **Exam ready**

Properties of waves

A wave transfers energy without transferring matter. You need to understand the properties of waves.

10 Properties of a wave

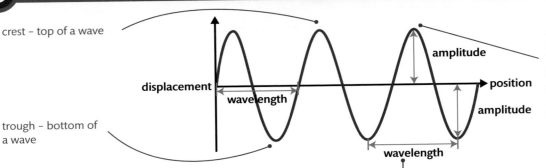

crest – top of a wave

amplitude

displacement

wavelength

position

amplitude

trough – bottom of a wave

wavelength

Amplitude – the maximum displacement. This is the height, in metres, of a wave measured from the middle of the undisturbed position.

Wavelength, λ – the length of one complete wave. It can be measured from anywhere on the wave to the next equivalent point, but crest to crest or trough to trough are the easiest to find and measure.

Figure 1 The main features of a wave

- **Wavelength**, λ, is measured in metres, but may be given in centimetres depending on the type and size of wave.
- **Period**, T, is the time to complete one full wave, measured in seconds, s.
- **Wave velocity**, v, is the speed at which energy is transferred (or the wave moves) through the medium, measured in m/s.
- **Frequency**, f, is the number of waves passing a point per second, measured in hertz, Hz.
- **Wave front** is a line on which all points are at the same displacement and at the same distance from the source.

2 Refraction and reflection

All waves can be refracted or reflected.

Refraction happens when a wave passes through a boundary between different materials. If a light wave passes from air into glass, it will change direction.

Reflection happens when a wave meets a reflective surface (such as when a light wave meets a mirror or a water wave meets a solid obstacle).

2 Worked example | Grade 5

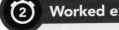

(a) It takes 1.51 s for a sound wave to travel 500 m. Calculate the speed of sound. **[2 marks]**

$$speed = \frac{distance}{time} = \frac{500}{1.51} = 331 \, m/s$$

(b) The sound wave has a frequency of 100 Hz. What is its period? **[2 marks]**

$$period = \frac{1}{frequency}$$

$$period = \frac{1}{100 \, Hz} = 0.01 \, s$$

5 Key equations

- wave speed (m/s) = frequency (Hz) × wavelength (m)
  $v = f\lambda$

- speed (m/s) = $\frac{distance \, (m)}{time \, (s)}$

  $v = \frac{s}{t}$

- frequency (Hz) = $\frac{1}{period \, (s)}$

10 Exam-style practice | Grade 5

1 It takes 0.03 s for a sound to travel 174 m in steel.

  (a) State the equation linking distance, speed and time. **[1 mark]**

  (b) Calculate the speed of sound in steel. **[2 marks]**

2 Waves on the sea approach a harbour wall. Use your knowledge of the properties of waves to describe what happens to the waves as they meet the wall. **[2 marks]**

3 The distance between the first and last ripples of 20 ripples on a pond is measured to be 15 cm.

  (a) Calculate the wavelength in cm. **[2 marks]**

  (b) The frequency of these waves is 4.0 Hz. Calculate the speed of these waves in cm/s. **[2 marks]**

 Made a start   Feeling confident   Exam ready

Practical: Investigating waves

These practicals investigate the speed, frequency and wavelength of waves in a ripple tank and in solids.

(10) Waves in a ripple tank

1 Time how long it takes for one wave to travel from the paddle to the edge of the ripple tank.

2 Measure the distance.

3 Calculate the wave speed.

$$\text{wave speed (m/s)} = \frac{\text{distance (m)}}{\text{time (s)}}$$

4 Time 10 rotations of the motor and divide by 10 to get the period. Calculate the frequency.

$$\text{frequency (Hz)} = \frac{1}{\text{period (s)}}$$

5 Calculate the wavelength.

$$\text{wavelength (m)} = \frac{\text{wave speed (m/s)}}{\text{frequency (Hz)}}$$

6 Alternatively, hold a ruler next to the water and try to estimate the distance from one ripple to the next.

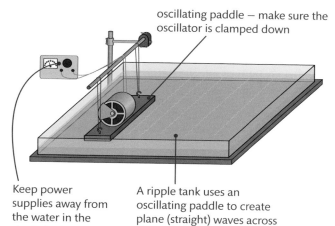

oscillating paddle – make sure the oscillator is clamped down

Keep power supplies away from the water in the ripple tank.

A ripple tank uses an oscillating paddle to create plane (straight) waves across shallow water.

Figure 1 Using a ripple tank to measure the speed of waves

(10) Waves on a string

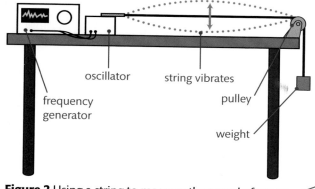

frequency generator

oscillator

string vibrates

pulley

weight

Figure 2 Using a string to measure the speed of waves

1 Using the frequency generator attached to the oscillator, adjust the frequency until you get a wave on the string as shown.

2 Read the frequency from the frequency generator.

3 Measure the length, L, of the string from oscillator to pulley. This is half a wavelength, so $\lambda = 2L$.

4 Calculate wave speed using:

wave speed (m/s) = frequency (Hz) × wavelength (m)

You could use a wire instead of string.

(2) Worked example — Grade 5

A student investigates water waves in a ripple tank. They take three different measurements of a single wavelength. Their results are 2.5 cm, 2.0 cm and 2.2 cm. Explain how they could improve their results. **[2 marks]**

The student should measure the distance between the first and last of a number of wave fronts. Then divide by the number of waves to get the wavelength.

(1) Working scientifically

- Wear goggles if you use wire.
- Keep clear of hanging weights.

(5) Exam-style practice — Grade 5

For the waves on a string investigation, explain what the weight is used for. **[2 marks]**

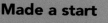 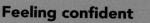

Types of electromagnetic waves

Waves on the electromagnetic spectrum are continuous but are grouped according to their wavelength and frequency. You need to know the properties of electromagnetic waves.

 Properties of electromagnetic waves

Electromagnetic (EM) waves have properties that depend on their wavelength. All waves on the electromagnetic spectrum are transverse and transfer energy from the source to an absorber. All electromagnetic waves travel at the same speed through a vacuum or air. The harmful effects of radiation depend on the type of radiation and its frequency.

Radio waves are produced by vibrations of electrons in electrical circuits. They have low energy so are harmless.

Microwaves have slightly higher frequencies than radio waves. They can cause a heating effect in water and internal heating of body cells.

Infrared radiation is emitted from hot objects. It can burn skin.

Visible light is seen as different colours by the human eye depending on its wavelength. Very bright light (such as from the Sun) can permanently damage eyesight.

Ultraviolet (UV) light is present in sunlight. It can damage cells in the skin, causing skin cancer, and parts of the eye, causing eye conditions.

X-rays pass through soft tissue but are absorbed by denser bones. X-rays are ionising radiation. Ionising radiation can change genes, which can cause cancers and kill cells.

Gamma rays are produced by changes to the nucleus of an atom. Gamma rays are also ionising radiation. Ionising radiation can change genes, which can cause cancers and kill cells.

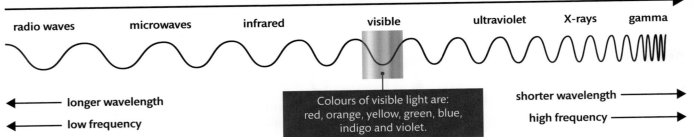

increasing energy

radio waves — microwaves — infrared — visible — ultraviolet — X-rays — gamma

← longer wavelength
← low frequency

Colours of visible light are: red, orange, yellow, green, blue, indigo and violet.

shorter wavelength →
high frequency →

Figure 1 Electromagnetic waves

The speed of light is 3×10^8 m/s (300 000 000 m/s).
You can use the wave equation $v = f\lambda$.
wave speed (m/s) = frequency (Hz) × wavelength (m)

 Worked example Grade 5

The wavelength of visible light ranges from 4×10^{-7} m to 7×10^{-7} m. Calculate the range of frequencies of visible light. **[2 marks]**

$$f = \frac{v}{\lambda} = \frac{3 \times 10^8}{4 \times 10^{-7}} = 7.5 \times 10^{14} \text{ Hz}$$

$$f = \frac{v}{\lambda} = \frac{3 \times 10^8}{7 \times 10^{-7}} = 4.3 \times 10^{14} \text{ Hz}$$

 Exam-style practice Grades 4–5

1 Give **two** examples that show that electromagnetic waves transfer energy. **[2 marks]**

2 Give some risks posed by sunbathing. **[2 marks]**

3 Explain why hospitals use X-rays despite the risk of cell damage. **[2 marks]**

4 The recommended maximum yearly dose of radiation for a person is 50 millisieverts (mSv). A patient having an X-ray receives a 0.1 mSv dose.

(a) Calculate the maximum number of X-rays a patient would be allowed to have in one year. **[2 marks]**

(b) Explain why a patient would be advised to have far fewer than this. **[1 mark]**

 Made a start   **Feeling confident**   **Exam ready**

Practical: Investigating refraction

When light passes from one material to another, the velocity of the light wave changes. You need to know how to investigate refraction of a light wave when it interacts with an air-to-glass boundary.

Experiment to investigate refraction

1. Make sure the slit is inserted into the ray box then switch the ray box on to produce a narrow ray of light.

2. In the centre of a sheet of paper, draw around a rectangular glass block using a pencil.

3. Draw a straight line perpendicular to the longer side of the block and label this 'N' for 'normal'.

4. Use the ray box to shine a ray of light at the point where the normal line meets the longer side of the glass block. Label this as the incident ray.

5. Measure the angle of incidence between the normal line and the incident ray. Record this in a suitable table.

6. Mark the path of the ray as it emerges from the block.

7. Remove the block and draw a line joining where the ray enters and leaves the glass block.

8. Use this line to measure the angle of refraction. This is the angle between the joining line and the normal line.

9. Repeat the procedure for different angles of incidence.

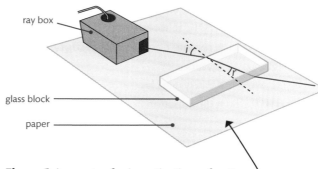

Figure 1 Apparatus for investigating refraction

Worked example — Grade 5

When a light ray enters a glass block at an angle, it is refracted towards the normal.

Suggest what you would expect to happen to the light ray as it leaves the glass block and enters the air once again. **[2 marks]**

The light ray would change direction away from the normal as it leaves the glass block and enters the air.

Working scientifically

Be careful: the ray box will get very hot. Disconnect it between experiments and allow it to cool down before you handle it.

Exam-style practice — Grade 5

Refraction of waves can be investigated using a light ray and a rectangular glass block. In this investigation, different angles of incidence are used and the path of the light ray plotted through the block.

(a) Name the independent variable in this investigation. **[1 mark]**

(b) As the angle of incidence is increased, state what you would expect to happen to the angle of refraction. **[1 mark]**

(c) Explain why it is important to use a slit when producing a light ray from a ray box. **[2 marks]**

Applications of EM waves

Electromagnetic waves have many different uses. You should be able to explain why each type of electromagnetic wave is suited to its applications.

⑮ Electromagnetic wave applications

Increasing frequency → Increasing wavelength

Type of wave	Applications	Further details
radio waves	• broadcasting • communications • satellite transmissions	The frequency of radio waves allows them to be transformed into electrical signals when received by aerials, and allows aerials to produce radio waves using electrical signals.
microwaves	• cooking • communications • satellite transmissions	Certain frequencies of microwaves are absorbed by water, so can be used to heat most food. They penetrate food up to about 1 cm, which means that they cook food faster than infrared.
infrared	• cooking • thermal imaging • short-range communications • optical fibres • remote controls and security systems	Infrared waves may be absorbed at the surface of some objects, transferring energy and increasing the temperature of the objects. Modern communications rely on infrared lasers sending information along optical fibres.
visible light	• vision • photography • illumination	Visible light waves have a frequency that interacts with cells in the eyes, causing signals to be sent to the brain that enable us to see. Light sensors in cameras detect visible light waves to form photographic images. Fibre optic cables transmit information through internal reflection.
ultraviolet (UV)	• security marking • fluorescent lamps • detecting forged bank notes • disinfecting water	UV can pass into skin cells and cause skin burns and skin cancer. UV can be absorbed by some substances, such as invisible ink, which then re-emit the energy as visible light. In strip lights, an electrified gas emits UV, which is absorbed by a powder that glows emitting visible light.
X-ray	• observing the internal structure of objects • airport security scanners • medical scans	X-rays can pass through soft materials like skin and suitcases. They are absorbed by dense materials like bones and metal. This makes them ideal for seeing inside bodies and luggage.
gamma	• sterilising food and medical equipment • detection of cancer • treatment of cancer	Gamma radiation is very high frequency and can kill cells and bacteria easily. As it can pass through most materials, a weak source can be used for medical scans and large doses can target cancer cells deep within the body.

Notice how the potential danger of electromagnetic waves increases with increasing frequency.

① Walkie-talkies

radio wave produced ——→ radio wave detected

electrical circuit produces a radio wave

radio wave produces an electrical signal

Figure 1 Radio waves

② Worked example — Grade 4

Suggest why people should use UV tanning lamps for only short periods of time. **[2 marks]**

Short doses of UV radiation tan the skin, but longer/larger doses can cause skin burns and skin cancer.

⑩ Exam-style practice — Grade 5

1 Give an example of each type of wave used for communication. **[3 marks]**

2 Explain why medical scanners that use X-rays should only be switched on for very short periods of time. **[2 marks]**

✓ **Made a start** ✓ **Feeling confident** ✓ **Exam ready**

The structure of an atom

You need to know the structure of an atom, in terms of electrons, protons and neutrons.

⑩ Structure

Electrons have a negative charge and orbit the nucleus in different energy levels at different distances from the nucleus. Electrons are very small and have a tiny mass, but occupy most of the volume of the atom. This means the atom is mostly empty space.

Atoms that are electrically neutral (have no overall charge) contain equal numbers of electrons and protons.

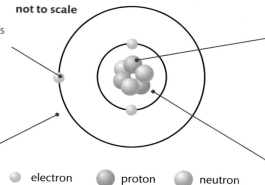

not to scale

● electron ● proton ● neutron

The number of protons in an atom determines what element it is. An atom is carbon if it has six protons. If it had seven, it would be nitrogen.

The **nucleus** contains positive protons and neutral neutrons. It contains most of the mass, but its radius is one ten-thousandth of the radius of the atom. Protons and neutrons have similar masses. The particles here are shown much larger relative to the size of the atom than they are in reality.

Figure 1 Atoms are around 1×10^{-10} m in radius. Small molecules are usually 2 or 3 atoms big, so approximately 3×10^{-10} m in diameter.

	Particle			
	proton	neutron	electron	positron
Relative mass	1	1	negligible	negligible
Relative charge	+1	0	–1	+1

Table 1 Mass and charges of particles

② Worked example — Grade 5

The radius of an atom is 1×10^{-10} m. What is the radius of a nucleus? **[2 marks]**

$10\,000 = 1 \times 10^4$ m

Radius of nucleus $= 1 \times 10^{-10} \div 1 \times 10^4$
$= 1 \times 10^{-14}$ m

⑤ Absorption and emission of electromagnetic radiation by electrons

When an electron in an atom absorbs electromagnetic radiation, it moves to a higher energy level, an orbit further away from the nucleus. The electron may later fall back to its original energy level, causing electromagnetic radiation to be emitted.

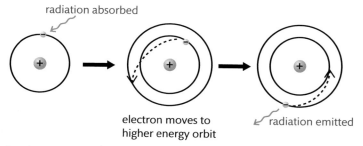

radiation absorbed

electron moves to higher energy orbit

radiation emitted

Figure 2 An electron that absorbs electromagnetic radiation moves to a higher energy level. The electron may then emit electromagnetic radiation and move back to a lower energy level.

⑩ Exam-style practice — Grade 5

❶ A neutral magnesium atom has 12 protons. How many electrons does it have? Explain your answer. **[2 marks]**

❷ A student says that if you add a proton to the nucleus of a magnesium atom, it is still magnesium. Is this statement true? Explain your answer. **[2 marks]**

❸ State **two** differences between electrons and protons. **[2 marks]**

❹ State **two** similarities between protons and neutrons. **[2 marks]**

Mass number, atomic number and isotopes

Every atom has a mass number and an atomic number. You can use these numbers to work out how many protons and neutrons are in an atom's nucleus.

 Particles in an atom

number of protons = atomic number

number of neutrons = mass number − atomic number

$^{14}_{7}N$ has 7 protons and 7 neutrons (14 − 7). A nitrogen atom has 7 electrons.

$^{7}_{3}Li$ has 3 protons, 3 electrons and 4 neutrons (7 − 3).

$^{19}_{9}F$ has 9 protons, 9 electrons and 10 neutrons (19 − 9).

The mass number is equal to the total number of protons and neutrons.

$$^{14}_{7}N$$

The atomic number is equal to the number of protons.

Figure 1 An atomic symbol

Isotopes

Isotopes are forms of particular elements with the same atomic number (number of protons) but different mass numbers (protons + neutrons). As the number of protons is the same, this means there is a different number of neutrons.

Carbon $^{12}_{6}C$ has six protons and six neutrons. An atom is carbon only if it has six protons. Carbon $^{14}_{6}C$ is an isotope of carbon. It has six protons and eight neutrons. As $^{14}_{6}C$ has six protons, it is still carbon, but it is heavier because of the extra neutrons. The protons in the nucleus give the element its characteristic positive charge.

 Ionisation

If an atom loses electrons, it becomes a positively charged **ion**.

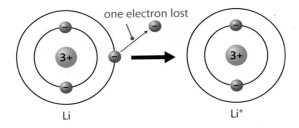

Li atom with 3 electrons Li⁺ ion with only 2 electrons

Figure 2 If an atom loses one or more electrons, it becomes a positive ion

 Worked example **Grade 5**

An ion has 14 protons, 14 neutrons and 12 electrons. State the atomic number, the mass number and the charge on the ion. **[2 marks]**

Atomic number 14, mass number 28. The neutral atom would have 14 electrons, so it has lost two, resulting in charge 2+.

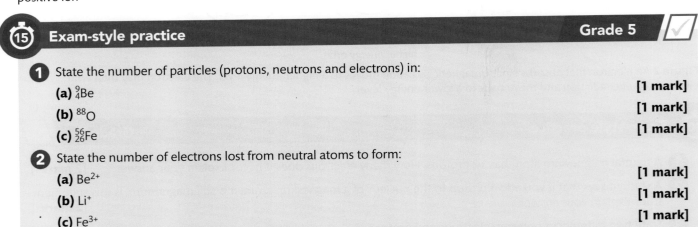

Exam-style practice **Grade 5**

1 State the number of particles (protons, neutrons and electrons) in:

(a) $^{9}_{4}Be$ **[1 mark]**

(b) ^{88}O **[1 mark]**

(c) $^{56}_{26}Fe$ **[1 mark]**

2 State the number of electrons lost from neutral atoms to form:

(a) Be^{2+} **[1 mark]**

(b) Li^{+} **[1 mark]**

(c) Fe^{3+} **[1 mark]**

3 The most common form of carbon has six protons, six neutrons and six electrons. State an example of how these numbers can change but the atom can remain a carbon atom. **[2 marks]**

Made a start | Feeling confident | Exam ready

Development of the atomic model

Scientists' theories about the atom changed as new experimental evidence was discovered. You need to know how the model of the atom has developed over time.

 Developing the model of the atom

1. Before electrons were discovered, it was thought that atoms were tiny spheres that could not be divided into anything else.

2. The **plum pudding model** was proposed by scientists who thought that the atom was like a positively-charged 'pudding', with electrons like 'plums' embedded in it.

3. Rutherford, Geiger and Marsden tested the plum pudding model by aiming a beam of positively-charged alpha particles at a very thin sheet of gold foil (scattering experiment). Some of the alpha particles were repelled by positively-charged particles that were concentrated in the centre of the atom (the nucleus). Most alpha particles passed through unaffected, showing that the nucleus was only a very small part of the atom. This evidence gave rise to the **nuclear model**.

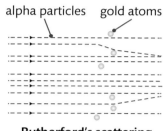

alpha particles   gold atoms

Rutherford's scattering experiment

4. Niels Bohr adapted the nuclear model. Using theoretical calculations alongside experimental observations, Bohr suggested that electrons travel in circular orbits around the nucleus. Further research showed that the nucleus was actually composed of smaller particles with equal amounts of positive charge. These became known as protons. About 20 years after the nuclear model became accepted, neutrons were discovered in the nucleus.

 Worked example **Grade 5**

Explain how the alpha particle scattering experiment showed that the mass of an atom is concentrated at the centre and that atoms are mostly empty space. **[2 marks]**

Most of the alpha particles passed straight through without hitting anything, showing that atoms are mostly empty space. Occasionally they were deflected or bounced back, showing they were repelled by the positive nucleus.

Exam-style practice **Grade 5**

1 Describe the plum pudding model of the atom. **[3 marks]**

2 Give the differences between the plum pudding model and the nuclear model. **[2 marks]**

3 The nuclear model of the atom helps to explain how ionisation of an atom happens.

(a) Describe what is meant by 'ionisation of an atom'. **[2 marks]**

(b) Suggest why the nuclear model helps to explain ionisation of an atom. **[2 marks]**

 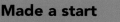

Ionising radiation

In radioactive decay, atoms with unstable nuclei can emit alpha or beta particles, neutrons or gamma rays.

⑤ Radioactive decay

Radioactive isotopes are atoms with unstable nuclei. An unstable nucleus will decay by emitting radiation. Decay is random; there is no way to tell which atom will decay next or when an atom will decay.

All radiation is emitted from the nucleus of the atom, not the outer part.

This radiation is known as **ionising radiation**. Ionising radiation can cause damage to cells that it comes into contact with. Alpha and beta radiation consist of particles. The bigger and more highly charged the particles, the more they can ionise and damage molecules in cells.

⑤ Types of radiation

❶ An alpha particle is the same as a helium nucleus. It contains 2 protons and 2 neutrons.

❷ A beta particle is a fast-moving electron.

❸ Gamma radiation consists of a high frequency, short wavelength electromagnetic wave.

⑩ Properties of radiation

Radiation	Particle	Relative charge	Ionisation ability	Penetrative ability
alpha	two protons, two neutrons (a helium nucleus)	+2	high	low
beta-minus	fast-moving electron (from the nucleus)	−1	medium	medium
beta-plus	positron	+1	medium	medium
gamma	electromagnetic wave	0	low	high

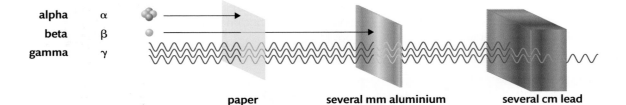

paper | several mm aluminium | several cm lead

② Worked example Grade 5

Alpha particles cannot pass through the skin, but if a source of alpha particles is swallowed, it can cause very serious health problems. Explain why alpha particles pose such a risk inside the body. **[2 marks]**

Alpha particles are the largest and most highly charged form of ionising radiation. This means that the ionising power of alpha particles is very high. If they are emitted inside the body, they can cause damage to cells within the body.

⑩ Exam-style practice Grade 5

❶ A company has designed a medical device that treats cancer using gamma rays. They need to produce a shield that will protect health workers using the device. Which material should they use for the shield? **[1 mark]**

☐ **A** thick glass

☐ **B** several sheets of paper

☐ **C** several mm of aluminium

☐ **D** several cm of lead

❷ Explain why alpha particles have a higher ionising power than beta particles or gamma rays. **[2 marks]**

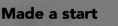 **Made a start** 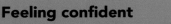 **Feeling confident** **Exam ready**

Background radiation

You need to know how ionising radiation can be detected, its units of measurement, and how background radiation affects measurements.

5 Detecting radiation

A **Geiger–Müller** (G-M) tube is used to detect ionising radiation by detecting the ions formed in a chamber of low-pressure gas when radiation passes through it.

Radioactivity can also be measured using photographic film. For example, health workers who carry out X-ray scans wear a film badge dosimeter to measure the radiation they are exposed to when carrying out their job.

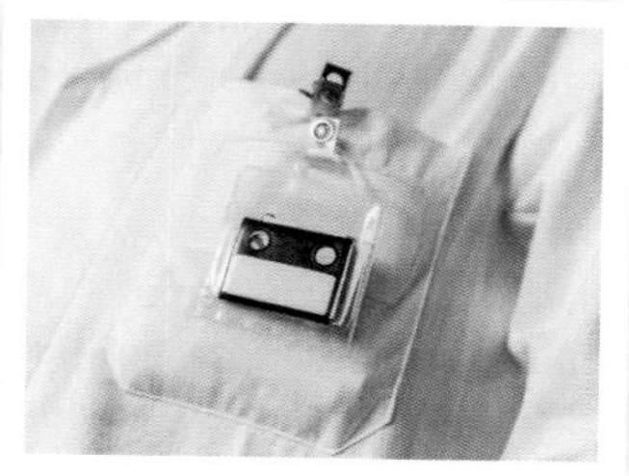

Figure 1 A film badge dosimeter measures radiation

5 Measuring radiation

The **activity** is the rate at which atoms in a radioactive source decay.
Activity is measured in becquerels (Bq). 1 Bq means 1 decay per second.

The **count rate** is the number of decays recorded per second by a detector such as a G-M tube.

5 Background radiation

Background radiation is radiation that is not due to a specific radioactive source. It comes from many sources, both from Earth and space, including food and drink, the air and the ground.

Radon is a gas given out by some rocks, such as granite. It emits alpha particles, and humans can inhale it. There are also cosmic rays from space that contribute to background radiation. Nuclear power stations and medical procedures also contribute to background radiation. In most places, the level of background radiation is low and so does not pose a serious risk to health.

There is always some background radiation present, so when you are measuring a count for a radioactive source, you must first measure the background count and then subtract it from your final measurement.

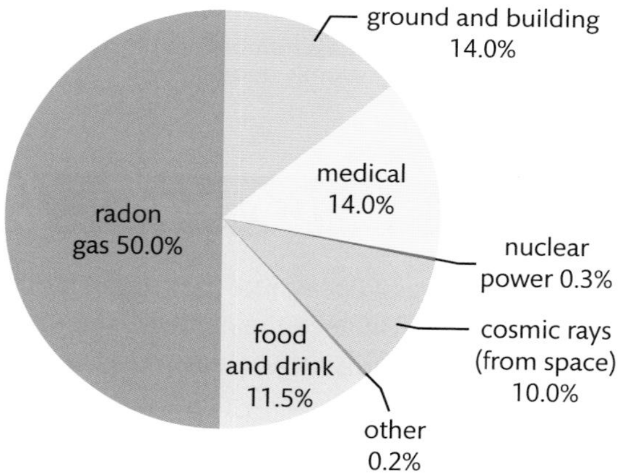

Figure 2 Sources of background radiation

2 Worked example — Grade 4

(a) Give the full name of the device used to detect ionising radiation. **[1 mark]**

A Geiger–Müller tube.

(b) Suggest a reason why this device cannot measure all the radiation produced by a source. **[2 marks]**

The radiation goes in all directions so not all of it reaches the detector.

10 Exam-style practice — Grades 4–5

1. A scientist wants to investigate the radioactivity of a source. She notices that the G-M tube detects radiation in the laboratory all the time, even when a source is not in the room. Explain where this radiation is coming from. **[2 marks]**

2. Radioactive sources need to be kept securely in a lead-lined box. Explain the potential dangers of leaving a gamma source out in the school laboratory. **[2 marks]**

Made a start | Feeling confident | Exam ready

Beta decay

Beta decay is one type of radioactive emission from an unstable nucleus.

 ## β– decay

β– particles are electrons that are moving very fast. They are emitted from the nuclei of some unstable atoms when one of the neutrons changes into a proton and an electron.

Changes as a result of β– decay

The β– particle has a relative charge of –1. This means that the atomic number of an atom emitting a β– particle increases by one. This makes sense, because a neutron has changed to become a proton.

However, the β– particle has a tiny mass compared to a neutron, and the mass of a neutron is almost exactly the same as the mass of a proton. This means that the mass number of the atom after emission of the β– particle remains the same.

β+ decay

β+ particles are positrons. They have the same mass as an electron but a relative charge of +1. They are emitted from the nucleus of some unstable atoms when a proton changes into a neutron and a β+ particle.

Changes as a result of β+ decay

The β+ particle has a relative charge of +1. When it is emitted from the nucleus of an atom, the atomic number of the remaining atom decreases by one.

The β+ particle, just like the electron, has a tiny mass compared to a neutron, so the mass number of the atom after β+ emission remains the same.

	p	n	e⁺
mass number	1	1	0
atomic number	1	0	–1

Figure 3 β+ decay

Figure 1 β– decay

After the β– decay, the nucleus still has the same total number of protons and neutrons, so the mass number does not change. As there is an extra proton, the atomic number increases by one. This means that the nucleus is a new element.

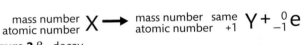

$$^{\text{mass number}}_{\text{atomic number}} X \rightarrow ^{\text{mass number same}}_{\text{atomic number} +1} Y + ^{0}_{-1}e$$

Figure 2 β– decay

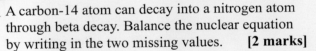 ## Worked example　　　Grade 5

A carbon-14 atom can decay into a nitrogen atom through beta decay. Balance the nuclear equation by writing in the two missing values. **[2 marks]**

$$^{14}_{6}C \rightarrow ^{14}_{7}N + ^{0}_{-1}e$$

Notice how the atomic number of the nitrogen has increased by one and the mass number has remained the same.

The mass numbers and atomic numbers balance on each side of the equation:

$14 = 14 + 0$

$6 = 7 - 1$

Exam-style practice　　　Grades 4–5

1 Carbon-11 is an isotope of carbon. It has 6 protons, 6 electrons and 5 neutrons.

Carbon-11 can decay into boron by β+ decay.

A ^{11}C nucleus undergoes β+ decay. State the change in:

(a) atomic number **[1 mark]**

(b) mass number. **[1 mark]**

2 The symbol for a β– particle can be written as $^{0}_{-1}e$.

Describe what each part of the symbol tells you. **[3 marks]**

 Made a start　　 Feeling confident　　 Exam ready

Nuclear decay

When a nucleus undergoes radioactive decay, there may be changes to the atomic and/or mass number of the atom.

(5) Changes to the atomic and mass numbers

Type of decay		Change to atomic number	Change to mass number
alpha	α or $^4_2$He	decreases by 2	decreases by 4
beta-minus	$\beta-$ or $^0_{-1}$e	increases by 1	no change
beta-plus	$\beta+$ or $^0_{+1}$e	decreases by 1	no change
gamma	γ	no change	no change
neutron	$^1_0$n	no change	decreases by 1

(5) Alpha decay

When a nucleus undergoes **alpha decay**, it loses two protons and two neutrons. The mass number of the nucleus decreases by four and the atomic number and the charge on the nucleus decrease by two. The nucleus becomes a new element.

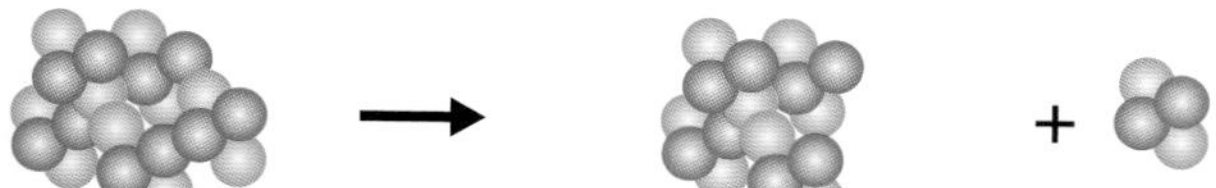

$$\text{mass number} \atop \text{atomic number}\ X \longrightarrow {\text{mass number }-4 \atop \text{atomic number }-2}\ Y + {^4_2}\alpha$$

Figure 1 Alpha decay

Remember that these decays happen randomly. The products, or daughter nuclei, created may be radioactive isotopes that decay again.

(2) Gamma decay

Nuclei that have undergone alpha, $\beta-$ or $\beta+$ decay are often left in a high-energy unstable state and undergo nuclear rearrangement in order to make the remaining nucleus more stable. In this rearrangement, some energy is lost from the nucleus in the form of gamma radiation.

(2) Neutron decay

In **neutron emission**, a neutron is emitted from the nucleus. The mass decreases by 1 and another isotope of the same element is formed. For example, beryllium-13 decays to form beryllium-12 by emitting a neutron.

$$^{13}_4\text{Be} \rightarrow {^{12}_4}\text{Be} + {^1_0}\text{n}$$

In all **nuclear changes**, mass and charge are conserved.

(2) Worked example — Grade 4

Thorium-232 has 90 protons. It decays into radium-228, which has 88 protons.

(a) State the change in the atomic number. **[1 mark]**

The atomic number has decreased by 2 (90 to 88).

(b) State the change in the mass number. **[1 mark]**

The mass number has decreased by 4 (232 to 228).

(c) Use your answers to part **(a)** and part **(b)** to determine the type of nuclear decay. **[1 mark]**

The decay is alpha decay.

(10) Exam-style practice — Grade 5

1 Fill in the gaps.

  (a) $^{239}_{94}$Pu $\rightarrow$ $^{\square}_{\square}$U + $^4_2\square$ **[2 marks]**

  (b) $^{16}_5$B $\rightarrow$ $^{\square}_5$B + $^1_0\square$ **[2 marks]**

2 Uranium-238 ($^{238}_{92}$U) decays into thorium-234 ($^{234}_{90}$Th).

  (a) Calculate the changes in atomic number and mass number. **[2 marks]**

  (b) Determine the particle that is emitted in this decay. **[1 mark]**

3 Lead-212 ($^{212}_{82}$Pb) decays into bismuth-212 ($^{212}_{83}$Bi).

  (a) Calculate the changes in atomic number and mass number. **[2 marks]**

  (b) Determine the particle that is emitted in this decay. **[1 mark]**

Half-lives

Half-life is a measure of how radioactive a source is. It can be anything from a fraction of a second to many thousands of years. You need to be able to determine a substance's half-life from a graph or table of data.

 **Half-life**

The half-life of a radioactive source is the time taken for either:

- the **count rate** (activity) to fall to **half** its initial value *or*
- half the radioactive nuclei in a sample to decay.

Half-life is an average time, resulting from the random nature of radioactive decay. Looking at the half-life of a radioactive source allows us to predict the activity of a large number of nuclei during radioactive decay.

Time (minutes)	Number of radioactive nuclei
0	1000
2	842
4	681
6	540
8	428
10	353

Table 1 Half-life can be estimated from data

 Worked example | **Grade 5**

The activity after a nuclear accident is 150 Bq. The area is considered safe when the activity drops under 75 Bq. The radioactive source has a half-life of 20 years. Determine how long it will take for the area to become safe. **[2 marks]**

1 half-life ➔ $\frac{1}{2}$ initial value = 75 Bq

This is the safe level, so the time taken will be one half-life = 20 years.

The number of nuclei halves to 500 between 6 and 8 minutes. This means the half-life is between 6 and 8 minutes. You can use a graph to find a more accurate answer.

 Half-life graphs

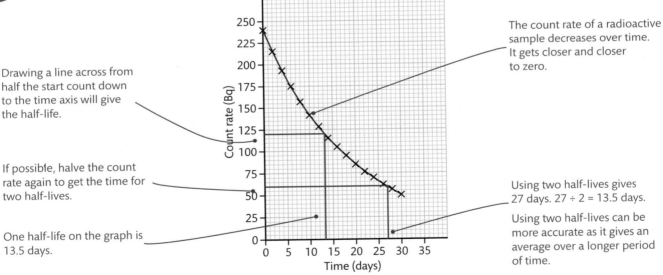

Drawing a line across from half the start count down to the time axis will give the half-life.

If possible, halve the count rate again to get the time for two half-lives.

One half-life on the graph is 13.5 days.

The count rate of a radioactive sample decreases over time. It gets closer and closer to zero.

Using two half-lives gives 27 days. 27 ÷ 2 = 13.5 days.

Using two half-lives can be more accurate as it gives an average over a longer period of time.

Figure 1 Finding a half-life from a graph

 Exam-style practice | **Grades 4–5**

1. State the fraction of a radioactive isotope left in a sample after one half-life. **[1 mark]**

2. A sample with a half-life of 10 mins has an activity of 45 Bq. Calculate the activity after 10 minutes. **[2 marks]**

3. A scientist measures the activity of a sample. The activity drops from 640 Bq to 320 Bq in 36 seconds. It takes another 38 seconds to drop to 160 Bq. Estimate the half-life by calculating the average of these two readings. **[2 marks]**

 Made a start **Feeling confident** **Exam ready**

Dangers of radioactivity

Ionising radiation can be useful to us, but it also poses some dangers. It is important to understand and minimise the risks to ensure the safety of people exposed to radiation.

5 Dangers of ionising radiation

Ionising radiation has both direct and indirect dangers for humans. Direct damage can be caused to body tissues if radiation affects the cells. Indirect damage can occur if the radiation causes ions to be produced. These ions can destroy cells in our bodies or they can mutate the genes within our cells.

During the Fukushima nuclear disaster in Japan in 2011, both caesium-137 and iodine-131 were released. Caesium-137 has a half-life of about 30 years, so the ground and the water surrounding the plant site will remain contaminated for many decades to come. Iodine-131 has a half-life of 8 days, so the dangers posed by iodine are severe, but short-lived.

Figure 1 A major earthquake in March 2011 caused a tsunami that affected the power supply and cooling to the Fukushima nuclear power station and caused a nuclear accident

5 Precautions to ensure safety

Radioactive isotopes are frequently used in the diagnosis and treatment of medical conditions. For example, technetium-99 is widely used as a tracer that allows doctors to detect abnormalities in internal organs. Technetium-99 is also used to treat some cancers; some tumours can be destroyed using very high doses of gamma radiation.

It is important that the dose a patient receives is as small and targeted as possible, to limit unnecessary exposure. Medical staff who regularly administer such treatments are required to wear badges that record the amount of radiation they are exposed to. The staff also limit their exposure, for example, by sheltering behind a lead screen or wearing protective clothing such as lead-lined aprons.

5 Radiation dose

The amount of radiation an object is exposed to is called the **dose**. For small doses, such as radiation treatment in hospitals, the risks are much less than the benefit from the treatment.

A dose can be reduced by:

- reducing the exposure time
- using a source of lower activity
- wearing protective clothing and/or staying behind a screen
- keeping your distance from sources, for example, using long tweezers, tongs or robotic arms.

Ultraviolet rays and X-rays can have a similar hazardous effect on the body as gamma rays, although they are less ionising and less penetrating. UV can cause premature ageing of the skin and increase the risk of skin cancer.

5 Worked example — Grade 4

Workers in nuclear power stations use many different ways to stay safe. Suggest **three** ways they can use. **[3 marks]**

They can work for short periods of time. They can wear protective clothing. They can wear badges that record the amount of radiation they are exposed to.

5 Exam-style practice — Grade 5

X-rays are used in hospitals to take pictures of broken bones. The X-rays pass through a person's soft tissue but are blocked by bone.

(a) Explain why it is important to limit the time that a patient is exposed to X-rays. **[2 marks]**

(b) Explain why the person operating the X-ray equipment goes behind a lead shield each time they take a picture. **[2 marks]**

 Made a start **Feeling confident** **Exam ready**

Radioactive contamination and irradiation

Contamination and irradiation are both harmful to living things. You need to know about the measures taken to avoid radioactive contamination and also understand the difference between contamination and irradiation.

(5) Irradiation

To be **irradiated** means to be exposed to a source of ionising radiation, such as alpha, beta or gamma radiation, X-rays or ultraviolet. The irradiated object does not become radioactive. Irradiation can cause damage to cells, alter genes and cause mutations that can lead to cancer. When you move away from the source of radiation, irradiation stops.

(5) Contamination

Touching a source can leave traces of radioactive material on you or an object. If this radioactive material is unwanted, it is called **contamination**. Contamination is dangerous, especially for living things, as you continue to be irradiated by the radioactive material that is in contact with you. The level of hazard depends on the type of radiation. Contamination should be cleaned off immediately. Removing contaminated materials from skin can be difficult.

Avoid contamination by avoiding direct contact with sources. The same precautions as for reducing irradiation will also help reduce the risk of contamination. Liquid and powdery sources are particularly risky and need to be kept in sealed containers.

(5) Peer review and scientific research

Before a scientist publishes their research, their work is checked and evaluated by other scientists (the scientist's peers). This process is known as **peer review**. During this process, scientists check the findings, assess the methods and comment on the conclusions. This process makes scientists more confident about each other's findings.

It is important to understand the effects of radiation on human beings in order to protect and treat anyone exposed to high levels of radiation. There is a lot of scientific research conducted in this area. This means that people who work with radiation are better able to protect themselves and treat anyone who may have been contaminated or received a high dose of radiation.

There is more about reducing radiation doses on page 181.

(3) Worked example — Grades 4–5

1 State **two** ways that contamination can be removed. **[2 marks]**

Clean contamination off by thorough washing. Dispose of/throw away clothing that may be contaminated.

2 A person is receiving treatment for cancer that means they are irradiated by gamma rays. After their treatment, they are worried that they will be radioactive. Explain why they do not need to worry about this. **[3 marks]**

The person is only being irradiated when they are exposed to the source of radiation. When they move away from the source, the irradiation stops. They do not become radioactive themselves.

(10) Exam-style practice — Grade 5

1 A science teacher is using radioactive rocks. Explain why the teacher is at risk from both contamination and irradiation and what they can do to reduce the risk. **[4 marks]**

2 **(a)** Describe the difference between irradiation and contamination. **[2 marks]**

(b) One way to stop being irradiated is to move away from the source of radiation. Explain why this does not work with radioactive contamination. **[2 marks]**

Made a start | Feeling confident | Exam ready

Revising energy transfers

Appliances transfer energy from one store to another. Some energy transfers are useful, others are not. The law of conservation of energy states that energy can neither be created nor destroyed, but is transferred from one form into another. This means that there is no overall (net) change to the total energy in a system.

 ## Changes in energy stores

When an object is moving upwards, its kinetic energy (energy stored due to its movement) is transferred into its gravitational potential energy store:

$\Delta GPE = mg\Delta h = \Delta KE = \frac{1}{2}m\Delta v^2$

Energy is always conserved, but it is not always transferred in a useful store.

For example, when a driver brakes to slow a car, the kinetic energy is transferred into thermal energy in the brakes, which dissipates into the surroundings.

A television usefully transfers energy to the surroundings by light and sound. It also transfers energy by heating, which is not useful.

Energy is transferred to an electric kettle by electricity. The electricity transfers energy to the kettle and water by heating. Useful energy is transferred to the water. Energy is transferred to the body of the kettle by heating and is dissipated to the surroundings. A little energy is transferred by sound. An efficient kettle maximises the fraction of energy transferred usefully into the water.

> Look at pages 161 and 162 where GPE and KE are explained in more detail.

 ## Sankey diagrams

Sankey diagrams can be used to represent energy transfers.

Figure 1 shows that 80% of the energy transferred by the television is transferred by light and sound. The remaining 20% of the energy is dissipated as thermal energy.

The width of the arrow represents the amount of energy.

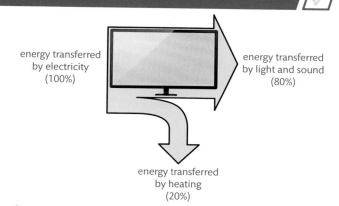

energy transferred by electricity (100%)

energy transferred by light and sound (80%)

energy transferred by heating (20%)

Figure 1 A Sankey diagram for energy transfers by a television

 ## Worked example — Grade 5

1500 J is transferred to a kettle by electricity. 1000 J is stored as thermal energy in the water in the kettle.

(a) Calculate the amount of energy transferred to the kettle body and its surroundings. **[1 mark]**

1500 – 1000 = 500 joules

(b) Complete the Sankey diagram to represent this energy transfer. **[3 marks]**

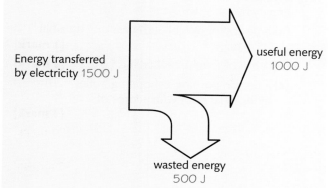

Energy transferred by electricity 1500 J

useful energy 1000 J

wasted energy 500 J

 ## Exam-style practice — Grade 6

A light bulb has 40 J of energy transferred to it by electricity every second. 15 J are transferred to the surroundings by light.

(a) Calculate the amount of energy that is wasted. **[1 mark]**

(b) Complete the Sankey diagram to show the energy transfers. **[3 marks]**

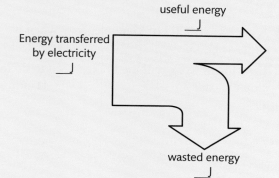

useful energy

Energy transferred by electricity

wasted energy

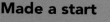

Work done and energy transfer

Work done is energy transferred when a force moves an object through a distance. You need to be able to calculate work done, given the force and distance.

Calculating W

work done (J) = force (N) × distance moved in the direction of the force (m)

$W = F \times d$

One joule of work is done when a force of one newton is applied over a distance of one metre.

> Distance is measured along the line of action of the force.

When calculating work done, the force is measured along the same line of action as the distance. You may need to resolve forces to calculate work done.

As work done = force × distance, you can give the unit for work done as newton metres (Nm) instead of joules.

Energy transfer

If you do work pushing an object, it will gain **kinetic energy**. If you do work lifting an object, it gains **gravitational potential energy**.

Force × distance would have the unit newton metres, Nm, which is equal to work done measured in joules. So one newton metre is equal to one joule.

When a potential difference makes a current flow by 'pushing' charge around a circuit, it is doing work. Work done against friction heats up the moving object. When surfaces rub together, there is friction between the two surfaces, which causes the objects to heat up. This unwanted energy transfer can be reduced by lubricating the surfaces.

Worked example Grades 4–5

1 A person lifts a heavy box from the floor onto a table.

Describe the energy change that has taken place for the box. **[2 marks]**

The box has gained height, so its gravitational potential energy has increased.

2 **Figure 1** shows a person who weighs 650 N. Calculate how much work the person has to do against gravity to climb the stairs. **[2 marks]**

> The person has weight 650 N, so the force they must use to climb the stairs must match their weight: 650 N.
>
> As they are applying an upward force, you are only interested in the upwards motion; the 1.1 m is not used in the calculation.

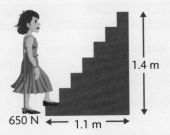

1.4 m

650 N ← 1.1 m →

Figure 1 A person climbing stairs

W = F × d = 650 × 1.4 = 910 J

3 A car has 20 000 J of kinetic energy when it starts to brake.

How much work will the brakes need to do to stop the car? **[1 mark]**

20 000 J

Exam-style practice Grades 4–5

1 A person pushes a heavy box sideways along the floor.

(a) Name the energy that the person supplies. **[1 mark]**

☐ **A** kinetic energy

☐ **B** gravitational potential energy

☐ **C** thermal energy

☐ **D** work

(b) What energy has the box gained? **[1 mark]**

2 Calculate how much work is done against or by gravity by:

(a) a person of weight 500 N walking up a hill 35 m high **[1 mark]**

(b) a ball of weight 20 N falling 1.5 m **[1 mark]**

(c) a person pushing a shopping trolley 120 m along a flat floor with a force of 25 N. **[1 mark]**

☐ **Made a start** ☐ **Feeling confident** ☐ **Exam ready**

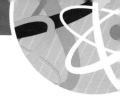

Power

Power is a measure of the rate of energy transfer. It tells you how much energy is transferred per second. You need to know how to calculate power using two different equations.

2 Calculating power

You can calculate power with the equations:

$$\text{power (W)} = \frac{\text{work done (J)}}{\text{time (s)}}$$

$$\text{power} = \frac{\text{energy transferred}}{\text{time}} \qquad P = \frac{E}{t}$$

Power is the **rate** of energy transfer. It measures how quickly work is done, or energy is transferred. A power of 1 watt means 1 joule is being transferred every second. A 1000 W heater will transfer 1000 J of electrical energy into heat and waste energy every second.

5 Worked example — Grade 5

An electric heater uses 24 000 J of energy every minute.

(a) Calculate the power of the heater. **[3 marks]**

$$\text{power (W)} = \frac{\text{energy transferred (J)}}{\text{time (s)}} = \frac{24\,000}{60}$$

$$= 400\,\text{W}$$

(b) How much energy will the heater use if it is left switched on for 1 hour? Give your answer in standard form. **[3 marks]**

energy (J) = energy in 1 min × number of minutes

= 24 000 × 60

= 1 440 000 J

= 1.44×10^6 J

Watch the units.

The time needs to be in seconds; 1 min = 60 s and 1 hour = 60 min = 3600 s.

Energies can get very large so you must be prepared to use standard form. Make sure you know how to put standard form into your calculator and how to read it.

Exam focus

Notice that the question asked for standard form, so you must state your answer in that form. Make sure you read questions carefully.

5 Units

$$\text{power (W)} = \frac{\text{energy transferred (J)}}{\text{time (s)}} = \frac{\text{work done (J)}}{\text{time (s)}}$$

so the unit for power, watts, is the same as joules per second or 1 W = 1 J/s

Many appliances have large powers which are measured in kilowatts. 1 kW = 1000 W

Likewise for energy: 1 kJ = 1000 J

If you use kilojoules in the equation, the power will be in kilowatts. The time must still be in seconds.

10 Exam-style practice — Grade 5

1. A motor transfers 4800 J of electrical energy in one minute. Calculate its power. **[2 marks]**
2. An athlete lifts herself 40 times in 90 s.

   (a) If each lift takes 30 J of work, calculate the total amount of work that the athlete does in 90 s. **[2 marks]**

   (b) Calculate the athlete's useful power output. **[2 marks]**

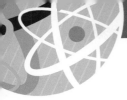

Forces

A force is a push or pull that acts on an object due to its interactions with another object. You need to know about forces that require contact to exert the force and forces that can act at a distance (non-contact).

2 Contact forces

- friction
- normal contact force
- air resistance
- water resistance
- tension
- lift
- upthrust

2 Non-contact forces

- gravitational force (weight)
- electrostatic force
- magnetic force

2 Resultant forces

When two forces act on the same object at the same time, we need to determine the combined effect of those forces.

- If two forces act in the same direction, we add them up.
- If two forces act in opposite directions, we subtract one force from the other.

In both cases, the total force is called the resultant force.

For example, a motor boat has a force pushing it forwards provided by the motor. There is a force pushing it backwards because of water resistance. The forwards force is larger than the water resistance, so the resultant force moves the boat forwards.

2 Normal contact force

An object pushing against a surface experiences a force pushing back on it. We call this a 'normal contact force' because its direction acts at 90° to the surface.

For example, a book placed on a flat table pushes downwards against the table because of the book's weight. The normal contact force pushes upwards on the book.

5 Reducing friction

Friction is a contact force. The amount of friction between two solid objects depends on how rough the surfaces in contact are. Friction increases as the roughness increases.

This can cause problems in machines with many moving parts, such as engines. Over time, friction causes the parts to wear away.

We can reduce the amount of friction and reduce the amount of wear by making the surfaces of parts smoother. One way to do this is to add lubrication.

Some types of liquid oil are designed to reduce friction between the parts of engines. This means the parts slide over each other more easily.

2 Exam focus

When talking about forces, use 'weight' or 'gravitational force' instead of 'gravity'.

10 Worked example — Grade 5

A skydiver falls through the air towards the ground. They are speeding up.

(a) Describe the **two** forces acting on the skydiver, including their directions. **[4 marks]**

The weight of the skydiver acts downwards.
The force of air resistance acts upwards.

(b) State whether each of the **two** forces is a contact or a non-contact force. **[2 marks]**

weight = non-contact

air resistance = contact

(c) Describe the resultant force. In which direction does it act? How does its size compare with the skydiver's weight? **[2 marks]**

The resultant force acts downwards. It is smaller than the skydiver's weight.

10 Exam-style practice — Grade 5

1. A student suggests that air resistance is a non-contact force. Explain why the student is incorrect. **[1 mark]**
2. Explain what a 'non-contact force' is. Include an example. **[2 marks]**
3. Sort the following forces into 'contact' and 'non-contact' forces. **[2 marks]**

friction	magnetic force	upthrust	weight

Circuit diagrams

You need to be able to recognise and draw the universal symbols used to represent the components of a circuit.

5 Circuit components and their symbols

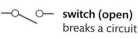

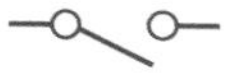
switch (open)
breaks a circuit

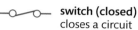

switch (closed)
closes a circuit

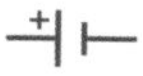

cell
provides energy to the circuit

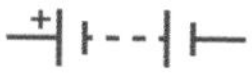

battery
more than one cell in series

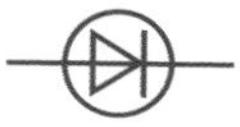
diode
only lets charge flow in the direction shown by the arrow

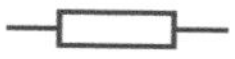
resistor
reduces the current

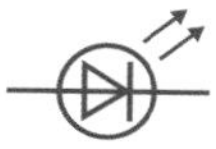
LED (light emitting diode)
lights up when charge flows in the direction of the arrow

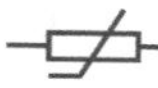
thermistor
resistance decreases as temperature increases; used in devices such as thermostats or electronic thermometers

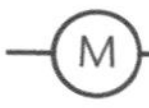

motor
transfers electrical to kinetic energy

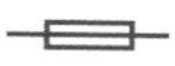
fuse
melts and breaks the circuit if the current gets too high

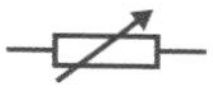
variable resistor
a resistor you can change

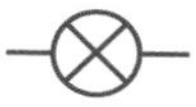
lamp
lights up when charge flows

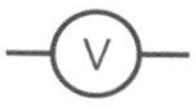

voltmeter
connected to a circuit in parallel, measures the potential difference

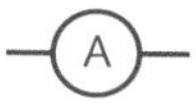

ammeter
connected to a circuit in series, measures the current

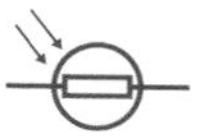
LDR (light-dependent resistor)
resistance decreases as light intensity increases; can be used to control light-sensitive devices such as street lights that come on when it's dark

5 Circuits

For charge to flow, there must be a complete circuit. We use the convention that current is from positive to negative (even though the electrons flow the opposite way – see page 173 for electrons in atoms). This is particularly important when dealing with diodes and LEDs.

Test circuits

Circuits powered by a cell carry direct current (d.c.). A **test circuit** allows the current and potential difference across a component to be measured. You could replace the lamp with any other component. A voltmeter is connected in parallel with (across) the component being measured. It is used to measure the potential difference across a component. Voltage is an alternative term for potential difference.

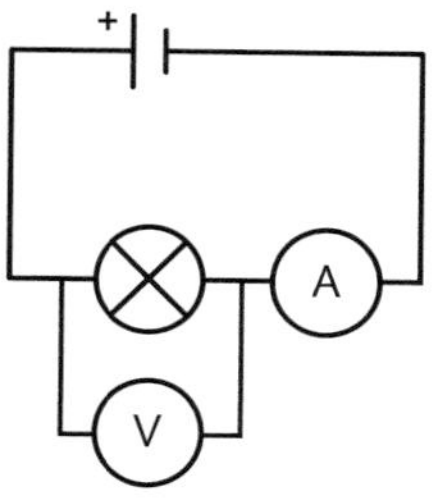

Figure 1 A test circuit

An ammeter is connected in series with (in line with) the component being measured. It is used to measure the current in a component.

5 Worked example — Grade 5

Look at the circuit diagram shown in **Figure 2**.

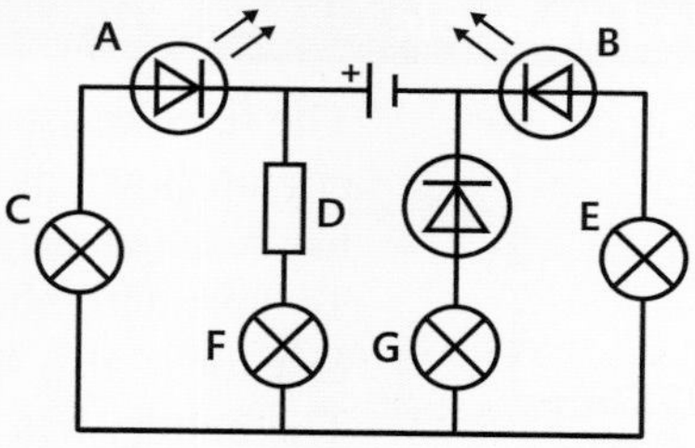

Figure 2

Which of the components **A–G** will receive a flow of charge? Explain your answer. **[3 marks]**

D, F, G, E and B, as the current can pass through all the LEDs and diodes in the right direction.

LED A is the wrong way around and would conduct no current so charge cannot flow to lamp C.

15 Exam-style practice — Grade 5

1. Look at the circuit diagram shown in **Figure 3**. When the switch is closed, state if the lamps **A**, **B**, **C** or the LED (**D**) would light up. Explain your answer. **[4 marks]**
2. Draw a circuit diagram for a circuit containing a cell and:
   (a) a lamp in parallel with an LDR **[2 marks]**
   (b) a resistor in series with a variable resistor. **[2 marks]**

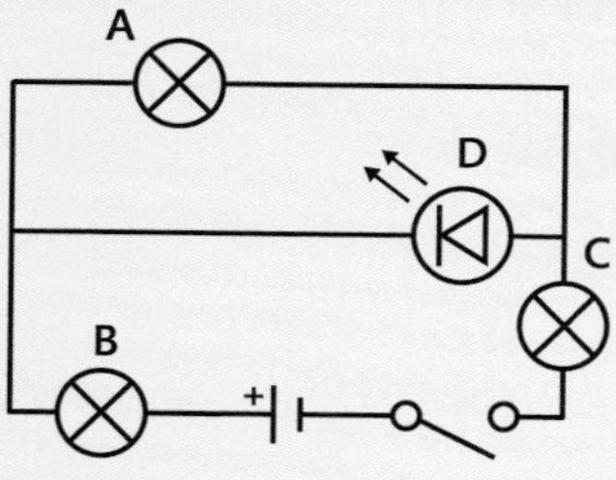

Figure 3

Made a start | Feeling confident | Exam ready

Current, resistance and potential difference

You need to understand current, resistance and potential difference to understand the basics of electrical circuits.

 Key definitions

Current is the rate of flow of charge (page 189). In metal wires, the charge that flows consists of electrons. Electrical current is always conserved at a junction in a circuit. Also, no current is 'lost' through components.
Potential difference (pd), measured in volts, is the energy transferred per unit charge passed and therefore the volt is a joule per coulomb (the unit of charge; see page 189). You will sometimes hear pd referred to as *voltage*.
Resistance reduces the current. It is measured in ohms or Ω (for example, 10 ohms or $10\,\Omega$). Resistance is caused by electrons colliding with the metal ions inside a wire.

 $V = IR$

When there is a pd in a closed circuit there will be a current.
potential difference (V) = current (A) × resistance (Ω)
$V = I \times R$
When the potential difference is increased and the resistance remains constant, more energy is given to the charge, increasing the current.
If you increase the resistance, it becomes harder for charge to flow. If the pd is kept the same, the current decreases.

 Maths skills

Potential difference is proportional to current.
$V \propto I$ (for ohmic conductors where R is constant)
If you double V, you also double I for the same resistance.
If V is kept constant, then current is inversely proportional to resistance.
$I \propto \dfrac{1}{R}$
If you double the resistance, you halve the current.

 Worked example **Grades 4–5**

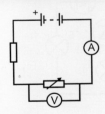

Figure 1

The fixed resistor in the circuit shown in **Figure 1** has resistance $15\,\Omega$.
To start with, the variable resistor is also set to $15\,\Omega$.
The battery has a potential difference of 3 V.

You will need to understand resistances in series circuits for these questions. Go to page 190 to revise resistance. Remember, the potential difference is split across components. If they are identical, they will take an equal share.

(a) Give the reading on the voltmeter. **[1 mark]**
1.5 V

(b) Calculate the total resistance. **[2 marks]**
R = 15 + 15 = 30Ω

(c) Calculate the current in the circuit. Use the equation $V = IR$. **[3 marks]**
3 = I × 30
So current, I = $\dfrac{3}{30}$ = 0.1 A

(d) Describe the effect on the current if the resistance of the variable resistor is increased. **[1 mark]**
The current would decrease.

 Exam-style practice **Grades 4–5**

1 State the potential difference measured across the lamp in the circuit shown in **Figure 2**. **[1 mark]**

2 Calculate the resistance of the lamp. Use the equation $V = IR$. **[3 marks]**

3 A second identical lamp is added in series with the first.
 (a) State the potential difference across the battery. **[1 mark]**
 (b) Calculate the potential difference that would be measured across each lamp. **[2 marks]**

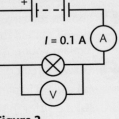

Figure 2

 Made a start **Feeling confident** **Exam ready**

Charge, current and energy

Electrical current is rate of flow of charge, usually carried by electrons in wires. You need to be able to calculate charge, given the current and time the charge has been flowing.

Charge and current

The size of the electrical current (I) is the rate of flow of the electrical charge (Q). Charge is measured in coulombs (C) and current is measured in amps (A), which is the number of coulombs of charge per second.

The equation to work these quantities out is

charge (C) = current (A) × time (s)

$Q = I \times t$

An ammeter can be used to measure the current over a period of time, and this equation can be used to work out the electrical charge.

Charge and potential difference

The energy transferred to a component (E) is given by the charge moving through the component (Q) multiplied by the potential difference across the component (V).

energy transferred = charge moved × potential difference
(J)   (C)   (V)

$E = Q \times V$

Exam focus

The equations on this page won't be on your exam sheet, so you need to be able to remember them. Make sure you know how to rearrange the equations as well.

Worked example   Grade 5

Figure 1 shows a circuit diagram with two lamps in series.

Figure 1

(a) A current of 0.6 A flows for five minutes. Calculate the amount of charge transferred.
[2 marks]

Make sure you convert 5 minutes to 300 s before you use the equation.

→ $Q = I \times t = 0.6 \times 300 = 180\,C$

(b) How much charge will pass through each lamp in this time?   **[1 mark]**

Remember that the current is the same in all places in a series circuit. This also means that the amount of charge flowing through each bulb is the same.

→ $180\,C$

(c) The potential difference of the cell is 1.5 V. Calculate the amount of energy transferred by the cell to the circuit components.   **[2 marks]**

$E = Q \times V = 180 \times 1.5 = 270\,J$

(d) Calculate the current if 30 C of charge flows in 20 s.   **[1 mark]**

$I = \dfrac{Q}{t} = \dfrac{30}{20} = 1.5\,A$

Exam-style practice   Grade 5

1 The current in a car starter motor needs to be 60 A to start the car. If it needs to transfer 30 C of charge, calculate how long it needs to be switched on.
[2 marks]

2 An ammeter is connected in a circuit before two lamps connected in series. It reads 0.6 A.
(a) What does the ammeter read when placed between the lamps?   **[1 mark]**
(b) Calculate the charge transferred in 15 s.   **[2 marks]**

 Made a start **Feeling confident** 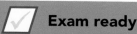 **Exam ready**

Series and parallel circuits

Electrical components can be joined either in series or in parallel. You need to know the differences between series and parallel circuits.

 Series and parallel circuits

Potential difference and current behave differently in series and parallel circuits.

	Series circuit	Parallel circuit
Current	same through all components	current split through each loop of the circuit
Potential difference (pd)	split across components	same across each component
Total resistance	sum of all resistances (equivalent to a single resistor with the same value)	less than the smallest resistance

 Resistors in series

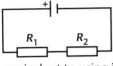

Any components connected in the same loop are in series. The resistances can be added together to give a total resistance equivalent to using just one resistor of that size.

$R_{total} = R_1 + R_2$

In series, each added component increases the resistance and decreases the current. This is because every additional component makes it more difficult for charge to flow. The potential difference is divided evenly when the resistances are the same.

 Resistors in parallel

Components connected in different loops are in parallel. In parallel circuits, every new loop gives the current a new route to get around the circuit. Even though each loop contains a component, it is easier overall for the charge to flow, decreasing the overall resistance. The total resistance of two resistors in parallel is always less than the resistance of the smaller of the two resistors. The current through the cell is the sum of the currents in the different loops.

 Worked example **Grade 5**

Two identical lamps are connected **(i)** in series and **(ii)** in parallel.

(i)
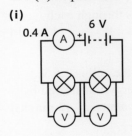

(ii)
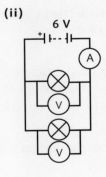

(a) State the reading on each voltmeter in each circuit. **[2 marks]**

(i) Each voltmeter reads 3 V. The pd splits up evenly as the lamps are identical.

(ii) Each voltmeter reads 6 V as they get the same pd.

(b) State and explain what the current is in each lamp in circuit **(i)**. **[2 marks]**

0.4 A, current is the same in every component.

(c) Each lamp in circuit **(ii)** conducts 0.3 A of current. State the reading on the ammeter. **[1 mark]**

0.6 A, the two currents are combined.

 Exam-style practice **Grade 5**

1 A series circuit has two resistors, $R_1 = 12\,\Omega$ and $R_2 = 4\,\Omega$. Calculate the total resistance. **[1 mark]**

2 Two lamps are connected in series with a battery.

(a) Predict what will happen to the brightness of the lamps if another lamp is connected in series with the first two. **[1 mark]**

(b) The original two lamps are now connected in parallel with each other, using the same battery. Predict how the brightness of each lamp will compare with when they were connected in series. **[1 mark]**

Practical: Resistance

This practical investigates the factors affecting the resistance of electrical circuits. You need to be familiar with the method and results.

⑤ Potential difference, current and resistance

1 Set up a circuit with a power supply, ammeter, voltmeter, variable resistor and a fixed resistor.

2 Use the variable resistor to change the potential difference across the resistor. Record the current in the resistor for five different potential differences across the resistor.

3 Change the fixed resistor to a filament lamp. Repeat step 2 to find the current in the filament lamp for five different potential differences.

4 Draw a graph for each set of results. Plot values of current (on the y-axis) against potential difference (on the x-axis).

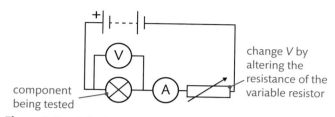

Figure 1 Circuit for investigating the potential difference and current in a filament lamp

⑤ Resistors in series and parallel

1 Set up a circuit with a power supply, ammeter, voltmeter and a single resistor (or filament lamp, which acts as a resistor).

2 Note the readings from the ammeter and voltmeter. Use them to calculate the resistance of the resistor using $R = \frac{V}{I}$.

3 Change the resistor and repeat step 2 to determine the resistance of the second resistor.

4 Arrange the two resistors in series and repeat step 2 to determine the total resistance of the resistors in series.

5 Arrange the two resistors in parallel and repeat step 2 to determine the total resistance of the resistors in parallel.

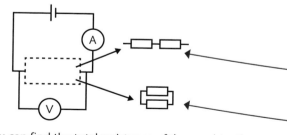

Figure 2 You can find the total resistance of the combination of resistors using $R = \frac{V}{I}$

⑤ Worked example   Grade 5

A student measures the current through a resistor for eight different values of potential difference across the resistor. The results are plotted as a graph of current against potential difference.

(a) State **two** advantages of plotting a graph to show the results. **[2 marks]**

It is easier to identify a pattern from a graph than from a table, and it is easier to spot any results that may be errors or that do not follow the pattern.

(b) The graph is a straight line through the origin. Explain what this shows. **[2 marks]**

This shows that the current is directly proportional to the potential difference across the resistor.

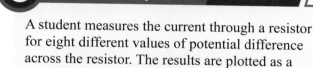

For resistors in series, the total resistance is equal to the sum of the individual resistances, $R_{total} = R_1 + R_2$.

For resistors in parallel, the total resistance is less than the resistance of the smallest resistor.

⑩ Exam-style practice   Grade 7

A student investigates the total resistance of two resistors **(i)** when they are connected in series and **(ii)** when they are connected in parallel. Compare the total resistance you would expect to find in each case. **[2 marks]**

Resistors

Some components have constant resistance. The resistance of other components, such as lamps, diodes, thermistors and LDRs, changes. The resistance of a thermistor changes with temperature and the resistance of an LDR changes with light intensity. You need to be able to interpret an *I–V* graph to study the resistance of a component.

(5) Fixed resistor

I–V graphs for resistors at constant temperature

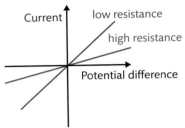

Figure 1 An *I–V* graph

The gradient of the *I–V* graph indicates the resistance. The **higher** the gradient, the **lower** the resistance.

If the resistance is constant, then the graph will be a straight line.

> Review the effect of temperature on resistance on page 193.

(5) Diodes

Diodes are like electrical valves. They only let current flow one way. Above a small pd the diode conducts. If the current is reversed, the graph is flat and shows a very high resistance, so no current can flow.

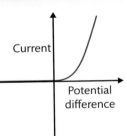

Figure 2 An *I–V* graph for a diode

> The *I–V* graph for a diode is non-linear.
> The *I–V* graphs for ohmic conductors are linear.

(5) LDRs and thermistors

The resistance of a **light-dependent resistor (LDR)** is high in the dark. The resistance gets less if light shines on it. The brighter the light, the lower the resistance.

The resistance of a **thermistor** depends on its temperature. The higher the temperature, the lower the resistance.

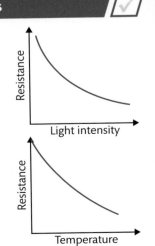

Figure 3

(10) Worked example — Grades 3–4

1 Look at **Figure 4**, the *I–V* graph for a filament lamp, and describe how the resistance changes as the pd increases. **[4 marks]**

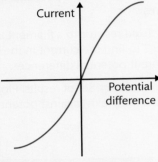

Figure 4

The gradient decreases as the potential difference increases or decreases from O. Resistance is indicated by $\frac{1}{gradient}$. This means that the resistance gets higher as the potential difference increases.

2 As potential difference is increased across a filament bulb, it causes an increase in current.
  (a) Describe what happens to the temperature of the filament as the current is increased. **[1 mark]**

Temperature of the filament increases.

  (b) Describe the effect this has on the resistance of the filament bulb. **[1 mark]**

Resistance of the filament bulb increases.

(10) Exam-style practice — Grades 4–5

1 Identify the component needed to produce each of the following effects in a circuit.

  (a) Cause current to only flow in one direction. **[1 mark]**

  (b) Change the current as the temperature changes. **[1 mark]**

2 Some cars have headlights that switch on automatically when it gets dark. Suggest the component that is needed in the lighting circuit to achieve this. **[1 mark]**

Practical: *I–V* characteristics

You need to be able to plot an *I–V* graph for a filament bulb, a diode, a thermistor and a resistor.

⑤ Plotting an *I–V* graph

To plot a graph for current against pd:

- Change the potential difference across the component and measure the current passing through it.
- Switch the direction by changing the pd from positive to negative. The current and potential difference will be negative values in this direction. Diodes do not behave the same in both directions, although most other components do.
- Plot potential difference on the *x*-axis and current on the *y*-axis.

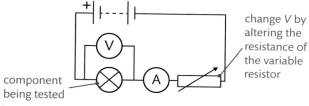

component being tested

change *V* by altering the resistance of the variable resistor

Figure 1 This circuit is a bit more complex than the circuit used to find the resistance of components, as you need to be able to change the potential difference across the component

② Resistor and diode

Resistor

Allow the resistor to cool between readings (e.g. by switching the circuit off) in order to keep the temperature constant.

It should give a straight line showing constant resistance.

Diode

In one direction the resistance will be tiny, meaning a large current can flow. A large current will damage the diode. Use an extra resistor in series to keep the current low and protect the diode.

② Gradient and resistance

A general straight line equation is *y* = *mx* + *c*, where:

- *m* is the gradient
- *c* is the *y*-intercept.

Rearrange the equation *V* = *IR* to give:

$$\begin{matrix} I \\ y \end{matrix} = \begin{matrix} \frac{1}{R} \\ m \end{matrix} \begin{matrix} V \\ x \end{matrix} + c$$

The gradient is $\frac{1}{\text{resistance}}$ so resistance is $\frac{1}{\text{gradient}}$.

Even for curves, the gradient still indicates the resistance. Where the gradient is lower at larger potential differences, the current increases more slowly as potential difference increases, showing that the resistance increases.

⑤ Thermistors and LDRs

You can investigate how the resistance of a thermistor varies with temperature. Replace the variable resistor in **Figure 1** with a fixed resistor. Measure the potential difference across the thermistor, and the current, at different temperatures. Use these results to calculate the resistance at different temperatures. You can also use this circuit to investigate how the resistance of an LDR varies with light intensity.

② Reducing errors

- If doing repeat readings, make sure the component has a chance to cool down between tests. Do this by switching the circuit off between readings.
- For wires and resistors, keep the potential difference low to reduce heating from large currents.

① Exam focus

- Make sure you know what the shape of the graph would be for each component and what this tells you about the resistance.
- A constant gradient means constant resistance.
- For curves, link the change in resistance to the pd.

③ Worked example   Grade 5

A student produces an *I–V* graph for a component.

(a) State which variable should be changed by the student.   **[1 mark]**

Potential difference

(b) State which variable should be measured by the student.   **[1 mark]**

Current

⑩ Exam-style practice   Grade 5

A student produces an *I–V* graph for a length of wire, shown in **Figure 2**. The graph should have produced a straight line.

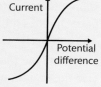
Current
Potential difference

(a) Explain what a straight line on an *I–V* graph tells us.   **[2 marks]   Figure 2**

(b) The curved line produced by the student suggests that the length of wire was heating up. Suggest **two** ways the student could avoid this happening.   **[2 marks]**

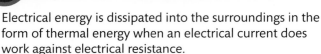

Energy transfer in circuits

In any electrical circuit, there are wanted and unwanted energy transfers.

⑤ Energy transfers in resistors

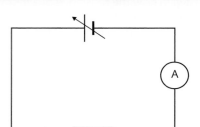

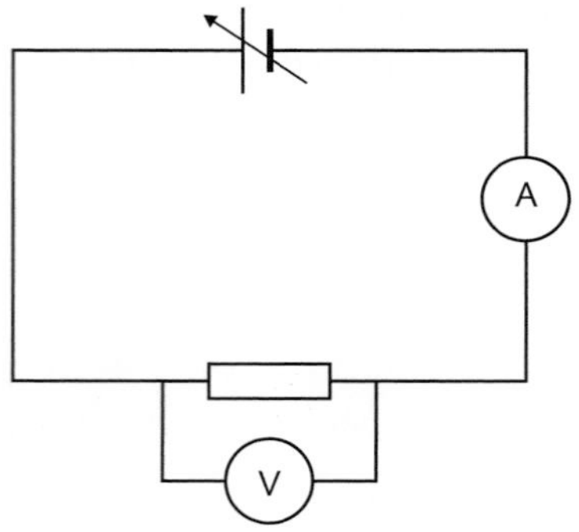

Figure 1 A circuit containing a resistor

When there is an electric current in a resistor, there is an energy transfer that causes the resistor to heat up. This is due to collisions between the moving electrons (the electric current) and the ions in the metal lattice of the resistor.

⑤ Energy dissipation

Electrical energy is dissipated into the surroundings in the form of thermal energy when an electrical current does work against electrical resistance.

This waste is usually undesirable, particularly when trying to transmit lots of power, such as through the National Grid. Using low-resistance (high-voltage) cables reduces the energy loss.

In an electric heater or a hairdryer, however, you do want energy transferred to the surroundings as thermal energy.

For more about the National Grid go to page 200.

⑤ Advantages and disadvantages of heating effect

Advantages:

- 👍 Tungsten light bulbs: the tungsten filament glows white-hot when a current flows and the temperature rises, emitting light.
- 👍 Heaters, kettles: electrical current is transferred into thermal energy.
- 👍 Fuses: heating effect of the current increases the temperature of the wire, melting the fuse wire above a certain current, breaking the circuit for safety.

Disadvantages:

- 👎 Component lifespan: the heating effect of the electric current can shorten the life of components in a circuit, meaning they have to be replaced more regularly.
- 👎 Wastage: energy is wasted in power transmission because of the heating effect of an electric current.
- 👎 Cooling systems and heat sinks: if these have to be added to circuits to stop overheating, the cost of manufacture is increased.

⑤ Calculating energy transferred

The energy transferred in a circuit can be calculated using the equation:

energy transferred (joule, J) = current (ampere, A) × potential difference (volt, V) × time (second, s)

$E = I \times V \times t$

⑤ Worked example　Grade 5

An electric kettle is connected to the mains electricity supply with a potential difference of 230 V. It takes three minutes for the kettle to boil the water inside it. The current flowing through the kettle is 12 A.

Calculate the total energy transferred by the kettle. Use the equation $E = I \times V \times t$. **[3 marks]**

$t = 3 \times 60 = 180$ seconds

$E = 12 \times 230 \times 180 = 496\,800$ J or 496.8 kJ

⑤ Exam-style practice　Grade 5

A microwave oven is connected to the mains electricity supply with a potential difference of 230 V. If it draws a current of 4.5 A and is used for five minutes, calculate the energy transferred. Use the equation $E = I \times V \times t$. **[3 marks]**

Electrical power

Electricity transfers energy from a source to its components via an electrical circuit. Power is a measure of how quickly the energy is transferred. You need to be able to calculate power from several different equations. Some domestic devices transfer energy from batteries to motors. Others transfer energy from the a.c. mains supply instead.

2 Power

$$\text{power (W)} = \frac{\text{energy transferred (J)}}{\text{time (s)}}$$

$$P = \frac{E}{t}$$

1 W = 1 J/s; 1 joule of energy is transferred per second.

Many electrical appliances have power ratings measured in kilowatts. 1 kW = 1000 W.

10 Worked example — Grade 5

Two kettles boil 1 litre of water each.

Kettle	Power	Time to boil
A	6.0 kW	70 s
B	2.4 kW	3 min 50 s

Note the units are kW. You may need to convert these to W.

This must be changed to seconds. 3 × 60 s = 180 s
180 s + 50 s = 230 s

(a) Calculate the total energy used by kettle A. **[2 marks]**

$E = P \times t = 6 \times 70 = 420$ kJ

You can leave the power in kW if you give the answer in kJ. Read the question to check if you need to give different units with your answer.

(b) Calculate the total energy used by kettle B. **[3 marks]**

$E = P \times t = 2.4 \times (3 \times 60 + 50)$
$= 2.4 \times 230 = 552$ kJ

(c) Compare the two values you have calculated. Which kettle is more efficient? **[1 mark]**

Kettle B uses more energy for the same task, so kettle A is more efficient.

5 Electrical power equations

electrical power (W) = current (A) × potential difference (V)

$P = I \times V$

electrical power (W) = current^2 (A) × resistance (Ω)

$P = I^2 \times R$

The larger the potential difference across a component, or the higher the current through it, the more power it uses. The power of a circuit tells us how quickly it transfers energy.

This shows why using high-voltage cables reduces energy loss in the National Grid: for a given amount of energy over a given time, a higher voltage means a lower current, so less heating effect.

10 Exam-style practice — Grade 5

1. A television uses 230 V and 0.5 A. Calculate its power rating. **[3 marks]**
2. A battery gives out an average current of 0.4 A and has potential difference 1.5 V.
   (a) Calculate its average power output. **[1 mark]**
   (b) The battery keeps a bulb lit for 6 hours. Determine how much energy the battery stored. State your answer in kilojoules to 1 decimal place. **[3 marks]**

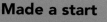

Mains electricity

A direct voltage can vary in magnitude, but it does not change direction. A direct current is one which is always in the same direction. An alternating voltage causes an alternating current, which continually changes direction. The UK mains supply is an alternating (a.c.) supply.

 ## Alternating and direct currents

- **Alternating current (a.c.)**: movement of charge changes constantly from one direction to the opposite direction and back.
- **Direct current (d.c.)**: charge moves in one direction.

Mains electricity in the UK uses a.c. with a frequency of 50 Hz. The current changes direction 50 times a second.

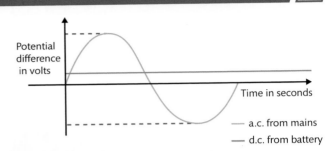

Figure 1 Batteries provide d.c. while mains electricity uses a.c.

 ## Three wires in a plug

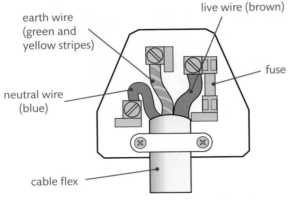

Figure 2 Appliances are connected to the mains using a three-core cable and a plug

The **live wire** carries the a.c. pd at +/−230 V.

The **neutral wire** has a pd of 0 V. It completes the circuit.

The **earth wire** is at 0 V. It only carries a current if there is a fault. It 'earths' a casing that has accidentally become live, reducing the risk of an electric shock. The earth wire is only required to earth a metal casing.

The earth wire connects the outer case to the ground. If the case becomes live, the current is conducted by the earth wire rather than shocking a person who touches it. The low resistance of the connection to earth results in a large current that breaks the fuse and switches the current off.

 ## Worked example   Grade 3

Metal parts of appliances are connected to the earth wire. In a modern building, a circuit breaker is connected to the live wire of the mains supply. Explain why this is done.   **[2 marks]**

If there is a fault and the live wire touches the metal casing, a very large current flows to the earth. The earth wires for all devices connect to the mains earth wire. A large current in the mains supply causes the circuit breaker to operate, cutting off the mains supply.

 ## Electrical safety

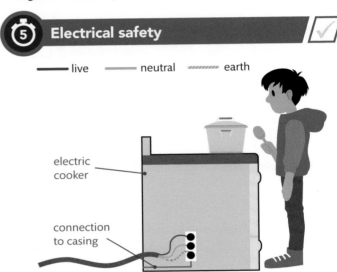

Figure 3 Take care when handling electrical equipment

If you touch a live wire while the appliance is on, you can get an electric shock. This is because you are completing a new circuit between the live wire and the ground. If there is a fault, the metal outer casing might become live. If someone touches the casing, they would receive an electric shock as the charge flows through them to the ground.

When an appliance is earthed, the live wire touches the earth wire, which has a low resistance and causes a large current. This breaks the fuse and disconnects the appliance. It can also cause a fire. This is why switches and fuses must be connected to the live wire.

 ## Exam-style practice   Grades 4–5

1 Explain why an appliance with outer material only made from plastic does not need an earth wire.   **[2 marks]**

2 The potential difference in a circuit increases and decreases repeatedly from 0 V to 120 V. Explain if the current is a.c. or d.c.   **[2 marks]**

Energy transfers in appliances

All electrical appliances transfer energy in useful processes; however, some energy is always dissipated in wasteful processes.

 Energy stores

Energy cannot be created or destroyed, only transferred. All the energy going into an appliance has to go somewhere.

- Mains appliances transfer energy provided by the electricity supply into other **energy stores**.
- Battery-powered appliances transfer energy stored in the battery to produce a potential difference, then into other energy stores.

Work is done when charge flows in a circuit.

 Energy transfers

The appliances shown below transfer energy provided by a supply of electricity (mains or battery) into other energy stores as part of useful processes. Some energy is also transferred by wasteful processes. The amount of energy transferred depends on the power of the appliance and how long it is switched on for.

The useful processes are in blue, and wasteful processes are in red.

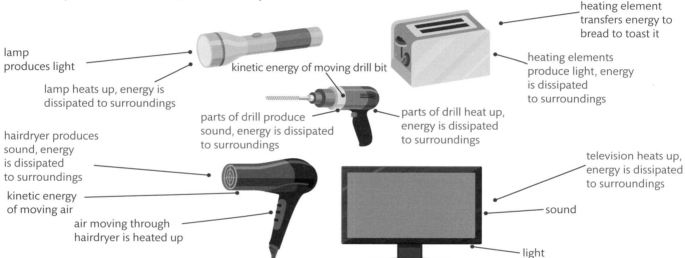

lamp produces light

lamp heats up, energy is dissipated to surroundings

kinetic energy of moving drill bit

parts of drill produce sound, energy is dissipated to surroundings

parts of drill heat up, energy is dissipated to surroundings

heating element transfers energy to bread to toast it

heating elements produce light, energy is dissipated to surroundings

hairdryer produces sound, energy is dissipated to surroundings

kinetic energy of moving air

air moving through hairdryer is heated up

television heats up, energy is dissipated to surroundings

sound

light

Wasted energy

It is important to always identify all the types of energy that are transferred, whether or not they are useful. Energy is often wasted when friction between moving parts causes heating, increasing the temperature of the appliance and the surroundings. A small amount of energy may be wasted as sound.

 Worked example Grades 4–5

1 Explain why devices with moving parts all have wasteful processes that dissipate energy. **[2 marks]**

Any device with moving parts will produce friction as parts rub together. This heats the parts up and causes energy to be dissipated to the surroundings.

2 Device A has a power rating of 1000 W. Device B has a power rating of 1.3 kW. Which device will transfer more energy in one minute? **[1 mark]**

1.3 kW = 1300 W. Device B will transfer more energy in one minute.

 Exam-style practice Grades 3–4

1 Give the useful processes and wasteful processes that transfer energy for:
(a) a radio **[1 mark]**
(b) an electric fan **[1 mark]**
(c) an electric car motor **[1 mark]**
(d) a mobile phone. **[1 mark]**

2 State the wasteful processes that cause energy to dissipate into the surroundings in an electric heater. **[2 marks]**

3 A torch uses 1000 J of energy and 800 J is transferred in the process that produces light. State how much energy is transferred in wasteful processes. **[1 mark]**

 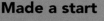

Magnetic fields

A magnetic field is the region around a magnet where forces are exerted on another magnet or on materials with magnetic properties. A magnet can attract or repel another magnet, but always attracts magnetic materials.

(10) Magnetic fields and forces

Magnets do not have to touch to exert forces. Magnetism is a non-contact force. The closer the magnets, the stronger the force. The magnetism gets weaker as the magnets get further apart. Compasses point in the direction of a **magnetic field**. Like poles repel and unlike poles attract.

The field is strongest at the poles.

The direction of magnetic field lines is from north to south. This is the direction of the force on another north pole near the magnet.

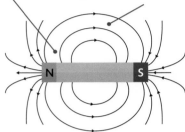

Figure 1 A magnetic field

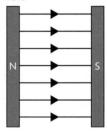

Figure 2 A uniform magnetic field

Because compasses point in the direction of magnetic fields, they can be used as evidence of Earth's magnetic field.

Figure 3 Earth's magnetic field is the same shape as the field around a bar magnet. It is produced by the rotating iron core.

Permanent magnets (like bar magnets) produce their own magnetic field. They can cause objects made from magnetic materials such as cobalt, iron, nickel and steel (remember CoINS) to become **induced magnets**.

Figure 4 An induced magnet

Induced magnets do not stay magnetic like permanent magnets. The magnetic force is always attractive. Uses of permanent magnets include: motors, generators, loudspeakers, compasses, door closers on fridges and fridge magnets. Uses of temporary magnets include: electromagnets, circuit breakers, magnetic relays and electric bells.

(5) Mapping field lines

plotting compass

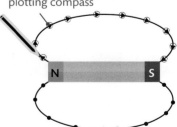

Figure 5 Drawing field lines around a magnet

1. Place a plotting compass at the north pole of a magnet. It will point away in the direction of the field. Draw a dot where it points.

2. Move the compass so the back of the needle is on the dot and draw another dot.

3. Repeat until the compass reaches the other side of the magnet.

4. Join all the dots together. Don't forget to put an arrow showing the direction of the field, north to south. This shows the direction the compass is pointing.

(2) Worked example — Grade 4

Describe how **Figure 1** shows that the magnetic force is stronger at the poles. **[2 marks]**

The closer together the lines are, the stronger the field. At the poles, the lines are closer together, so the force must be stronger.

(10) Exam-style practice — Grades 4–5

1. Describe how you could find the north pole of an unmarked bar magnet. **[2 marks]**

2. Describe how you could demonstrate that the magnetic force of attraction is non-contact. **[2 marks]**

3. State the difference between a permanent magnet and an induced magnet and give an example of each. **[2 marks]**

Electromagnetism

Electromagnets are made from coils of wire. You need to know the shape of a magnetic field around a straight wire and a coil of wire.

(5) Electrical wires

Wires carrying an electrical current produce a magnetic field. The strength of the magnetic field depends on the current through the wire and the distance from the wire. Conventional current is from the positive to the negative terminal of a cell.

The magnetic field around a wire is circular.

Using your right hand, if your thumb shows the direction of the current, your fingers wrap around the wire in the direction of the field.

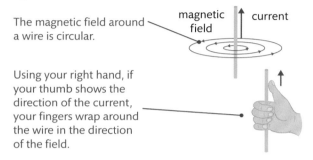

Figure 1 A magnetic field around a wire

You can show the magnetic effect of a wire carrying a current by holding a compass near the wire and turning the current on and off.

(2) Electromagnets

- Electromagnets can be switched off.
- Their strength can be altered easily by controlling the current.
- Increasing the number of coils increases the strength of the field.

(5) Electromagnetic fields

You can test the strength of an electromagnet by seeing how many paperclips it picks up as you change factors like current and number of coils.

Direction
The current flow is positive to negative. Curl the fingers of your right hand as shown in **Figure 1**, with your fingers pointing in the direction of the current. Your thumb will point in the direction of the north pole of the magnet.

(5) Solenoids

A **solenoid** is a coil of wire carrying a current that produces a magnetic field like the field around a bar magnet. This is called an electromagnet. When you add an iron core, the field is strengthened.

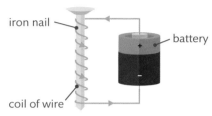

Figure 2 You can make an electromagnet by coiling wire around an iron nail and passing an electrical current through the wire

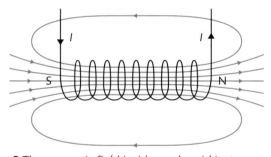

Figure 3 The magnetic field inside a solenoid is strong and uniform

Inside a solenoid the fields from individual coils add together to form a very strong almost uniform field along the centre of the solenoid.

Outside the solenoid the fields cancel to give a weaker field.

(2) Worked example — Grade 4

Describe how you would find the direction of the magnetic field on an electromagnet. **[2 marks]**

Hold a compass over the magnet. The arrow will point in the direction of the magnetic field from north to south.

(10) Exam-style practice — Grade 4

1. A scrapyard uses an electromagnet rather than a permanent magnet. Explain why. **[2 marks]**
2. Sketch the magnetic field of the electromagnet in **Figure 2**. **[3 marks]**
3. Suggest how you would change the direction of the magnetic field in an electromagnet. **[1 mark]**

The National Grid and transformers

You need to know how the National Grid transfers electrical energy around the country.

 The National Grid

The National Grid uses a system of cables and transformers to transfer electrical energy from power stations to consumers. When a current flows through a wire some energy is lost by heating. The National Grid transmits electricity at a low current to minimise heat loss. This requires a high voltage.

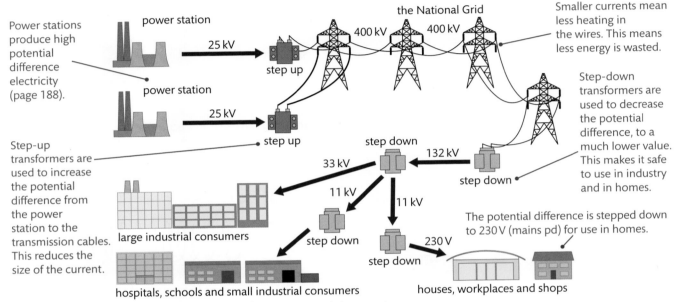

Power stations produce high potential difference electricity (page 188).

Step-up transformers are used to increase the potential difference from the power station to the transmission cables. This reduces the size of the current.

Smaller currents mean less heating in the wires. This means less energy is wasted.

Step-down transformers are used to decrease the potential difference, to a much lower value. This makes it safe to use in industry and in homes.

The potential difference is stepped down to 230 V (mains pd) for use in homes.

Figure 1 The National Grid transports electrical energy around the country

 Transformers

A transformer is a device with two coils. When an alternating potential difference is applied to the primary (first) coil, an alternating potential difference is created in the secondary coil. Changing the relative numbers of turns in each coil changes the size of the output potential difference compared to the input.

A step-up transformer increases potential difference.
A step-down transformer reduces potential difference.

Power out of secondary coil = power into primary coil

Primary potential difference × primary current = secondary potential difference × secondary current

$$V_s \times I_s = V_p \times I_p$$

 Worked example **Grade 5**

Explain why step-down transformers are used between the National Grid and homes. **[2 marks]**

The potential difference across the National Grid is very high. A step-down transformer reduces the potential difference of mains electricity so it is safer to use in homes.

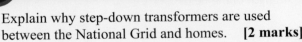 **Exam-style practice** **Grade 5**

1 Heating in wires is caused by the current and resistance in the wire. Other than reducing the current to very small values, suggest how the energy lost to heating might be reduced. **[2 marks]**

2 A transformer is used in a mobile phone charger to turn 230 V mains pd into 12 V to charge a battery. Give the name of this type of transformer. **[1 mark]**

  **Made a start** **Feeling confident** **Exam ready**

Density

You need to know how to calculate density, the amount of mass per unit volume.

2 Calculating density

Density is a property of a substance. You can work out the density of a substance using the equation:

$$\text{density (kg/m}^3\text{)} = \frac{\text{mass (kg)}}{\text{volume (m}^3\text{)}} \qquad \rho = \frac{m}{V}$$

Gases have a lower density than solids because the particles in a gas are spread further apart, increasing the volume and so decreasing the density.

5 Worked example — Grade 5

Figure 1 shows a copper cube with sides 25 cm. The mass of the cube is 140 kg.

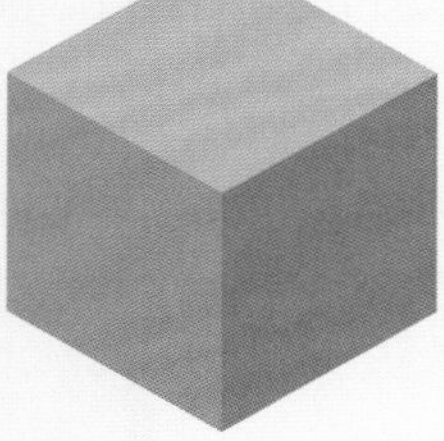

Figure 1

(a) Calculate the volume of the cube in m^3. **[2 marks]**

25 cm = 0.25 m

$V = 0.25\text{ m} \times 0.25\text{ m} \times 0.25\text{ m} = 0.0156\text{ m}^3$

(b) Calculate the density of copper. **[2 marks]**

$\rho = \frac{m}{V} = \frac{140}{0.0156} = 8974\text{ kg/m}^3$

(c) Calculate the volume of a copper cube of mass 2.2 kg. **[2 marks]**

$V = \frac{m}{\rho} = \frac{2.2}{8974} = 2.5 \times 10^{-4}\text{ m}^3$ (=0.00025 m^3)

Convert the lengths to metres before working out the volume; it is more complicated to convert them later.

The volume of a cube is the (length of a side)^3.

Maths skills

You can calculate the volume of a cuboid using $V = abc$

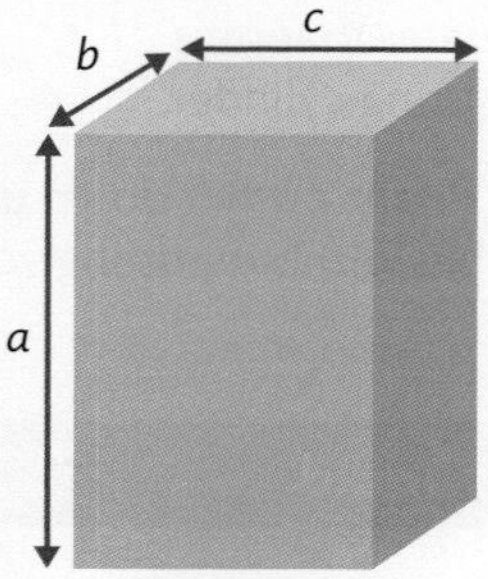

Figure 2 Cuboid with sides a, b and c

As the density is a property of the material, any size piece of copper will have the same density.

Small volumes measured in m^3 will be very small numbers and are best expressed in standard form. Make sure you know how to enter standard form into your calculator and read it off.

10 Exam-style practice — Grades 4–5

1 The volume of water in a bucket is twice the volume in a bottle. Compare the density and mass of the water in the bucket with the water in the bottle. **[2 marks]**

2 **(a)** The density of water is 1000 kg/m^3. An object will float in water if its density is less than water. State which of these objects will float in water. **[5 marks]**

Object	apple	hollow steel box	solid plastic cube	human
Mass (kg)	0.074	1.3	0.5	70
Volume (m^3)	1.04×10^{-4}	2×10^{-3}	4.1×10^{-4}	0.071

(b) Find the mass of an apple with volume 1.5×10^{-4} m^3. **[3 marks]**

Practical: Density of materials

You need to know how to accurately measure the mass and volume of an object so that you can calculate its density.

② Measuring density

$$\text{density (kg/m}^3) = \frac{\text{mass (kg)}}{\text{volume (m}^3)}$$

Go to page 201 to practise calculating density.

The mass of the object can be found using a top pan balance. Using a top pan balance with a higher level of precision will improve the precision of the answer.

Measuring the volume of an object depends on the size and shape of the object.

② Density of irregular shapes

You can find the volume of an irregularly-shaped object by measuring the volume of water that the object displaces.

displacement can

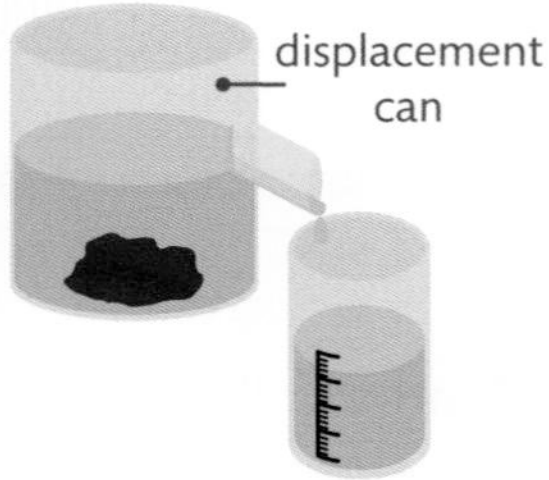

1 Fill the displacement can to the spout.

2 Place the object in the can.

3 Collect the water that runs off in a measuring cylinder.

Figure 1 Apparatus

4 If the object floats, push it down until it is all below the surface, but without putting your finger into the water.

② Density of liquid

1 Find the mass of the liquid by measuring the mass of the empty measuring cylinder on a digital balance. Make sure the measuring cylinder is completely dry.

2 Measure the mass of the measuring cylinder again with the liquid inside. The mass of the liquid will be the difference between the two measurements.

3 Measure the volume of liquid using the scale on the measuring cylinder.

② Worked example — Grades 4–5

A student wants to find the mass and volume of a sample of liquid.

(a) Name a piece of equipment they could use to measure the volume of liquid. **[1 mark]**

Measuring cylinder

(b) Explain why the student should carefully dry this piece of equipment before adding the sample. **[2 marks]**

To avoid the sample mixing with any liquid left behind and giving a false reading.

⑤ Measuring objects

To get an accurate volume, you need to measure the dimensions of a regular object to as high a precision as possible.

The size of a large object can be measured using a ruler or tape measure. Smaller objects can be measured using vernier calipers. They will measure to 0.01 mm.

volume of a cuboid = length × width × depth

Remember to convert the lengths to metres to get the volume in m³.

② Reducing errors

- Suspend the object from a piece of string so it can be lowered carefully into the water to avoid making a splash.
- Stand the measuring cylinder on a flat surface.
- Make sure your eyes are at the same level as the water.
- Read the level of the water, ignoring the meniscus created at the edge.

water level

Figure 2 Taking a reading from a measuring cylinder

⑩ Exam-style practice — Grade 5

1 Name a piece of equipment you could use to find the volume of a rough piece of rock. **[1 mark]**

2 Describe the method for finding the volume of a rough piece of rock. **[3 marks]**

Made a start Feeling confident Exam ready

Changes of state

You need to know about the three states of matter: solid, liquid and gas.

(5) States and state changes

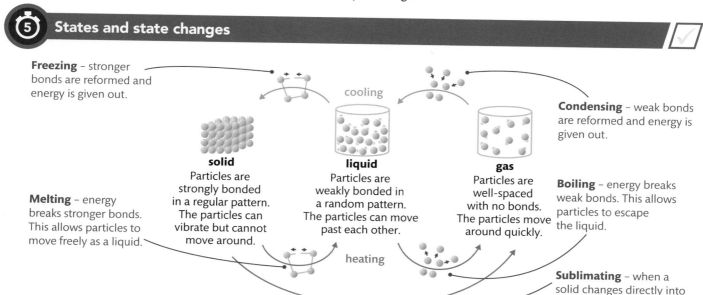

Freezing – stronger bonds are reformed and energy is given out.

cooling

Condensing – weak bonds are reformed and energy is given out.

solid
Particles are strongly bonded in a regular pattern. The particles can vibrate but cannot move around.

liquid
Particles are weakly bonded in a random pattern. The particles can move past each other.

gas
Particles are well-spaced with no bonds. The particles move around quickly.

Melting – energy breaks stronger bonds. This allows particles to move freely as a liquid.

Boiling – energy breaks weak bonds. This allows particles to escape the liquid.

heating

Sublimating – when a solid changes directly into a gas.

Figure 1 The particle model of matter

(2) State changes: key facts

- The temperature a substance both melts and freezes at is called the **melting point**.
- The temperature a substance both condenses and boils at is called the **boiling point**.
- Changes of state are physical and reversible. The material recovers its original properties.
- Particles in a solid are usually arranged more closely than in a liquid, so solids tend to have higher density.
- Particles in gases are very far apart, so gases have very low densities.
- The properties of a substance may change when it changes state. Its density and volume may alter, but the mass will stay the same. This is because the number of particles does not change. Mass is conserved.

(5) Heating and cooling curves

Thermal energy is transferred to kinetic energy in the particles, raising the temperature.

At the melting and boiling points, thermal energy is absorbed and causes the particle bonds to break. The temperature remains constant as the state changes.

Heating curve

Temperature (°C) / Time (minutes)

boiling

melting

Cooling curve

Temperature (°C) / Time (minutes)

condensing

freezing

Thermal energy is given out. Particles lose kinetic energy and temperature decreases.

Thermal energy is given out as bonds reform. Temperature does not decrease until the state has finished changing.

(15) Exam-style practice

Grades 4–5

1 Water is heated to its boiling point of 100 °C. The water is heated further but the temperature stays constant. Explain what is happening to the energy. **[2 marks]**

2 Describe the motion of particles in a solid, a liquid and a gas. **[5 marks]**

3 An ice cube is placed in a glass of water. Describe the change in the arrangement of particles in both the ice and the water. **[4 marks]**

Specific heat capacity

The specific heat capacity, c, is the energy needed to raise the temperature of 1 kg of a substance by 1 °C. It is measured in joules per kilogram per degree Celsius.

5 Calculating specific heat capacity

change in thermal energy (J) = mass (kg) × specific heat capacity (J/kg °C) × temperature change (°C)

$\Delta Q = mc\Delta\theta$

Δ (delta) means 'change in' and θ (theta) means temperature. The greater the specific heat capacity, the more energy it takes to raise the temperature of a given mass through a given temperature rise. Energy is stored in a system as internal energy, which is the total of all the kinetic and potential energy of the particles.

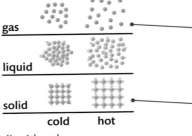

gas
liquid
solid
cold   hot

A higher temperature means the particles in a substance have greater kinetic energy. The particles will move around faster, or vibrate faster.

Energy added to a system is either used to break bonds and change the state or increase the energy of the particles and raise the temperature.

Figure 1 Particles in a solid, liquid and a gas

10 Worked example — Grade 5

Liquid	Melting point (°C)	Boiling point (°C)	Specific heat capacity as a liquid (J/kg °C)
A	15	80	200
B	0	100	4200
C	−12	15	2150

(a) The three liquids in the table are heated by a 1 kW heater. Identify which liquid's temperature would rise most quickly. Explain why. **[3 marks]**

Liquid A, it has the lowest specific heat capacity so it takes the least energy to warm up.

(b) 3 kg of liquid A is heated from 20 °C to boiling point. Calculate how much energy it would take. **[2 marks]**

$\Delta Q = mc\Delta\theta = 3 \times 200 \times 60 = 36\,000\,J$

2 Exam focus

Use this equation to help you remember the unit for specific heat capacity:

$c = \dfrac{\Delta Q}{m\Delta\theta} \rightarrow \dfrac{J}{kg\,°C} = J/kg\,°C$

Look carefully at the headings in a table of data so you are familiar with all the information it gives before you read the question.

Liquid A has the lowest specific heat capacity. This means it takes very little energy to increase the temperature, so it would warm up the fastest.

Work out the temperature change 20–80 °C first. Then use the equation.

5 Exam-style practice — Grade 5

1 2 kg of a liquid was heated from 30 °C to 70 °C. The specific heat capacity of the liquid is 2500 J/kg °C. Calculate the total amount of energy needed. **[3 marks]**

2 A second liquid was heated from 30 °C to 70 °C. The specific heat capacity of this liquid is 5000 J/kg °C. State the effect this will have on the energy required compared to question **1**. **[1 mark]**

☐ **A** stay the same ☐ **B** halved ☐ **C** doubled ☐ **D** four times

Made a start   Feeling confident   Exam ready

Specific latent heat

Specific latent heat, L, is the energy required to change the state of 1 kg of a substance with no change in temperature.

② Calculating L

energy for a change of state = mass × specific latent heat
$$(J) \qquad (kg) \qquad (J/kg)$$

$Q = m \times L$

The **specific latent heat of fusion** is the energy required to melt 1 kg of a substance or the energy given out when 1 kg of a substance freezes.

The **specific latent heat of vaporisation** is the energy required to evaporate or boil 1 kg of a substance, or the energy given out when 1 kg of a substance condenses.

⑩ Worked example — Grade 5

1.2 kg of metal is heated to its melting point.

(a) The melting point of the metal is 1500 °C. Explain why the temperature will not increase until all of the metal has melted. **[3 marks]**

The heat energy is used to break bonds between metal atoms and change their state. The temperature will increase when the energy is used to increase the kinetic energy of the metal atoms. This will not happen until all the bonds have broken and all the metal is liquid.

(b) The specific latent heat of the metal is 4500 J/kg. Calculate the energy needed to melt the metal. **[2 marks]**

$Q = m \times L = 1.2 \times 4500 = 5400\,J$

(c) How much energy would be given out as 1.2 kg of molten metal turned solid? **[1 mark]**

5400 J

② Latent heat and particles

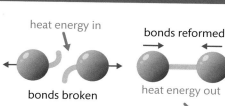

heat energy in — bonds broken — bonds reformed — heat energy out

Figure 1 When a substance changes state, energy is used to break bonds or is given out as the bonds reform

As something cools down, energy is released from it. When it condenses or freezes, the temperature stays constant because all the energy given out is produced by the bonds forming between the particles, and does not come from a reduction in their kinetic energy.

> The temperature of any substance will stay constant while it changes state, whether it is being heated or cooled.

Exam focus
The units for specific latent heat are J/kg.
You can use the equation to help you remember the unit:

$$L = \frac{Q\,(J)}{m\,(kg)} \rightarrow J/kg$$

> Energy is always conserved, so if you have to put 5400 J in to melt 1.2 kg of metal, when you freeze 1.2 kg of molten metal you will get 5400 J of energy back out.

⑩ Exam-style practice — Grade 6

1 Copper has a specific latent heat of 206 000 J/kg.
   (a) Calculate the energy required to melt 0.5 kg of copper. **[2 marks]**
   (b) Gold has a specific latent heat of 64 000 J/kg. State which requires less energy to melt completely, 0.5 kg of gold or 0.5 kg of copper. **[1 mark]**

2 Tin has a melting point of 232 °C and a specific latent heat of 227 000 J/kg. Explain why more than 227 000 J of energy is needed to completely melt a 1 kg block of tin that is initially at room temperature (20 °C). **[2 marks]**

Practical: Properties of water

You need to know how to determine the specific heat capacity of water and produce a temperature–time graph for melting ice. This practical investigates a method for each.

Experiment 1: Specific latent heat

1. Put 50 g of crushed ice into a calorimeter.
2. Place the immersion heater into the central hole in the lid of the calorimeter.
3. Clamp the thermometer so that its bulb is in the ice but near to the top.
4. Record the temperature of the ice.
5. Connect the heater to the power supply and joulemeter, turn it on and record the temperature every 20 seconds. If no joulemeter is available, connect an ammeter and a voltmeter instead.
6. Continue heating until no more ice is present.
7. Plot a graph of temperature against time and identify where the ice melted.
8. Use the reading on the joulemeter to determine the energy supplied to the ice.
9. Calculate latent heat using the equation:
$$\text{latent heat} = \frac{\text{energy supplied to ice}}{\text{mass of ice}}$$

Experiment 2: Specific heat capacity

1. Put 1 kg (1 litre) of water into a calorimeter.
2. Place the immersion heater into the central hole in the lid of the calorimeter.
3. Clamp the thermometer into the smaller hole with a stirrer next to it.
4. Wrap the calorimeter completely in an insulating material.
5. Record the initial temperature of the water.
6. Connect the heater to the power supply and a joulemeter and turn it on for 10 minutes. If no joulemeter is available, connect an ammeter and a voltmeter instead. Stir the water regularly.
7. After 10 minutes, switch the heater off. The temperature of the water will rise further before it begins to cool. Record the highest temperature it reaches. Use this value to calculate the temperature rise during the experiment and determine the specific heat capacity.
8. Calculate specific heat capacity using the equation:
$$c = \frac{\Delta Q}{m \times \text{temperature change}}$$

Worked example — Grade 5

1. Describe the safety factors you must consider in each experiment described above. **[4 marks]**

- Do not touch the heating element directly.
- Do not overfill the container; wait until cooled before moving it, and keep the temperature low.
- Mop up any spills immediately and keep the water away from electrical equipment (apart from the heater).
- Do not lean the thermometer in a beaker of water in case it pulls it over.

2. For Experiment 2, explain why it is important to keep taking measurements after the heater has been switched off. **[2 marks]**

The temperature of the water continues to rise after the heater has been switched off. It is important to measure the full temperature rise of the water.

Reducing errors

- Measure the temperature of water in the middle, as hot water rises to the top. Make sure not to touch the heater.
- Insulate the water. A lid on the water also reduces energy and mass loss by evaporation.
- Take the mass of ice or water before and after heating, and calculate an average.
- Limit heat loss to the environment by keeping heating time short.
- Reduce the initial temperature of the water to allow a greater increase in temperature. A temperature change of only a few degrees makes the result very inaccurate.
- The hotter the water gets, the more energy it will lose to the environment.

Some of these points work against each other, but it is acceptable to mention them all if asked in the exam.

Exam-style practice — Grades 4–5

1. Suggest why it is important to measure the mass of ice or water used in these experiments. **[2 marks]**
2. Explain why putting the water in an insulated container with a lid reduces errors in the experiments. **[2 marks]**
3. For Experiment 1, describe how you can identify where the ice melted on the graph (step 7). **[3 marks]**

 Made a start **Feeling confident** **Exam ready**

Particle motion in gases

Gas molecules are in constant random motion. You need to be able to explain the effect of temperature and type of container on particle motion in gases.

 **Heating gases**

When a gas is heated, the particles gain kinetic energy. They move faster than in liquids and solids. As there are very weak forces between the particles they spread out as far as possible. This means the volume of the gas can increase.

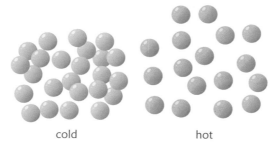

cold   hot

Figure 1 Heating a gas

 Gas in containers

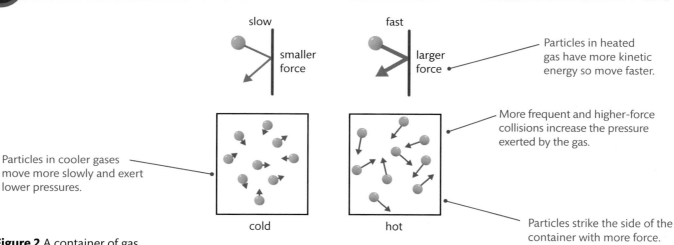

slow

smaller force

Particles in heated gas have more kinetic energy so move faster.

fast

larger force

More frequent and higher-force collisions increase the pressure exerted by the gas.

Particles in cooler gases move more slowly and exert lower pressures.

cold   hot

Particles strike the side of the container with more force.

Figure 2 A container of gas

 Worked example **Grade 4**  **Absolute zero**

Describe the changes to the collisions between particles that take place in a gas when it is heated. **[2 marks]**

The collisions become more frequent and take place with higher force.

The kelvin scale starts at absolute zero. There is no movement of particles at absolute zero, so it is not possible to get any colder. Absolute zero is –273 °C, or 0 K. To convert from degrees Celsius to kelvin, you need to add 273. For example, 25 °C is 298 K.

 **Exam-style practice** **Grades 4–5**

1. A sample of hot gas is used to fill a fixed container. Explain what forces cause the pressure inside the container to increase. **[2 marks]**

2. A container full of hot gas is left to cool. The pressure inside the container reduces.
   (a) Describe what happens to the collisions between gas particles inside the container as it cools. **[2 marks]**
   (b) Suggest how you could cause the pressure to increase again, without opening the container. **[1 mark]**

 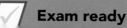

Forces and elasticity

Forces can cause objects to change shape permanently or temporarily, by bending, stretching or compressing them. You need to know the effects of forces on elastic objects like springs.

 Types of distortion

Distortion is the term used to describe an object changing shape. Distortion can be elastic or inelastic:

- **Elastic distortion** – an object changes shape when a force is applied but returns to its original shape when the force is removed.
- **Inelastic distortion** – an object changes shape when a force is applied but does not return to its original shape when the force is removed.

The amount an object changes shape is the **extension** or **compression**. To cause an object to compress, stretch or bend, you usually need two forces working against each other. If you try to squash a rubber ball, you have to push from both sides or the ball will simply move.

 Linear elastic distortion

The extension of an elastic object is directly proportional to the force applied to it:

force applied (N) = spring constant (N/m) × extension (m)

$F = k \times x$

- The force, F, is the load or weight applied to the object being deformed.
- The spring constant, k, is a measure of how stiff the spring or object is.
- Extension or compression, x, is the amount the object changes shape. It is the stretched length minus the original length.

This equation works for the straight-line part of a force–extension graph.

 Springs

Force against extension of a spring

An object that obeys the equation for linear elastic distortion has a straight line on a force–extension graph. If the object is stretched too far, the force–extension graph curves and the object is permanently distorted.

The gradient gives you the spring constant, but be careful to only use the straight-line section.

Energy stored by a stretched spring

Anything that stretches, compresses or bends stores elastic potential energy.

energy transferred = 0.5 × spring constant × extension²
in stretching (J)　　　　(N/m)　　　　(m)

$E = \frac{1}{2}kx^2$

When released, the spring moves so the stored energy is usually transferred into the kinetic energy store of the spring.

This is true for the linear part of the graph. In the non-linear part, work is being done in permanently distorting the spring.

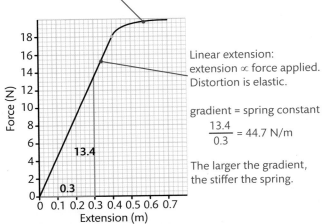

Non-linear extension: there is a large increase in extension for a small increase in force. Distortion is inelastic.

Linear extension: extension ∝ force applied. Distortion is elastic.

gradient = spring constant
$\frac{13.4}{0.3}$ = 44.7 N/m

The larger the gradient, the stiffer the spring.

Figure 1 A graph showing how the extension of a spring changes when different forces are applied

 Worked example　　**Grade 5**

A force is applied to a spring so that it is distorted elastically. The spring constant k is 50 N/m.

(a) Calculate the force that must be applied to cause an extension of 36 cm.　　**[2 marks]**

$k = \frac{F}{x}$ so $F = k \times x = 50 \times 0.36 = 18$ N

(b) Calculate the total elastic potential energy stored in the spring at this extension. **[3 marks]**

$E = \frac{1}{2}kx^2 = 0.5 \times 50 \times 0.36^2 = 3.24$ J

 Exam-style practice　　**Grades 4–5**

Look at **Figure 1**.

(a) Explain what the straight-line section of the graph tells us about the distortion of the spring at lower values of force. **[1 mark]**

(b) Name the quantity that the gradient of the graph gives in this straight-line section. **[1 mark]**

(c) Give the maximum force that the spring can take before being damaged. **[1 mark]**

(d) The curved part of the graph shows inelastic distortion. Explain what 'inelastic distortion' means. **[2 marks]**

 Made a start　　 **Feeling confident**　　 **Exam ready**

Practical: Force and extension

You need to know how to investigate the relationship between force and extension with a spring.

5 Method

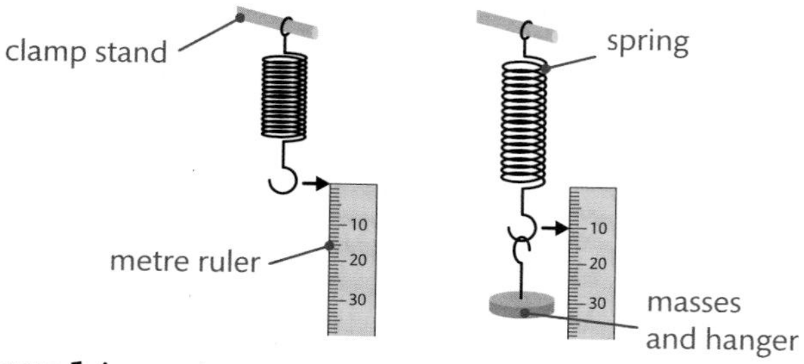

Figure 1 Apparatus

1. Clamp a ruler so that the zero mark is next to the end of the spring.
2. Hang a range of masses from the spring.
3. Record the force, which is the weight of each mass.
4. Record the extension of the spring for each force.
5. Plot a graph of force (*y*-axis) against extension (*x*-axis).
6. You can then use the graph to estimate the weight of another object that is hung from the spring by measuring the extension.

Maths skills

The force is in newtons, N, and the extension (x) in metres, m, so the gradient is N/m. The gradient is also the spring constant, calculated from $F = kx$. If the graph is plotted with the axes reversed, remember that the spring constant $= \frac{1}{\text{gradient}}$

If the spring is distorting inelastically, the graph will be a curve.

2 Reducing errors

- Measure the spring length from the same point on the spring each time.
- Make sure the spring is at eye level when measuring it.
- Repeat each extension by removing and rehanging the mass in case larger masses distort the spring inelastically.

5 Worked example — Grade 5

Look at **Figure 2,** a graph showing the force and extension of springs A and B.

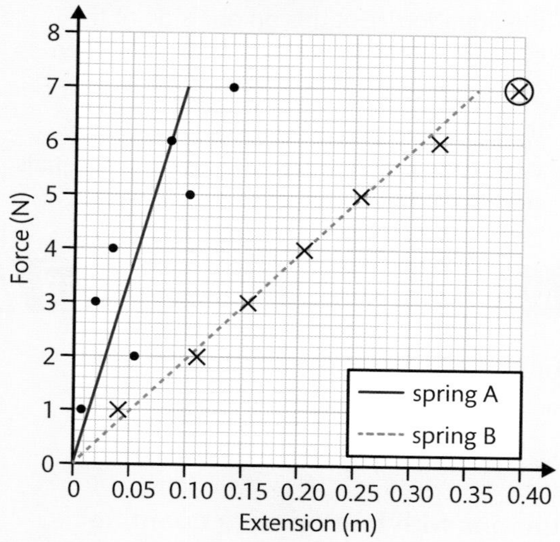

Figure 2

(a) The points for spring A are further away from the line of best fit than the points for spring B. Explain what this tells us about the errors in the investigation of each spring. **[2 marks]**

The errors in the investigation of spring A are greater than the errors in the investigation of spring B.

(b) The gradient of the line for spring A is 70. Give the unit for the gradient. **[1 mark]**

N/m

(c) Describe a method for checking whether a spring is distorting inelastically after a mass is added. **[2 marks]**

After taking the measurement of extension, remove the mass and allow the spring to return to its natural length. If it does not return to its original length, it has been distorted inelastically.

10 Exam-style practice — Grade 5

Look at **Figure 2**.

(a) Calculate the gradient of the green dashed line for spring B. **[2 marks]**

(b) State the spring constant for spring B, including the units. **[1 mark]**

(c) The final plotted point for spring B is circled. This is because the spring has started to be distorted inelastically. Explain what 'distorted inelastically' means. **[2 marks]**

Equations

You need to know which equations to use and how to rearrange them to answer questions in the exam. You will be given a formulae sheet with some equations on in the physics exams.

(2) Three rules for rearranging

1. Decide what you want to work out (subject of the equation). Get this on one side of the equation and everything else on the other.
2. Make sure the value you want to find is not on the bottom of a fraction.
3. When you move something across the equals sign, the operation needs to be reversed.

(10) Maths skills

Equations with three quantities

If you needed to calculate the mass, m:

$F = ma \rightarrow \dfrac{F}{a} = m \rightarrow m = \dfrac{F}{a}$

Equations with four or more quantities

$\Delta GPE = mgh \rightarrow \dfrac{\Delta GPE}{mg} = h \rightarrow h = \dfrac{\Delta GPE}{mg}$

Divide both sides of the equation by mg.

Equations with squares

$KE = \dfrac{1}{2}mv^2 \rightarrow v^2 = \dfrac{KE}{\frac{1}{2}m} \rightarrow v = \sqrt{\dfrac{KE}{\frac{1}{2}m}}$

First rearrange for v^2, you can move the $\dfrac{1}{2}$ and m as normal, then square root both sides.

$v^2 = u^2 + 2as$

To find u, first rearrange so that u^2 is on its own:

$u^2 = v^2 - 2as \rightarrow u = \sqrt{v^2 - 2as}$

To find a, first rearrange so that $2as$ is on its own:

$v^2 - u^2 = 2as \rightarrow \dfrac{v^2 - u^2}{2s} = a \rightarrow a = \dfrac{v^2 - u^2}{2s}$

(2) Exam focus

In the exam, you can save time by using symbols rather than words. For example, use:

$F = ma$ rather than *force = mass × acceleration* as it is quicker to write and rearrange.

Take your time when rearranging equations and allow time to check your calculations to ensure you have written the correct answer.

1. Find out what you are being asked to find (current).
2. Identify which values you have been given in the question and what their units are: a potential difference (V), a resistance (Ω) and a power (W).
3. Think of the equation that includes the thing you want to find and the numbers that you have.
4. Rearrange the equation to isolate the unknown value on one side and replace the symbols with the known values.
5. Check whether you need to convert the unit.

(5) Worked example   Grades 4–5

A 12 V motor has resistance 30 W. Calculate the current in the motor.

$P = IV$ **[2 marks]**

power = potential difference × current

$P = IV \rightarrow 30 = I \times 12 \rightarrow I = \dfrac{30}{12} = 2.5\,A$

Alternatively, rearrange the equation first, then put the numbers in.

$P = IV \rightarrow 30 = I \times 12 \rightarrow I = \dfrac{30}{12} = 2.5\,A$

(10) Exam-style practice   Grade 5

1. Rearrange the following equations for each of the other quantities.

   (a) $\rho = \dfrac{m}{V}$ **[1 mark]**

   (b) $E = \dfrac{1}{2}kx^2$ **[1 mark]**

   (c) $\Delta Q = mc\Delta\theta$ **[1 mark]**

   (d) $a = \dfrac{\Delta v}{t}$ **[1 mark]**

2. Give the name and units for each of the quantities in question **1**.   **[4 marks]**

Pages
62, 74,
149, 164
LINKS

BBC

GCSE Science | Exam skills

Converting units

You need to know how to convert quantities to the standard unit.

 Prefixes

Prefix	nano	micro	milli	centi	kilo	mega	giga
Example unit	nm	µm	mm	cm	km	Mm	Gm
Standard form	1×10^{-9}	1×10^{-6}	1×10^{-3}	1×10^{-2}	1×10^{3}	1×10^{6}	1×10^{9}
Factor	0.000 000 001	0.000 001	0.001	0.01	1000	1 000 000	1 000 000 000
Example	atom 0.1 nm	cells 1–100 µm	ball bearing few mm	pencil 15 cm	Mount Everest 9 km	Earth 13 Mm	Moon orbit 0.4 Gm

Converting units

To convert 30 mm to m, first figure out what the conversion factor is between mm and m. There are 1000 (10^3) mm in one metre (m).

Then decide if you need to multiply or divide.

30 mm is much smaller than a metre so your answer should be a very small number:

30 mm ÷ 1000 = 0.03 m

Complex units

To convert the spring constant 4.5 N/cm to N/m, first work out what the conversion factor is between cm and m (100).

4.5 N/cm × 100 = 450 N/m

Now, check logically: if it takes 4.5 N to stretch the spring 1 cm, you would expect a lot more force to stretch it 1 m, so 450 N makes sense.

Time

Remember, that when dealing with time you need to multiply or divide by 60, not 100.

1 hour = 60 minutes, 1 minute = 60 seconds

Area and volume

When converting areas, take the normal conversion factor and square it.

Convert cm² to m²

250 cm² ÷ 100² = 0.025 m²

For volumes, cube the usual factor:

Convert m³ to mm³

1.2 m³ × 1000³ = 1 200 000 000 mm³

or 1.2 ×10⁹ mm³

Standard form is written in terms of powers of 10. Negative numbers mean you divide by 10 that many times and positive numbers mean you multiply by 10 that many times. For example: 1×10^9 is equal to 1 000 000 000.

Worked example Grades 4–5

Convert:

(a) 0.56 kg to g **[1 mark]**

0.56 × 1000 = 560 g

(b) 12 mm to m **[1 mark]**

12 ÷ 1000 = 0.012 m

(c) 25 MJ to J **[1 mark]**

25×10^6 = 25 000 000 J or 2.5×10^7 J

(d) 0.037 mm to µm **[1 mark]**

$0.037 \div 10^3$ = 3.37 µm

Matching units

$$\text{velocity} = \frac{\text{displacement}}{\text{time}}$$

Normally, the velocity is in m/s, so the displacement and time need to be converted into metres and seconds to match.

However, if the displacement is in kilometres and the time in hours, the velocity will be in km/h. Check which units you should use in your calculation and answer.

Exam-style practice   Grade 6

1 Convert:
 (a) 200 µg to g **[1 mark]**
 (b) 10 N/kg to N/g **[1 mark]**
 (c) 330 J/minute to J/s. **[1 mark]**

2 Calculate how many orders of magnitude larger 10 kg is than 1 g. **[1 mark]**

Making estimations

You need to know how to estimate the results of simple calculations.

5 Estimating speeds and masses

Speeds
You need to have an idea of how fast some objects move.

- Cars move at around 20 m/s up to 30 m/s at motorway speeds.
- People walk at around 1–2 m/s and run at around 3 m/s and sprint at up to 10 m/s.
- Jet planes can fly up to around 250 m/s.

Try to picture an object moving and estimate how far you think it would get in 1 second. Use this to estimate its speed.

Masses
You need to have an idea of the masses of certain objects.

The following are rough estimates and vary with size:

You can estimate the mass of an object by comparing it with objects of a similar mass.

- a person: 50–70 kg
- a car: 1000 kg
- 1 litre of water: 1 kg
- a dog: 5–25 kg
- a mobile phone: 100–200 g.

1 Exam focus

If a question instructs you to 'calculate', you should work out the answer exactly using a calculator. It is good practice to then estimate the answer to check it is correct.

10 Worked example — Grade 4

1 Estimate the kinetic energy of a person sprinting in a race. **[3 marks]**

kinetic energy = ½ × mass × speed²
mass ~ 60 kg and speed ~ 10 m/s
kinetic energy = ½ × 60 kg × (10 m/s)² = 3000 J

2 Calculate the increase in potential energy of a 1.45 kg mass lifted 9.5 m (g = 9.8 N/kg). **[3 marks]**

ΔGPE = mgh = 1.45 × 9.8 × 9.5 = 135 J

Check the answer is correct by rounding the numbers and working out an approximate answer.
1.5 × 10 × 10 = 150, so this answer is about right.

1 Maths skills

If you are asked to estimate the area under a curve, you do not need to try and calculate the area. First, work out the value of each square, then count roughly how many squares there are on the graph and then multiply these two numbers together.

5 Worked example — Grade 5

3 The time it takes a beaker of hot water wrapped in different thicknesses of insulation to cool down by 5 °C is recorded in the table below.

Thickness of insulation (mm)	2	4	6	8
Time to cool (s)	250	569	603	798

(a) Another beaker of hot water with 3 mm thick insulation is cooled by 5 °C. Use the table to estimate the time this took. **[1 mark]**

400 seconds (between 250 and 569 seconds)

(b) The results are plotted on the graph in **Figure 1**. Use the line of best fit on the graph to estimate the time taken for a beaker with 7 mm of insulation to cool by 5 °C. **[1 mark]**

700 seconds

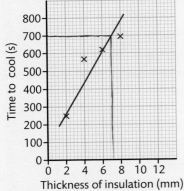

Figure 1

10 Exam-style practice — Grade 4

Use **Figure 1** to estimate the time it takes for the beaker to cool by 5 °C with 5 mm of insulation. **[2 marks]**

Made a start | Feeling confident | Exam ready

Interpreting data

In the exam, you will need to demonstrate that you can interpret data from a range of equipment, tables, charts and graphs.

Correlations

Scatter graphs show patterns, **outliers** and **anomalies** in numerical data. Anomalies do not fit the pattern at all, and outliers fit poorly. You may need to discount these results when finding an average for your data.

A **correlation** is a relationship between two variables that can easily be seen by drawing a line of best fit on a scatter graph. If the line is straight, then the relationship is linear. If it also goes through the origin (0,0), you can say that the measurements are proportional. A lot of scatter can indicate random error affecting your experiment. Think about how you can reduce this.

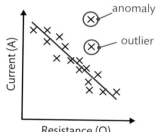
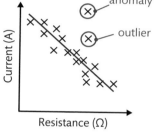

If the line of best fit should go through (0,0) and does not, this indicates a systematic error. All of your readings are likely to be too high or too low by the same amount.

The closer together the results are, the more precise they are.

Data in tables

If you are given data in a table, it is helpful to first of all look for a pattern to work out the relationship between the variables. In the table below, as speed increases, braking distance increases.

Speed (m/s)	5	10	15	20	25	30
Braking distance (m)	4	16	36	64	100	144

Now, look for further patterns. What happens when one of the quantities is doubled? As you double any speed, the distance gets four times bigger.

You can make estimates for other speeds based on the values in the table. For example, the braking distance at a speed of 12 m/s would be between 16 m and 36 m.

As one measurement doubles, if the other:

- doubles, they are **directly proportional**
- halves, they are **inversely proportional**.

Averages

$$\text{mean} = \frac{\text{sum of numbers}}{\text{amount of numbers}}$$

Use the **mean** for repeat readings. This is the most commonly used average in science. However, it should not be used where the range includes extremely large or small numbers that would affect the mean.

The **mode** is the number or measurement that occurs most often. It could be used with measurements that are not numbers, like average eye colour.

The **median** is the middle number when values are placed in order of increasing size.

Worked example   Grade 4

Give the volume of the liquid in the measuring cylinder.   **[1 mark]**

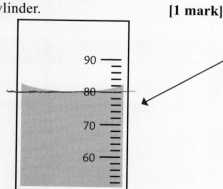

When measuring a volume of liquid, make sure you take your reading from the **bottom** of the meniscus (the curved line that the skin of the liquid makes). If this comes up in an exam, draw a line across the bottom of the meniscus to help you find the right value.

80 ml or 80 cm³

Make sure to use the correct units. If measuring volume, you can use ml or cm³. Remember that area will use squared units.

Exam-style practice   Grades 4–5

Puppies in a litter have masses of 1.1 kg, 1.2 kg, 1.2 kg, 1.3 kg, 3.3 kg.

(a) Give the mean, mode and median for the mass of these puppies.   **[3 marks]**

(b) Explain why the mean gives the least accurate idea of the mass of the majority of the puppies.   **[2 marks]**

Using charts and graphs

Pages
12, 145, 209
LINKS

Graphs are commonly used in science, particularly line and scatter graphs. You need to know how to interpret and draw a graph.

5 Types of graphs and charts

Pie charts
Pie charts show the proportional measurements that make up a total. For example, percentage use of energy resource.

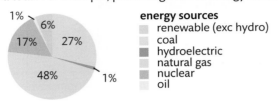

energy sources
- renewable (exc hydro)
- coal
- hydroelectric
- natural gas
- nuclear
- oil

Bar charts
Bar charts should only be used to show information about discrete data. For example, the strength of the gravitational field on different planets. They are not to be confused with histograms, which show continuous data.

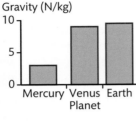

Gravity (N/kg)

Mercury Venus Earth
Planet

Graphs
Graphs, such as scatter graphs, show the relationship between two variables. For example, length of wire and resistance, weight and mass.

Weight

Mass

5 Worked example — Grade 5

The table shows a student's results for an investigation.

Time (s)	0	10	20	30	40	50	60
Temperature (°C)	5	6	11	17	35	72	180

(a) Use these results to draw a line graph. **[3 marks]**

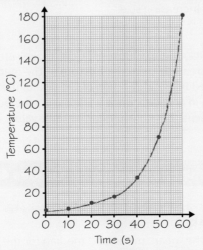

(b) Determine how long it took to reach 100 °C.
[1 mark]

53 seconds

10 Interpreting graphs

Straight line graphs
The general equation of a straight line is $y = mx + c$, where:
- x and y are values on the x and y axes
- m is the gradient
- c is where the line meets the y-axis.

A straight line represents a linear relationship. The equation for the line in the graph in **Figure 1** is $y = 0.5x + 2.5$. You can replace x and y with the quantities you have plotted.

The meaning of the gradient depends on the quantities being divided. For example, with speed on the y-axis and time on the x-axis the gradient is speed ÷ time = acceleration.

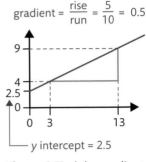

$$\text{gradient} = \frac{\text{rise}}{\text{run}} = \frac{5}{10} = 0.5$$

y intercept = 2.5

Figure 1 Find the gradient

Tangents
You can find the gradient of a curve at any point by drawing a tangent at that point.
Find the gradient of the tangent but remember that the gradient is different at every point on the curve.

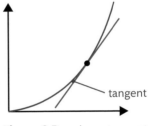

tangent

Figure 2 Drawing a tangent

Areas under the line
You can figure out what the area under the line represents by looking at the quantities that are being multiplied together. If the axes are speed and time, speed × time = distance. The area represents distance.

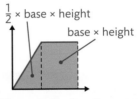

$\frac{1}{2}$ × base × height

base × height

Figure 3 Finding the area under a line

10 Exam-style practice — Grades 4–5

1 Name a suitable type of graph to show:

  (a) the braking distances of different cars at 10 m/s
  [1 mark]

  (b) the mass of salt that dissolves in water at different temperatures
  [1 mark]

  (c) the percentage of energy lost from the windows, doors, walls and floors in a house.
  [1 mark]

2 A straight line graph has the equation distance = 4 × time + 10 in the form $y = mx + c$. Give the gradient and the y intercept of the line.
[1 mark]

 Made a start Feeling confident Exam ready

Using diagrams

You could be asked to draw or label a diagram in the exam. Diagrams can also help you to organise information to answer a question.

Key questions

- ☑ Do you need to use a ruler?
- ☑ Do you need to label any parts?
- ☑ Should you add arrows to show direction?

- ☑ Should you draw anything to scale?
- ☑ Do you need to use symbols (like circuit symbols)?
- ☑ Do you need to use a particular shape or position?

Worked example

Grades 4–5

1 Draw a diagram of an animal cell and label the following features:

- nucleus
- ribosome
- mitochondrion
- cell membrane.

[4 marks]

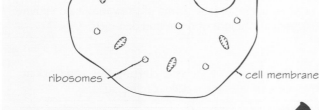

Exam focus

When asked to add a label to a diagram, make sure you think carefully about the position and draw your lines in exactly the right places.

The crest is just one position, but amplitude and wavelength must indicate between two positions.

The wavelength needs to be indicated exactly from the crest of one wave to the crest of the next and the amplitude from the centre line to the very highest point.

2 Find the acceleration of a car of mass 1200 kg if the engine force is 1000 N and it experiences 350 N of air resistance and 200 N of friction.

[3 marks]

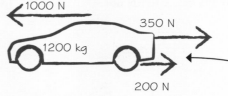

Resultant force = 1000 − 350 − 200 = 450 N

acceleration = $\frac{force}{mass} = \frac{450}{1200}$ = 0.375 m/s^2

This sketch isn't part of the answer but it helps to organise all the numbers in the question.

3 Look at the wave shown in **Figure 1**.

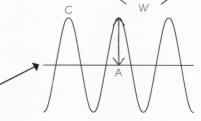

Figure 1

(a) Label the crest of a wave with **C**. **[1 mark]**

(b) Indicate the amplitude and label it **A**. **[1 mark]**

(c) Indicate a wavelength and label it **W**. **[1 mark]**

Exam-style practice

Grade 5

1 Sketch a skydiver of weight 600 N experiencing 300 N air resistance upward and a 200 N side wind. **[3 marks]**

2 Draw a circuit diagram that could be used to find the resistance of a light bulb. **[3 marks]**

Planning practicals

Pages
8, 46,
106, 171
LINKS

You need to know how to write a plan for a practical, including an equipment list, a method and details about control and safety measures.

 Worked example Grades 4–5

A student makes the hypothesis that the average speed of a trolley rolling down a ramp increases with the height of the ramp.

(a) Identify the variables needed to compare the speed of the trolley with the height of the ramp. **[3 marks]**

> The variables are speed and height. You either have to measure speed directly or measure distance and time for speed to be calculated.

Change the height of the ramp and measure the distance the trolley moves and the time it takes to reach the bottom.

$$\text{average speed} = \frac{\text{distance down ramp}}{\text{time}}$$

(b) Draw a diagram to show the equipment needed. List any other items not shown. **[3 marks]**

> Your equipment needs to reflect the variables you are going to measure.
>
> You could suggest using two light gates and a data logger set up for timing here instead. A sonic distance sensor and data logger could measure the speed of the trolley directly so no need to measure time and distance individually. This would also be a way to remove the reaction time uncertainty mentioned in **(c)**.

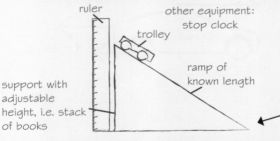

ruler
other equipment: stop clock
trolley
ramp of known length
support with adjustable height, i.e. stack of books

> The diagram is meant to save you wasting space in a method describing the layout of equipment. Not every single piece needs to be shown, but every piece needs mentioning in an equipment list.
>
> It can be useful to label some of the variables on your diagram like height of ramp and distance.

(c) Explain why there is an uncertainty involved in using a stop clock in this experiment. **[1 mark]**

The reaction time of the person who judges when the trolley reaches the bottom will affect the measurement of time.

> There would also be an issue starting the stop clock at the same time as the trolley is released.

(d) Suggest how the uncertainty in **(c)** could be reduced. **[2 marks]**

Use two light gates at a set distance and a data logger set to measure the speed directly.

> Using a longer ramp and small heights would increase the time. This would make the uncertainty in reaction time less significant.

(e) Identify **one** hazard and suggest how this hazard could be reduced. **[2 marks]**

The trolley may roll onto the floor and become a trip hazard. Someone should catch it at the end of the ramp.

> This is a low-risk experiment, but even experiments without acid or fire have a small hazard. Keep your experiments simple and avoid getting too inventive.

 Exam-style practice Grades 4–5

A student carries out an experiment to test how the thickness of insulation around a beaker of hot water affects the temperature change.

For the experiment:

(a) identify the variables that need measuring and controlling **[2 marks]**

(b) list the equipment needed to take the measurements **[2 marks]**

(c) give **two** safety precautions the student should take. **[2 marks]**

Comparing data

You need to know how to compare data and be able to discuss the advantages and disadvantages of different ideas.

 Worked example | **Grades 4–5**

The table shows the estimated figures for the percentage of electricity produced from different resources in Spain and the UK.

Resource	Electricity production (%)	
	UK	Spain
wind turbine	2.3	26.4
solar	0.2	2.6
hydroelectric	0.6	23.9
biomass	1.7	0.2
fossil fuel	87.4	17.9
nuclear	7.8	29.0

(a) Compare the percentage of renewable resources in each country. **[2 marks]**

4.8 per cent of electricity in UK comes from renewable resources compared to 53.1 per cent in Spain, which is over ten times higher.

(b) Suggest a reason for the difference in solar electricity production by each country. **[2 marks]**

Spain may have more hours of sunshine, or fewer clouds, making solar power a more useful resource.

(c) The percentage of electricity produced by nuclear power in Spain is just over three times the percentage in the UK. A student says that this means Spain has three times more nuclear power stations than the UK. Explain whether or not you agree with this statement. **[4 marks]**

No. The percentage just means that a larger fraction of Spain's energy comes from nuclear power. A percentage does not tell us how much energy is actually produced in each case. Also, power stations can produce different amounts of energy so number of power stations does not necessarily indicate power output.

Percentages just tell us how much of the total something makes up. It does not tell us how much energy is actually used.

If the two countries used different amounts of energy in total, then one resource having the same percentage in both countries does not mean they actually produce the same amount of energy. Therefore, having three times the percentage does not mean you have three times the energy.

 Comparing data

- Look for patterns in the data.
- Identify any similarities or differences, and what they mean.
- Consider the advantages and disadvantages of different variables.

Exam focus

When comparing data, look at the table's headings. Make sure you know exactly what the data is before answering the question.

When comparing, make sure you refer to both values and clearly state which is greater. Look for any patterns, e.g. if something is approximately ten times larger.

First, look at what the difference is, then apply what you know about solar power to try to explain it.

 Exam-style practice | **Grades 4–5**

A tyre manufacturer wants to compare the performance of two tyres. Using the same car and driver, they perform emergency stops at different speeds with each set of tyres, A and B.

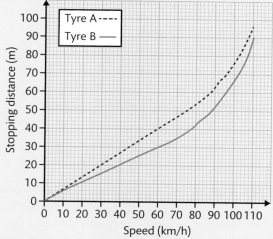

(a) Give **one** similarity and **one** difference between the two graphs. **[2 marks]**

(b) Describe how the stopping distances would change if the tyres were tested on a wet road. **[2 marks]**

(c) Deduce which tyre has the best performance in this test. Explain your answer. **[3 marks]**

Working scientifically

Pages 8, 12, 129
LINKS

You need to demonstrate the ability to work scientifically through your experimental skills, analysis and evaluation of data.

Experimental skills and strategies

Experiments are designed to test hypotheses (ideas or explanations).

Scientists use experiments to find data, such as the specific heat capacity of a material. They also test how one measured quantity affects another: one variable (the independent variable) is changed and another variable (the dependent variable) is measured.

Planning

Being able to choose the correct equipment and method to carry out a practical is an important skill for scientists. A plan should include an equipment list and a step-by-step method, as well as details about any control or safety measures.

Analysis and evaluation

After making and recording their observations, scientists process and present data in a way that enables them to evaluate the validity of a hypothesis.

It is important to use scientific theories and explanations to explain data and reflect on whether patterns and observations support the original hypothesis.
The evaluation should also include suggestions on how the practical could be improved.

Development of scientific ideas

As new evidence comes to light, scientists change and develop their theories and knowledge. These changes may have ethical, social, environmental or economic implications.

Experimental results are published for peer review. This means other scientists can check the findings and carry out further experiments based on the original results.

Worked example   Grades 4–5

1 A student makes a hypothesis that the greater the light intensity, the taller a plant will grow.

(a) Identify the dependent and independent variables.   **[2 marks]**

The independent variable is the level of light intensity, which needs changing. The height of the plant needs to be measured. This is the dependent variable.

> The variables need to come from the hypothesis. In this case, light intensity and height can be measured directly. However, for variables like speed, you might need to measure distance and time and then calculate the variable you are investigating.

(b) Give **three** factors that need to be controlled.   **[3 marks]**

Type of plant, time allowed and growing conditions (e.g. water and temperature)

> There are lots of other factors, but these three are important and you should always choose the most obvious first. Others could include: carbon dioxide concentration or soil pH.

(c) Describe the best graph to plot the data on.   **[3 marks]**

A scatter graph of light intensity on the x-axis and height of plant on the y-axis with a line of best fit.

> A scatter or line graph is best for any experiment that tests the relationship between two numerical variables.

2 Scientists are researching a cure for Parkinson's disease using embryonic stem cells. Evaluate the advantages and disadvantages of this method of stem cell treatment.   **[4 marks]**

The advantages are that it will replace the patient's damaged cells with healthy cells, which may help them to recover. It is also easier to extract cells from an embryo, which saves time and money. One disadvantage is that some people have ethical issues with the use of embryos in stem cell research, as embryos cannot consent to being used.

> Consider the ethical, social, environmental and economic aspects. They may not all be relevant.

Exam-style practice   Grades 4–5

1 A student wants to find out which metal is the best conductor of electricity. Describe a method to find which of four different metals has the highest resistance.   **[6 marks]**

2 Discuss the possible effects of developing more efficient cars powered by solar cells.   **[3 marks]**

 Made a start   **Feeling confident**   **Exam ready**

Extended-response questions

You will be expected to answer questions worth 4–6 marks as part of your biology, chemistry and physics exams.

 Worked example Grade 5

1 Explain, in terms of structure and bonding, why sodium chloride, NaCl, is a solid at room temperature but chlorine, Cl_2, is a gas at room temperature. **[6 marks]**

Sodium chloride is an ionic substance. It is made up of positive sodium ions and negative electrostatic ions. In the solid, the ions form a giant lattice. As the ions are oppositely charged, there are strong forces of attraction between the ions, meaning that large amounts of energy are needed to overcome these forces and melt the substance. This means that, at room temperature, NaCl will be a solid.

Chlorine is a small covalent molecule. It has a strong covalent bond between the two atoms of chlorine, but much weaker intermolecular forces between the separate molecules of chlorine. It is these intermolecular forces that need to be overcome in order to melt and boil chlorine. As the forces are weak, it does not take very much energy to do this. This means that, at room temperature, Cl_2 will be a gas.

> Be sure to answer the question fully: the student has stated the type of structure and bonding of each substance and has then explained the difference in melting and boiling points in terms of the bonding in these structures.

> Break your answer down to give it a logical order: the student writes about sodium chloride first, and then chlorine. Each paragraph states the structure and the bonding and then explains the effect on melting and boiling point.

2 Compare alpha, beta and gamma radiation in terms of their penetrating and ionising powers. **[6 marks]**

Alpha radiation can be stopped by skin or paper. It is the most ionising type of radiation as it is the largest and has the highest charge.

Beta radiation can be stopped by a few mm of aluminium. It is moderately ionising as, although it is small, it has a charge.

Gamma radiation is the most penetrating. It takes a few centimetres of lead or a few metres of concrete to stop it. It is the least ionising as it is very small and has no charge.

> It is often useful to include a diagram in extended-response questions, such as **Figure 1**:

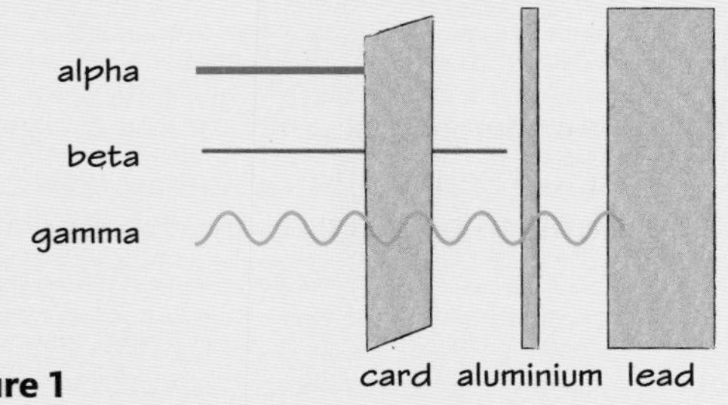

alpha
beta
gamma

card aluminium lead

Figure 1

3 Gases can be compressed but solids cannot. Use ideas about particles to explain why. **[4 marks]**

The particles in a gas are spread out, with a lot of space between them. This means that gas particles can be pushed closer together. Solid particles are tightly packed together: there is no space between them, which means that they cannot be pushed closer together.

4 Explain why reactivity decreases going down Group 7. **[4 marks]**

Group 7 elements all have 7 electrons in their outer shell. When they react, they will gain an electron. The reactivity decreases down the group because the size of the atoms increases as you go down the group. This increase in size means that the outer-electron shell is further away from the nucleus. This means that the 'incoming' electron feels less pull from the nucleus.

 Exam-style practice Grade 4

Describe the levels of organisation within the human circulatory system. **[4 marks]**

Improving results

Pages
8, 28,
136, 167
LINKS

It is important to be able to suggest improvements to practical methods.

⑤ Types of error

Systematic errors are consistent throughout a practical investigation and are caused by the measuring equipment, for example, calibration errors. They lead to all measured values being either greater than or lower than the true value.

Random errors are those that are unpredictable. The effect of random errors can be reduced by taking repeat readings and then calculating a mean.

Zero errors occur when a piece of measuring equipment gives a reading when the true value is zero.

⑩ Worked example
Grade 6

❶ **Figure 1** shows the equipment used to measure the specific heat capacity of an aluminium block.

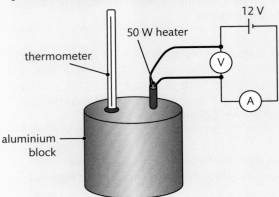

Figure 1

Suggest **one** change that could be made to the equipment that would allow more accurate measurements to be taken. Explain your choice. **[2 marks]**

Some of the heat from the heater will be lost to the surroundings as opposed to heating up the aluminium block. In order to minimise this heat loss, the block could be wrapped in some insulating material.

❷ **Figure 2** shows the equipment used by a student to investigate the relationship between force on a spring and extension of the spring.

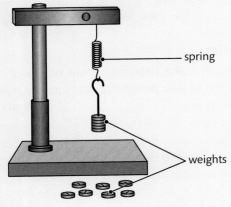

Figure 2

Suggest **one** change to the equipment shown that would allow the student to measure the length of the spring consistently and so calculate the extension. Explain your suggestion. **[2 marks]**

The student should clamp a ruler behind the spring. This would mean that they are always measuring from the same point each time.

⑩ Exam-style practice
Grades 4–5

Figure 3 shows the apparatus used by a student to investigate the behaviour of light shining through a clear plastic block.

(a) Add a label to the diagram to indicate which line shows the normal as the light enters the block.
[1 mark]

(b) Suggest a piece of equipment that could be used to measure the angles of incidence and refraction.
[1 mark]

(c) Explain why the light beam needs to be narrow to produce more accurate results. **[2 marks]**

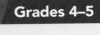

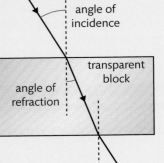

angle of incidence

transparent block

angle of refraction

Figure 3

 Made a start   Feeling confident   Exam ready

Answers

Page 1 Levels of organisation

1. A

2. The circulatory system is an organ system made up of several organs, the heart and blood vessels working together. The organs consist of different types of tissue: epithelial, muscle, connective tissue. The tissues are made up of cells, such as red blood cells.

Page 2 Eukaryotic and prokaryotic cells

cell membrane – controls what enters and leaves cell;

flagella – enable cell to move;

nucleus – contains DNA;

ribosome – where proteins are made;

cell wall – protects cell

All correct = 4 marks; 3 correct = 3 marks; 2 correct = 2 marks; 1 correct = 1 mark

Page 3 Animal and plant cells

chloroplast – 3;

mitochondrion – 2;

nucleus – 4;

permanent vacuole – 5;

ribosome – 1

All correct = 2 marks; at least three in correct sequence = 1 mark

Page 4 Specialised animal cells

(a) Any two from: egg cells have: cytoplasm containing nutrients needed for growth; a cell membrane that changes after fertilisation so that only one sperm cell can enter; a haploid nucleus to combine with the sperm cell nucleus during fertilisation.

(b) Any two from: sperm cells have: an acrosome containing enzymes needed to digest the outer layers of the egg cell; a tail for movement; mitochondria to provide energy for movement; a haploid nucleus to combine with the egg cell nucleus during fertilisation.

(c) Ciliated epithelial cells have: cilia to move mucus containing dirt and bacteria away from the lungs; mitochondria to provide energy for the cilia to move.

Page 5 Microscopy

1. 20 cm = 200 mm

   magnification = $\dfrac{200}{0.1}$ = 2000

2. 15 × 50 = × 750

Page 6 Practical: Using microscopes

1. To produce an image that the eye can see, light needs to be able to pass through the tissue. If the tissue is made of many layers of overlapping cells, it is difficult to see individual cells clearly.

2. To make the cells, or parts of the cells, easier to see.

Page 7 Enzyme action

The active site of the enzyme has a complementary shape to the substrate molecule, so will only attach to that substrate.

Page 8 Practical: Enzymes

1. Any one from: concentration of substrate/starch solution; concentration of enzyme/amylase solution.

2. Any one from: take the drops more frequently, e.g. every 15 seconds; have a colour reference to compare the samples to.

Page 9 Digestion and enzymes

So the molecules are small enough, or soluble enough, to be absorbed through the intestine wall into the bloodstream.

Page 10 Diffusion

higher; lower

Page 11 Osmosis

water; dilute; concentrated; permeable

Page 12 Practical: Osmosis

1. Different-sized potato chips would have different surface areas, which would affect the rate of osmosis. It is the effect of concentration that is being investigated so all other variables should be kept the same (controlled).

2. The hypothesis was only partly correct. The change in mass only increased in sugar concentrations above about 42 g dm³.

Page 13 Active transport

1. Any two from:
   - active transport uses energy/diffusion does not use energy
   - active transport moves substances from a low to a high concentration/diffusion moves substances from a high to a low concentration
   - active transport uses carrier molecules/diffusion does not use carrier molecules.

2. Answers may vary, e.g.
   - plant roots absorbing mineral ions from the soil
   - humans absorbing glucose from the small intestine.

Page 14 Mitosis and the cell cycle

1. Any two from: the cell grows larger; chromosomes/DNA/genetic material replicates/is copied; sub-cellular structures/ribosomes/mitochondria replicate/increase in number.

2. The cell (that has two new nuclei) divides into two (genetically identical) daughter cells.

Page 15 Importance of mitosis

asexual reproduction – producing offspring from one parent only;

growth – getting larger;

repair – replacement of damaged cells

All correct – 2 marks; 2 or 1 correct – 1 mark

Page 16 Cell differentiation and growth

cell differentiation – when cells become specialised;

cell division – when cells split into two;

cell elongation – when cells become bigger

All correct – 2 marks; 2 or 1 correct – 1 mark

Page 17 Stem cells

No risk of rejection; donor gives consent.

Page 18 The human nervous system

Image showing stimulus: heat/hot oven; → receptor: skin; → coordinator: spinal cord; → effector: muscles in arm/hand; → response: removes hand

Page 19 Meiosis

meiosis; four; half; different

Page 20 The structure of DNA

It is made of two strands, coiled together in a spiral.

Page 21 DNA and the genome

1. D

2. gene, chromosome, nucleus, cell
   All correct – 2 marks; all correct except for one error – 1 mark

3. DNA from blood (white blood cells) could be analysed to find out who it came from.

Page 22 Genetic inheritance

alleles; phenotypic

Page 23 Genetic diagrams

(a)

blue eyes

		b	b
heterozygous brown eyes	B	Bb brown eyes	Bb brown eyes
	b	bb blue eyes	bb blue eyes

Probability is 50% or ½ or 0.5.

(b) No, because both parents would be bb, so all children would also be bb.

Page 24 Sex determination

1. (a) A
   (b) C

2. 50% or $\frac{1}{2}$ or 0.5.

Page 25 Variation and mutation

1. C

2. C

Page 26 Evolution by natural selection

1. Natural selection

2. Some animals were faster runners than others. The faster animals caught more food and were better able to survive.

They therefore had more offspring who inherited the alleles for running faster. Over many generations, the species as a whole became faster runners.

Page 27 Evidence for human evolution

(a) The tools became slimmer/smaller/more sophisticated.

(b) They were becoming more intelligent, and had better coordination/dexterity.

Page 28 Classification

1. Less confusing as each species just has one name.

2. Any one from:
   - improvements to microscopes
   - DNA analysis and sequencing
   - improved understanding of biological processes.

Page 29 Selective breeding

1. Any two from: better quality meat; better quality wool; increased hardiness, docility.

2. Any two from: lack of variation; increased susceptibility to disease; inbreeding/genetic defects.

Page 30 Genetic engineering

1. Selective breeding can only work within a species. Genetic engineering can introduce characteristics from other species.

2. Farmers may use more herbicide and the herbicide may harm people who eat the crops. It may also cause a herbicide-resistant weed to develop.

Page 31 Health issues

1. Communicable diseases can be passed on by, or caught from, another person, non-communicable diseases cannot. Communicable diseases are caused by pathogens; non-communicable diseases have other causes.

2. Pathogens are microorganisms that cause disease.

Page 32 Communicable diseases

1. A disease that can be passed from one person to another.

2. Infectious microorganisms can be breathed in without coming into contact with the infected person. Microbes can be breathed out by one person and breathed in by many people who are nearby.

Page 33 Viral diseases

1. Viruses are much smaller than bacteria. They consist of small genes surrounded by protein. When a virus invades a cell, the genes in the virus instruct the cell to make more copies of the virus.

2. By avoiding sexual contact; by using a condom.

Page 34 Bacterial diseases

1. Toxins, which damage or kill cells.

2. Any two from: avoiding sexual contact; using a condom; regular screening followed by treatment if necessary.

Page 35 Fungal diseases

1. It is killing ash trees and harming other species that depend on ash trees.

2. Cut down infected trees. Burn, bury or compost infected leaves.

Page 36 Protist diseases

1. D

2. Any two from: mosquito nets; mosquito repellent; insecticides (to kill mosquitoes); drain stagnant water (where mosquitoes breed).

Page 37 Human defence systems

1. Some white blood cells engulf bacteria and kill them (phagocytosis); other white blood cells produce antibodies.

2. Any two from: provides a barrier; forms scabs (if cut); secretes antimicrobial substances.

Page 38 Immunisation

1. C

2. The pathogens are dead or inactive, so cannot reproduce and cause the symptoms of the disease.

Page 39 Antibiotics

1. Antibiotics work by inhibiting cell processes in bacteria. Viruses are not living things and are not made of cells.

2. Bacteria develop resistance to antibiotics by natural selection. Some bacteria have mutations which make them resistant to a particular antibiotic. These resistant bacteria will survive and reproduce rapidly. The bacteria that are susceptible to the antibiotic will be destroyed. Eventually, only bacteria that are resistant to the antibiotic will exist.

3. So that the doctor can prescribe an antibiotic that will work specifically just against that type of bacteria. This avoids prescribing antibiotics that work against many different types of bacteria, as it is the overuse of this type of antibiotic that is the main cause of the spread of antibiotic resistance in bacteria.

Page 40 Development of drugs

1. The work of a scientist, or a group of scientists, is checked by others, to make sure that it is correct.

2. 9 to 16 years

3. Clinical trials involve testing on human volunteers or patients, to check a new drug's safety, its effectiveness and the optimum dose. Preclinical trials involve testing on cells, tissues or animals to make sure the new drug has the wanted effect and that it's safe to start testing on humans.

Page 41 Non-communicable diseases

(a) People aged less than 30

(b) People who have never smoked can still get lung cancer.
The older you are when you stop smoking, the more likely you are to get lung cancer (or the reverse).

(c) (i) 0.4 per cent

(ii) 5.6 per cent

Page 42 Effects of lifestyle

1. Teenagers are still growing, so their heights and BMI may be changing quite dramatically. This is quite normal.

2. Poor diet can lead to being obese or malnourished.

Page 43 Cardiovascular disease

1. Any two from: stop smoking; drink less alcohol; more healthy diet; more exercise.

2. Any two from: a stent; drugs such as statins or warfarin; by-pass surgery.

Page 44 Photosynthesis

1. B

2. A

Page 45 Rate of photosynthesis

Increasing carbon dioxide concentration can increase the rate of photosynthesis because – increasing the concentration of one of the reactants will increase the rate of reaction.

Increasing light intensity can increase the rate of photosynthesis because – more energy is provided for this endothermic reaction.

Increasing temperature can increase the rate of photosynthesis because – molecules move more quickly increasing the rate of reaction.

all 3 correct – 2 marks; 1 correct – 1 mark

Page 46 Practical: Photosynthesis

1. Measuring the volume will give more accurate results, because not all bubbles will be the same size. Counting bubbles is not as accurate, but is a quick and easy method that still gives fairly accurate results.

2. It is easier to measure oxygen production underwater because you can see the bubbles / collect the gas.

Page 47 Specialised plant cells

1. A root hair cell contains many mitochondria to provide the energy needed for the absorption of mineral ions by active transport. It also has a large surface area to increase the rate of water and mineral ion absorption.

2. Translocation is the movement of sucrose through the phloem up and down a plant.

Page 48 Transpiration

1. C

2. Water vapour, carbon dioxide and oxygen.

Page 49 Water uptake in plants

1. D

2. The stomata open to allow carbon dioxide to enter for photosynthesis.

Page 50 Human endocrine system

1. The pancreas.

2. A hormone is a substance secreted by an endocrine gland, that travels through the blood to its target organ(s), and helps regulate processes in the body.

Page 51 Hormones in reproduction

(a) Oestrogen causes the lining of the uterus to develop and thicken (repair) during the early part of the menstrual cycle.

(b) Progesterone maintains the thickened uterus lining during the latter part of the menstrual cycle.

Page 52 Contraception

1. The hormones it contains prevent any eggs being released, so fertilisation and pregnancy cannot occur.

2. Sperm and egg cannot meet, so fertilisation and pregnancy cannot occur.

Page 53 Control of blood glucose

B

Page 54 Diabetes

Type 1 diabetes is where the pancreas does not produce sufficient insulin. Type 2 is where the cells in the body no longer respond to insulin.

Type 1 diabetes is controlled by injections of insulin. Type 2 is mainly controlled by diet.

Obesity is a risk factor for Type 2 diabetes but not for Type 1.

Page 55 Transport in animals

1. surface area : volume = $(6 \times 4 \times 4) : (4 \times 4 \times 4)$

$$= 96 : 64$$
$$= 3 : 2$$
$$= 1.5 : 1$$

2. The places in an organism where substances are moved across a surface, such as a cell membrane.

Page 56 Alveoli

1. Large surface area, thin walls, good blood supply.

2. B

Page 57 The blood

1. B

2. D

Page 58 Blood vessels

1. Blood entering the arteries has only just been pumped by the heart (unlike the blood in veins which is returning to the heart). The thick elastic and muscular walls of the arteries then maintain the pressure. The high pressure is necessary to make sure the blood circulates around the whole body.

2. Veins carry blood at low pressure, usually upwards back to the heart against the force of gravity. Valves are needed to ensure blood will not flow backwards. The pressure in the other vessels is high enough to keep the blood flowing in the correct direction, so they do not need valves.

Page 59 The heart

1. (right ventricle →) pulmonary artery → lungs → pulmonary vein (→ left atrium)

2. The atria only need to force blood into the ventricles. The ventricles have to pump blood much further, to the lungs and the rest of the body.

Page 60 Aerobic and anaerobic respiration

Anaerobic respiration does not use oxygen, aerobic does; anaerobic produces lactic acid, aerobic produces carbon dioxide and water; anaerobic releases less energy than aerobic (from the same amount of glucose).

Page 61 Practical: Rate of respiration

1. Respiration is a chemical reaction. If the temperature increases, the reactant molecules will have more energy so move faster and collide and react more frequently, so the rate of respiration increases.

2. To absorb any carbon dioxide produced.

Page 62 Response to exercise

1. Cardiac output will rise during exercise and then fall after exercise.

2. Stroke volume = $\dfrac{\text{cardiac output}}{\text{heart rate}} = \dfrac{4}{60} = 0.067$ litres

Page 63 Communities

1. all the oak trees – population;

all the oak trees and the animals living in them – community;

single oak tree – organism

All correct – 2 marks; 2 or 1 correct – 1 mark

2. B

Page 64 Abiotic factors

1. A

2. Cold temperatures (in Europe)

Page 65 Biotic factors

1. Any valid example, e.g. predation of seals by polar bears.

2. Abiotic factors: temperature, carbon dioxide levels, wind intensity.

Biotic factors: new pathogens, food availability, predators.

3. Grey squirrels compete with red squirrels for food and territory, causing a great decrease in the population of red squirrels.

Page 66 Practical: Population studies

The plants are competing with the tree for light, water and mineral ions. Further away from the tree trunk there is less competition, for example, there is less competition for light as there is less shading from the tree branches.

Page 67 Biodiversity

3, 5, (1,) 6, 2, 4

All correct – 2 marks; at least 3 in correct sequence – 1 mark

Page 68 Maintaining biodiversity

1. C

2. Endangered animals are bred in captivity and then released into the wild. This increases the number of species in the wild which leads to greater biodiversity.

Page 69 Carbon cycle

1. carbon dioxide used to make glucose – photosynthesis;

glucose broken down making carbon dioxide – respiration;

glucose converted to other compounds such as proteins – growth

all 3 correct – 2 marks; 1 or 2 correct – 1 mark

2. B

Page 70 Water cycle

1. It may be sea water. It may contain harmful microorganisms or toxins.
2. When water falls from clouds as rain, snow or hail.

Page 71 Nitrogen cycle

(a) Denitrifying bacteria

(b) Decomposers and nitrifying bacteria

Page 72 Atoms, elements and compounds

1. It cannot be chemically broken down into anything simpler.
2. Al
3. (a) Sodium
   (b) (i) Hydrogen, H
      (ii) hydrogen + chlorine → hydrogen chloride

Page 73 The model of the atom

1. Neutron
2. The current model contains smaller particles.

Page 74 Subatomic particles

1. Positive
2. Protons and neutrons
3. (a) protons: 2, neutrons: 2, electrons: 2
   (b) There are the same number of positive protons as there are negative electrons.

Page 75 Size and mass of atoms

(a)

Subatomic particle	Relative mass	Relative charge
electron	$\frac{1}{1836}$	−1
neutron	1	0
proton	1	+1

(b)

Particle	Number of protons	Number of neutrons	Number of electrons
fluorine	9	10	9
fluoride	9	10	10

Page 76 Isotopes and relative atomic mass

(a) Different atoms of the same element containing the same number of protons but a different number of neutrons in the nuclei.

(b) ^6_3R and ^7_3M

Page 77 Developing the periodic table

(a) Any three from: carbon, silicon, titanium, zirconium.

(b) A

(c) He realised that some undiscovered elements must exist with properties like those of the rest of their groups.

(d) Elements are grouped by their properties, which are linked to electronic structure, and not by their relative atomic mass.

Page 78 The periodic table

1. (a) Group 5
   (b) Period 3
   (c) Nitrogen or any other named Group 5 element
2. (a) Group 2   (b) Period 3
3. The elements are arranged in the periodic table in increasing number of protons in the nucleus (atomic number).

Page 79 Electronic configuration

(a) C   (b) A and B   (c) D   (d) C

Page 80 Metals and non-metals

1. (a) It is the division which separates the metals and the non-metals.
   (b) Carbon is a non-metal. It is positioned to the right of the zigzag line.
2. Element A is a metal because it only has two electrons in its outer shell. Element B is a non-metal because it has six electrons in its outer shell. The more outer electrons, the further to the right an element will be placed in the periodic table (where the non-metals are placed).
   Element B has six outer electrons (so is in Group 6), will be positioned to the right of the table and so is most likely to be the non-metal.

Page 81 Chemical bonds

(a) (i) metallic; (ii) ionic; (iii) covalent

(b) Metallic bonding and ionic bonding

Page 82 Ionic bonding

potassium ion

fluoride ion

Page 83 Ionic compounds

1. 2
2. potassium bromide; KBr
3. Sodium chloride forms a giant ionic lattice held together by strong electrostatic forces of attraction.
4. (a) Ionic
   (b) Limitation: the diagram incorrectly suggests there are gaps between the atoms/the ions are not to scale/ the ionic bonds are represented by straight lines when they are actually forces of attraction.
      Advantage: the diagram shows the positions of the ions in space/the layout of the bonds between the atoms.

Page 84 Properties of ionic compounds

1. (a) sodium + chlorine → sodium chloride
   (b) Sodium chloride forms a regular lattice structure made up of sodium ions and chloride ions.
2. (a) Magnesium oxide is an ionic compound with a lattice structure held together by strong electrostatic forces of attraction between oppositely charged ions. A diagram showing these points would also be acceptable.
   (b) Ions are free to move.
   (c) High

Page 85 Covalent bonding

1. Covalent bonds/shared pair of electrons.
2. There are two (covalent) bonds between each oxygen and the carbon atom.
3.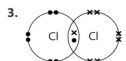

Page 86 Properties of simple molecular substances

1. **(a)** H_2

   (b)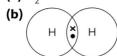

2. Covalent
3. The substance must be heated to provide enough energy for intermolecular forces between molecules to be overcome.

Page 87 Giant covalent structures

1. Three
2. Four
3. giant covalent structure
4. Slippery/soft; conductor of electricity; high melting or boiling point
5. Diamonds are hard so they can cut through different materials.

Page 88 Diamond

1. B
2. D
3. **(a)** C

   (b) Any three from: hard; high melting/boiling point; does not conduct electricity; clear/transparent; solid at room temperature; insoluble in water

   (c) Drill bits/cutting tools
4. The atoms are held firmly in place and this does not allow the substance to slide and act as a lubricant.

Page 89 Graphite

(a) It conducts electricity and it has a high melting point.

(b) Giant covalent structure; covalent bonding

(c) A

(d) Electrodes, lubricant and in pencils

Page 90 Graphene and fullerenes

1. Carbon
2. Graphene and carbon nanotubes both contain covalent bonds and make a giant covalent structure. Graphene forms as layers but nanotubes are in the form of hollow tubes.

Page 91 Polymers

1. Covalent bonds made from shared pairs of electrons between neighboring atoms.
2. C
3. No free-moving charged particles/delocalised electrons/ ions to carry the charge.

Page 92 Metals

1. C
2. Conductor
3. Metallic bonds are very strong. It takes a lot of energy to break these bonds so that a metal can melt/boil.

Page 93 Relative formula mass

1. **(a)** C = 1; H = 4

   (b) $M_r = 1 \times C + (4 \times H)$
   $= 1 \times 12 + (4 \times 1)$
   $= 16$

2. $M_r = 1 \times C + (2 \times O)$
   $= 1 \times 12 + (2 \times 16)$
   $= 44$

Page 95 Balancing equations

1. **(a)** carbon + oxygen $\rightarrow$ carbon monoxide

   (b) $2C + O_2 \rightarrow 2CO$

2. Any one from: Balanced equations give the formulas of substances. They show how many molecules of each substance are involved in the reaction.

3. Chemical equations should always balance because mass cannot be created or destroyed in a chemical reaction.

4. $4Na + O_2 \rightarrow 2Na_2O$

Page 96 Conservation of mass

1. **(a)** zinc carbonate $\rightarrow$ zinc oxide + carbon dioxide

   (b) Carbon dioxide gas produced in the reaction escaped.

   (c) 50 g/the same/no change in mass

2. $C_2H_5OH + 3O_2 \rightarrow 2CO_2 + 3H_2O$

Page 97 Calculating masses in reactions

1. 50 g
2. **(a)** magnesium carbonate $\rightarrow$ magnesium oxide + carbon dioxide

   (b) 84 g = 40 + ?
   84 − 40 = 44 g of carbon dioxide

Page 98 Concentrations of solutions

1. **(a)** $\frac{1500}{1000} = 1.5\,dm^3$

   (b) $\frac{60}{1.5} = 40\,g\,dm^{-3}$

2. concentration $= \dfrac{mass}{volume}$

   $10 = \dfrac{mass}{5}$

   mass = 5 × 10
   = 50 g

Page 99 States of matter

1. LiCl – solid

   CCl_4 – liquid

   OCl_2 – gas

2. Liquid

Page 100 Pure substances

(a) The temperature where a solid becomes a liquid or a liquid becomes a solid.

(b) Decreases because the ice melts at a lower temperature.

(c) Boiling point would be slightly higher than 100 °C.

Page 101 Mixtures

1. ink and water – simple distillation

   sand and water – filtration

   sugar and water – crystallisation

2. W – conical flask; X – filter paper; Y – filter funnel

Page 102 Chromatography

(a) Chromatography

(b) Three; yellow, red and blue

(c) The R_f value is the ratio of the distance moved by a substance (from the centre of its spot at the base line) to the distance moved by the solvent.

Page 103 Practical: Investigating inks

(a) Condenser

(b) Any one from:

- heating liquids could burn – wear eye protection
- breaking glass could cut – alert teacher/use dust pan and brush
- spilled liquids someone could slip over – wipe up immediately.

(c) The thermometer measures the boiling point of the solvent. This can then be compared to known samples to work out the substance.

Page 104 Potable water

1. Distillation

2. Chlorine

3. It contains large amounts of dissolved solids/salt.

4. Rainwater

5. Any three from:
   - rainwater
   - groundwater
   - rivers
   - lakes
   - oceans.

Page 105 The pH scale and neutralisation

1. hydrochloric acid + sodium hydroxide →

   sodium chloride + water

2. **(a)** alkali/base

   (b) OH^-

Page 106 Practical: pH change

(a)

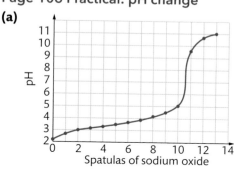

Spatulas of sodium oxide

1 mark for labelled axes

1 mark for plotted points

1 mark for smooth curve through all/most points

(b) The pH starts low/pH 2.2 and then increases as more sodium oxide is added.

(c) Cross at ph 7 on graph, between 10 and 11 spatulas

Page 107 Salt production

1. Potassium nitrate

2. Neutralisation

3. Hydrochloric acid

4. sodium carbonate + hydrochloric acid →

   sodium chloride + water + carbon dioxide

5. $2NaOH + H_2SO_4 \rightarrow 2H_2O + Na_2SO_4$

Page 108 Reactions of acids with metals

1. magnesium + hydrochloric acid → magnesium chloride + hydrogen

2. H_2

3. magnesium metal/magnesium hydroxide/magnesium oxide and sulfuric acid

4. Calcium nitrate

Page 109 Soluble salts

1. Filtration

2. C

3. copper nitrate

Page 110 Practical: Making salts

1. Any five relevant stages:
   - Warm the dilute hydrochloric acid and add copper oxide.
   - Stir to ensure the reaction is complete.
   - Filter the solution (retaining the filtrate).
   - Heat the solution (gently) until it begins to evaporate.
   - Stop heating when crystals begin to form (to the point of crystallisation).
   - Allow to cool so more crystals form.
   - Dry the crystals (between two pieces of filter paper).

2. Copper chloride

Page 111 Titration

1. Salt and water

2. The salt would be coloured/not pure.

Page 112 Solubility rules

1. A substance that can dissolve in a solvent, e.g. water.

2. **(a)**

liquid and insoluble solid

filter paper

filter funnel — filtered solid – residue

filtered liquid – filtrate

(Filter paper and filter funnel must be labelled.)

(b) To remove soluble impurities.

Page 113 Electrolysis

1. electrolyte – liquid used for electrolysis
   electrode – solid, electrical conductor
   anode – electrode with a positive charge
   cathode – electrode with a negative charge
2. The cathode/negative electrode

Page 114 Electrolysis of molten ionic compounds

1. (a)

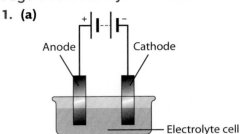

   (b) $PbBr_2 \rightarrow Pb + Br_2$
   (c) Bubbles (of bromine gas)
2. (a) cathode = lead;   anode = iodine
   (b) cathode = zinc;   anode = bromine
   (c) cathode = magnesium;   anode = oxygen
   (d) cathode = lithium;   anode = chlorine

Page 115 Electrolysis of aqueous solutions

(a) The solution conducts electricity.
   The ions move to oppositely charged electrodes.
   Bubbles are seen at the anode because chlorine gas is produced.
   The cathode becomes coated in pink/brown copper.
(b) Copper and chlorine
(c) $CuCl_2 \rightarrow Cu + Cl_2$

Page 116 Practical: Electrolysis of copper sulfate

Oxygen at the anode and copper at the cathode.

Page 117 The reactivity series

1. Metal D as there are the most bubbles.
2. The easier it is for the metal to become an ion by losing outer-shell electrons, the more reactive the metal is.
3. calcium + water → calcium hydroxide + hydrogen

Page 118 Extraction of metals and reduction

1. (a) lead oxide + carbon → lead + carbon dioxide
   (b) Reduction
   (c) Lead is less reactive than carbon/lower in the reactivity series than carbon.
2. Calcium is above carbon in the reactivity series. Metals can only be extracted by elements that are more reactive than them.

Page 119 Electrolysis to extract metals

1. Large amounts of energy are needed to melt the magnesium chloride. Energy is also needed to generate an electric current.
2. It is dissolved in cryolite.

Page 120 Metal oxides

(a) iron + oxygen → iron oxide
(b) Ionic bonding
(c) Electrostatic force of attraction between oppositely charged ions.

Page 121 Recycling and life-cycle assessment

1. Less energy and less pollution for reuse than recycling.
2. To assess the environmental impact of a product.
   To compare environmental impact of products with the same use.
3. Recycling needs energy to melt the product down. Burning fossil fuels to power this process releases carbon dioxide into the atmosphere, leading to global warming.
   Transporting the products to and from the recycling plant requires the burning of fuel to power the vehicle used to transport the products. This produces greenhouse gases and may also produce nitrogen oxides and sulfur dioxide, leading to global warming and acid rain.

Page 122 Reversible reactions

1. The products of the reaction can react to form the original reactants.
2. (a) By reversing the reaction (adding water) the original substance (hydrated copper sulfate) is formed.
   (b) hydrated $\rightleftharpoons$ anhydrous + water
        copper sulfate   copper sulfate

Page 123 Dynamic equilibrium and the Haber process

(a) 450 °C; 200 atmospheres; iron catalyst
(b) Gases are cooled and the ammonia turns to liquid/condensation.
(c) The unreacted gases are recycled to save money and energy.

Page 124 Group 1

1. As you move down the group the elements become more reactive.
2. Any three of the following: bubbles/fizzing/effervesces; metal floating; metal skimming across the surface of the water; metal reducing in size.
3. The rubidium will react explosively with the water and catch fire.

Page 125 Group 7

1. (a) 2.8.7
   (b) Chlorine has seven outer-shell electrons and readily accepts one electron to become an anion with a full outer shell. Thus it forms ionic compounds with positively-charged metal ions.
   (c) Fluorine is more reactive than chlorine so it will react more vigorously.
2. (a) Any number less than 7 but equal to or greater than 0.
   (b) Turns red.
      Turns white/bleaches.

Page 126 Group 7 reactivity

1. potassium iodide + bromine → potassium bromide + iodine

2. Chlorine is more reactive than iodine because it is higher in the group. This means that its outer shell is closer to its nucleus, which can therefore more easily attract and hold an extra electron than iodine can.

3. Iodine

Page 127 Group 0

1. All Group 0 atoms have a full outer shell.

2. **(a)** The atomic mass increases because there are more protons and neutrons in the atom.

   (b) Because their outer shells are full, noble gas atoms are unreactive.

3.

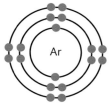

Page 128 Calculating rate of reaction

(a) cm^3/s

(b) $120\,cm^3 \div 120\,s = 1\,cm^3/s$

Page 129 Factors affecting rate of reaction

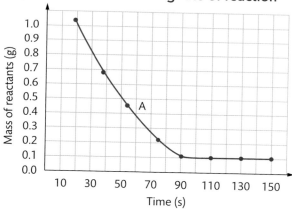

(a) Line A on graph. 1 mark for correct axes with units. 2 marks for correct plotting – lose one mark per incorrect plot. 1 mark for the line of best fit – smooth curve passing through or very close to each point.

(b) Increase the concentration of hydrochloric acid. Increase the surface area of the marble chips.

Page 130 Practical: Monitoring rate of reaction – colour change

(a) Particles would have more energy, so there would be more collisions in the same amount of time and also each collision would be of a higher energy. Therefore, there would be more successful collisions in the same time and so an increase in the rate of reaction.

(b) Independent variable – temperature

Dependent variable – the time taken for cross to disappear

Control variables – concentration and volume of hydrochloric acid, concentration and volume of sodium thiosulfate.

Page 131 Practical: Monitoring rate of reaction – gas production

The greater the surface area, the higher the rate of reaction.

Page 132 Collision theory and activation energy

1. The rate of reaction will increase. This is because the particles have more energy and therefore will move quicker, increasing the chance of collisions.

2. The gas particles become more crowded, so there is more chance of successful collisions and a higher rate of reaction.

Page 133 Reaction profiles

1. Energy

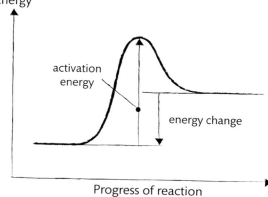

- 1 mark for correctly labelled axes
- 1 mark to show the position of the reactants and products - with the products having more energy than the reactants
- 1 mark for the labelling and arrow for activation energy
- 1 mark for labelling the energy change.

2. **(a)** Exothermic

   (b) Because the energy of the products is less than the energy of the reactants.

   (c)

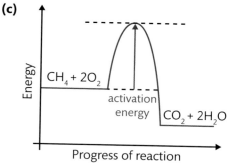

Page 134 Catalysts

1. Iron

2. Enzymes

Page 135 Exothermic and endothermic reactions

1. Exothermic

2. Decrease/drop/reduce

Page 136 Temperature changes

$-6.3\,°C$

Page 137 Crude oil and hydrocarbons

1. A limited supply of something that is not being made any more, or which is being made extremely slowly.

2. A group of organic compounds that have the same general formula (differ only by the number of CH_2 units in the main carbon chain), have the same chemical properties and show a gradual variation in physical properties, such as their boiling points.

Example: alkanes/alkenes/alcohols/halogenoalkanes.

3. C_6H_{14}

Page 138 Fractional distillation

1. Crude oil is heated to evaporate the hydrocarbons. The column has a temperature gradient/is cooler at the top than the bottom. The gaseous fractions travel up the column until they reach their boiling point. The fractions then condense and can be collected/run off.

2. X – evaporation

Z – condensation

Page 139 Properties of hydrocarbons

1. Water and carbon dioxide.

2. propane + oxygen → carbon monoxide + carbon + water

3. As molecular size increases, viscosity increases too.

4. Because in the combustion of a hydrocarbon both the carbon and the hydrogen atoms gain oxygen.

Page 140 Atmospheric pollutants

1. $S(s) + O_2(g) \rightarrow SO_2(g)$

2. A substance which may harm health or the environment.

3. Any three from: carbon monoxide, carbon/soot, sulfur dioxide/acid rain, oxides of nitrogen/nitrogen oxide/nitrogen dioxide.

Page 141 Comparing fuels

If hydrogen is produced from natural gas/crude oil derivatives and steam, it is still using non-renewable resources. If produced by electrolysis, electricity is required, which is usually generated using fossil fuels, which are non-renewable and release carbon dioxide into the atmosphere causing global warming.

Hydrogen is difficult to store safely in a small space in a vehicle.

Page 142 Cracking and alkenes

(a) Gases, petrol and diesel oil

(b) 12%

(c) Petrol, because there is a very large demand for it that cannot be satisfied from the supply of uncracked crude oil.

Page 143 Earth's early atmosphere

(a) 3.5

(b) There are no plants to carry out photosynthesis and produce oxygen.

Page 144 Oxygen and carbon dioxide levels

1. Approximately 20%

2. Levels of carbon dioxide reduced as plants took in carbon dioxide and some dissolved in the oceans.

Page 145 Gases in the atmosphere

1. 78–80%

2. The fraction of oxygen is about 20%, which is $\frac{20}{100}$.

Divide both by a common factor to get the lowest values:

$20 \div 20 = 1$

$100 \div 20 = 5$

So oxygen is $\frac{1}{5}$

Page 146 Greenhouse gases

1. Methane, carbon dioxide and water vapour

2. Absorb heat radiation from the Earth which re-radiates energy initially absorbed from the Sun.

3. By volcanoes

Page 147 Human contribution to greenhouse gases

1. Any two from:
- increased combustion of fossil fuels
- increased population
- increased waste
- deforestation.

2. There are other greenhouses gases/Methane and water are also greenhouse gases. There may be changes in the amount of other greenhouses gases in the atmosphere which may affect global temperatures.

Page 148 Global climate change

1. Any two from:
- rising sea levels
- heatwaves
- change in precipitation patterns
- increasing storm intensity.

2. An increase in greenhouse gases in the atmosphere contributing to increasing global temperatures.

3. Digestion in cattle (livestock farming)

Page 149 Key concepts in physics

1. B

2. (a) 0.0001 m or 1.0×10^{-4} m

(b) B

Page 150 Scalar and vector quantities

1. Displacement has size (magnitude) and **direction**. This means displacement is a **vector**. Distance only has size, so distance is a **scalar**.

2. C

Page 151 Distance and speed

(a) Distance = 200 km

Displacement = 200 km west

(b) Distance = 260 m

Displacement = 100 m up

(c) Distance = 700 m

Displacement = 0 m

Page 152 Speed and velocity

1. $3 \times 700 = 2100$ m (or 2.1 km)

2. (a) $200 \div 10 = 20$ m/s

(b) C is fastest on average.

Page 153 Distance–time graphs

1. The line would be less steep/half as steep; the final point would be (7, 21) instead of (7, 42).

2. **(a)**

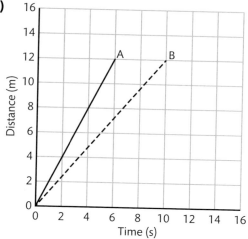

(b) Vehicle A has a higher average speed.

Page 154 Uniform acceleration

1. $10 = (v - 0) / 1.5$, $1.5 \times 10 = 15 \, \text{m/s}$
2. $5 = (65 - 0) / t$, $5 \times t = 65$, $65 \, \text{m/s} \div 5 \, \text{m/s}^2 = 13 \, \text{s}$
3. $(30 - 20) / 100 = 0.1 \, \text{m/s}^2$

Page 155 Velocity–time graphs

(a) From 0 to 20 seconds the golf cart is accelerating. From 20 to 45 seconds the golf cart is still accelerating but at a reduced rate (because the graph is less steep).

(b) At 10 s the gradient is $0.5 \, \text{m/s}^2$.

Page 156 Gravity

1. Using a calibrated spring-balance or force meter (like a newtonmeter)
2. weight = mass × gravitational field strength
3. $12000 \, \text{N} = m \times 10 \, \text{N/kg}$; rover mass = 12000 / 10 = 1200; $1200 \times 1.6 = 1920 \, \text{N}$

Page 157 Newton's laws of motion

1. D
2. force = $0.06 \times 500 = 30 \, \text{N}$

Page 158 Practical: Investigating acceleration

1. The force accelerating the trolley is found by calculating the weight of the masses using the equation:
   weight = mass × gravitational field strength
2. Any sensible safety precaution. Examples include: wearing safety goggles, avoiding overloading the cord or wire, removing the masses when the equipment is not in use, standing clear of the end of the desk.

Page 159 Stopping distance

1. C ($s = d/t$, $31 = d/0.6$, $0.6 \times 31 = 18.6$)
2. **(a)** Both results show that the 'distracted' time is much longer than/about double the 'concentrating' time.
   (b) Longer reaction times mean that the thinking distance increases, so a car's stopping distance is increased. It is best to be concentrating at all times when driving, to keep the stopping distance to a minimum.

Page 160 Factors affecting braking distance

1. Brakes heat up when they are applied to slow a car down. Racing cars travel much faster than road cars, so they need brakes that can heat up much more than brakes on road cars, and still function properly.

2. Kinetic energy = $\frac{1}{2} \times$ mass × speed^2.
   Doubling the speed increases the kinetic energy by four times. The brakes have to do four times the work to stop the car, so the car has to travel four times further when braking. Therefore, the braking distance is four times larger. Doubling the speed doubles the distance the car travels while the driver reacts, so the thinking distance is doubled.

Page 161 Gravitational potential energy

1. A
2. $70 \times 10 \times 100 = 70\,000 \, \text{J}$
3. **(a)** As the ball falls its height decreases, which means its GPE decreases. The GPE is being transferred to kinetic energy, which increases. Therefore, its speed increases.
   (b) An object's GPE transfers to kinetic energy as it falls. An object dropped from a greater height begins with more GPE to transfer, so will have more kinetic energy when it reaches the ground. Therefore, it will hit the ground faster.
4. Twice the change in height, so twice the increase in GPE: $1000 \times 2 = 2000 \, \text{J}$

Page 162 Kinetic energy

1. **(a)** KE = $0.5 \times 10 \times 20 \times 20 = 2000 \, \text{J}$
   (b) C: $2250 \, \text{J}$
2. **(a)** $0.5 \times 1200 \times 20^2 = 240\,000 \, \text{J}$
   (b) $240\,000 \, \text{J}$
3. The van has twice the mass of the car, so would have twice the kinetic energy if they were travelling at the same speed.
   However, the car has twice the speed of the van, which multiplies the kinetic energy by a factor of four. Overall, the car has twice as much kinetic energy.

Page 163 Conservation of energy

1. **(a)** chemical $\rightarrow$ thermal + kinetic + sound
   (b) chemical $\rightarrow$ kinetic (dissipated as light + thermal + sound) $\rightarrow$ gravitational potential energy
   (c) chemical $\rightarrow$ kinetic + thermal + sound
2. Thermal energy is wasted when water is heated to make steam, in the wires and through friction between moving parts. This could be reduced by insulation or reusing the wasted energy for heating, lubricating the moving parts, and using thicker wires to reduce resistance.
3. The jumper is thick and the wool traps air. Air has poor thermal conductivity, so reduces the jumper's rate of heat loss.

Page 164 Efficiency

1. Useful energy = 400 − 150 = 250 J
   Efficiency = $250 \div 400 = 0.625$
2. 85% of the energy produced is used to heat the house, and 15% is wasted.

3. Appliance A: 35 ÷ 100 = 0.35

   Appliance B: 35 ÷ 50 = 0.70

   Appliance B has the higher efficiency because it uses a greater proportion of the input power usefully.

4. Efficiency of 60%

   60 ÷ 100 = 0.6 as a decimal

   input energy = useful output energy ÷ efficiency

   2000 ÷ 0.6 = 3333 J.

5. LEDs are much more efficient/waste less energy; LEDs need less energy input.

Page 165 Renewable energy resources

1. A; D

2. Wind: only works when windy; can't be used in storms.

   Hydroelectricity: more reliable as doesn't depend on weather/nature to work.

3. Advantage: any one from: reliable; high power output.

   Disadvantage: any one from: fuel crops can drive up cost of food; environmental impact if spaces are cleared to make room for crops.

Page 166 Non-renewable energy resources

1. Nuclear and coal-fired power stations are equally as reliable and both have a high power output. Nuclear power stations are clean and do not produce any smoke or greenhouse gases. However, they do produce nuclear waste that must be stored safely; if there is an accident, there is a risk of radiation getting into the environment. Coal-fired power stations do produce smoke, greenhouse gases and sulfur dioxide. This can cause respiratory diseases, increase global warming and cause acid rain. They also need a large amount of coal to be transported.

2. Any four from:
   - non-renewables are running out so renewables need to be used to satisfy the demand for energy
   - other than biofuel, renewables produce little chemical pollution
   - no renewable resource adds to carbon emissions (biofuels do produce CO_2 when burned, but are carbon neutral overall) and so do not contribute to global warming, whereas fossil fuels do
   - nuclear accidents can affect a large area for a long period of time, but renewable resources tend to be safer
   - while the cost of building some renewable power sources is still high, the running costs or fuel costs are cheaper and in some cases virtually free, compared to the rising cost of non-renewable resources, especially as they become rarer
   - people are more interested in saving the environment so it has become popular for individuals to use renewable resources to generate electricity in their own home or use biofuels in cars
   - governments are under pressure to reduce the carbon emissions produced by their countries, which has caused a shift towards more renewable resources like wind farms and solar cells
   - farms are using spare land to generate electricity by creating wind or solar farms to generate additional income.

Page 167 Types of wave

1. Using speed = distance/time the student can use distance = 100 m (distance to the wall and back) and time = the time recorded. Inputting these into the equation will give the speed of sound.

2. The main source of error is the reaction time involved in starting and stopping the stop clock. A further source of error is being sure that the stop clock is stopped at the same point in the clap/echo each time. To improve the experiment, microphones and data loggers could be used instead.

3. There are no particles for sound to transfer through.

Page 168 Properties of waves

1. (a) speed = $\dfrac{\text{distance}}{\text{time}}$ Also accept distance = speed × time

   (b) $\dfrac{174}{0.03}$ = 5800 m/s

2. The waves reflect off the harbour wall and travel back in the opposite direction.

3. (a) wavelength: 20 waves are 15 cm long, so one wave is

   $\dfrac{15 \text{ cm}}{20 \text{ waves}}$ = 0.75 cm (0.0075 m)

   (b) wave speed = frequency × wavelength

   4.0 Hz × 0.0075 m = 0.03 m/s = or 3 cm/s

Page 169 Practical: Investigating waves

The weight causes there to be a force/tension in the string. This makes sure that the string is kept taut/stretched.

Page 170 Types of electromagnetic waves

1. Microwaves: cause a heating effect in water

   Infrared: can burn skin (accept other sensible examples)

2. Any two from:
   - premature ageing of the skin
   - skin cancer (caused by UV light)
   - sunburn.

3. Patients are exposed to very small doses of radiation, so the risk of cell damage only increases slightly. This is considered less of a risk than being unable to diagnose and treat conditions.

4. (a) $\dfrac{50}{0.1}$ = 500 X-rays per year

   (b) This number is not considered safe, because greater exposure to X-rays means greater risk. X-rays are kept to a minimum to keep the risk as low as possible.

Page 171 Practical: Investigating refraction

(a) Angle of incidence

(b) Angle of refraction increases.

(c) If the beam from the light/ray box spreads out widely, each part of the beam will be refracted by different amounts, making measurements difficult/less accurate. A slit reduces the width of the beam/ray.

Page 172 Applications of EM waves

1. Radio: TV, radio, two-way radio

   Microwaves: mobile phones, satellites, satellite TV

   Infrared: remote controls, wireless links between computers

Visible light: car indicators, warning lights, flashing torches, optical fibres

2. X-rays are harmful. Using the scanner only for a very short amount of time reduces the amount of X-rays a person receives, making harm less likely to occur.

Page 173 The structure of an atom

1. It will have 12 electrons. As an atom, it has neutral charge and so must have equal numbers of electrons and protons.

2. No this is not true. The atom needs to have 12 protons to be magnesium. An atom with 13 protons is aluminium.

3. Differences: electrons are negative and have a very small mass; protons are positive and have a larger mass. They are also found in different places in the atom.

4. Similarities: protons and neutrons have similar masses and are both found in the nucleus.

Page 174 Mass number, atomic number and isotopes

1. (a) 4 protons, 4 electrons, 5 neutrons

   (b) 8 protons, 8 electrons, 8 neutrons

   (c) 26 protons, 26 electrons, 30 neutrons

2. (a) 2 electrons

   (b) 1 electron

   (c) 3 electrons

3. The number of neutrons can be different if it is an isotope of carbon. The number of electrons can change if it is an ion.

Page 175 Development of the atomic model

1. The atom is a positively-charged sphere with tiny negatively-charged electrons embedded in it.

2. Unlike the plum pudding model, the nuclear model puts the majority of the mass and the positive charge at the centre, the outside carries the negative charge and the rest is empty space.

3. (a) Ionisation is where at least one electron is removed from or added to an atom, giving the atom an overall electric charge.

   (b) The nuclear model places electrons in orbits around the nucleus, making it easier for electrons to be added or removed.

Page 176 Ionising radiation

1. D

2. Alpha particles are larger and have a greater charge, meaning they have a higher ionising power.

Page 177 Background radiation

1. This is background radiation, which comes from a number of sources, including the ground, the air and from space.

2. Gamma radiation passes easily into the body and may cause damage to cells.

Page 178 Beta decay

1. (a) decreases by one

   (b) stays the same

2. Letter 'e' means the particle is an electron. Number '0' is mass number.

   Number '−1' is atomic number.

Page 179 Nuclear decay

1. (a) $^{235}_{92}U + ^4_2\alpha$ (b) $^{15}_5B + ^1_0n$

2. (a) atomic number decreases by 2, mass number decreases by 4

   (b) alpha particle/helium nucleus

3. (a) atomic number increases by 1, mass number does not change

   (b) beta particle/electron

Page 180 Half-lives

1. half or $\frac{1}{2}$

2. 22.5 Bq (accept 22 Bq or 23 Bq)

3. Average = $\frac{(36 + 38)}{2}$ = 37 s

Page 181 Dangers of radioactivity

(a) X-rays are harmful. Limiting the time of exposure reduces the risk of harm.

(b) A lead shield stops all the X-rays. This means that the person operating the equipment receives no harmful X-rays.

Page 182 Radioactive contamination and irradiation

1. They are at risk of irradiation because they are quite close to the rocks. They are at risk of contamination because the rocks may produce dust particles that would stick to their skin if they came into contact. They should not touch the rocks and should keep them in a sealed container to avoid contamination. To reduce their dose they should keep their distance from the sources, use them at arm's length by using long tongs or tweezers and only be near them when actually using them.

2. (a) Irradiation is being exposed to a source of radiation. Contamination is when a radioactive material is in contact with a person or other material and some of it remains on the person or material.

   (b) Contamination moves with the person so the person continues to be irradiated.

Page 183 Revising energy transfers

(a) 40 − 15 = 25 J

(b)

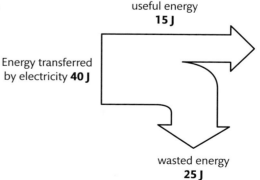

useful energy
15 J

Energy transferred by electricity **40 J**

wasted energy
25 J

Page 184 Work done and energy transfer

1. (a) D

   (b) kinetic energy

2. (a) $500 \times 35 = 17\,500\,\text{J}$

  (b) $20 \times 1.5 = 30\,\text{J}$

  (c) $120 \times 25 = 3000\,\text{J}$

Page 185 Power

1. $P = \dfrac{E}{t} = \dfrac{4800}{60} = 80\,\text{W}$

2. (a) Total work done $= 40 \times 30 = 1200\,\text{J}$

  (b) $P = \dfrac{E}{t} = \dfrac{1200}{90} = 13.3\,\text{W}$

Page 186 Forces

1. Air resistance is caused by air particles hitting a moving object. The particles have to touch the object to apply the force, so it is a contact force.

2. A force that acts over a distance/does not have to touch an object to affect it. Any example from: gravitational force (weight), electrostatic force, magnetic force.

3. Contact: friction, upthrust. Non-contact: weight, magnetic force.

Page 187 Circuit diagrams

1. Lamps A, B and C would light up, but the LED (D) would not light. The LED would allow current to flow anticlockwise around the loop, but the current from the cell would flow clockwise.

2. (a)

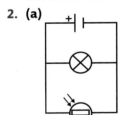

  (b)

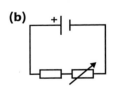

Page 188 Current, resistance and potential difference

1. 6 V

2. $V = IR$ so $6 = 0.1 \times R$. Then $R = \dfrac{6}{0.1} = 60\,\Omega$

3. (a) 6 V

  (b) The potential difference would be shared between the two lamps, so they would get 3 V each.

Page 189 Charge, current and energy

1. $t = \dfrac{Q}{I} = \dfrac{30}{60} = 0.5\,\text{s}$

2. (a) 0.6 A

  (b) $Q = It = 0.6 \times 15 = 9\,\text{C}$

Page 190 Series and parallel circuits

1. $12 + 4 = 16\,\Omega$

2. (a) As another lamp is added in series, they become less bright.

(b) In parallel, they both have the full 6 V potential difference across them, so they are brighter than when in series.

Page 191 Practical: Resistance

(i) When the resistors are connected in series, the combined resistance is the two resistances added together/more than each resistor on its own.

(ii) When the resistors are connected in parallel, the total resistance is less than either of the resistances connected on their own.

Page 192 Resistors

1. (a) diode

  (b) thermistor

2. light-dependent resistor

Page 193 Practical: *I–V* characteristics

(a) The current increases in direct proportion to the potential difference.

(b) Allow the components to cool down between each measurement.

  Keep the potential difference low to reduce heating from large currents.

Page 194 Energy transfer in circuits

$E = 230 \times 4.5 \times 300 = 310.5\,\text{kJ}$

Page 195 Electrical power

1. power rating $= 230 \times 0.5 = 115\,\text{W}$

2. (a) Power $= 1.5 \times 0.4 = 0.6\,\text{W}$

  (b) $E = P \times t = 0.6 \times 6 \times 60 \times 60 = 12\,960 = 13.0\,\text{kJ}$ to 1 d.p.

Page 196 Mains electricity

1. If the appliance has a case made of plastic (or another insulating material), it cannot conduct electric current. So even if there is a fault inside, the casing cannot become live and shock a person who touches it, so there is no need for an earth wire.

2. The potential difference goes up and down. However, it is always positive, so always flows the same direction and is therefore d.c.

Page 197 Energy transfers in appliances

1. *Wasted energy is underlined.*

  (a) Energy from electrical supply or battery produces sound and thermal energy that dissipates into the surroundings.

  (b) Energy from electrical supply transfers to movement of the fan (kinetic energy store) and sound and thermal energy that dissipate to the surroundings.

  (c) Energy stored in the car's battery produces movement in the motor (kinetic energy store within motor), which in turn produces movement of the car (kinetic energy store of car) and sound and thermal energy that dissipates into the surroundings.

  (d) Energy stored in the battery produces light and sound but also thermal energy that dissipates into the surroundings.

, Not all of the heat it produces will go into warming up the room. Some is used to warm up parts of the heater first and some of the heat might escape from the room.

3. 200 J must have been transferred and wasted by being dissipated into the surroundings.

Page 198 Magnetic fields

1. Place a compass near one of the poles. If the north arrow on the compass points towards the pole, it is the south. If it points away, it is the north.

   Or:

   Place the north pole of another bar magnet near one pole. It will be attracted to the south pole and repelled by the north.

2. Use a magnet to repel or attract another without touching it.

   Or:

   Show how a magnet moves a compass arrow without touching it.

3. A permanent magnet always has a magnetic field. An induced magnet only has one when placed near another magnet.

   A bar magnet is a permanent magnet. An induced magnet is an object made of cobalt, iron, nickel or steel that is being attracted to a magnet, for example, a fridge door with a magnet stuck to it.

Page 199 Electromagnetism

1. It can be switched off to put objects down, and its strength can be increased to pick up heavier objects.

2.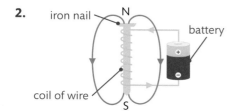

   North is at the top.

3. Change the direction of the electric current.

Page 200 The National Grid and transformers

1. Reduce the resistance by using wires with a wider diameter, or multiple wires in parallel. The wires could also be made from metals that are better conductors.

2. The potential difference is being decreased, so it is a step-down transformer.

Page 201 Density

1. The density stays the same as it is a property of water. The volume of the water in the bucket is greater as there is a higher capacity than in the bottle. The mass of water in the bucket will therefore be greater.

2. **(a)** Densities:
   - apple: $\dfrac{0.074}{1.04 \times 10^{-4}} = 712\,\text{kg/m}^3$ – floats
   - hollow steel box: $\dfrac{1.3}{2 \times 10^{-3}} = 650\,\text{kg/m}^3$ – floats
   - solid plastic cube: $\dfrac{0.5}{4.1 \times 10^{-4}} = 1220\,\text{kg/m}^3$ – sinks

- human: $\dfrac{70}{0.071} = 986\,\text{kg/m}^3$ – floats

(b) $m = \rho \times V = 712 \times 1.5 \times 10^{-4} = 0.107\,\text{kg}$

Page 202 Practical: Density of materials

(a) displacement can

(b) Fill the displacement can up to the level of the spout. Place a measuring cylinder under the spout to catch water that is displaced. Place the piece of rock in the displacement can. Take a reading of the volume of water displaced into the measuring cylinder.

Page 203 Changes of state

1. At its boiling point, the water will start to evaporate. The energy is used to break the weak bonds between water molecules, to make steam rather than going into kinetic energy of the particles that would increase the temperature.

2. Solid – stuck in place, so they will vibrate but not move around.

   Liquid – loosely bonded together and allowed to move around randomly. They will collide with each other.

   Gas – very well spaced out and fast moving, free to move around with no bonds between particles. They will collide with each other.

3. The energy will flow from the water (higher temperature) to the ice (lower temperature). The particles in the water will collide with the particles in the ice and lose kinetic energy. The water particles will slow down as the temperature decreases. The particles in the ice will gain kinetic energy and vibrate more quickly. When the ice reaches melting point (0 °C), the energy lost from the kinetic energy in the water particles is passed to the ice by collision. This will be used to break bonds between particles in the ice and cause it to melt and therefore change state.

Page 204 Specific heat capacity

1. **(a)** $\Delta Q = mc\Delta\theta = 2 \times 2500 \times (70 - 30) = 200\,000\,\text{J}$ (200 kJ)

2. C

Page 205 Specific latent heat

1. **(a)** $Q = m \times L = 0.5 \times 206\,000 = 103\,000\,\text{J}$ (or 103 kJ)

   (b) 0.5 kg of gold

2. Energy is required both to increase the temperature to the melting point, and to change the state of the tin when it reaches the melting point.

Page 206 Practical: Properties of water

1. The specific heat capacity of a substance is per unit of mass/per kg, so we must know the mass each time to make the correct calculation.

2. As the water heats up, it loses energy to the surroundings, which makes the results contain errors. Insulation and a lid reduces the amount of energy lost, so reduces the errors.

3. There will be a section of horizontal line where the ice reaches its melting point and all the energy is then used to melt the ice, and not raise the temperature.

Page 207 Particle motion in gases

1. The particles move faster so they collide with each other and the inside of the container more frequently and with higher forces.

2. **(a)** The collisions become less frequent and with smaller forces.

   (b) Heat the gas/supply energy.

Page 208 Forces and elasticity

(a) Elastic distortion/spring returns to original length when load removed.

(b) spring constant

(c) About 18 N

(d) If the load/mass is removed, the spring does not return to its original length.

Page 209 Practical: Force and extension

(a) gradient = $\dfrac{7}{0.36}$ = 19.4 N/m

(b) spring constant = 19.4 N/m

(c) The force is no longer proportional to extension and the spring will not return to its original shape when the force is removed.

Page 210 Equations

1. **(a)** $m = \rho V$, $V = \dfrac{m}{\rho}$

   (b) $k = E \div \left(\dfrac{1}{2}x^2\right)$, $x = \sqrt{\dfrac{V}{\frac{1}{2}k}}$

   (c) $m = \dfrac{\Delta Q}{c\Delta\theta}$, $c = \dfrac{\Delta Q}{m\Delta\theta}$, $\Delta\theta = \dfrac{\Delta Q}{mc}$

   (d) $\Delta v = at$, $t = \dfrac{\Delta v}{a}$

2. m – mass kg, ρ – density kg/m^3, V – volume m^3, E – energy J, k – spring constant N/m, x – extension m, $\Delta\theta$ – change of temperature °C, a – acceleration m/s^2, t – time s, ΔV – change in velocity m/s.

Page 211 Converting units

1. **(a)** $200\,\mu g \div 10^6 = 2\times10^{-4}\,g$

   (b) $10 \div 1000 = 0.01$ N/g

   (c) $330 \div 60 = 5.5$ J/s

2. 1 kg is 1000 so 10^3 or three orders of magnitude larger. So 10 kg is 4 orders of magnitude larger than 1 g.

Page 212 Making estimations

From **Figure 1**, around 500 s.

Page 213 Interpreting data

(a) mean = 1.62 kg $\left(\dfrac{(1.1 + 1.2 + 1.2 + 1.3 + 3.3)}{5} = 1.62\,\text{kg}\right)$

   mode = 1.2 kg

   median = 1.2 kg

(b) There is one large puppy and this makes the mean larger than most of the puppies.

Page 214 Using charts and graphs

1. **(a)** Bar chart – different cars are a discrete variable.

(b) Line graph (or scatter graph with line of best fit) – they best show the relationship between two quantities.

(c) Pie chart – they are best for showing the proportions of something that can be compared.

2. gradient = 4, y intercept = 10

Page 215 Using diagrams

1.

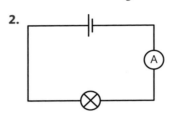

air resistance = 300 N

side wind
200 N

weight = 600 N

2.

Page 216 Planning practicals

(a) Measuring: thickness of insulation; temperature change
Controlling: volume of water; size and material of beaker; insulating material

(b) Thermometer; ruler

(c) Care with hot water; wipe up spills

Page 217 Comparing data

(a) Similarities: Both show that stopping distance increases with speed.
The stopping distances of both tyres increases more rapidly at higher speeds.
Differences: Tyre A has a greater stopping distance for any speed.
Speed and stopping distance stays proportional for tyre A for much longer.

(b) We would expect that the wet road would make the stopping distances much longer. Water on the road means there is less friction and therefore a lower braking force, meaning the car has to travel further to stop.

(c) Tyre B has the best performance as the stopping distances are shorter which means it is safer or stops over shorter distances. (Even though tyre A is more consistent, the stopping distances are greater making it a worse tyre.)

Page 218 Working scientifically

1. The best conductor would have the lowest resistance. To measure the resistance, you would need to measure the potential difference across the sample with a voltmeter and current through the sample of metal with an ammeter after connecting it to a power supply.

   resistance = $\dfrac{\text{potential difference}}{\text{current}}$

To reduce errors, keep the current low to avoid heating, repeat the readings several times and take an average. Use a ruler to keep the length of each sample the same and a calliper to check that the width of each sample is the same.

2. More people would be able to use solar powered rather than fossil fuel powered or rechargeable electric cars, which would reduce carbon emissions and reduce the effect of global warming. Countries with variable day lengths or poor daylight through frequent poor weather would be better able to use the technology where previously they did not generate enough power to operate the cars.

Page 219 Extended-response questions

The circulatory system is an organ system made up of several organs, including the heart and blood vessels, working together. The organs consist of different types of tissues, epithelial, muscle, nervous or connective tissues. The tissues are made up of cells, such as red blood cells.

Page 220 Improving results

(a)

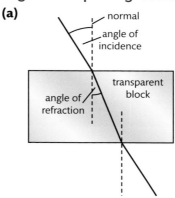

(b) A protractor.

(c) If the ray is wider, it is only possible to measure a range of angles. A narrow ray means the measurement of the angles will be more precise.

Equations for physics

In the exam, you could be asked about any of the equations on this page. Make sure you know how to rearrange each of the equations and learn the units that match each quantity.

🔟 Equations to learn

Word equation	Symbol equation
weight = mass × gravitational field strength	$W = m \times g$
work done = force × distance moved in the direction of the force	$E = F \times d$
force exerted on a spring = spring constant × extension	$F = k \times x$
distance travelled = average speed × time	
acceleration = change in velocity ÷ time taken	$a = \dfrac{(v - u)}{t}$
force = mass × acceleration	$F = m \times a$
kinetic energy = $\frac{1}{2}$ × mass × (speed)^2	$KE = \frac{1}{2} \times m \times v^2$
change in gravitational potential energy = mass × gravitational field strength × change in vertical height	$\Delta GPE = m \times g \times \Delta h$
power = energy transferred (J) ÷ time taken	$P = \dfrac{E}{t}$
power = work done ÷ time taken	$P = \dfrac{E}{t}$
efficiency = $\dfrac{\text{(useful energy transferred by the device (J))}}{\text{(total energy supplied to the device (J))}}$	
wave speed = frequency × wavelength	$v = f \times \lambda$
wave speed = distance ÷ time	$v = \dfrac{x}{t}$
charge = current × time	$Q = I \times t$
potential difference = current × resistance	$V = I \times R$
electrical power = current × potential difference	$P = I \times V$
electrical power = (current)^2 × resistance	$P = I^2 \times R$
energy transferred = charge moved × potential difference	$E = Q \times V$
density = mass ÷ volume	$\rho = \dfrac{m}{V}$

5️⃣ Physics equation sheet

You will be given a list of some of the more complicated equations in the exam.

Word equation	Symbol equation
(final velocity)^2 − (initial velocity)^2 = 2 × acceleration × distance	$v^2 - u^2 = 2 \times a \times x$
change in thermal energy = mass × specific heat capacity × change in temperature	$\Delta Q = m \times c \times \Delta\theta$
thermal energy for a change of state = mass × specific latent heat	$Q = m \times L$
energy transferred = current × potential difference × time	$E = I \times V \times t$
For transformers with 100% efficiency, potential difference across primary coil × current in primary coil = potential difference across secondary coil × current in secondary coil	$V_p \times I_p = V_s \times I_s$
energy transferred in stretching = 0.5 × spring constant × (extension)^2	$E = \frac{1}{2} \times k \times x^2$

 Made a start   **Feeling confident**   ☑ **Exam ready**

Periodic table

1	2												3	4	5	6	7	0
																		4 **He** Helium 2
7 **Li** Lithium 3	9 **Be** Beryllium 4												11 **B** Boron 5	12 **C** Carbon 6	14 **N** Nitrogen 7	16 **O** Oxygen 8	19 **F** Fluorine 9	20 **Ne** Neon 10
23 **Na** Sodium 11	24 **Mg** Magnesium 12												27 **Al** Aluminium 13	28 **Si** Silicon 14	31 **P** Phosphorus 15	32 **S** Sulfur 16	35.5 **Cl** Chlorine 17	40 **Ar** Argon 18
39 **K** Potassium 19	40 **Ca** Calcium 20	45 **Sc** Scandium 21	48 **Ti** Titanium 22	51 **V** Vanadium 23	52 **Cr** Chromium 24	55 **Mn** Manganese 25	56 **Fe** Iron 26	59 **Co** Cobalt 27	59 **Ni** Nickel 28	63.5 **Cu** Copper 29	65 **Zn** Zinc 30		70 **Ga** Gallium 31	73 **Ge** Germanium 32	75 **As** Arsenic 33	79 **Se** Selenium 34	80 **Br** Bromine 35	84 **Kr** Krypton 36
85 **Rb** Rubidium 37	88 **Sr** Strontium 38	89 **Y** Yttrium 39	91 **Zr** Zirconium 40	93 **Nb** Niobium 41	96 **Mo** Molybdenum 42	98 **Tc** Technetium 43	101 **Ru** Ruthenium 44	103 **Rh** Rhodium 45	106 **Pd** Palladium 46	108 **Ag** Silver 47	112 **Cd** Cadmium 48		115 **In** Indium 49	119 **Sn** Tin 50	122 **Sb** Antimony 51	128 **Te** Tellurium 52	127 **I** Iodine 53	131 **Xe** Xenon 54
133 **Cs** Caesium 55	137 **Ba** Barium 56	139 **La** Lanthanum 57	178 **Hf** Hafnium 72	181 **Ta** Tantalum 73	184 **W** Tungsten 74	186 **Re** Rhenium 75	190 **Os** Osmium 76	192 **Ir** Iridium 77	195 **Pt** Platinum 78	197 **Au** Gold 79	201 **Hg** Mercury 80		204 **Tl** Thallium 81	207 **Pb** Lead 82	209 **Bi** Bismuth 83	[201] **Po** Polonium 84	[210] **At** Astatine 85	[222] **Rn** Radon 86
[223] **Fr** Francium 87	[226] **Ra** Radium 88	[227] **Ac** Actinium 89	[261] **Rf** Rutherfordium 104	[262] **Db** Dubnium 105	[266] **Sg** Seaborgium 106	[264] **Bh** Bohrium 107	[277] **Hs** Hassium 108	[268] **Mt** Meitnerium 109	[271] **Ds** Darmstadtium 110	[272] **Rg** Roentgenium 111								

Key

relative atomic mass
atomic symbol
name
atomic (proton) number

1
H
Hydrogen
1

Elements with atomic numbers 112–116 have been reported but not fully authenticated.

* The Lanthanoides (atomic numbers 58–71) and the actinides (atomic numbers 90–103) have been omitted.
Relative atomic massses for copper and chlorine have not been rounded to the nearest whole number.

Published by BBC Active, an imprint of Educational Publishers LLP, part of the Pearson Education Group, 80 Strand, London, WC2R 0RL.

www.pearsonschools.co.uk/BBCBitesize

© Educational Publishers LLP 2020

BBC logo © BBC 1996. BBC and BBC Active are trademarks of the British Broadcasting Corporation.

Typeset by Newgen KnowledgeWorks Pvt. Ltd., Chennai, India

Produced and illustrated by Newgen Publishing UK

Cover design by Andrew Magee & Pearson Education Limited 2020

Cover illustration by Darren Lingard / Oxford Designers & Illustrators

The rights of Sam Holyman, Aidan Gill and Mike Smith to be identified as authors of this work have been asserted by them in accordance with the Copyright, Designs and Patents Act 1988.

First published 2020

23 22 21 20

10 9 8 7 6 5 4 3 2 1

British Library Cataloguing in Publication Data

A catalogue record for this book is available from the British Library

ISBN 978 1 406 68575 6

Printed and bound in Slovakia by Neografia.

The Publisher's policy is to use paper manufactured from sustainable forests.

Acknowledgements

Content written by Karen Bailey and Jen Randall is included.

Text credits:

BBC: PP1–218 © 2019.

Photo Credits:

(Key: T-top; B-bottom; C-centre; L-left; R-right)

123RF: Sirikorn Thamniyom 30, Jarun Ontakrai 57; **Alamy Stock Photo:** Peter Hermes Furian 6, Marcus DeYoung 26, The Natural History Museum 27, Mediscan 33, Geogphotos 35, PR BOUREE/BSIP SA 36, Chronicle 39, Wayne Lynch/All Canada Photos 64, AfriPics. com 65t, Image Quest Marine 65b, Xinhua/Xue Yubin 68, Nigel Cattlin 71, David J. Green 88; **Getty Images:** Iryna Imago/iStock 44; **Shutterstock:** Aldona Griskeviciene 27, Matej Hudovernik 28, Zcw 30, GraphicsRF 33, CLIPAREA I Custom media 43, Luis Santos 44, Number-one/Shutterstock 57, Josep Curto 91, Dario Lo Presti 177, Fly_and_Dive 181.

Notes from the publisher

1. While the publishers have made every attempt to ensure that advice on the qualification and its assessment is accurate, the official specification and associated assessment guidance materials are the only authoritative source of information and should always be referred to for definitive guidance. Pearson examiners have not contributed to any sections in this resource relevant to examination papers for which they have responsibility.

2. Pearson has robust editorial processes, including answer and fact checks, to ensure the accuracy of the content in this publication, and every effort is made to ensure this publication is free of errors. We are, however, only human, and occasionally errors do occur. Pearson is not liable for any misunderstandings that arise as a result of errors in this publication, but it is our priority to ensure that the content is accurate. If you spot an error, please do contact us at resourcescorrections@pearson.com so we can make sure it is corrected.

Websites

Pearson Education Limited is not responsible for the content of third-party websites.